Children's
Literature
Review

Guide to Gale Literary Criticism Series

For criticism on	Consult these Gale series
Authors now living or who died after December 31, 1959	*CONTEMPORARY LITERARY CRITICISM (CLC)*
Authors who died between 1900 and 1959	*TWENTIETH-CENTURY LITERARY CRITICISM (TCLC)*
Authors who died between 1800 and 1899	*NINETEENTH-CENTURY LITERATURE CRITICISM (NCLC)*
Authors who died between 1400 and 1799	*LITERATURE CRITICISM FROM 1400 TO 1800 (LC)* *SHAKESPEAREAN CRITICISM (SC)*
Authors who died before 1400	*CLASSICAL AND MEDIEVAL LITERATURE CRITICISM (CMLC)*
Authors of books for children and young adults	*CHILDREN'S LITERATURE REVIEW (CLR)*
Dramatists	*DRAMA CRITICISM (DC)*
Poets	*POETRY CRITICISM (PC)*
Short story writers	*SHORT STORY CRITICISM (SSC)*
Black writers of the past two hundred years	*BLACK LITERATURE CRITICISM (BLC)*
Hispanic writers of the late nineteenth and twentieth centuries	*HISPANIC LITERATURE CRITICISM (HLC)*
Native North American writers and orators of the eighteenth, nineteenth, and twentieth centuries	*NATIVE NORTH AMERICAN LITERATURE (NNAL)*
Major authors from the Renaissance to the present	*WORLD LITERATURE CRITICISM, 1500 TO THE PRESENT (WLC)*

140.00

ISSN 0362-4145

volume 62

Children's Literature Review

Excerpts from Reviews,
Criticism, and Commentary
on Books for Children
and Young People

Michelle Lee
Deborah J. Morad
Editors

GALE GROUP

Detroit
New York
San Francisco
London
Boston
Woodbridge, CT

STAFF

Michelle Lee, *Editor*

Jennifer Baise, Vince Cousino, Deborah J. Morad, Elisabeth Gellert, Thomas Ligotti, *Contributing Editors*

Maria Franklin, *Permissions Manager*
Kimberly F. Smilay, *Permissions Specialist*
Shalice Shah-Caldwell, Kelly A. Quin *Permissions Associates*
Sandy Gore, *Permissions Assistant*

Victoria B. Cariappa, *Research Manager*
Andrew Guy Malonis, Barbara McNeil, Gary J. Oudersluys, Maureen Richards,
Cheryl L. Warnock, *Research Specialists*
Patricia T. Ballard, Tamara C. Nott, Tracie A. Richardson, *Research Associates*
Phyllis Blackman, Timothy Lehnerer, *Research Assistant*

Mary Beth Trimper, *Production Director*
Stacy Melson, *Buyer*

Michael Logusz, *Graphic Artist*
Randy Bassett, *Image Database Supervisor*
Robert Duncan, *Imaging Specialists*
Pamela Reed, *Imaging Coordinator*

Library of Congress Catalog Card Number 76-46132
ISBN 0-7876-3227-9
ISSN 0362-4145

Printed in the United States of America
10 9 8 7 6 5 4 3 2 1

Contents

Preface   vii

Acknowledgments   xi

Preface

Literature for children and young adults has evolved into both a respected branch of creative writing and a successful industry. Currently, books for young readers are considered among the most popular segments of publishing. Criticism of juvenile literature is instrumental in recording the literary or artistic development of the creators of children's books as well as the trends and controversies that result from changing values or attitudes about young people and their literature. Designed to provide a permanent, accessible record of this ongoing scholarship, *Children's Literature Review (CLR)* presents parents, teachers, and librarians—those responsible for bringing children and books together—with the opportunity to make informed choices when selecting reading materials for the young. In addition, *CLR* provides researchers of children's literature with easy access to a wide variety of critical information from English-language sources in the field. Users will find balanced overviews of the careers of the authors and illustrators of the books that children and young adults are reading; these entries, which contain excerpts from published criticism in books and periodicals, assist users by sparking ideas for papers and assignments and suggesting supplementary and classroom reading. Ann L. Kalkhoff, president and editor of *Children's Book Review Service Inc.,* writes that "*CLR* has filled a gap in the field of children's books, and it is one series that will never lose its validity or importance."

Scope of the Series

Each volume of *CLR* profiles the careers of a selection of authors and illustrators of books for children and young adults from preschool through high school. Author lists in each volume reflect:

- an international scope.

- representation of authors of all eras.

- the variety of genres covered by children's and/or YA literature: picture books, fiction, nonfiction, poetry, folklore, and drama.

Although the focus of the series is on authors new to *CLR*, entries will be updated as the need arises.

Organization of This Book

An entry consists of the following elements: author heading, author portrait, author introduction, excerpts of criticism (each preceded by a bibliographical citation), and illustrations, when available.

- The **Author Heading** consists of the author's name followed by birth and death dates. The portion of the name outside the parentheses denotes the form under which the author is most frequently published. If the majority of the author's works for children were written under a pseudonym, the pseudonym will be listed in the author heading and the real name given on the first line of the author introduction. Also located at the beginning of the introduction are any other pseudonyms used by the author in writing for children and any name variations, including transliterated forms for authors whose languages use nonroman alphabets. Uncertainty as to a birth or death date is indicated by question marks.

- An **Author Portrait** is included when available.

- The **Author Introduction** contains information designed to introduce an author to *CLR* users by presenting an overview of the author's themes and styles, biographical facts that relate to the author's literary career or critical responses to the author's works, and information about major awards and prizes the author has received. The introduction begins by identifying the nationality of the author and by listing the genres in which s/he has written for children and young adults. Introductions also list a group of representative titles for which the author or illustrator being profiled is best known; this section, which begins with the words "major works include," follows the genre line of the introduction. For seminal figures, a listing of major works about the author follows when appropriate, highlighting important biographies about the author or illustrator that are not excerpted in the entry. The centered heading "Introduction" announces the body of the text.

- **Criticism** is located in three sections: **Author's Commentary** (when available), **General Commentary** (when available), and **Title Commentary** (commentary on specific titles).

  - The **Author's Commentary** presents background material written by the author or by an interviewer. This commentary may cover a specific work or several works. Author's commentary on more than one work appears after the author introduction, while commentary on an individual book follows the title entry heading.

  - The **General Commentary** consists of critical excerpts that consider more than one work by the author or illustrator being profiled. General commentary is preceded by the critic's name in boldface type or, in the case of unsigned criticism, by the title of the journal. *CLR* also features entries that emphasize general criticism on the oeuvre of an author or illustrator. When appropriate, a selection of reviews is included to supplement the general commentary.

  - The **Title Commentary** begins with the title entry headings, which precede the criticism on a title and cite publication information on the work being reviewed. Title headings list the title of the work as it appeared in its first English-language edition. The first English-language publication date of each work (unless otherwise noted) is listed in parentheses following the title. Differing U.S. and British titles follow the publication date within the parentheses. When a work is written by an individual other than the one being profiled, as is the case when illustrators are featured, the parenthetical material following the title cites the author of the work before listing its publication date.

    Entries in each title commentary section consist of critical excerpts on the author's individual works, arranged chronologically by publication date. The entries generally contain two to seven reviews per title, depending on the stature of the book and the amount of criticism it has generated. The editors select titles that reflect the entire scope of the author's literary contribution, covering each genre and subject. An effort is made to reprint criticism that represents the full range of each title's reception, from the year of its initial publication to current assessments. Thus, the reader is provided with a record of the author's critical history. Publication information (such as publisher names and book prices) and parenthetical numerical references (such as footnotes or page and line references to specific editions of works) have been deleted at the discretion of the editors to provide smoother reading of the text.

- Centered headings introduce each section, in which criticism is arranged chronologically; beginning with Volume 35, each excerpt is preceded by a boldface source heading for easier access by readers. Within the text, titles by authors being profiled are also highlighted in boldface type.

- Selected excerpts are preceded by **Explanatory Annotations,** which provide information on the critic or work of criticism to enhance the reader's understanding of the excerpt.

- A complete **Bibliographical Citation** designed to facilitate the location of the original book or article precedes each piece of criticism.

- Numerous **Illustrations** are featured in *CLR*. For entries on illustrators, an effort has been made to include illustrations that reflect the characteristics discussed in the criticism. Entries on authors who do not illustrate their own works may also include photographs and other illustrative material pertinent to their careers.

Special Features: Entries on Illustrators

Entries on authors who are also illustrators will occasionally feature commentary on selected works illustrated but not written by the author being profiled. These works are strongly associated with the illustrator and have received critical acclaim for their art. By including critical comment on works of this type, the editors wish to provide a more complete representation of the artist's career. Criticism on these works has been chosen to stress artistic, rather than literary, contributions. Title entry headings for works illustrated by the author being profiled are arranged chronologically within the entry by date of publication and include notes identifying the author of the illustrated work. In order to provide easier access for users, all titles illustrated by the subject of the entry are boldfaced.

CLR also includes entries on prominent illustrators who have contributed to the field of children's literature. These entries are designed to represent the development of the illustrator as an artist rather than as a literary stylist. The illustrator's section is organized like that of an author, with two exceptions: the introduction presents an overview of the illustrator's styles and techniques rather than outlining his or her literary background, and the commentary written by the illustrator on his or her works is called "illustrator's commentary" rather than "author's commentary." All titles of books containing illustrations by the artist being profiled are highlighted in boldface type.

Other Features: Acknowledgments, Indexes

- The **Acknowledgments** section, which immediately follows the preface, lists the sources from which material has been reprinted in the volume. It does not, however, list every book or periodical consulted for the volume.

- The **Cumulative Index to Authors** lists all of the authors who have appeared in *CLR* with cross-references to the biographical, autobiographical, and literary criticism series published by Gale Research. A full listing of the series titles appears before the first page of the indexes of this volume.

- The **Cumulative Index to Nationalities** lists authors alphabetically under their respective nationalities. Author names are followed by the volume number(s) in which they appear.

- The **Cumulative Index to Titles** lists titles covered in *CLR* followed by the volume and page number where criticism begins.

A Note to the Reader

CLR is one of several critical references sources in the Literature Criticism Series published by Gale Research. When writing papers, students who quote directly from any volume in the Literature Criticism Series may use the following general forms to footnote reprinted criticism. The first example pertains to material drawn from periodicals, the second to material reprinted from books.

¹T. S. Eliot, "John Donne," *The Nation and the Athenaeum,* 33 (9 June 1923), 321-32; excerpted and reprinted in *Literature Criticism from 1400 to 1800,* Vol. 10, ed. James E. Person, Jr. (Detroit: Gale Research, 1989), pp. 28-9.

¹Henry Brooke, *Leslie Brooke and Johnny Crow* (Frederick Warne, 1982); excerpted and reprinted in *Children's Literature Review,* Vol. 20, ed. Gerard J. Senick (Detroit: Gale Research, 1990), p. 47.

Suggestions Are Welcome

In response to various suggestions, several features have been added to *CLR* since the beginning of the series, including author entries on retellers of traditional literature as well as those who have been the first to record oral tales and other folklore; entries on prominent illustrators featuring commentary on their styles and techniques; entries on authors whose works are considered controversial; occasional entries devoted to criticism on a single work or a series of works; sections in author introductions that list major works by and about the author or illustrator being profiled; explanatory notes that provide information on the critic or work of criticism to enhance the usefulness of the excerpt; more extensive illustrative material, such as holographs of manuscript pages and photographs of people and places pertinent to the careers of the authors and artists; a cumulative nationality index for easy access to authors by nationality; and occasional guest essays written specifically for *CLR* by prominent critics on subjects of their choice.

Readers who wish to suggest authors to appear in future volumes, or who have other suggestions, are cordially invited to contact the editor. By mail: Editor, *Children's Literature Review,* Gale Research, 835 Penobscot Bldg., 645 Griswold St., Detroit, MI 48226-4094; by telephone: (800) 347-GALE; by fax: (313) 961-6599; by E-mail: CYA@Gale.com.

Acknowledgments

The editors wish to thank the copyright holders of the criticism included in this volume and the permissions managers of many book and magazine publishing companies for assisting us in securing reproduction rights. We are also grateful to the staffs of the Detroit Public Library, the Library of Congress, the University of Detroit Mercy Library, Wayne State University Purdy/Kresge Library Complex, and the University of Michigan Libraries for making their resources available to us. Following is a list of the copyright holders who have granted us permission to reproduce material in this volume of *TCLC*. Every effort has been made to trace copyright, but if omissions have been made, please let us know.

COPYRIGHTED ESSAYS IN *CLR*, VOLUME 62, WERE REPRODUCED FROM THE FOLLOWING PERIODICALS:

Alan Review, v. 18, Spring, 1991. Reproduced by permission.—*American Book Review*, v. 19, November-December, 1997. © 1997 by The American Book Review. Reproduced by permission.—*American Music Teacher*, v. 41, April-May, 1992. Reproduced by permission. *Black American Literature Forum*, v. 11, Spring, 1977 for "To Make These Bones Live: History and Community in Ernest Gaines's Fiction" by Jack Hicks; v. 18, Fall, 1984 for "The Individual and the Community in Two Short Stories by Ernest J. Gaines" by John W. Roberts. Copyright © 1977, 1984 by the authors. Both reproduced by permission of the publisher and the author.—*Booklist*, v. 64, December 15, 1967; v. 67, July 15, 1971; v. 72, April 1, 1976; v. 73, July 1, 1977; v. 76, July 1, 1980; v. 78, September 15, 1981; v. 78, January 1, 1982; v. 81, September 15, 1984; v. 82, November 15, 1985; v. 82, March 1, 1986; v. 82, April 1, 1986; v. 83, October 1, 1986; v. 84, April 15, 1988; v. 84, July, 1988; v. 85, November 15, 1988; v. 85, December 1, 1988; v. 85, May 1, 1989; v. 86, January 1, 1990; v. 86, June 15, 1990; v. 87, March 1, 1991; v. 87, April 1, 1991; v. 87, June 1, 1991; v. 88, November 15, 1991; v. 88, February 15, 1992; v. 88, May 1, 1992; v. 89, March 1, 1993; v. 89, March 15, 1993; v. 89, June 1 & 15, 1993; v. 90, December 1, 1993; v. 90, March 1, 1994; v. 90, March 15, 1994; v. 91, October 15, 1994; v. 92, December 1, 1995; v. 92, September 15, 1995; v. 93, December 1, 1996; v. 93, April 15, 1997; v. 94, December 15, 1997; v. 94, May 1, 1998; v. 94, May 15, 1998; v. 95, September 15, 1998. Copyright © 1967, 1971, 1976, 1977, 1980, 1981, 1982, 1984, 1985, 1986, 1988, 1989, 1990, 1991, 1992, 1993, 1994, 1995, 1996, 1997, 1998 by the American Library Association. All reproduced by *permission. The Booklist*, v. 67, January 1, 1971; v. 70, December 1, 1973; v. 71, December 15, 1974; v. 73, November 15, 1976; v. 74, October 1, 1977; v. 76, September 1, 1979; Copyright © 1971, 1973, 1974, 1976, 1977, 1979 by the American Library Association. All reproduced by permission.—*The Booklist and Subscription Books Bulletin*, v. 75, July 15, 1969. Copyright © 1969 by the American Library Association. Reproduced by permission.—*Books for Keeps*, September, 1986; September, 1987; January, 1989; March, 1992; May, 1992; November, 1992; July, 1993; November, 1993; July, 1994; July, 1995; January, 1996; September, 1996; January, 1997; January, 1998; © School Bookshop Association 1986, 1987, 1989, 1992, 1993, 1994, 1995, 1996, 1997, 1998. All reproduced by permission.—*Books for Your Children*, v. 11, Summer, 1976; v. 13, Winter, 1977; v. 18, Spring, 1983; v. 28, Spring, 1993. © Books for Your Children 1976, 1977, 1983. All reproduced by permission.—*Bulletin of the Center for Children's Books*, v. 23, September, 1969; v. 24, April, 1971; v. 47, v. 25, February, 1972; v. 26, May, 1973; v. 28, April, 1975; v. 30, April, 1977; v. 30, May, 1977; v. 31, March, 1978; v. 32, January, 1979; v. 35, May, 1982; v. 36, April, 1983; v. 39, October, 1985; v. 40, December, 1986; v. 40, February, 1987; v. 42, September, 1988; v. 42, October, 1988; v. 44, October, 1990; v. 45, v. 45, October, 1991; April, 1992; v. 46, March, 1993; v. 47, February, 1994; v. 47, April, 1994; v. 48, February, 1995; v. 49, April, 1996; v. 51, November, 1997; v. 50, June, 1997; v. 51, October, 1997; v. 51, March, 1998. Copyright © 1969, 1971, 1972, 1973, 1975, 1977, 1978, 1979, 1982, 1983, 1985, 1986, 1987, 1988, 1990, 1991, 1992, 1993, 1994, 1995, 1996, 1997, 1998 by The Board of Trustees of the University of Illinois. All reproduced by permission.—*Chicago Tribune Books*, May 9, 1993. © 1993 Tribune Media Services, Inc. All rights reserved. Reproduced by permission.—*Christian Science Monitor*, v. 38, October 15, 1946. © 1946, renewed 1974 by The Christian Science Publishing Society; v. 46, May 13, 1954. © 1954, renewed 1982 The Christian Science Publishing Society.; v. 46, November 11, 1954. © 1954, renewed 1982 by The Christian Science Publishing Society./ v. 77, March 1, 1985. © 1985 The Christian Science Publishing Society. All rights reserved. All reproduced by permission from The Christian Science Monitor. All rights reserved.—*English Journal*, v. 79, January, 1990 for "Probably Nick Swansen" by Alleen Nilsen and Ken Donelson. Copyright © 1990 by the National Council of Teachers of English. Reproduced by permission of the publisher and the author.—*The Five Owls*, v. viii, September-October, 1993; v. ix, September-October, 1994. Both reproduced by permission.—*Growing Point*, v. 15, November, 1976 for a review of "The Nickle Nackle Tree" by Margery Fisher; v. 15, December, 1976 for a review of "Friends" by Margery Fisher; v. 16, January, 1978 in a review of "Suzanne and Nicholas at the Market" by Margery Fisher; v. 18, September, 1979 in a review of "Suzanne and Nicholas and the Four Seasons" by Margery Fisher; v. 20, September, 1981 in a review of "Let's Play" by Margery Fisher; v. 22, January, 1984 for a review of "Hairy Maclary from Donaldson's Dairy" by Margery Fisher; Reproduced by permission of the Literary Estate of Margery Fisher; v. 25,

Children's
Literature
Review

Alma Flor Ada
1938-

Cuban-American author of fiction.

Major works include *La moneda de oro* (1991; U.S. edition as *The Gold Coin*), *The Rooster Who Went to His Uncles Wedding: A Latin American Folktale* (retold by Ada, 1992), *My Name is María Isabel* (1993; Spanish version as *Me Llamo María Isabel,* 1994), *Dear Peter Rabbit: Querido Pedrín* (1994), *Where the Flame Trees Bloom* (1994; Spanish version as *Donde florecen los flamboyanes*), *Mediopollito: Half-Chicken: A New Version of a Traditional Story* (retold by Ada, 1995).

INTRODUCTION

Over the span of her prolific career, Ada has created a vast collection of vibrant stories in English and Spanish designed to entertain preschoolers and primary graders while educating them about language, multiculturalism, identity, and acceptance. With a distinctive emphasis on making learning fun, Ada's work deftly balances a celebration of the uniqueness of the individual with the importance of community and cultural understanding. Many critics have praised the author for her ability to present serious ideas, and what Susan Dove Lempke referred to as "explorations of character and values," with fun, light-hearted tones that are easily accessible to children. A number of Ada's works employ pleasing rhythms and rhymes, making them ideally suited for reading aloud.

Ada's complete scope of work combines retellings of favorite folk and fairy tales, many of which were first told to her by family in her native Cuba, with original stories that exhibit a folkloric style and, often, a moral theme. Her love for Latin American culture and its oral traditions comes through in works such as *Where the Flame Trees Bloom*, a collection of stories that shows her fondness for her childhood and her homeland, which she clearly wishes to share with children everywhere. Critic Marilyn Long Graham noted that "[w]armth and love for a treasured childhood exude from the pages" of Ada's work. Often, her books emphasize the importance of heritage and encourage youngsters to cherish the unwritten stories imparted by grandparents, parents, and other relatives and community members. Many of her stories are enriched by illustrations that reflect a variety of traditional Latin American and Spanish folk-art styles.

A notable feature of Ada's wide range of work is its versatility, equally successful when set in timeless Latin American landscapes or in contemporary classrooms. Several original stories, such as *Dear Peter Rabbit: Querido Pedrín*, feature fanciful casts of animal characters in what Joy Fleishhacker referred to as "a convincing and intriguing make-believe world." Others, such as *My Name is*

María Isabel, take place in modern-day settings and focus on the challenges today's children face in confronting cultural misunderstanding while learning to take pride in their heritage. Much of her later work reflects the lives of her own family. *I Love Saturdays y Domingos (1995)*, for instance, depicts her grandchildren's experience of having two sets of grandparents, each from very different cultural backgrounds. A *Publishers Weekly* reviewer observed that Ada's "carefully drawn characterizations avoid stereotypes, thus increasing their appeal and believability."

Perhaps Ada's most distinguishing literary quality is her facility in both English and Spanish. Her bilingual approach has allowed her to write a number of books incorporating both languages, exposing beginning readers to bilingual vocabulary as well as multicultural themes. In addition to her original stories, Ada's retelling and translation of tales such as *Mediopollito: Half-Chicken* and *The Rooster Who Went to His Uncle's Wedding*, have significantly impacted children's literature by making traditional Latin-American favorites accessible to both Spanish and English speaking children. Overall, Ada's work has ensured that children learning either language can access fun, enjoyable stories, not just traditional textbooks.

As the author stated in *Something about the Author* (*SATA*): "I made a firm commitment while in the fourth grade to devote my life to producing schoolbooks that would be fun—and since then I am having a lot of fun doing just that!"

Biographical Information

Born in Cuba, Ada's upbringing had a profound impact on her decision to teach and write for children. Ada learned to read at a very early age, taught by her grandmother who wrote out the names of local flora and fauna in the earth with a stick. Her father, mother, grandmother, and uncle were master storytellers who read to her frequently, inventing tales to educate her about her history, culture, and environment. For Ada, these lessons helped foster a love of the Cuban landscape and heritage that comes through in much of her work. By the time she reached grade school, Ada was easily bored by what she felt to be dry, lifeless textbooks that were no match for the vibrant stories she had waiting for her at home. As a young girl, Ada committed herself to writing stories for children that would make learning fun.

Fueled by her passion for language and learning, Ada went on to become a distinguished scholar, teacher and writer. She earned her undergraduate degree in 1959 from the Universidad Central de Madrid in Spain, a master's degree in 1963, and her doctorate in 1965 from Pontifica Universidad Catolica del Peru. Additionally, Ada pursued post-doctoral studies at Harvard University. During her doctoral studies in Peru, Ada began teaching Spanish at the university level. After completing her work at Harvard, she returned to teaching in Peru for two years before making her permanent home in the United States. Ada has held professorships in Romance languages and bilingual studies at a number of American post-secondary institutions. In 1979, she became a professor of education at the University of San Francisco, where she has remained for over 20 years.

It was in Peru that Ada launched her writing career with the publication of several stories and poems in Spanish in 1974. She first established herself in the United States as a translator of English stories into Spanish, and went on to write many stories in both languages throughout the 1990s. While Ada's upbringing, scholarship, and active promotion of bilingualism have always influenced her writing, she told (*SATA*) that her children and grandchildren have always been a "constant source of inspiration." Ada's daughter Rosalma Zubizarreta, an author in her own right, has translated many of her mother's books into both English and Spanish.

Major Works

La moneda de oro (U.S. edition as *The Gold Coin*), an original story set in South America, is an early example of Ada's thematic focus on growth and self-renewal through community. The tale is centered on the transformation of Juan, a career thief, sallow and stooped from many years of creeping about his village. Peering through a window one night, Juan spies elderly Doña Josefa holding up a gold coin and proclaiming that she is "the richest person in the world." Once the old woman leaves, Juan ransacks her hut in search of her supposed treasures. Finding nothing, Juan trails Doña Josefa as she tours the countryside helping people in need. As he encounters those who have benefited from Doña Josefa's kindness, Juan's own health and attitude slowly begin to improve. Juan finally catches up with Doña Josefa and demands her gold, only to realize that he, too, has been touched by her goodness. In the end, Juan returns the gold as a gift for the next person in need. Critics have applauded this tale for its treatment of a lofty moral subject in a manner that children can comprehend and appreciate. Caroline Phelan praised the book for presenting "ideals of love and honor without becoming too sweet or stuffy."

Also set in Latin America, *The Rooster Who Went to His Uncle's Wedding* is Ada's lively adaptation of a classic folktale that had been frequently told to her by her grandmother. Here a well-groomed rooster on his way to his uncle's wedding risks spoiling his clean appearance when he spots a delicious-looking kernel of corn nestled in the mud. After dirtying his gleaming beak by gobbling the kernel, the rooster must figure out how to clean himself before the wedding. One by one, the rooster is turned down by a long list of surrounding characters, including festively attired blades of grass and a lamb in a ruffled dress. Only his friend the Sun agrees to help him in the end. Critics have commended this book for its colorful, fun approach to a dilemma that many a child would relate to. A critic for *Publishers Weekly* noted, "Through harmonious repetition and sing-song rhythms, Ada's leisurely, conversational tale neatly mimics the cadences of a traditional storyteller."

Ada retells another traditional folktale in *Mediopollito: Half-Chicken: A New Version of a Traditional Story*, a humorous account of the origins of the weathervane. Presented here in both English and Spanish on facing pages, the story teaches about the perils of haughtiness and the importance of kind deeds. As his name implies, Half-Chicken has only one eye, one wing, and one leg. Accustomed to being admired for his unusual appearance, Half-Chicken decides to visit the palace to impress the viceroy. On his way, Half-Chicken helps a number of neighbors, including a blocked stream, a tangled breeze, and a dwindling fire. Upon his arrival, Half-Chicken does not receive the hero's welcome he expects, but is instead greeted by a cook eager to turn him into a tasty chicken soup. Remembering Half-Chicken's good deeds, the elements come to his rescue. Finally, the wind carries him to the top of the palace where remains forever as a weathervane. Ada employs repetition, simple rhythms and abundant humor to make both languages accessible for children. Reviewer Annie Ayres called the story "a jewel that will add a spicy sparkle to any folktale collection."

Ada offers her own take on the fairy tale tradition in *Dear Peter Rabbit: Querido Pedrín*. This funny, fanciful tale unfolds through a series of letters written by familiar storybook characters, including Goldilocks McGregor, Baby Bear, the Little Pigs, the infamous Peter Rabbit, and others. Through their correspondence, readers discover that Peter is unable to attend the straw-housewarming party thrown by Pig One because he is in bed with a cold. Meanwhile, Baby Bear invites his new friend Goldilocks to visit, as she complains to Peter of vegetables missing from her father's garden. In the end, all characters meet face-to-face at Pig Two's stick house and the story is recorded by Red Riding Hood in a letter to her grandmother. Critics have commended Ada's clever intertwining of classic stories to create a seamless and imaginative plot. As reviewer Joy Fleishhacker commented, "Children will be enchanted by the opportunity to meet familiar faces in new settings." The story is appropriately complemented by Beatrix Potter-style illustrations.

Ada shifts from rural landscapes to a modern-day setting with *My Name is María Isabel*, an original story that explores the importance of identity and cultural understanding. María Isabel Salazar López has always taken great pride in the name given to her in honor of her two grandmothers, her grandfather, and her father. When María Isabel moves with her family to the United States from Puerto Rico, adjusting to a new school and new friends is made even more difficult when her teacher insists on calling her "Mary" to avoid confusion with two other Marias already present in the classroom. Matters are made worse by the teacher's dissatisfaction when María Isabel fails to respond to a name she does not recognize as her own. The situation is finally resolved when María Isabel explains the importance of her name in an essay. The story serves as a reminder of the importance of compassion and acceptance, and also of finding a voice for one's identity. Many critics praised the book for its heart-felt depiction of an experience common for children new to America. A *Language Arts* reviewer noted that, "Important understandings about language and cultural identity can be gained by reading this book." Ann Welton commented that the book "reads aloud well and could certainly be used . . . to illustrate the Hispanic culture that is part of the lives of many contemporary children."

In *Where the Flame Trees Bloom*, a volume of 11 short stories, Ada reaches back into her childhood to bring to life well-loved tales and family memories she frequently heard as a girl in Cuba. Centering around her family's own experiences, the stories reveal the strengths and values Ada admires most in her relatives and vividly illustrates her love for her homeland. As she reminisces about her grandmother's kindness to fellow villagers, her uncle's care for his pupils, and her father's dedication to his family in the face of adversity, Ada paints a vibrant picture of the rich surroundings and warmth of the Cuban countryside and its people. Martha V. Parravano described the collection as "valuable not only for its authentic voice but also for Ada's re-creation of truly memorable characters." Susan Dove Lempke also noted that "Reading the book to young listeners . . . could prompt them to share moments from their own family stories."

Awards

Ada received a Christopher Award in 1992 and NCSS/CBC Notable Children's Trade Book in the Field of Social Studies, both for *The Gold Coin. Dear Peter Rabbit: Querido Pedrín* won the Parents' Choice Honor in 1995. *Mediopollito: Half-Chicken: A New Version of a Traditional Story* made the Aesop Accolade List in 1996.

TITLE COMMENTARY

LA MONEDA DE ORO (translated by Bernice Randall as *The Gold Coin,* 1991)

Kirkus Reviews

SOURCE: A review of *The Gold Coin,* in *Kirkus Reviews,* Vol. LIX, No. 1, January 1, 1991, p. 42.

Juan, a confirmed thief, overhears old Doña Josefa referring to herself as "the richest person in the world"; moreover, he sees a gold coin in her hand. But before he can steal it, she hurries away with two men, leaving nothing of value that he can find in her humble hut. Juan follows her trail, only to discover that she has gone on another errand of mercy just before he arrives. The people she's helped are willing to lead him to her—but each time there is work to be finished first, and Juan (hoping to hurry his guide) joins in. As he labors and shares food with these humble folk, Juan becomes healthier in body and mind; still, when he finally catches up with Doña Josefa, he demands her gold. She gives it to him freely—thus completing his moral transformation: he returns it as a gift for the next patient.

Like a folk tale, this original story builds naturally to its satisfying conclusion; its long text should appeal well beyond the picture-book age. [Neil] Waldman's watercolors, with stylized forms displayed against varying backgrounds of romantic sunset hues, gently suggest both the story's universal tone and its Latin American setting.

Publishers Weekly

SOURCE: A review of *The Gold Coin,* in *Publishers Weekly,* Vol. 238, No. 2, January 11, 1991, p. 103.

An elderly woman, Doña Josefa, sits in her hut, holding a gold coin. "I must be the richest woman in the world," she says to herself. But unbeknownst to her, a thief, Juan, crouches at her window, watching and listening. When Doña Josefa leaves, Juan ransacks the hut but fails to find her treasure. Tracking the woman across the countryside, he misses her again and again—coming instead upon many people who have been helped by her. And when the thief finally does catch up with her, he is surprised to find that he, too, has been touched by her simple goodness. Set in South America, this beautifully designed book features an unusual, rewarding fable and Waldman's lovely, stylized watercolors. It's a rich collaboration, worthy of repeated readings.

Carolyn Phelan

SOURCE: A review of *The Gold Coin,* in *Booklist,* Vol. 87, No. 13, March 1, 1991, pp. 1395-96.

Set in Central America, this original story concerns the salvation of a thief through his contact with goodness. When Juan peers into Doña Josepha's hut one night, he sees a gold coin shining in the old woman's hand and decides to steal it. Doña Josepha, a beloved healer, travels from sickbed to sickbed, giving comfort and offering her gold coin, which each invalid refuses to take from her. Following her for days, Juan comes to know the good families who revere Doña Josepha. When he finds the healer, she gives him the coin freely. Changed by his experiences, he gives it back. The book presents ideals of love and honor without becoming too sweet or stuffy. While longer than the usual picture-book story, this satisfying tale could be read aloud to primary-grade children. Waldman . . . contributes a series of fluid watercolor illustrations, large and small, which come together into a well-designed whole.

Ann Welton

SOURCE: A review of *The Gold Coin,* in *School Library Journal,* Vol. 37, No. 4, April, 1991, p. 88.

Juan has been a thief for many years. He is pale and bent from creeping about at night, and that's what he's doing the night he peeks into Doña Josefa's hut. She is holding a gold coin and says that she must be the richest woman in the world. Then and there, Juan determines to steal that coin, and any others she may have. It is a decision that changes Juan's life forever. This gentle story of redemption, ably translated by Randall, is structurally at once cumulative and circular, and is ideally suited for memorization and telling. It will work well as a read-aloud, too. Waldman's clean, pale watercolors have an art nouveau feel, and are large enough to be seen at story times. Whether told, read to a group, or shared one-on-one, the tale of Juan's search for an old woman's treasure makes an important point in a concise and satisfying manner.

SERAFINA'S BIRTHDAY (translated by Ana M. Cerro, 1992)

Caroline Ward

SOURCE: A review of *Serafina's Birthday,* in *The Horn Book Guide,* Vol. IV, No. 1, July-September, 1992, p. 18.

On the way to his friend's birthday party, Sebastian, an absent-minded rabbit, forgets the present. The culminating

theme—that guests are the most valuable present—and his attempts to rectify the situation are reminiscent of *Dandelion* by Don Freeman; however, the wordy text and ordinary, cartoonlike illustrations (by Louise Bates Satterfield) are no match for Freeman's classic.

Alexandra Marris

SOURCE: A review of *Serafina's Birthday,* in *School Library Journal,* Vol. 38, No. 9, September, 1992, p. 196.

The rabbit Sebastian has overslept and is late for Serafina's birthday party. To make matters worse, he forgets her gift as well. His trip to her home is fraught with mishaps: he almost misses his train stop, he is chased out of several gardens, he is scolded by irate squirrels, and he is pecked by crows. The party is winding down when he finally arrives, but he consoles himself by sitting down to tell the others about his adventures. While the plot strives to build action and excitement, Sebastian's conflict begins to feel more and more like an exercise in frustration; his continuing difficulties take on an aura of futility. Meanwhile, his conversations with himself echo with self-defeated overtones; he appears overly concerned about what others think of him. As a character, the little brown rabbit doesn't emanate any unique personality. The illustrations, line drawings with bright watercolor washes, are adequate but on the cloyingly sweet side.

THE ROOSTER WHO WENT TO HIS UNCLE'S WEDDING: A LATIN AMERICAN FOLKTALE (retold by Ada, 1992)

Maria Cecilia Silva-Diaz

SOURCE: A review of *The Rooster Who Went to His Uncle's Wedding: A Latin American Folktale,* in *The Horn Book Guide,* Vol. IV, No. 2, January-June, 1993, p. 324.

The rooster needs to clean his beak in time for a wedding, but the grass refuses to help him, so he asks the lamb to eat the grass. So begins a cumulative folktale narrated in a rhythmic cadenza. Bold illustrations [by Kathleen Kuchera] create a colorful tropical world, but the challenge of representing inanimate characters such as water and grass is unsatisfactorily resolved.

Graciela Italiano

SOURCE: A review of *The Rooster Who Went to His Uncle's Wedding: A Latin American Folktale,* in *Booklist,* Vol. 89, No. 13, March 1, 1993, p. 1231.

This delightful cumulative tale introduces a perfectly groomed rooster, with a gleaming beak, who's on his way to his uncle's wedding. As hunger overcomes him, he ponders, whether to "Peck or not peck?" while looking at "a single golden kernel of corn" lying in a puddle of mud. Peck he does, and he muddies his beak as he gobbles the kernel down. Now, how to get his beak clean? The velvety grass won't do it, but the rooster thinks perhaps he can scare the grass into helping, if he asks the lamb to eat the grass. The list of characters who refuse to help is long. Finally, the rooster's good friend, the Sun, comes to his rescue. Each character, when threatened by a natural adversary, does what it is supposed to do, which, in the end, helps the rooster. The rooster, a universal folk character humanized in many cultures, is appealing here. The story, which was told to Ada by her grandmother in Cuba, will delight young children with the sheer joy of its repetitive rhythms, and it is particularly appropriate to be told aloud. The illustrations, bright with tropical colors, depict a Latin American setting. An interesting addition to the folktale collection.

Publishers Weekly

SOURCE: A review of *The Rooster Who Went to His Uncle's Wedding: A Latin American Folktale,* in *Publishers Weekly,* Vol. 240, No. 17, April 26, 1993, p. 76.

The author of **The Gold Coin** retells a Latin American version of a familiar cumulative folk story, illustrated in the vibrant colors of the tropics. In a narrative line reminiscent of Rosanne Litzinger's *The Old Woman and Her Pig,* Ada tells of a rooster who muddies his beak en route to his uncle's wedding feast; he implores the grass to give it a cleaning, but is refused. As the brightly colored spreads become increasingly crowded with other recalcitrant creatures—lamb, dog, stick, fire, water—the feathered hero is finally saved by the sun, which sets off a chain reaction that solves the problem. Through harmonious repetition and singsong rhythms, Ada's leisurely, conversational tale neatly mimics the cadences of a traditional storyteller. Kuchera's geometric illustrations in intense hues of orange and chartreuse evoke the designs of Latin American folk art with their flat edges, sharp lines, zigzags and whorls. Frequent use of multiple panels on a single spread occasionally makes the detailed images difficult to interpret—though the artist deserves kudos for her animated rendering of such normally static objects as a stick and a blade of grass.

Lauralyn Person

SOURCE: A review of *The Rooster Who Went to His Uncle's Wedding: A Latin American Folktale,* in *School Library Journal,* Vol. 39, No. 5, May, 1993, p. 92.

Rooster, en route to his uncle's wedding, struggles with the dilemma of whether he should risk getting dirty in order to obtain a kernel of corn. His hunger overcomes his better judgment and, of course, he winds up " . . . with a beak full of mud." This leads into a cumulative tale that will be familiar to anyone who knows "The Old Woman and Her Pig" or any number of its variants. In this case, his quest to get clean is nicely circular: the sun, just coming

up as the book begins, is the one who agrees to break the chain of refusal, to repay the rooster for greeting him each morning. Ada's lively adaptation uses economical language with just enough detail to move things along. Vivid hand-colored prints illustrate the story well. All of the characters are festively arrayed: the blades of grass, for example, play musical instruments, and one is wearing a gaucho hat and a cape. The sheep wears a ruffled dress and has a bowl of fruit on her head, a la Carmen Miranda. The plain white borders contribute to the clean pleasing design. The stylized patterns, with lots of diamonds and zigzags, have the look of Central and South American folk art. A solid addition to folklore collections and a story hour hit as well.

MY NAME IS MARÍA ISABEL (translated by Ana M. Cerro, 1993; Spanish version as Me Llamo María Isabel, 1994)

Ann Welton

SOURCE: A review of *My Name Is María Isabel,* in *School Library Journal,* Vol. 39, No. 4, April, 1993, p. 117.

This gentle story tells of María Isabel Salazar López, who finds herself dubbed "Mary López" when her family moves and she is placed in a class with two other Marias. María Isabel finds it hard to respond to a name that does not seem like hers. Her teacher doesn't understand why it is so difficult for her to answer to "Mary" until the child is inspired to address her paper on "My Greatest Wish" to the topic of her name. The result is not only a happy ending, but also an affirming study of heritage and how it is integrally bound up in an individual's sense of self. The brief text, adequately extended by line drawings [by K. Dyble Thompson], reads aloud well and could certainly be used in conjunction with Gary Soto's *The Skirt* to illustrate the Hispanic culture that is part of the lives of many contemporary children.

Publishers Weekly

SOURCE: A review of *My Name Is María Isabel,* in *Publishers Weekly,* Vol. 240, No. 16, April 19, 1993, p. 62.

Armed with her new blue bookbag, María Isabel bravely faces her first day at a new school. But when she meets her new teacher, she is told there are already two other Marias in the class. "Why don't we call you Mary instead?" her teacher suggests, unaware that María was named for both her grandmothers, a grandfather and her father. María's inability to respond to "Mary" leads to more problems. Simply told, this story combines the struggle of a Puerto Rican family's efforts to improve their life with a shared sense of pride in their heritage. The author's carefully drawn characterizations avoid stereotypes, thus increasing their appeal and believability. An essay involving a wish list gives María a chance to reclaim her name, and allows her teacher to make amends. Abetted by Thompson's straightforward black-and-white drawings, this contemporary serves as a good reminder that no two names are really alike.

Irvy Gilbertson

SOURCE: A review of *My Name Is María Isabel,* in *The Five Owls,* Vol. VIII, No. 1, September-October, 1993, p. 14.

María Isabel Salazar López and her family have moved again. This means María Isabel must go to a new school and make new friends, which concerns her, since the school year has already begun. When María Isabel arrives at school, the teacher decides to call her Mary López because there are already two Marias in class. María Isabel is devastated. She has always been proud of her name, which her mother has explained this way: María is for her grandmother, whom she did not know, Isabel is for her other grandmother, whom she knows and loves, Salazar is for her father and, of course her grandfather Antonio, and López is for her mother and her grandfather Manuel. María Isabel has trouble recognizing the name the teacher has assigned to her and often fails to respond. As a result, the teacher thinks she is indifferent and María Isabel also misses the chance to participate in the Winter Pageant. The link of María Isabel's name with her heritage is an important theme in this story. As much as María Isabel wants to please her teacher, the name Mary López has no meaning in her life. María Isabel grows throughout the story. The reader realizes that the teacher's remedy to having three Marias in class has caused unnecessary problems for María Isabel and undermined her self-esteem. In a writing assignment, María Isabel explains her feelings; happily, the teacher addresses María Isabel by her given name and makes last-minute changes in the Winter Pageant to include her.

Translated from the Spanish by Ana M. Cerro, this multicultural book is written from an insider's perspective. The author was born in Cuba and lived in Spain and Peru before coming to the United States. Selected Spanish words are used to expose the reader to a different culture, yet the feelings of uncertainty, insecurity, and frustration are universal. Each chapter contains a black-and-white illustration to lend visual substance to the characters. The spider web depicted on the front and back of the jacket is an allusion to *Charlotte's Web,* which María Isabel is reading; she finds she is not the only one who has problems.

This is an excellent short chapter book that is accessible to beginning readers. The satisfying conclusion offers hope to children faced with the challenge of fitting into a new situation.

Language Arts

SOURCE: A review of *Me Llamo María Isabel,* in *Language Arts,* Vol. 73, No. 3, March, 1996, p. 207.

Alma Flor Ada's chapter book with black-and-white pencil illustrations is written totally in Spanish and is well suited for children in first through fourth grades. Ada uses straight-forward, graceful, and simple language to develop the story of an experience that is all too common among the immigrant children of the United States. In the López Salazar family's struggle to improve their life, they move to a school where María Isabel must attend classes in English. María Isabel's school progress is impeded by her teacher's insistence on calling her Mary López, a name she refuses to recognize as her own. The little girl's struggle to adjust to her new school and friends is exacerbated by her teacher's insensitivity. Important understandings about language and cultural identity can be gained by reading this book. Clearly communicated is María Isabel's sense of pride in her given name, which represents her Puerto Rican cultural heritage. During a writing assignment, María Isabel is able to reveal to the teacher her wish to be called María Isabel and to participate in the class drama presentation. An English version of this book is also available.

DEAR PETER RABBIT (Spanish version as *Querido Pedrín,* 1994)

Publishers Weekly

SOURCE: A review of *Dear Peter Rabbit,* in *Publishers Weekly,* Vol. 241, No. 8, February 21, 1994, p. 253.

Reminiscent of Janet and Allan Ahlberg's hugely successful *The Jolly Postman,* this clever picture book creates a fictitious flurry of correspondence between such familiar characters as Goldilocks (here given the surname McGregor, with a wink and a nod to Beatrix Potter), the Three Pigs, Baby Bear, Red Riding Hood and Peter Rabbit. As the plot thickens (will Goldilocks make a return visit to the Bears' house? Will Peter Rabbit be well enough to attend the Three Pigs' housewarming party?), Ada inventively weaves together the criss-crossing letters, neatly tying up the loose ends with a finale wherein the entire assembly (except for the now-tailless wolf) shows up for Goldilocks's birthday party. Ada clearly had fun extrapolating the characters' private lives, and her sunny treatment finds ready companionship in [Leslie] Tryon's delicately colored, lovingly detailed pen-and-ink and watercolor art. A Spanish edition, *Querido Pedrín,* is being issued simultaneously.

Kirkus Reviews

SOURCE: A review of *Dear Peter Rabbit,* in *Kirkus Reviews,* Vol. LXII, No. 5, March 1, 1994, p. 297.

The events in four familiar tales are cleverly intertwined and reported in a dozen letters. "Pig One" invites Peter Rabbit to a housewarming, but he can't go because he's in bed sipping camomile; Baby Bear wants his new friend Goldilocks McGregor to visit; Pigs One and Two report that they're now safely with Pig Three; Peter gets an unexpected invitation from Goldilocks and compliments the three pigs on the wolf's-tail soup served at the housewarming they finally managed to celebrate; the wolf orders a new tail and swears off pigs and little girls. Red Riding Hood wraps up events in a letter to her grandmother, while Tryon visualizes them in an inviting fairy-tale world, gently recalling both Gustave Doré and Beatrix Potter with entrancing, delicately colored crosshatched detail. In addition to more obvious uses, try a dramatic reading of these pleasingly childlike letters. Also available in Spanish.

Roger Sutton

SOURCE: A review of *Dear Peter Rabbit,* in *Bulletin of the Center for Children's Books,* Vol. 47, No. 8, April, 1994, p. 249.

What's going on here with all this clever deconstructing of favorite fairy tales? The Ahlbergs (with *The Jolly Postman* and *Ten in a Bed*), Scieszka and Smith (*The True Story of the Three Little Pigs* and *The Stinky Cheese Man*), Trivizas and Oxenbury (*The Three Little Wolves and the Big Bad Pig*) and many others are taking a new look at old tales, shifting allegiances, subverting endings, and introducing the most unlikely characters to each other. Like *The Jolly Postman, Dear Peter Rabbit* exchanges letters, here between Pig One and Peter Rabbit, as well as between Goldilocks (McGregor) and Baby Bear; a closing party brings everybody together, as well as occasioning a letter from Little Red Riding Hood: "Dear Grandma . . . Goldilocks has very interesting friends." Ada's book is as clever as most in the genre, and kids will enjoy putting together the narrative pieces from the various stories. Leslie Tryon's observant and fully-packed line-and-watercolor paintings have a romantic tone that softens the edges of the gimmick. John Barth has called parody "the literature of exhaustion," and this particular trend in children's books will probably wear itself out fairly quickly. So—where do we go from here?

Joy Fleishhacker

SOURCE: A review of *Dear Peter Rabbit,* in *School Library Journal,* Vol. 40, No. 7, July, 1994, p. 73.

A series of lively letters penned by beloved storybook characters tells an entertaining and imaginative tale. As the Big Bad Wolf lurks just out of sight, Pig One writes to Peter Rabbit, inviting him to a housewarming party at his newly built straw house. Meanwhile, Baby Bear sends Goldilocks a note asking her to visit, admonishing her to "knock on the door first before you come in." In reply, Goldilocks McGregor writes about vegetables missing from the garden and the "tiny jacket" and "tiniest pair of shoes" found by her father. Peter sends his regrets to Pig One; he caught cold while hiding from Mr. McGregor in a "half-full" watering can. Not to worry, due to uncontrollable

circumstances the party will take place at Stick House at a later date. The chatty correspondence continues, culminating in a birthday party that brings the characters face to face. Carefully weaving together the lives of these literary favorites into a seamless plot, Ada uses familiar elements to create a convincing and intriguing make-believe world. In addition to being fun to read, the letters move events along quickly and create a unique voice for each author. Tryon's inviting illustrations, rendered in pen and ink with watercolors, add both detail and dimension. Whether author or recipient is depicted, the pictures include and expand on the contents of each letter. Drawings of Peter Rabbit and Mr. McGregor are appropriately reminiscent of Beatrix Potter's originals. Children will be enchanted by this opportunity to meet familiar faces in new settings.

EL UNICORNIO DEL OESTE (translated by Rosa Zabizarreta as *The Unicorn of the West,* 1994)

Jane Marino

SOURCE: A review of *The Unicorn of the West,* in *School Library Journal,* Vol. 40, No. 6, June, 1994, p. 94.

A gentle story that can be effectively shared on many levels. A young unicorn who has never before met any other creatures of the forest tries to discover who he is. With each season, he meets a different animal: a spring robin, a summer butterfly, an autumn squirrel. But it's not until winter approaches that he hears a "melody" that seems to beckon him to a place where he meets the Unicorns of the East, South, and North. They tell him that he is the Unicorn of the West and that every seven years on the solstice, the four meet to insure that each corner of the world will always know love and beautiful dreams. The unicorn returns home, content to know his identity and with the knowledge that he has true friends. In *The Gold Coin* and *My Name Is María Isabel,* Ada employed similar themes of self-discovery. Here, it is interwoven with the idea that both friendship on an individual level and peace on a universal level are important. The story is well told and folkloric in its approach as a pattern is developed and repeated with each encounter with a different animal. The [Abigail Pizer] watercolor illustrations are soft without being pale and portray an apt world for this original fable.

Rose Zertuche Treviño

SOURCE: A review of *The Unicorn of the West,* in *School Library Journal,* Vol. 40, No. 8, August, 1994, p. 181.

Every evening, a unicorn wanders through the forest seeking his identity. He meets a robin, a butterfly, and a squirrel, each of whom decides to help him find another creature like himself. Most children are fascinated by unicorns and the magic that surrounds them, and they won't be disappointed with this tale that's illustrated with lovely, bright watercolors. A good choice for independent reading or primary-grade storytimes.

WHERE THE FLAME TREES BLOOM
(Spanish version as *Donde Florecen Los Flamboyanes,* 1994)

Martha V. Parravano

SOURCE: A review of *Where the Flame Trees Bloom,* in *The Horn Book Guide,* Vol. VI, No. 1, July-December, 1994, p. 72.

The collection of eleven short stories, reminiscences of the author's childhood in rural Cuba, is valuable not only for its authentic voice but also for Ada's re-creation of truly memorable characters: her uneducated but wise great-grandmother; her grandfather, who let a fortune slip through his fingers rather than leave the side of his dying wife. Black-and-white sketches [by Antonio Martorell] accompany the text.

Susan Dove Lempke

SOURCE: A review of *Where the Flame Trees Bloom,* in *Bulletin of the Center for Children's Books,* Vol. 48, No. 6, February, 1995, p. 190.

Ada explains in an introduction to these family memories that her family lived in Cuba, spending their evenings telling the stories Ada retells here (she adds a few paragraphs to provide background explanations as needed). Most of the stories either reveal qualities that Ada admires in her relatives, as in the story about her grandmother encouraging her school pupils to talk to a lonely-looking man, or they tell about turning points in lives, as when her uncle realizes the importance of his teaching job when he mistakenly believes that his pupils have been killed by lightning. Ada skillfully depicts the country of her childhood with its coconuts, flame trees, and heat, and her writing evokes the warmth and character of her family. However, the stories are mostly low-key, quiet explorations of character and values (the one with a family friend dangling beneath a train being a notable exception), and they generally stay true to life in having no grand finale. The descriptive passages may turn readers with a taste for more action away, and the ink wash drawings, while in keeping with the tone of the stories, don't add much child appeal. Reading the book to young listeners, though, could prompt them to share moments from their own family stories.

Marilyn Long Graham

SOURCE: A review of *Where the Flame Trees Bloom,* in *School Library Journal,* Vol. 41, No. 2, February, 1995, p. 96.

Those who wonder what "family values" really are may possibly find the answer in this slim volume of short stories. Telling of her childhood in Cuba, Ada begins with an introduction to her homeland followed by 11 episodes about her family and her community. One story tells of her grandfather Modesto's courage and loyalty in the face of the death of his beloved wife and the simultaneous collapse of the Cuban economy. Another tells of her great-grandmother Mina, who continued to make rag dolls for the village children even after she had lost her sight. And a third tale tells of a Japanese street vendor who sold ice cream for a living, but gave generous samples to children who could not afford to pay. Warmth and love for a treasured childhood exude from the pages. The writing is elegant, but not overly sweet. Each selection stands well on its own. Children can read this book independently or enjoy listening to it read aloud.

Miriam Martinez and Marcia F. Nash

SOURCE: A review of *Where the Flame Trees Bloom,* in *Language Arts,* Vol. 72, No. 7, November, 1995, pp. 542-43.

In *Where the Flame Trees Bloom,* Alma Flor Ada remembers stories from her childhood in Cuba. In one story, she tells of her grandmother, a teacher, whose greatest lesson was teaching her students to reach out to others. In another, a lightning strike shows a teacher the importance of believing in his students' future. In yet another, a surveyor uses his wits to save himself when stranded in the middle of a railroad bridge with a train hurtling toward him. These are poignant stories about courage, determination, faith, and love. Some are based on the author's own experiences, while others were told to her by family members. Whatever the source, each clearly comes from the heart and gives readers the opportunity to meet the people of Cuba from an earlier era.

MEDIOPOLLITO: HALF CHICKEN: A NEW VERSION OF THE TRADITIONAL STORY
(retold by Ada; translated by Rosa Zubizarreta, 1995)

Kirkus Reviews

SOURCE: A review of *Mediopollito: Half Chicken: A New Version of the Traditional Story,* in *Kirkus Reviews,* Vol. LXIII, No. 14, July 15, 1995, p. 1020.

A traditional Spanish tale of how the weathervane came to be, set in Mexico and told in Spanish on the left page of each spread, and English on the right. Half-Chicken, a hatchling with only one eye, one wing, and one leg, is treated as a marvel by everyone, and becomes so vain that he decides to go impress the viceroy in Mexico City with his uniqueness. Along the way he turns a few good deeds: He untangles the wind, fans a guttering flame, releases an impounded stream. At the viceroy's palace, Half-Chicken isn't received with the pomp he expected, and escapes the stew pot with the help of the elements; fire, water, and wind take him out of harm's way, up to a rooftop where he can be found to this day. Both texts have a good simple beat, with enough repetition to allow readers in one language to comfortably sample the other. [Kim] Howard's stylized, two-dimensional pictures demand closer viewing than story-hour sharing will allow; recalling Mexican mural art, they have a weathered, antique texture, as if some of the chunky blocks of color have been rubbed with ash.

The message is universal and bears repeating: Neighborliness is its own reward, but paybacks come in handy.

Annie Ayres

SOURCE: A review of *Mediopollito: Half-Chicken: A New Version of the Traditional Story,* in *Booklist,* Vol. 92, No. 2, September 15, 1995, p. 165.

Hip hop hip hop, Half-Chicken is off to Mexico City to see the court of the viceroy. Along the way, he helps the stream, the fire, and the wind, and they, in turn, help Half-Chicken when the viceroy's cook tries to turn him into chicken soup. Finally, the wind blows Half-Chicken to safety a top a palace tower. "And from that day on, weathercocks have stood on their only leg, seeing everything that happens below, and pointing whichever way their friend the wind blows." Ada gives her riotous retelling of this traditional folktale about the vain but helpful Half-Chicken a flavorful colonial Mexican setting. Howard matches the frolicsome mood and Hispanic setting with exuberant and glowing illustrations inspired by the patterns and textures of Mexican murals. Presented in a bilingual format and brimming with silliness and the simple repetition that children savor, this picture book is a jewel that will add a spicy sparkle to any folktale collection.

Graciela Italiano

SOURCE: A review of *Mediopollito: Half Chicken: A New Version of the Traditional Story,* in *School Library Journal,* Vol. 41, No. 11, November, 1995, p. 87.

An adaptation of a Spanish folktale that explains the origin of weather vanes. The hatching of a chick with only one wing, one leg, one eye, and half the usual number of feathers raises quite a stir on a colonial Mexican ranch. All of the attention encourages the vain Mediopollito, Half-Chicken (as he is called), to seek his fortune. He encounters, in turn, fire, water, and wind and assists each of them during the course of his trip "to Mexico City to see the court of the viceroy!" In return, the elements come to the fowl's aid and Half-Chicken finds his rightful place in the scheme of things. The repetitive and predictable nature of the tale makes it an appropriate read-aloud choice. The translation retains the meaning and flavor of the original Spanish, which appears alongside the English on each double-page spread. The folksy and brightly colored illustrations, "inspired by the patterns and texture of Mexican murals," provide lively and interesting visual information. While the characters are at times a bit caricatured, this title remains a good addition to folklore collections.

Martha V. Parravano

SOURCE: A review of *Mediopollito: Half-Chicken: A New Version of the Traditional Story,* in *The Horn Book Magazine,* Vol. LXXI, No. 6, November-December, 1995, pp. 749-50.

Noted translator and writer Ada has set her bilingual retelling of this traditional tale from Spain in colonial Mexico. As the humorous rather offbeat story opens, a mother hen hatches a chick with "only one wing, only one leg, only one eye, and only half as many feathers as the other chicks." Half-Chicken, as he comes to be known, gets a swelled (half) head from all the attention he attracts and decides to travel to Mexico City to show his uniqueness to the viceroy. Off he hops, stopping on his urgent quest only to unblock a stream impeded by branches, fan a small fire that is about to go out, and untangle a wind caught in some bushes. Half-Chicken finally reaches the viceroy's palace, but instead of the hero's welcome he expects, the little rooster is greeted with jeers and ignominiously thrown into a kettle on the kitchen fire. The good deeds Half-Chicken performed on his journey, however, literally get him out of hot water: the grateful fire tells the water to jump on him and put him out, and the water complies. Then, tossed out the window by the frustrated cook, Half-Chicken is again rescued, this time by the wind, who blows him to the top of a tower. There, transformed into a weather vane, he is forever safe from the cooking pot. Ada's liberal use of repetition, especially in describing Half-Chicken's gait—"hip hop hip hop"—and the convention of the three helpers keep this rather unusual story grounded, while Howard's vibrant, jaunty illustrations, rich in warm reds and golds and lively with pattern and texture, move the tale forward with great energy. Her humorous depiction of poor scrawny Half-Chicken is particularly successful.

JORDI'S STAR (1996)

Amy E. Brandt

SOURCE: A review of *Jordi's Star,* in *Bulletin of the Center for Children's Books,* Vol. 50, No. 4, December, 1996, p. 126.

There is little vegetation on the deforested hillsides in Catalonia where the bearded Jordi herds his goats, and when he attempts to dig a well, the rocky ground yields no water. The effect of a sudden rainstorm changes his solitary, workaday life when he discovers a fallen star in the pool made by rainwater in his well hole. Touched that the star has chosen him for a companion, Jordi honors their friendship with gifts of quartz, moss, and wildflowers that he places in and around the pool. Jordi eventually replants the entire mountainside, learning to reach out to people along the way (à la *Miss Rumphius* and *The Selfish Giant*). Unfortunately, Ada's explanation of Jordi's misunderstanding of the star's reflection denies readers the suspension of disbelief necessary in a folktale-like story. This defensive action weakens our opinion of Jordi, making his croonings to the star sound sentimental and silly. [Susan] Gaber expresses the rocky, unpredictable landscape with dark hues of blue, brown, and green, lightening her palette as Jordi's relationship with the star grows. Small details supplement narrative events, as when starlight from the sky-bound star shines through Jordi's window as he sleeps, while Jordi himself is a broad and solid figure at home in his environment, whether barren or beautified.

Joy Fleishhacker

SOURCE: A review of *Jordi's Star,* in *School Library Journal,* Vol. 42, No. 12, December, 1996, p. 84.

A solitary shepherd finds a special kind of magic. On a hillside stripped bare by woodcutters, Jordi tends his goats. Hoping to save a trip to the river, he digs a hole in the ground, but the would-be well remains dry. An intense rainstorm fills the hole, creating a pool that mirrors the night sky. Gazing at its reflection, Jordi truly believes that a star has fallen into the pool. Overcome with happiness, he attempts to make his new friend comfortable, gradually bringing rocks, flowers, and other gifts from nature. As the years pass, the now-lush hillside flourishes and both Jordi and his star shine with contentment. Written with strong emotion and a sense of wonder, this story has the tone and resonance of a folktale. Because Jordi is presented with dignity and simple wisdom, his belief in the star does not seem foolish, but rather an act of faith powerful enough to change his life. Done with acrylics on coquille board, Gaber's paintings are pleasing. Jordi is the only splash of color against a barren background; his bearded, square-jawed face is painted with deep emotion as, touched by starlight, he smiles in his sleep, or gazes lovingly into the pool. Landscape scenes are varied with close-up pictures, and changes in the perspective add detail and depth to the illustrations. A moving, beautifully told story.

Susan Dove Lempke

SOURCE: A review of *Jordi's Star,* in *Booklist,* Vol. 93, No. 7, December 1, 1996, p. 652.

Jordi lives a difficult, lonely life on a rocky hill, tending a herd of goats. The terrain is bleak, and even getting water is difficult. When the hole he digs to try to open a well fills with water during a thunderstorm, Jordi's life is forever altered. That night he sees a star shining in the pool, and he gazes on it enraptured. He is certain the star has gone to sleep when it disappears from the pool the next day, and sure enough, that night the star reappears. Feeling an urge to nurture his new friend, he begins bringing it things—large rocks, which he puts together with soft moss, shiny quartz pebbles, which he tosses into the bottom of the pool; and "some tiny blue flowers he had never noticed before." Day by

day, he brings more gifts to the star, gradually transforming his landscape and himself: "Jordi could not understand how life had once seemed so sad and lonely to him, filled as it was with so many beautiful things to discover." This touching, lyrically told story is given substance by Gaber's earthy illustrations, which show Jordi as a poignantly real man, his broad face and large hands in sharp contrast to the delicate flowers and the twinkling star. The book is appropriate for any picture-book collection, but one particular illustration, which shows Jordi sleeping as starlight shining in the window illuminates a cross and an icon, makes this an especially fine choice for church and parochial school libraries.

GATHERING THE SUN: AN ALPHABET IN SPANISH AND ENGLISH (translated by Rosa Zubizarreta, 1997)

Ann Welton

SOURCE: A review of *Gathering the Sun: An Alphabet in Spanish and English,* in *School Library Journal,* Vol. 43, No. 3, March, 1997, pp. 169-70.

An alphabet book with exceptional illustrations and excellent poetry that gives voice to the experience of Hispanic agricultural workers. Each letter is matched with a Spanish word (for example, "Arboles" for "A") and accompanied by a poem in both Spanish and English that describes how the plant, fruit, vegetable, person, or feeling functions in the lives of these workers. Zubizarreta's English translations are informed and graceful, but predictably cannot match the Spanish originals in rhythm, assonance, or meter. [Simón] Silva's vibrant, double-page, gouache illustrations are reminiscent of the artwork of Diego Rivera and José Clemente Orozco. The colors are brilliant, and the scope has a certain larger-than-life sense to it. This is a book that begs to be read aloud to all students, whether they are Spanish speaking or not. The sound of the poems will draw them in. The touching elegy for César Chávez successfully imparts the impact of a heroic man on his people. Whether used to show the plight of migrant workers or the pride Hispanic laborers feel in their heritage, this is an important book.

Annie Ayres

SOURCE: A review of *Gathering the Sun: An Alphabet in Spanish and English,* in *Booklist,* Vol. 93, No. 16, April 15, 1997, p. 1431.

Using the Spanish alphabet as a template, Ada has written 27 poems that celebrate both the bounty of the harvest and the Mexican heritage of the farmworkers and their families. The poems, presented in both Spanish and English, are short and simple bursts of flavor: **"Arboles/ Trees," "Betabel/Beet," "Cesar Chavez,"** etc. Silva's sun-drenched gouache paintings are robust, with images sculpted in paint. Brimming with respect and pride, the book, with its mythic vision of the migrant farm worker, will add much to any unit on farming or Mexican American heritage.

Janice M. Del Negro

SOURCE: A review of *Gathering the Sun: An Alphabet in Spanish and English,* in *Bulletin of the Center for Children's Books,* Vol. 50, No. 10, June, 1997, pp. 348-49.

A series of expository poetic pieces on the lives of migrant farm workers is arranged according to the Spanish alphabet in this bilingual picture book. From *Arboles* (Trees) to *Zanahoria* (Carrot), Ada selects various elements from the itinerant lives of farmworkers and creates short verses, most of which commemorate the fruits of the harvest and the closeness of family. Each double-page spread features two letters; each letter is in a red-bordered text box accompanied by a short piece in Spanish, with the English translation alongside it. Silva's paintings are garish with summer colors, the verdant green fields aflame with red fruits and flowers, and, except for the spread where it's raining on a field of lettuce, even the sky is a hot summer blue. While there is little differentiation between the old faces and the young ones, the massive compositions have an elemental appeal. Both the format and text dogmatically serve the theme, although Ada's over-earnest approach to giving children a look at their own and other people's lives is understandably sympathetic.

George R. Bodmer

SOURCE: A review of *Gathering the Sun: An Alphabet in Spanish and English,* in *American Book Review,* Vol. 19, No. 1, November-December, 1997, pp. 12-13.

Gathering the Sun is a bilingual alphabet book from the perspective of a Hispanic migrant farm worker; the book carries a distinct political point of view (the letter C honors Cesar Chavez) and describes the work with pride and lush detail. Once again, the impulse here is to educate as well as to expose the young reader to a segment of our population he or she might not have been aware of. The food we eat is the result of human labor unseen in the city: "Empty boxes/ wait for us/ to bend our backs and fill them up." Writer Ada emphasizes the pride of the workers for their jobs and the history of the people: "Honor is the work/ we do in the fields./ Honor is a family/ who loves and cares for one another./ Honor is being true to myself/ as I wake up each morning." This book is overwhelmingly positive, without any sense that there are abuses or difficulties to this life in the fields. The gouache paintings of Simón Silva, who himself grew up in a migrant farmworker family, are dominated by the oranges and earth tones of Mexican mural painting, and stress even more than the text the closeness of the farmworkers' families and their honoring of the children.

LA LAGARITAA Y EL SOL: CUENTO TRADICIONAL EN INGLÉS Y ESPAÑOL (translated by Rosa Zubizarreta, as *The Lizard and the Sun: A Folktale in English and Spanish,* 1997)

Janice M. Del Negro

SOURCE: A review of *The Lizard and the Sun: A Folktale in English and Spanish,* in *Bulletin of the Center for Children's Books,* Vol. 51, No. 2, October, 1997, p. 40.

Once, in ancient Mexico, the sun disappeared. For days the anxious people wait for the sun to return, but it does not. When lizard discovers a rock glowing with an inner light, she tells the emperor, and they awaken the sleeping sun; it returns to the sky, shedding light and warmth on all the earth. Ada retells this traditional tale with graceful language and read-aloud rhythms, juxtaposing images of the tenacious, questing lizard against the darkness of jungle, marketplace, and palace. [Felipe] Dávalos's paintings are rich with color and expression as the bright green lizard traverses the torchlit night in balanced compositions that spring to bright life with the discovery of the brilliant, sleeping sun. The bilingual book has English text on the left-hand page and Spanish text on the right. An author's note states that Ada remembers this story from a fragment in an old reading textbook, and it gives some cultural context although no specific written source.

Julie Corsaro

SOURCE: A review of *The Lizard and the Sun: A Folktale in English and Spanish,* in *Booklist,* Vol. 94, No. 8, December 15, 1997, p. 698.

Presented in both Spanish and English, this gentle traditional tale from Mexico shows how people working together can get the job done. When the sun disappears from the sky, it is lizard who discovers a rock that was "shining as though it had a light inside." Traveling to the distant city, she tells the emperor who orders her to move it. But when she is unable to, the emperor and the woodpecker help lizard release the reluctant sun trapped inside. The structure is different from many folktales, allowing more room for Ada's eloquent voice. Dávalos sets the story during the time of the Aztec empire; his stylistically detailed artwork is initially veiled in midnight blue but erupts in golden yellow when the sun finally returns to the sky. According to the author's note, Ada remembers this pourquoi story from an old reading text.

THE CHRISTMAS TREE: A CHRISTMAS RHYME IN SPANISH AND ENGLISH (Spanish version as *El Arbol de Navidad,* 1997)

Publishers Weekly

SOURCE: A review of *The Christmas Tree: A Christmas Rhyme in Spanish and English,* in *Publishers Weekly,* Vol. 244, No. 41, October 6, 1997, p. 54.

One by one, members of a family add decorations to their Christmas tree, and Ada's cumulative text charts their offerings—from Grandma's candle to Uncle Irineo's painted sleigh ornament. With a line of text in English followed by the line in rhyming Spanish, the quietly graceful narrative is complemented by [Terry] Ybáñez's folk-art style illustrations, rendered in acrylic on black paper. Simple borders start out incorporating a single visual element—candy canes, stars, a sprig of evergreen—and grow gradually more intricate as additional ornaments are added.

Kirkus Reviews

SOURCE: A review of *The Christmas Tree: A Christmas Rhyme in Spanish and English,* in *Kirkus Reviews,* Vol. LXV, No. 24, December 15, 1997, p. 1832.

A lilting Spanish text and its weak English counterpart relate a cumulative tale about the decorating of a tree, and provide a good argument against the use of bilingual texts.

"Look at the beautiful Christmas tree/with the bright candle/Grandma lit,/the candy cane/Grandpa hung,/and the sleigh/Uncle Irineo painted!" cannot compare to "¡Qué lindo el árbol de Navidad/adornado con la vela/que encendió Abuela,/con el caramelo/que le colgó Abuelo/y con el trineo/de tío Irineo!" These events are illustrated over several pages. The text is so brief that there are only five couplets in the last appearance of the rhyme, and only five ornaments on the large tree. A final page expresses the family's happiness that Christmas has arrived. A lengthy note describes various customs of the season from the author's childhood. The perspectives in the art are flat, more amateurish than naive, with static compositions that do not convey the joy expressed in the text. An unfortunate effort in almost every respect.

YOURS TRULY, GOLDILOCKS (translated by Rosa Zubizarreta, 1998)

Kitty Flynn

SOURCE: A review of *Yours Truly, Goldilocks,* in *The Horn Book Guide,* Vol. IX, No. 2, January-June, 1998, p. 282.

In this epistolary companion to *Dear Peter Rabbit,* Goldilocks, Red Riding Hood, Baby Bear, Peter Rabbit, and the three Pigs correspond about the Pigs' upcoming housewarming party. The letters weave bits from each characters' folktale into the story; the elaborate illustrations [by Leslie Tryon] provide plenty of detail (camouflaged wolves are spying in many of the pictures), but two wordless spreads of the climactic party scene interrupt the story's pace.

Ilene Cooper

SOURCE: A review of *Yours Truly, Goldilocks,* in *Booklist,* Vol. 94, No. 17, May 1, 1998, p. 1520.

In this sequel to *Dear Peter Rabbit*, a housewarming party is planned for the Three Little Pigs through a series of letters between the pigs, Goldilocks, Baby Bear, and Little Red Riding Hood. But the fairy tale characters aren't the only ones exchanging letters. Big, bad cousins Wolfy Lupus and Fer O'Cious have heard about the party and are writing each other with some plans that spell trouble for the party goers. The letter format is a bit confusing at first but will gain appeal as kids get the characters straight in their minds. Each attractive two-page spread features a letter and a facing full-page picture of the letter writer, often shown in some action that extends the story. Fans of the previous book or lovers of fractured fairy tales will be the book's natural audience.

Publishers Weekly

SOURCE: A review of *Yours Truly, Goldilocks,* in *Publishers Weekly,* Vol. 245, No. 21, May 25, 1998, p. 89.

In this sly picture book, Ada and Tryon make a return visit to the storybook backdrop of their *Dear Peter Rabbit.* While the sequel succeeds as a stand—alone, it offers double the fun in tandem with its predecessor. The exchange of letters among familiar characters—Goldilocks, the Three Little Pigs, Peter Rabbit, Little Red Riding Hood, Baby Bear and, of course, the Big Bad Wolf (aka Fer O'Cious)-continues as the pigs invite their pals to their new, wolf-proof home for a housewarming party. The wolf, however, has been spying on the pigs, and he hatches a plan of his own, suggesting that his cousin join him in an ambush. But the wolves haven't counted on Baby Bear's mother and her swift reflexes. The mixing and matching of nursery favorites provides a lively framework for the epistolary conceit and allows even the youngest readers access to the inside track. Amusing details, meanwhile, hook older readers (Goldilocks, for instance, is imagined as Mr. McGregor's daughter, and resides on Veggie Lane). Tryon enriches her delicate pen-and-ink and watercolor illustrations with an abundance of delicious visual tidbits, as in the cover art, which shows the wolf on a stakeout, peering through a telescope at his prey. The ending hints of more adventures to come—good news indeed.

Beth Tegart

SOURCE: A review of *Yours Truly, Goldilocks,* in *School Library Journal,* Vol. 44, No. 7, July, 1998, p. 64.

Like *Dear Peter Rabbit,* this charming book tells its story through an exchange of letters. Here Ada chronicles the attempt of the three little pigs to plan a housewarming party. Meanwhile the villains from the previous title are still up to no good, spying on the residents of the forest and planning an attack on the homeward-bound guests. Fortunately, the surprise is on them and the two wolves lose both their pride and their fur. This is fairy-tale fun at its best. Following these well-loved characters on a new adventure tickles the imagination with fanciful "what ifs."

Tryon's wonderfully intricate colored drawings, with their delightful details and carefully wrought scenarios, bring the action to life. Perspective plays an important role in many of the pictures, from the wolf's telescope-lens view of his victims, to an interior scene of Peter Rabbit's den. Warm colors and sharp details pull readers right into the Hidden Forest. The climactic scenes are on wordless double-page spreads that perfectly convey a sense of frivolity and fear, while the final letter leaves readers hoping for yet another installment. Get on the mailing list for these letters.

THE MALACHITE PALACE (translated by Rosa Zubizarreta, 1998)

Pat Matthews

SOURCE: A review of *The Malachite Palace,* in *Bulletin of the Center for Children's Books,* Vol. 51, No. 7, March, 1998, pp. 234-35.

The little princess living in the malachite palace is not allowed to consort with the "rude," "ignorant," and "common" children she hears playing outside the ornate iron gates of her home. The queen (in gold), the lady-in-waiting (in white), and the governess (in black), looking suspiciously like the long-lost cousins of Cinderella's step-relations, make sure of that. When a delicate yellow songbird flies through a palace window, they immediately cage it and try to seduce it into singing with chocolate, caviar, and a golden cage: "But in spite of all their efforts, the little bird remained silent." Nothing unforeseen happens in this new fairy tale that looks every inch the part: luminous acrylics [by Leonid Gore] create a delicate, hazy lushness and exude an air of elegance that is pretty to look at, but the fairy-tale plot elements remain caged in clichés. The three women are never menacing enough to create the required tension, and the bird's release by the princess, closely coinciding with her newly declared resolve to play with the children on the outside, is a foregone conclusion. While this lacks bite, it might satisfy those with a sweet tooth for frothy confections.

Kirkus Reviews

SOURCE: A review of *The Malachite Palace,* in *Kirkus Reviews,* Vol. LXVI, No. 9, May 1, 1998, p. 654.

From Ada an original fairy tale that is predictable, elevated to beauty by Gore's paintings.

A princess—a child—is isolated in a palace, away from the "rude," "ignorant," and "common" children who play outside her gates. One day an exquisite yellow bird visits her, singing a joyful tune; the princess cages it and its joy fades. She frees the bird, and eventually frees herself, joining the children outside. The message is heavy-handed, the telling is without style, the setting is nondescript. The illustrations, however, are ephemeral: The princess and her surroundings are depicted in Gore's paintings as if they are seen through gauze. The angles of the characters' faces, the sharp definition of the cage, the detailed scrollwork of the windows and gates are all in perfect contrast to the hazy existence of a friendless princess—an isolation based on prejudice and hearsay, and one to be willingly shattered.

Publishers Weekly

SOURCE: A review of *The Malachite Palace,* in *Publishers Weekly,* Vol. 245, No. 18, May 4, 1998, p. 212.

Gore's acrylic and ink illustrations, spun like gossamer and lit with an inner radiance, lend their magic to a tale about a lonely princess. Confined to the castle and forbidden to play with the children outside the gates (whom the queen, the governess and the lady-in-waiting deem common), the princess is delighted when a little yellow bird flies in through the window, filling the palace with "a light and joyful music." After it is captured and placed in a cage, however, the little bird ceases to sing. Only when she sets it free, turning its cage into a bird feeder so that it and its friends may come and go at will, does it sing joyfully again. Seeing the bird's happiness inspires the princess to seek her own, and she ventures for the first time beyond the palace gates to play with the other children. Ada puts a bit of a fresh spin on the tired metaphor of the bird in the gilded cage by having the girl take responsibility for her own freedom. But it is Gore's airy, diaphanous illustrations that lift the tale above the sum of its parts. Studies in the refinements of light and texture, they appear overlaid with a delicate, filmy gauze, and their weightless elegance imbues the translucent green walls of the malachite palace and the sun-dappled interiors with a mysterious, ethereal beauty.

Hazel Rochman

SOURCE: A review of *The Malachite Palace,* in *Booklist,* Vol. 94, No. 18, May 15, 1998, p. 1629.

An original fairy tale/fable, translated from Spanish, tells a touching story of a privileged child in a gilded cage, who sets herself free. The princess lives in splendor in the malachite palace, but she is shut in there. She hears the laughter of children playing in the fields outside the gates, but she is forbidden to join the "common, ignorant" crowd. Gore's full-page, acrylic-and-ink pictures, in rich, shimmering shades of green and red, show the angelic child nearly overwhelmed by her flamboyant care-givers: the arrogant queen, the repressive governess, the protective lady-in-waiting. Then a singing bird flies into the child's room; the ladies lock him into a silver cage, and he stops singing—until the princess opens the cage and lets him fly away. She transforms the empty cage into an open archway, and finally she opens the ornate palace gates for herself and runs outside to play with the children. The theatrical illustrations provide a lavish setting for the sturdy child's struggle to leave home.

UNDER THE ROYAL PALMS: A CHILDHOOD IN CUBA (1998)

Sylvia V. Meisner

SOURCE: A review of *Under the Royal Palms: A Childhood in Cuba,* in *School Library Journal,* Vol. 44, No. 12, December, 1998, p. 132.

This simple and graceful reminiscence of a childhood in Cuba in the 1940s is a companion to *Where the Flame Trees Bloom.* Although not wealthy, the author's family lived comfortably with aunts, uncles, and cousins in a large, shared family home in the small town of Camagüey. Here any event beyond the ordinary became the focus of everyone's attention and the fuel for many days of conversation. Each chapter includes an early memory or experience of Ada's: nursing the baby bats that fell onto her porch, the production of simple and inexpensive plaster figures for nativity scenes, etc. The author writes about the contrast of wealth and poverty in her country at that time and of the people who made an impression on her, including a ballet teacher who befriended her during a lonely year in a new school, and an uncle and aunt who worked with lepers. Her observations of people lead to a series of revelations that shaped her life. Black-and-white photographs of the author and her family appear throughout.

Publishers Weekly

SOURCE: A review of *Under the Royal Palms: A Childhood in Cuba,* in *Publishers Weekly,* Vol. 245, No. 49, December 7, 1998, p. 61.

In this handsomely designed companion volume to *Where the Flame Trees Bloom,* Ada once again draws upon her experiences growing up in post-war Cuba. In a short introduction, the author describes her hometown, Camagüey, as a "city of contrasts"—diverse religions and education and economic levels ("some had so much and others had very little"). The 10 stories that follow do not focus on these oppositions so much as the unique experiences of young Alma and her extended family. Several memories poignantly expose the disparity between those who have

and those who have not, such as "Explorers" in which young Alma and her cousin get lost in a marabu field and are aided and fed by a poverty-stricken family. Others illustrate life lessons (for example, the impossible but gleeful task of counting bats in flight for their nightly feeding taught Alma to appreciate the process of an endeavor, rather than its completion). But the best of these stories simply recreate a poignant or humorous moment from the author's girlhood: Alma sipping from a porron (a small clay pot) at school, lovingly filled with water by her mother; Alma's pride in her uncle's daring turning to grief when he dies in an airplane crash. Many of the stories stand well alone, but some take a meandering expository path to recount a history or explain a term. These more formal (though often graceful) tangents distance readers from the slices of life. Still, at the core of the collection, there is a heartfelt portrayal of a quickly disappearing culture and a vastly beautiful land.

THE THREE GOLDEN ORANGES (1999)

Kirkus Reviews

SOURCE: A review of *The Three Golden Oranges,* in *Kirkus Reviews,* Vol. LXVII, No. 9, May 1, 1999, p. 718.

Ada reworks the traditional story of Blancaflor, taking swipes at greed, vanity, and the practice of arranged marriages in the process. Some well-traveled types help make the points: older brothers full of themselves and not above treachery; the innocent, well-intentioned youngest brother; a wise older woman; and a young woman in dire circumstances, with the moral fiber to endure. Here the story revolves around three brothers wishing to wed, and how they seek the advice of an elderly woman and then ignore all her warnings. The two bad-of-heart brothers wind up in a castle jail, and then marriageless; Matías, the pure one, liberates a family under a sorcerer's spell, gains love and marriage, and fulfills his mother's wishes. Ada invests her lengthy retelling with a quiet musicality that softens the predictability of the narrative. Meanwhile, the Spanish countryside comes blazingly alive under the bold illustrations of [Reg] Cartwright's stylized, utterly transporting artwork.

Additional coverage of Ada's life and career is contained in the following sources published by The Gale Group: *Contemporary Authors,* Vol. 123 and *Something about the Author,* Vols. 43, 84.

Alice Dalgliesh

1893-1979

Trinidad-born American author of fiction, nonfiction, and picture books.

Major works include *The Silver Pencil* (1944), *The Bears on Hemlock Mountain* (1952), *The Courage of Sarah Noble* (1954), *The Thanksgiving Story* (1954), *The Columbus Story* (1955).

INTRODUCTION

The author of more than forty books for children and young people, Dalgliesh is praised equally for her fiction and nonfiction. She is also recognized as an editor, educator, and children's literature professional who devoted for life to bringing children and books together. Three of Dalgliesh's books were runners-up for the John Newbery Medal, and one of her books was a runner-up for the Caldecott Medal. As a writer, Dalgliesh created informational books, historical fiction, contemporary realistic fiction, and picture books. She is noted for her ability to make history come alive for young readers and is also acknowledged for creating authentic depictions of modern life. Dalgliesh directed most of her works to primary and middle graders, although two of her most well received books, the semi-autobiographical novel *The Silver Pencil* and its sequel *Along Janet's Road* (1946), are directed to young adults. Often commended for creating distinctive informational picture books for preschoolers and early readers, Dalgliesh is also credited for writing exceptional historical and contemporary realistic fiction. In addition, Dalgliesh wrote textbooks and primers and edited collections of stories, folktales, fairy tales, and Mother Goose rhymes as well as a collection of the horse stories of Will James. Her nonfiction is noted for encompassing a variety of subjects, locales, and periods as well as for its accessibility and thorough research.. In these works, Dalgliesh addressed such topics as the kings and queens of England, the discovery of America, the story of the first colonies, the background behind Thanksgiving and the Fourth of July, a South American travelogue, and the biographies of Christopher Columbus and Charles Lindbergh. Since she believed that nonfiction should not be dull or loaded with too much information, Dalgliesh offered stories with essential facts tucked into their storylines. Dalgliesh is often acknowledged for creating the first or best books on her subjects for her audience; in its day, her nonfiction was quite popular and went through several editions.

As with her nonfiction, Dalgliesh was praised for the diversity and accuracy of her historical fiction. Often drawing her inspiration from historical figures and incidents as well as from oral stories, she set several of her books in eighteenth-century America and England. Dalgliesh is perhaps best known as the author of *The Courage of Sarah Noble,* the story of an eight-year-old girl who leaves Massachusetts for the wilds of Connecticut in 1707 to accompany her father as his cook. As she adjusts to her new home, the first house in Milford, Connecticut, Sarah faces her loneliness and uncertainties and becomes friends with the Native Americans who live nearby. As a writer of realistic fiction, Dalgliesh is noted for describing family life with believability and humor. She is well known for writing the "Sandy Cove" stories, a trilogy that revolve around a group of children who live in the Nova Scotia community where she had a summer home; the "Smiths" books, stories about a family in a New York suburb; and *Three from Greenaways: A Story of Children from England* (1941), an account of how three English children come to America after the World War II raids begin and find a home with a Connecticut family. In both her contemporary and historical fiction, Dalgliesh makes children the pivotal characters, and she is often praised for her characterizations of the young. As a literary stylist, Dalgliesh is lauded for her facility with dialogue and for the smoothness of her prose, which is considered good for reading aloud; she is also credited for writing concisely but with color and drama in her informational books. Dalgliesh's works are often acknowledged as particularly attractive examples of bookmaking; she worked with a number of well known illustrators, such as Katherine Milhous, Helen Sewell, Leo Politi, Flavia Gag, Leonard Weisgard, and Berta and Elmer Hader. Although some of Dalgliesh's sequels were not as well received as the initial volumes of their series and several of her works are thought not to have aged well, she is usually considered a writer of varied, interesting, and engaging books that reflect her understanding of children and of what appeals to them. Writing in the *St. James Guide to Children's Writers,* Rachel Fordyce said, "Alice Dalgliesh's characters and stories are all given life and moment because of the author's attention to image, detail, and believability…. Behind all of Dalgliesh's work is a strong sense of the child audience for which it is written, and a delight in language, detail, situation, and action." According to Zena Sutherland and May Hill Arbuthnot in their *Children and Books,* Dalgliesh "had the ability to create realistic child characters and to make their concerns important to us without losing sight of the historical elements of her tales." Peter D. Sieruta of *Children's Books and Their Creators* concluded, "As an author, she is best remembered for her pleasantly appealing stories. Although some may now seem dated and precious in tone, her best books… remain fresh and enjoyable for today's readers."

Biographical Information

Many of Dalgliesh's works reflect elements from her life. Born in Trinidad, British West Indies, to John Dalgliesh, a Scottish businessman, and Mary Haynes Dalgliesh, the daughter of an English sugar-planter, Dalgliesh came from a seafaring tradition; consequently, her books often include the sea and ships. The family lived on a tropical island; during the dry season, Dalgliesh played outside, but in the rainy season she amused herself by reading. Her parents allowed Dalgliesh to choose the books she wanted, so she explored the works of authors such as Dickens, Scott, and Thackery as well as *Alice in Wonderland, The Swiss Family Robinson,* and the books of Kate Greenaway. While attending a one-room schoolhouse, Dalgliesh liked to listen to the English lessons being taught to the older students. Her class often did needlework while the teacher would read aloud; her father also read to her at home. Dalgliesh began writing stories at the age of six. When she was ten, Dalgliesh lost her father and went to live in England with her mother. At twelve, Dalgliesh won a prize—a five-pound box of chocolates—for a story that she had submitted to the children's page of a magazine. She wrote in her essay in *Junior Book of Authors,* "Filled with enthusiasm I wrote more stories and won two more prizes. Finally the editor of the magazine suggested that I had written enough stories."

At thirteen, Dalgliesh began to attend the Wimbledon Hill School. She wrote in *Junior Book of Authors,* "I loved summer vacations on the south coast, and the biggest thrill of all was to visit the places that made English history really mean something." At nineteen, Dalgliesh decided to become a kindergarten teacher. She wrote *in Junior Book of Authors,* "I thought that would be one way to find out more about writing for children." Dalgliesh moved to New York City and began studying at the Pratt Institute in Brooklyn. She went on to receive her bachelor's degree in education and her master's degree in English from the Teacher's College at Columbia University. While still a college student, her first books—*A Happy School Year* (1924), a reader based on the activities of her first-graders, and the story *West Indian Play Days* (1926)—were published. Dalgliesh taught elementary school for seventeen years, including teaching kindergarten at the Horace Mann School in New York. In 1931, she produced *The Blue Teapot,* the first volume of her "Sandy Cove" series; this work, which she once described as "[o]ne book of mine which I would like to have kept on living," is the first of the author's books for older children. In the early 1930s, Dalgliesh began teaching children's literature at Teachers College, Columbia University.

.
In 1934, Dalgliesh left teaching to join the staff of publisher Charles Scribner's Sons as Editor of Books for Young Readers. She also bought a summer home in Brookfield, Connecticut, which she used as the setting for some of her books; she considered Connecticut her adopted home state. At Scribner's, Dalgliesh discovered such talents as Marcia Brown and Genevieve Foster as well as two illustrators who later provided pictures for her books, Katherine Milhous and Leo Politi. Dalgliesh was also in charge of the children's book reviews for *Parents Magazine.* When she wasn't working, Dalgliesh enjoyed traveling, both in the United States and abroad. On a trip to Pennsylvania

with her friend, illustrator Katherine Milhous, she heard the tall tale about a boy who is protected from bears by the big iron pot that he is carrying. This story became the basis for *The Bears on Hemlock Mountain,* which the author described as "[o]ne of the books that has given me the most writing fun." Dalgliesh and Milhous also took a two-month trip by plane around South America, an experience that became the basis for *Wings around South America* (1941), an informational book about the continent, and *The Little Angel: A Story of Old Rio* (1943), a family story set in Brazil in the early nineteenth century. In 1960, Dalgliesh retired from Scribner's and became Contributing Editor of children's book reviews for *Saturday Review,* a position that she held for six years. Before her death in 1979, she became a naturalized citizen and served as the first president of the Children's Book Council. Dalgliesh stated in the *Horn Book Magazine,* "Children are my major interest; they come first; and second, books in relation to children; never *just books....* I write different kinds of stories for different kinds of children." She added in *Junior Book of Authors,* "I think that writing books for children is the most rewarding experience that anyone can have...."

Major Works

After producing a series of interactive picture books for very young children that strongly reflect her teaching background, Dalgliesh began to write stories and informational picture books and to edit collections of tales and rhymes. The first of her books to win a major award is *The Silver Pencil.* Partly autobiographical, this young adult novel follows the development of Janet Laidlaw, an English girl born in Trinidad who longs to be a writer. Janet's aspirations are noted by her father, who gives her a silver pencil as a gift. Janet goes to school in England, then goes to America and trains as a kindergarten teacher in New York. At the end of the story, Janet begins using the silver pencil to write her own works. Writing in the *Horn Book Magazine,* Alice M. Jordan said that Janet "will win many friends through this penetrating, often humorous portrayal of her character and problems." Ellen Lewis Buell of the *New York Times Book Review* noted the book's "sturdy honesty" and concluded that "beneath the surface there is humor and a fine sensitivity to people and places." A critic in *Kirkus Reviews* called *The Silver Pencil* "one of the finest stories of the season." In the sequel *Along Janet's Road,* Janet becomes an editor of books for children at a New York City publishing house. While describing the background of trade publishing, Dalgliesh outlines Janet's development as a woman as well as a writer and editor; at the end of the novel, Janet realizes that her boyfriend Perry is the most important person in her life.

In the regional folktale *The Bears on Hemlock Mountain,* eight-year-old Jonathan is sent by his mother to borrow a large pot from his aunt, who lives over Hemlock Mountain. On his way home in the dark, Jonathan encounters two bears; he protects himself by hiding under the pot until help arrives. Dalgliesh invests the tale with two elements beloved by young children, rhythm and repetition. A critic in *Bulletin of the Center for Children's Books* noted that the text has "the rhythmic quality and the humor of a folk tale" before calling *The Bears on Hemlock Mountain* "an exceptional book...." Writing in *the Horn Book Magazine*, Jennie D. Lindquist predicted that the story "will delight children because of its lively writing as well as its elements of suspense." Dalgliesh features another eight-year-old in *The Courage of Sarah Noble*. In this work, which is based on a true story, Sarah has left her mother and the rest of her family behind as she journeys to Connecticut to claim a homestead with her father. Living in a cave while her father works on the house, Sarah is alone and frightened. She is also terrified when she first encounters the Indian children who are her neighbors. However, she reads to them from her Bible, and they begin to play together and to learn from each other. At the end of the summer, the house is finished, and Sarah's father goes back to Massachusetts to retrieve the rest of his family. He leaves Sarah with the friendly Indians; although she is afraid, she learns to be at home with them. Olive Deane Hormel of the *Christian Science Monitor* stated, "This is a book unmarred by preachment, piety, or sentimentality—a book without flaw, it seems to me, which must become an American classic." Writing in *Virginia Kirkus' Bookshop Service*, a critic noted that *The Courage of Sarah Noble* "is simply told, with no embroidery or melodrama, but it carries the warmth of sincerity, and the wholesome appeal of true adventure." Virginia Haviland of the *Horn Book Magazine* concluded, "This is a remarkable book for younger readers—a true pioneer adventure, written for easy reading but without the sacrifice of literary quality or depth of feeling."

The Thanksgiving Story and *The Columbus Story* are two of Dalgliesh's most well received works of nonfiction. Framed in a fictional narrative, *The Thanksgiving Story* tells the story of the Pilgrims and describes the events that led up to the first Thanksgiving from the point of view of the Hopkins family, who have come over on the *Mayflower*. Writing in the *Horn Book Magazine*, Jennie D. Lindquist noted, "Everyone who has anything to do with children will want [*The Thanksgiving Story*] in time for Thanksgiving. It is the only really distinguished book we have on that holiday." Olive Deane Hormel of the *Christian Science Monitor* said, "[I]t has remained for Alice Dalgliesh to bring this important subject to the very young in a form both appealing and authentic," while a reviewer in *Bulletin of the Center for Children's Books* concluded by calling *The Thanksgiving Story* a "distinguished book" that recounts the facts with "great simplicity and dignity." A companion volume to *The Thanksgiving Story, The Columbus Story* is a purely historical account of the explorer's early life and first voyage. Jennie D. Lindquist of the *Horn Book Magazine* called the volume "[b]y far the best telling of the Columbus story I have ever read for younger children," while Louise S. Bechtel of the *New York Herald Tribune Book Review* said of Dalgliesh, who directs her book to children from five to eight, "Never has she

written with more insight into the imagination of this age, nor with more vivid delightful choice of facts and scenes that will interest them."

Awards

Dalgliesh received Newbery Medal runner-up designations for *The Silver Pencil* in 1945, for *The Bears on Hemlock Mountain* in 1953, and for *The Courage of Sarah Noble* in 1955. Four of Dalgliesh's books—*The Bears on Hemlock Mountain, The Courage of Sarah Noble, The Thanksgiving Story,* and *The Columbus Story*—were named Notable Books by the American Library Association in their respective years of publication. *The Thanksgiving Story* was named a Caldecott Medal Honor Book in 1955 for its illustrations by Helen Sewell.

TITLE COMMENTARY

AMERICA TRAVELS: THE STORY OF A HUNDRED YEARS OF TRAVEL IN AMERICA (1933)

Josette Frank

SOURCE: A review of *America Travels: The Story of a Hundred Years of Travel in America,* in *The Saturday Review of Literature,* Vol. X, No. 18, November 18, 1933, p. 271.

The past hundred years of travel in America—by stagecoach, sailboat, steamboat, covered wagon, and train—are pictured by Alice Dalgliesh in **America Travels.** The first part of the book, addressed to very young readers, is made up of pleasant little stories. Part II is straight exposition—dramatic in its own right because the historic facts are dramatic—and illustrated [by Hildegard Woodward] with truly fine sketches. These last are not only lovely to look at, but are especially valuable because they make available materials not to be found outside of scholarly source books.

The Booklist

SOURCE: A review of *America Travels: The Story of a Hundred Years of Travel in America, The Booklist,* Vol. 30, No. 4, December, 1933, p. 123.

In this book the history of transportation in America is presented in a manner that children of eight to ten will enjoy. Eight stories, telling how people traveled, each from the point of view of a child of the era, form the first part of the book. The second part gives more information about the ways of traveling than is told in the stories.

Line drawing illustrations contribute much to the interest of the book. Excellent format.

Anne T. Eaton

SOURCE: A review of *America Travels: The Story of a Hundred Years of Travel in America,* in *New York Review of Books,* December 3, 1933, p. 18.

Children enjoy book journeys and descriptions of ways of traveling are one of the best means of giving to young readers some comprehension of the differences between our own and other times. Up to now it has not been easy to find simple and interesting accounts of journeys taken long ago and Miss Dalgliesh deserves our gratitude for these pleasant little tales of travel by stage coach, packet boat, in the train drawn by the DeWitt Clinton engine, by canal and flat boat and Conestoga wagon, of a balloon ascension, a "buggy ride" in 1890 and one of the first automobiles in 1902. There is spontaneity and a knowledge of children's interest in these accounts of Deborah, who traveled alone by stage coach; of Hector crossing the Atlantic on a sailing ship; of David, who rode in the first train of the Mohawk & Hudson Railroad in 1831; of Harriet and her kitten on the canal boat, and all the rest.

The second half of the book consists of a "Picture Story of Travel" for children who want to know more about ways of traveling than is told in the stories. Here the interesting and accurate drawings and the brief text will adequately answer the questions children ask. To have kept the stories and the more strictly informational part of the book separate is a unique and admirable idea.

CHRISTMAS: A BOOK OF STORIES OLD AND NEW (compiled by Dalgliesh, 1934)

The Booklist

SOURCE: A review of *Christmas: A Book of Stories Old and New,* in *The Booklist,* Vol. 31, No. 4, December, 1934, p. 134.

An excellent selection of stories and poetry arranged under the following headings: Christmas stories and wonder tales, The first Christmas, Christmas in old-time America, Christmas in other lands. In general the book's appeal will be to children from eight to twelve, but, because of its subject, it will have a much wider range of interest. Attractive illustrations [by Hildegard Woodward] and format.

Virginia Kirkus' Bookshop Service

SOURCE: A review of *Christmas: A Book of Stories Old and New,* in *Virginia Kirkus' Bookshop Service,* Vol. XVIII, No. 18, September 15, 1950, p. 557.

A revised edition of the 1934 collection with additions and subtractions and heavy black and while illustrations by Hildegard Woodward. A satisfying collection for Christmas story hours—Christmas stories of the folklore and family pattern; stories of the first Christmas including the Bible text, poems and carols; Christmas as celebrated in early America; Christmas stories of other lands (of course *The Cratchit's Christmas Dinner* is here) and some information about the stories and the authors by the editor. Teachers and story tellers take note.

Louise S. Bechtel

SOURCE: A review of *Christmas: A Book of Stories Old and New,* in *The New York Herald Tribune Book Review,* November 19, 1950, p. 20.

Christmas: A Book of Stories Old and New, selected by Alice Dalgliesh, illustrated by Hildegard Woodward, now has a revised new edition. Since 1934, it has been in use by this reviewer, who recommends it heartily for family reading aloud, as well as many other uses in schools and libraries. Here you will find the complete text of that wonderful French picture book of *The Good Saint Florentin,* with older favorite stories, and modern ones, and a last section on "Christmas in Other Lands."

THE SMITHS AND RUSTY (1936)

May Lamberton Becker

SOURCE: A review of *The Smiths and Rusty,* in *The New York Herald Tribune Books,* August 23, 1936, p. 9.

It is like living in a cheerful, friendly family to read this amusing story of how the Smiths moved to a suburb and found a stray cocker spaniel almost as soon as they arrived; its effect lasts over for some time in the forms of a spontaneous chuckle whenever one gets so much as a glimpse of the jacket.

The Smiths—parents, son and daughter under ten, and a comparatively recent baby—have been fitting more and more closely into a New York flat for some seasons past. All at once they realise in a variety of striking ways, as people do when a small family grows larger, that the flat is not only outgrown but outworn. When a leg comes off the bath-tub and brings the plumbing with it, all that is needed is a little more money to bring to a head the determination to move far enough out of town to have a garden, keep pets, and otherwise be human. Father gets the money, Greg invests his first share of it in a pair of guinea-pigs, and off they go: "Rusty," as the name on this charming cocker's collar says, joins them directly.

The children go to a modern suburban school, organize the sort of plays every lone child loves to read about because they call for the co-operation of plenty of children, and generally spend their time in as entertaining a fashion as in any book for some time past. Their central interest, however, is in Rusty. Though they have advertised—with their hearts in their mouths—no one has claimed him, and they have begun to hope that no one will, long before his master does turn up. Fortunately this person has sense, and knows when a dog is well off. The story has thus a completely happy ending, with nobody chasing Rusty off the spare-room bed that night, but it has varied and spontaneous happiness all the way along. "An everyday American story," it is called on the jacket, and its charm as well as its usefulness is that it knows the pleasures possible to everyday American families, and shows them with unfailing sympathy and good humor. There are plenty of touches any parent will recognise as life-like, such as the general feeling toward a sweet child with lovely curls who embitters the feelings of the school by performing "Twinkle little star" on a radio amateur hour, or the way this young person surprises her little friends by unexpectedly showing sense for once. When a "Safety-first" cameraman is taking pictures in the neighborhood and Rusty and his family get in because the dog has been trained to stop at crossings for the word of command, the children are taken to Radio City Music Hall to see the result, and think themselves hardly used to have to sit through a Shirley Temple before they themselves, complete with dog, come on the screen. The temptation of a reviewer is to tell such incidents; in fairness, I should not do so, for the trick of the book is in the laughing, yet sensible, way in which these are told by the author.

This is a story to go directly to ten-year-olds or under who can read, or to be read aloud to children even younger. I am always on the lookout for simple records of our family joys, for young children, and I have seldom found a happier one.

WINGS FOR THE SMITHS (1937)

May Lamberton Becker

SOURCE: A review of *Wings for the Smiths,* in *The New York Herald Tribune Books,* August 29, 1937, p. 7.

When *The Smiths and Rusty* came out last year I hailed it, not only as a good funny story of a family who moved to the country and had a cocker spaniel, but as one more of a much-needed kind of reading matter for seven to ten or so—simple records of family joys. The children for whom it was written took to it at once, I am happy to say, and the present sequel (complete in itself) was really implicit in the first book. *Wings for the Smiths* has the same amusing parents, lively children, and comfortable home where pets are permitted: it has the same cocker and a new miniature schnauzer, and above all it has a new aeroplane.

The Smith family is happily at breakfast when an aviator makes a forced landing in their field. This brings to a boil father's simmering impulse to fly: he buys an outfit (which

he soon finds nobody but mechanics wear at the flying field) and takes lessons. Meanwhile the family and its friends organize a "Friends of Aviation" club, and to encourage this, a famous aviator offers a prize. It is open to the pupils of the local school, and is for the best drawing with which flying is in any way concerned. The winning pictures, reproduced, are really by an eleven-year-old artist. Father is given the new schnauzer to celebrate his taking the air, and in the last chapter even Grandma no longer holds out against being taken up as a passenger.

All very simple—yes, but very hard to do right, as children want and need it to be done, and as Miss Dalgliesh has done it.

AMERICA BEGINS: THE STORY OF THE FINDING OF THE NEW WORLD (1938)

Ellen Lewis Buell

SOURCE: A review of *America Begins: The Story of the Finding of the New World,* in *The New York Times Book Review,* April 3, 1938, p. 12.

This second volume in a series of historical picture books, of which *Long Live the King!* was the first, is designed to give the child in the elementary grades a connected view of the discovery and exploration which led to the settlement of the New World. Brief narratives, prefaced by a description of America before the white man came, describe the main events with admirable clarity, emphasizing the incidents which would be most memorable to children of that age, and each narrative is illustrated with full-page pictures, supplemented by smaller drawings in the style of the period described.

Thus we see the dragon ship of Leif the Lucky and Columbus dreaming on the wharves of Genoa, while the background of world exploration is given by such pictures as that of Marco Polo astride a camel beholding the lacquer red pagodas of the great Khan and Vasco de Gama being received in India. The second portion of the book deals with "The Great Treasure Hunt" of the Spanish, the French and the English for gold and furs, and the final section, "Homes in the New World," pictures the first settlements in Virginia and Canada.

The chapters are written concisely and simply, but with color and the touch of drama which transforms history into a subject of living interest. The illustrations [by Lois Maloy] are not only pleasing in design but contain the kind of detail which appeals to children of this age.

The Booklist

SOURCE: A review of *America Begins: The Story of the Finding of the New World,* in *The Booklist,* Vol. 34, No. 16, April 15, 1938, p. 304.

An attractive first book of the discovery and early exploration of America. For material both artist and author have searched sources. The book is divided into three sections: Finding a new world, The great treasure hunt, Homes in the new world. It is the second book of a series of picture histories of which *Long Live the King!* is the first. The pictures bring to a child the flavor and color of past days and the simple narrative will tempt him to read about them.

Florence Bethune Sloan

SOURCE: A review of *America Begins: The Story of the Finding of the New World,* in *The Christian Science Monitor,* Vol. XXX, No. 126, April 25, 1938, p. 7.

America Begins is an interesting book full of stories and pictures that bring to us events and people of those days long, long ago when men sailed across the ocean from Europe and found a new land, calling it first the New World and later America. Alice Dalgliesh tells the stories and Lois Maloy has made the pictures. They have searched through old records, many books, maps and pictures and have made their findings alive and fascinating in their own manner.

Beginning with the scene before the coming of the white men, we see the original American, the red man, the hunter in the forest, and the story of the discovery, the exploration of the new world and of the earliest settlements follows. Full page pictures in color, maps, and black-and-white drawings interpret the text. This fine book makes America's beginnings a thrilling story for boys and girls of today.

AMERICA BUILDS HOMES: THE STORY OF THE FIRST COLONIES (1938)

New York Herald Tribune Books

SOURCE: A review of *America Builds Homes: The Story of the First Colonies,* in *New York Herald Tribune Books,* November 13, 1938, p. 11.

On the last pages of *America Begins,* which came out last spring, first of a series of author-artist presentations of our history to little children, an Indian watched in wonder the rising habitations of the white man. At that point this second book begins, a trifle further advanced in style to suit the growing intelligence of the little reader, but with the same practical combination of simple narrative and lucid large-page drawings interspersed with color plates that spread across two large leaves. The scheme of this undertaking reveals itself as different from anything that preceded it and capable of further extension to take in the background of all America in the aspects most interesting to a young child and most likely to linger in his memory.

America Builds Homes tells how the first settlers came to live and build houses like those they had left, in Virginia,

New England, the New Netherlands, and the settlements in Pennsylvania and by the Swedes along the Delaware. John Smith has his proper place and so have other famous men, but the chief interest is in how everyday folks, including children, carried on everyday life in the new land. The research on which this is based has evidently been thorough: for instance, in the story of Miles Standish's red cow, here told for the first time to children, a system of trading is made clear and picturesque.

The pictures [by Lois Maloy] are noticeable for simplicity and for detail: that is, the details most needed to make all plain are brought out in simple, striking designs, on a scale large enough to be easy on young eyes—like the type.

The Booklist

SOURCE: A review of *America Builds Homes: The Story of the First Colonies,* in *The Booklist,* Vol. 35, No. 8, December 15, 1938, p. 139.

Historical events chosen from four of the early colonies are simply and effectively told, with a minimum of detail. The incidents have been selected with the younger child in mind. The illustrations do much to supplement the text; the book is a companion to *America Begins* and probably will arouse an interest in colonial history.

THE YOUNG AUNTS (1939)

May Lamberton Becker

SOURCE: A review of *The Young Aunts,* in *New York Herald Tribune Books,* Vol. 15, No. 30, March 26, 1939, p. 8.

Offer this book to any little girl you know—preferably one under ten but able to read—and see if you can get it away from her before the last page. The pictures will catch the attention, the story enchain it. This comes from two sources. It is a story in which our little girls will recognize themselves in their own environment, or at least one in which they would be glad to find themselves, and it is developed with the aid of dialogue of an infectious naturalness, and hearty enjoyment of the humors of everyday life.

There is something fascinating to children in the very idea of being anything so grown-up as an aunt or an uncle while yet they are young. There is always a glamour to small girls in a large wedding, and a small baby is to them a source of inexhaustible interest, a sort of live doll whose tricks and manners never pall—especially if all this takes place in a state of society in which there is a nurse or other grown-up to do the actual work. These are the three threads of the story. The twins figure as bridesmaids in a lifelike and very funny wedding procession. The baby comes into the story as a normal, everyday child expects him to come, some one confidently expected and eagerly welcomed. "Oh Dot, are we going to be aunts?" they cry.

They almost come to blows before the baby's actual arrival, over the proper color of the sweater for which they are shopping: the tactful floorwalker induces them to take white instead of either pink or blue. From the moment Dinkle claims the blue ribbons, from the breathless instant the nurse lets them get a good look at him, they follow his daily development with delight. So will a little girl reader.

The pictures are the work of [Charlotte Becker] whose work is new to me, but one whose gifts for showing the special charm of healthy, fat and energetic babyhood will be generally recognized. There are so many of these ingenious and lovable drawings that one is kept chuckling all the time. We need family stories of today for children who love to find themselves and their surroundings represented in books in a likable light.

Alice M. Jordan

SOURCE: A review of *The Young Aunts,* in *The Horn Book Magazine,* Vol. XV, No. 3, May 1939, p. 167.

A fresh and entertaining story for little girls of the twins, Terry and Chris, who became aunts at eight and took the liveliest interest in, and almost too much auntly responsibility toward, their older sister's baby. They go to the library to consult books on baby care, arrange a birthday party and send their nephew's picture secretly to a newspaper's baby-picture contest.

The Booklist

SOURCE: A review of *The Young Aunts,* in *The Booklist,* Vol. 35, No. 17, May 1, 1939, pp. 292-93.

The twins, Terry and Chris, become proud aunts and take their new responsibilities seriously. Their efforts at teaching Dinkie to crawl, their entering of his picture in a baby contest, and their squabbles seem natural, and make an amusing slight story. More realistic stories of modern home life are needed for this age reader. Appealing illustrations.

Charlotte Becker

SOURCE: A review of *The Young Aunts,* in *The Times Literary Supplement,* No. 1954, July 15, 1939, p. VII.

Aunt is a grown-up sort of word, so that the twins, Terry and Chris, were naturally very excited when they found out that they could be aunts themselves. They were even more excited when Dinkie was born, though Dinkie's mother (knowing the twins) was justifiably nervous until she saw how anxious they were to behave like proper, responsible aunts. They had one or two lapses, to be sure, but only because it *was* rather difficult to remember that they were aunts all the time. Dinkie was certainly the kind of baby that anybody would be proud to claim as a nephew. Miss Dalgliesh and Miss Becker are to be congratulated

on the result of their collaboration. The author succeeds in making the reader feel part of a charming family; the artist has an unusual gift for child drawing, and her many charcoal sketches are a delight in themselves. It is to be hoped that the twins are only starting on their career. Long may they be aunts!

Florence Bethune Sloan

SOURCE: A review of *The Young Aunts,* in *The Christian Science Monitor,* Vol. XXI, No. 208, July 31, 1939, p. 5.

Alice Dalgliesh, author of **The Blue Teapot, Relief's Rocker,** and many other books children like, has written a pleasant story that will appeal to seven to ten-year-old girls. *The Young Aunts* tells of Chris and Terry, twin sisters, who find, one day, that they are aunts, and are delighted with the new baby nephew who arrives. They feel he is almost as much theirs as their sister's, the baby's mother. The twins had always thought one had to be a grown-up before one could be an aunt, but they took their responsibilities very seriously and they both shared in bringing up that remarkable baby they nicknamed "Dinkie." There are many amusing incidents in the story and the charming illustrations by Charlotte Becker picture the twins and "Dinkie's" progress.

A BOOK FOR JENNIFER (1940)

Florence Bethune Sloan

SOURCE: A review of *A Book for Jennifer,* in *The Christian Science Monitor,* Vol. XXXII, No. 230, August 26, 1940, p. 7.

A Book for Jennifer, by Alice Dalgliesh, is an unusual and interesting book. It is a story of London children in the eighteenth century and of Mr. Newbery's Juvenile Library.

John Newbery is remembered because he printed many little books for children and put over his shop in St. Paul's Churchyard, London, the sign "Juvenile Library." He was a pioneer in children's book publishing, for up to this time very few books had been made especially for young readers. Two hundred years later this bookseller's name was given to the medal awarded annually to the most distinguished book written for children in America.

Modern boys and girls, for whom countless books are available, will be fascinated with this peek into the past through the story of the Bannister children, who lived in Gough Square. Here, too, lived the celebrated Dr. Samuel Johnson and his famous cat.

Miss Dalgliesh has brought Mr. Newbery and his shop to life in a book for boys' and girls' own reading. Katherine Milhous's ten drawings in gay colors enliven the story and they, together with cuts from old books with an epigram in verse adapted to each, provide authentic eighteenth century London atmosphere. Author and artist together have made an important contribution to the history of children's books.

May Lamberton Becker

SOURCE: A review of *A Book for Jennifer,* in *New York Herald Tribune Books,* September 8, 1940, p. 8.

My temptation was to reserve review of this charming book for the special Book Week number, which its subject and illustrations fit so well, but this would not be fair to book shops and libraries who should be told, well in advance, how well it suits displays and programs connected with this celebration. It is more than a mere "period piece," though in its fidelity to time, place and spirit it recreates a child's corner of London in the days of Dr. Johnson—the corner of St. Paul's Churchyard where stood the first bookshop for children, the famous one kept by John Newbery. It is more because books mean so much in little children's lives that this story of Jennifer's book is a story of her heart as well; as the ancient posy has it, the two "shall never part."

Newbery's library, fascinating as it was to its young audience, was meant above all to make children good. The book for Jennifer was chosen from a display of *Goody Two Shoes, A Little Pretty Pocket Book* and *Jack the Giant Killer,* given away with it was a pincushion in which to stick white pins for a good deed, black ones for a bad one. As Jennifer also received a "Moral Account," with parallel columns to note down good or bad actions, she was well provided for conscience's sake. An ingenious, affectionate and energetic child, her efforts to be good are so funny any one would love her; one of her adventures introduces no less a friend of children than Doctor Johnson himself. To his house in Gough Square go Jennifer and her brothers in a case involving the Great Lexicographer's famous cat Hodge. No literary shrine in London holds the presence of its owner more truly, and any American visitor will recognize it here. Feeling sure that the book would please Johnsonian authorities, I sent an advance copy to one in London. "What a gem of a book it is!" came the reply. "How rich and wise and understanding!"

Miss Milhous has made colored pictures in the same vein, and old woodcuts and facsimile verses blend with them happily. Even the cover is John Newbery's bright paper.

Alice M. Jordan

SOURCE: A review of *A Book for Jennifer,* in *The Horn Book Magazine,* Vol. XVI, No. 5, September-October 1940, p. 342-48.

In a strikingly attractive binding of "flowery and gilt" design, with title page in Eighteenth Century style and many amusing cuts from old books, the first story introducing John Newbery to children has appeared. It is indeed an achieve-

ment to have made this bit of social history seem so lifelike and real. Jennifer is truly a child of the period with her "moral account" book, her copies of *Giles Gingerbread* and *Little Goody Two Shoes,* but she is far more lively than the priggish children in the books of the time. She can stamp her foot at Dr. Johnson's cat, she can snip the wreaths from her mother's gown for the funeral of the mouse. Miss Dalgliesh has written a book that will appeal not only to little girls, but to older readers for whom the name of John Newbery and his Juvenile Library hold special significance. It is a charming addition to the history of children's literature.

Anne Carroll Moore

SOURCE: A review of *A Book for Jennifer,* in *The Horn Book Magazine,* Vol. XVI, No. 5, September-October, 1940, pp. 338-40.

It is, I think, a lovely and revealing book, and the key to it may be found in Alice Dalgliesh's **A Book for Jennifer,** by all odds the best and most discriminating work she has done as author or editor. London in the eighteenth century with John Newbery's Bookshop in St. Paul's Churchyard is the background.

While it is a book with a purpose—to make John Newbery more real to boys and girls who hear of the Newbery Medal award—Miss Dalgliesh has become so absorbed by the Newbery publications that she has achieved a book of unusual distinction. Her discriminating selection of verse and illustration from such a collection as that of Wilbur Macey Stone is worthy of note.

Booklist

SOURCE: A review of *A Book for Jennifer,* in *Booklist,* Vol. 37, No. 2, October 1, 1940, p. 39.

At the Newbery juvenile library in St. Paul's churchyard, Jennifer's brothers bought her the book, *The History of Little Goody Two-Shoes.* By it a lively little girl tried to mold her behavior and had great difficulty in balancing her "moral ledger" with good deeds. This story will not enjoy wide popularity. For the teacher or children's librarian to acquaint younger children with the familiar names of John Newbery and Dr. Samuel Johnson and eighteenth-century London life, it will prove useful. The 10 colored illustrations and the cuts from old books make for attractive format. The cloth cover reproduces a design from a Newbery "flowery and gilt" paper.

THREE FROM GREENWAYS : A STORY OF CHILDREN FROM ENGLAND (1941)

May Lamberton Becker

SOURCE: A review of *Three from Greenways: A Story of Children from England,* in *New York Herald Tribune Books,* March 23, 1941, p. 8.

Three English children, coming to America after raids began, settled for the duration with a family in Connecticut in which were two American children. This is the story of that adventure; it could not be simpler—or better. It moves to laughter and to tears, it has the humor, happiness and heartache, all in one, of the most touching gesture in national history—sending great numbers of English children to welcoming home, beyond the sea but still within the circle of a common cause. The book could easily have been so wrong, and it is so completely right! It has a child's outlook, a child's vocabulary, and the strong story interest that keeps a child reading and makes him remember. I wish every American child could read it before the year is out.

Nine-year-old Joan, with two younger brothers Peter and Timothy, came away from their beloved "Greenways," leaving Mum and Dad and Ruffy the pup. Three days out. . . .

> "I say, Joan," said Peter. "I do feel awfully funny. Do you?"
>
> "Yes," said Joan. "I'm homesick."
>
> "So'm I. What do we do about it?"
>
> "Get over it," said Joan fiercely. . . .

and just then she saw the man who owned Halfway House in Connecticut that was to be, though they didn't know it yet, their home. They greeted the Statue: Joan learned the Gettysburg Address out of *The Token of Freedom,* and when she talked it over with Mr. Stone it gave me the thrill Charles Laughton gave me in *Ruggles.* They became part of the family with the usual human adjustments. The first letter from home said that Ruffy, scared by a raid, had run away, but these children were among those who took part in the two-way broadcast, and Dad's first words to Timothy were that Ruffy had come back. The pictures [by Gertrude Howe] are lively and right: every statement in the book is taken from life.

All profits and royalties of this story go to children driven from their homes to seek refuge in another country: beneficiaries are named on the cover. That would be a good reason for getting the book: better ones for recommending it so strongly are that it is the best book in its field, that it is material for history, and that no child or grown-up can read it without being better and happier for the experience.

The Booklist

SOURCE: A review of *Three from Greenways: A Story of Children from England,* in *The Booklist,* Vol. 37, April 15, 1941, p. 392.

When their village was bombed, the three Martin children were sent from England to America for the duration of the war. Desperately in need of a father, they adopted a man aboard ship, and later found a home with him and his family in Connecticut. A short, unpretentious story which tells unemotionally of the uprooting of these children and their subsequent adjustment to American life.

WINGS AROUND SOUTH AMERICA (1941)

Alice M. Jordan

SOURCE: A review of *Wings around South America,* in *The Horn Book Magazine,* Vol. XVII, No. 6, November, 1941, p. 469.

A two months' trip by airplane down the west coast of South America by way of Panama, Ecuador, Peru and Chile and up the east coast by Argentina and Rio, furnished abundant material for author and artist. Lovely water colors and clever line drawings [by Katherine Milhous] make vivid the highlights of their journey, as told by Miss Dalgliesh with sympathy and appreciation. While they were less than ninety hours actually in the air, the plane dominates the picture. This beautiful book will be valuable in schools and libraries.

The Booklist

SOURCE: A review of *Wings around South America,* in *The Booklist,* Vol. 38, November 1, 1941, pp. 82-3.

The record of a two-months' trip by plane around South America, covering some 14,000 miles. This very subjective book, although little more than tourist impressions and obvious as to purpose, is colorful and will possibly serve as an introduction to that continent. The use of the present tense throughout will irritate many readers.

New York Herald Tribune Books

SOURCE: A review of *Wings around South America,* in *The New York Herald Tribune Books,* November 2, 1941, p. 11.

Bright with tropic color, moving swiftly as planes can make it, but succeeding in not being superficial, this trip around South America seems to me the best way for a young reader to make acquaintance not only with the continent but with the means by which alone the continent can be taken as a whole. Author and artist took this actual trip, which lasted for two unforgettable months. Miss Dalgliesh has not so much written about it as reproduced it: Miss Milhous's pictures—watercolor sketches in six colors and pencil drawings—have the convincing quality of being on the spot. The best way to write travel books for children is to create in the child a sense that he is traveling. That is the value of this journey, from before embarkation, when passports and inoculations make them ready, through successive stops to make friends along the way.

These stops are at Barranquilla; Panama (as that is neared, the plane is sprayed with insecticide, as no mosquitoes may be brought into Panama); over the equator to Quito; over the desert to Peru to Arequipa (in company with an American cardinal and a Peruvian baby); over a sea of cobalt blue to Chile; over the mountains to Argentina, leaving Buenos Aires at night looking like "the sky turned upside down"; over forests to Brazil, down to Rio, up the coast to Bahia and Para; home by way of the author's birthplace Trinidad—14,000 miles. They have not gone too fast, for they went like pilgrims, with a purpose; the Americas must learn to know each other and stand together. As Bolivar said to his weary soldiers: "The unity of the Americas is the hope of the universe." With all the first-hand information, all the brilliant pictures, the book's greatest value is the direction of both toward understanding, toward knowing how to get along with South America. For that reason, though ten-year-olds will grasp the book, they should not keep it away from their elders.

Florence Bethune Sloan

SOURCE: A review of *Wings around South America*, in *The Christian Science Monitor*, Vol. XXXIV, No. 15, December 11, 1941, p. 18.

A fascinating travel book, which recounts a two months' trip by air-plane to South America—covering Panama, Ecuador, Peru, and Chile, Argentine and Rio—is Alice Dalgliesh's *Wings around South America*, with remarkable water colors and line drawings by Katherine Milhous. Author and artist traveled together and both saw and have put down in words and pictures the live, interesting things that young people would most enjoy. Theirs is not the trite, all inclusive travelogue, but a real introduction to our neighbors in the "other America." Here is an attractive Christmas book for boy or girl!

THE LITTLE ANGEL: A STORY OF OLD RIO (1943)

Anne Carroll Moore

SOURCE: A review of *The Little Angel: A Story of Old Rio*, in *The Horn Book Magazine*, Vol. XIX, No. 6, November 1943, pp. 421-23.

Alice Dalgliesh has written an unusual and lovely story in *The Little Angel* and Katherine Milhous has illustrated it in color. The artist and author took their inspiration from prints and paintings of colonial life in Rio by the French painter Debret. The charm of the book lies in the naturalness of the large family, who seem contemporary, and their complete absorption in the life of their city and its festivals. In the Procession of Santo Antonio the little Maria appears as an angel. The pictures are delightful and a reminder that festivals are inseparable from the life of the countries in which they originate.

Margaret K. McElderry

SOURCE: A review of *The Little Angel: A Story of Old Rio*, in *The Christian Science Monitor*, Vol. XXXVI, No. 3, November 29, 1943, p. 12.

A book distinguished for its writing, its illustration and its format is *The Little Angel,* by Alice Dalgliesh. Rio de Janeiro in 1819 is the home of the Silva family whose daily life is pictured here with warmth, humor and great charm. Katherine Milhous, the artist, traveled through Brazil with the author, and has transmuted her understanding of the people and the period into remarkably fine illustrations.

Blanche Weber Shaffer

SOURCE: A review of *The Little Angel: A Story of Old Rio*, in *Saturday Review of Literature*, Vol. XXVI, No. 50, December 11, 1943, pp. 36-7.

Long after you have closed this book you will remember with a happy smile the da Silva family in early nineteenth-century Brazil.

"There is no finer family in all Rio," Senhor Silva sometimes said, looking over the handsome procession they made on Sundays when going to the public Promenade. And you really believe the proud Papai. You love Roberto, Paulo, and Pedro and are delighted with the pretty and mischievous Maria Luiza who punishes Santo Antonio. Maria da Gloria, the little sister, wins special affection on the great day when she walks in the Procession of Santo Antonio, dressed as an angel. The da Silva's celebration of Brazil's Independence Day, the gay street scenes like the "Battle of the Lemons," give rich local color to this simply family story, so full of gracious living and exotic charm. It is all infused with warmth and humor. We know that, while writing it, her own childhood came back to Alice Dalgliesh,—colorful years in Trinidad in a house overlooking the mountains of South America. Romance enters the story in the person of a curly-haired young Senhor who brings the "little angel" home when she has lost her way in searching for her kitten, Gatino. The kind Senhor will obviously become lovely Maria Luiza's husband.

Katherine Milhous went to Rio with the author and discovered Jean Baptiste Debret's pictures of colonial Brazil, which inspire her illustrations. Color, life, and humor make her pictures as captivating as the story. Every one will enjoy the festive Procession of Santo Antonio and the exciting scene after the Carnival. Both author and artist have succeeded in creating a book which is not only a very special contribution to stories of Latin America for North America, but a contribution to Latin American literature for children in general.

THE SILVER PENCIL (1944)

Virginia Kirkus' Bookshop Service

SOURCE: A review of *The Silver Pencil*, in *Virginia Kirkus' Bookshop Service*, Vol. XII, No. 18, September 15, 1944, p. 435.

Written as fiction, this reads as a "might-be-true" story of an English girl, born in Trinidad, who became an American citizen. With a good pace of plot—with unerring sense of the essential quality of each of the backgrounds that contributed to Janet Laidlaw's development,—Trinidad, England, the U.S., Nova Scotia—and with a penetrating and sympathetic insight into Janet's personality and the problems that grow out of it—the author has given us one of the finest stories of the season, a story that has much to give of basic internationalism and good will.

Alice M. Jordan

SOURCE: A review of *The Silver Pencil,* in *The Horn Book Magazine,* Vol. XX, No. 6, November, 1944, p. 483.

Alice Dalgliesh has written an outstanding story of a girl's choice of a career, based on her own unusual experiences. It began when Janet was a little girl on the tropical island of Trinidad, where she was born. Books held high place in the family life and her aspirations to be a writer herself were kindly looked upon by an understanding father. The silver pencil, long treasured, was his Christmas gift, the keynote of her ambition. Going to school in England was what all colonial children expected, and her first glimpses were like opening a picture book. In the midst of girls who knew no distinction between the West Indies and India, she came to see what England stood for in the building up of her people's way. But destiny called her to return to America and train as a kindergartner in New York, finally to become an American citizen. And yet she had not then found her true vocation. It was later to be borne upon her that her early urge was the compelling one and she turned to writing with joy. Janet is a girl who will win many friends through this penetrating, often humorous, portrayal of her character and problems. Her story may be confidently recommended to older girls.

Frances C. Darling

SOURCE: A review of *The Silver Pencil,* in *The Christian Science Monitor,* Vol. XXXVI, No. 293, November 9, 1944, p. 14.

The Silver Pencil, by Alice Dalgliesh, uses the varied backgrounds of the author's own life and, while it is not entirely autobiographical, it has all the warmth of personal experience, the charm of childhood in a foreign land happily remembered, and it is written by one who, like her heroine, decided that she wishes America to be her home and her country.

Janet Laidlaw (like Miss Dalgliesh) was born in the tropical island of Trinidad in the West Indies. It was there her father gave her the silver pencil, "for your stories," he said. Later Janet goes to England to school, to London "a fairytale in grey" and to Scotland with its scones and heather hills.

Then Janet comes to America, trains as a teacher, goes to college, and finds that this is the land where she wishes to live. Sometimes the silver pencil is forgotten, but at important moments Janet uses it, and it symbolizes the writing theme that runs through the story.

The Booklist

SOURCE: A review of *The Silver Pencil,* in *The Booklist,* Vol. 41, No. 5, November 15, 1944, p. 93.

Part fiction and part personal experience is this understanding story of the growing-up years of a girl's life in Trinidad, England, America, and Nova Scotia. Throughout her childhood, early school days, teacher's training, and teaching is the ever-present urge to write. Older girls will be charmed with this well-paced account of Janet's development, her successes and failures, her joys and heartaches. The fact that the book encompasses so much in time, place, and people will add to its interest.

REUBEN AND HIS RED WHEELBARROW (1946)

Virginia Kirkus' Bookshop Service

SOURCE: A review of *Reuben and His Red Wheelbarrow,* in *Virginia Kirkus' Bookshop Service,* Vol. XIV, No. 3, February 1, 1946, p. 66.

A Story Parade picture book in a series that can be counted on for good merchandise value. A very simple little story of a birthday gift for four year old Reuben, a new red wheelbarrow, which causes quite a stir in the household. Colorful, quaint illustrations by Ilse Bischoff show a large, lively Victorian family gay in pinks and lavenders, hoop skirts and bows. The general impression the book leaves is of a rather trivial story presented in attractive but mannered style.

Alice M. Jordan

SOURCE: A review of *Reuben and His Red Wheelbarrow,* in *The Horn Book Magazine,* Vol. XXII, No. 2, March, 1946, pp. 130-31.

Delightful colored pictures introduce an old-fashioned family in their activities behind the green-shuttered windows. Most important to the youngest readers is four-year-old Reuben who receives a fine red wheelbarrow for a birthday present. So pleased was Reuben with his gift that he was almost left out of the family group lined up for a long-planned daguerreotype. But Reuben did arrive, and with the wheelbarrow loaded most surprisingly. This pleasantly told Mid-Victorian story is just long enough for reading aloud to the picture-book age who will love it and the pictures.

Frances C. Darling

SOURCE: A review of *Reuben and His Red Wheelbarrow,* in *The Christian Science Monitor,* Vol. XXXVIII, No. 272, October 15, 1946, p. 10.

Reuben and His Red Wheelbarrow is an especially engaging book with its story by Alice Dalgliesh and its pictures by Ilse Bischoff. There is real originality in the recounting of Reuben's adventures on his fourth birthday and how, because of the gift of the little red wheelbarrow, he almost missed being in the long-planned photograph. The story is brief. I for one wish it might have been longer. I like those five brothers and sisters, and I like Reuben's enthusiasm in putting the wheelbarrow to use. Miss Bischoff's quaint drawings, humorously conceived, delicately tinted, cleverly stylized, match the story in charm, and help give the book real distinction.

ALONG JANET'S ROAD (1946)

Virginia Kirkus' Bookshop Service

SOURCE: A review of *Along Janet's Road,* in *Virginia Kirkus' Bookshop Service,* Vol. XIV, No. 10, May 15, 1946, p. 242.

When *The Silver Pencil* ended its record, Janet Laidlaw was a teacher. Now we follow a new road, as she shifts from her first chosen career to that of editor of books for children. Set in a general background of book publishing and editing, which could not but be convincing (with the author's own background), the book is the story of three girls living together, of the children they know, of romance and its trials and tribulations. As a story of budding maturity, it hasn't quite the note of authenticity that *The Silver Pencil* had—or perhaps it just isn't quite as fresh and novel a story. But the publishing background has much to offer the many young people whose private star is set in that particular sky. A good addition to career bookshelves. Decorations by Katherine Milhous. The setting shifts from New York City to Nova Scotia and back to New York again and Connecticut.

The Booklist

SOURCE: A review of *Along Janet's Road,* in *The Booklist,* Vol. 42, No. 19, June 15, 1946, p. 333.

In this continuation of *The Silver Pencil* Janet Laidlaw gives up teaching to take a job as juvenile editor in a publishing firm. As a sequel to an outstanding first book it is disappointing; as an independent story it seems quite superficial. The frequent telescoping of time is confusing and the author presupposes a considerable knowledge of and interest in editing and publishing. Older girls will probably like it as a story of three girls living together.

The Saturday Review of Literature

SOURCE: A review of *Along Janet's Road,* in *The Saturday Review of Literature,* Vol. XXIX, No. 24, June, 15, 1946, p. 43.

There is a satisfying quality about this sequel to *The Silver Pencil.* It can be read for itself alone, but it has greater value as a record of Janet Laidlaw's development—as a writer and editor and as a woman. At the close of this book we leave her secure in her work, happy in the culmination of her love story, rich in her friendships and sure of her part in the American scene. It was not altogether easy for her to leave the teaching that she loved to become editor of children's books with an old and well established firm. A writer herself, she knew a writer's problems. She had to learn that a publisher has problems, too. Her first day in the office is an amusing succession of situations, some very funny, some difficult, all a test of her poise and judgment. The honesty and courage that stood her in good stead in the early years help her through these trying first weeks. Budge, one of the two girls who live with her in the apartment on Morningside Heights, writes and illustrates her first book and Janet sees it through the editorial office and through the press. Here is an excellent picture of the making of a children's book. Janet's first conference with the salesmen, her effort to keep the balance between the books that she longs to publish and the books that she knows the public will buy, is obviously an actual experience, honestly and vividly told.

Her personal life, too, has its ups and downs. Budge and Ellen marry—Budge, the doctor, whose little daughter, Patsy, is one of the outstanding characters in the book. David, Janet's nephew, comes from Trinidad to have a serious operation on his eyes. Ellen's first baby is born. Finally Janet sells the house at Sandy Cove and buys an old farmhouse in Connecticut. On the hill above it is a great barn that has been fitted up as a guest house, and there are four acres of good New England land. The story ends there on Thanksgiving Day. Ellen and her husband and the baby, Budge the doctor, and little Paul and Patsy and David are all there. Then Perry, Janet's lover, comes back. There is no romantic scene between them. As she looks at Perry Janet knows, suddenly and surely, that he is the most important thing in her life. Perry tries to get her alone, but the little house is so filled with people that there are constant interruptions. Reading this homely, natural scene one is divided between irritation and laughter. The last of the unwelcome "interrupters" is Mrs. Snow, the cook. "There'll be lots of cold turkey," she remarks cheerfully. "What'll I do with it?" "Go and sit with it in the kitchen!" Perry answers fiercely.

Katherine Milhous has given the book dignity and beauty with her decorations.

Alice M. Jordan

SOURCE: A review of *Along Janet's Road,* in *The Horn Book Magazine,* Vol. XXII, No. 4, July, 1946, p. 269.

In this continuation of *The Silver Pencil* Miss Dalgliesh develops Janet's friendships in her New York business career, as well as in her home life and on vacation in Nova Scotia. There are other girls in the story and there is romance. Glimpses of the routine and rewards of working with books in a publishing house reflect the author's own experiences. But these later adventures of Janet provide a sequel that falls a little flat after so fine a book as *The Silver Pencil* and hurts rather than helps the earlier book.

THE DAVENPORTS ARE AT DINNER (1948)

The Saturday Review of Literature

SOURCE: A review of *The Davenports Are at Dinner,* in *The Saturday Review of Literature,* Vol. XXXI, No. 50, December 11, 1948, p. 38.

The Davenports are Kathy, Barbara, John, Ricky, their father, their new stepmother, and her own small daughter Lynette. In the beginning of the book they live in an old house which they love—but have to lose. The owner, as is the habit of owners nowadays, wanted to live in it himself. A kindly but rather "bossy" friend whom the Davenports call "Mrs. Waddletwaddle" offers them her barn. It is inconvenient and extremely small but the Davenports, being what they are, soon make it into a home. This is an unusually interesting family. Led by Kathy, they carry on a radio program, with conspicuous success, by means of including a large radio public as listeners in their ordinary dinner conversation. When the beloved White Horse (made of papier mâché but extremely stylish and handsome) is stolen from the harness shop they persist in their search until he is restored. When anything goes wrong they put their heads together and act. There isn't a selfish or lazy bone in them. They are plucky and funny and extraordinarily real. This is an honest picture of an American family in the complicated world of today. It is a book to read more than once. When you know them, the Davenports are not easy to forget.

May Lamberton Becker

SOURCE: A review of *The Davenports Are at Dinner,* in *New York Herald Tribune Weekly Book Review,* Vol. 25, No. 17, December 12, 1948, p. 8.

The Davenports are a family any person of sense would like to have for next-door neighbors; something to say for a family with four children and a father who writes children's books and illustrates them himself. Almost his only fault, according to his sons and daughters, is that he has a disturbing way of keeping things to himself until they are all settled. So when he announced that he was going to marry Emily and would bring her home on a certain day from Vermont the Davenports said "You know how Father is," hoped for the best and were delighted to find that was what Emily was. Father hadn't thought to mention that she was a widow with one child just the age of their youngest, and this shy Lynette, who looked at them with the eyes of a trapped rabbit and would hardly speak, was a problem. So was the discovery that, as he had not told his publishers what his book was about, they had

contracted for another on the same subject and that his would have to be held over at least three years. Even more was the housing shortage, which turned them out of their house in Penny Brook, Connecticut, into a one-room barn. But in the midst of all came Kathy's great idea.

It was that if two people could share their breakfast conversations with a radio audience the actual give-and-take of a lively family at dinner might be quite as interesting, especially on a small local station. How they carried it out makes as absorbing a family story as ten-year-olds have had for years. Flavia Gag's pictures show the family to the life.

THE BEARS ON HEMLOCK MOUNTAIN (1952)

Jennie D. Lindquist

SOURCE: A review of *The Bears on Hemlock Mountain,* in *The Horn Book Magazine,* Vol. XXVIII, No. 2, April, 1952, p. 99.

When Jonathan's mother sent him over Hemlock Mountain to borrow a large iron pot from Aunt Emma, he wasn't quite sure he liked the idea of going alone. Of course, he was a big boy—eight years old—but some people maintained that there were bears on the mountain. "Stuff and nonsense," said his mother. "Many's the time I've been over Hemlock Mountain and not a bear did I see." To tell whether Jonathan met any bears would be to spoil a story that will delight children because of its lively writing as well as its element of suspense.

Virginia Kirkus' Bookshop Service

SOURCE: A review of *The Bears on Hemlock Mountain,* in *Virginia Kirkus' Bookshop Service,* Vol. XX, No. 14, July 15, 1952, p. 404.

Legend in the making in the form of a sort of regional folk tale with the kind of rhythm and repeat construction small children love. Jonathan was eight, pretty small to be sent over Hemlock Mountain to borrow a big iron pot from his aunt on the other side. But he found he had friends in the squirrels and the birds and the rabbits, and all would have been well if he hadn't eaten too many of his aunt's cookies and drunk too much milk and slept too long so that it was dark when he started back with the big iron pot. What he discovered about the bears of Hemlock Mountain makes the climax of a story that is good read aloud material, and that second graders will be able to read to themselves. Helen Sewell's line drawings in black and blue make decorative borders. Her humans are pretty much stock figures but she has a nice feel for the Pennsylvania German decorative art quality.

Bulletin of the Center for Children's Books

SOURCE: A review of *The Bears on Hemlock Mountain,* in *Bulletin of the Center for Children's Books,* Vol. 6, No. 1, September, 1952, p. 4.

Eight years old was not very old to be going alone over Hemlock Mountain but Jonathan's mother needed to borrow Aunt Emma's big iron pot and there was no one but Jonathan to go after it. All would have been well had Jonathan not eaten too many cookies, drunk too much milk, and slept too long. That was how it happened that he had to come back over Hemlock Mountain after dark when every one knew—or at least suspected that there were bears on Hemlock Mountain. How the small animals and birds helped Jonathan keep up his courage and what happened when he really met the bears makes an exciting story. The text has the rhythmic quality and the humor of a folk tale and will be fun to read aloud in family groups or story hours. The illustrations [by Helen Sewell] are perfect for the story—emphasizing the humor and heightening the suspense. An exceptional book in quality of writing, illustrations and make-up.

The Booklist

SOURCE: A review of *The Bears on Hemlock Mountain,* in *The Booklist,* Vol. 49, No. 1, September 1, 1952, p. 19.

Based on a tale "told by the people," this is the story of a little boy sent by his mother to borrow an iron pot from an aunt who lived on the other side of Hemlock Mountain—really only a hill. Jonathan's mother did not believe that there were bears on Hemlock Mountain but Jonathan did; his adventures and discovery are told with suspense and with a touch of folk-tale quality. The two-color, somewhat stylized illustrations seem right for the story.

THE COURAGE OF SARAH NOBLE (1954)

Olive Deane Hormel

SOURCE: A review of *The Courage of Sarah Noble,* in *The Christian Science Monitor,* Vol. XLVI, No. 142, May 13, 1954, p. 9.

My favorite of this group—indeed, I think, my favorite of all the spring books—is *The Courage of Sarah Noble,* by Alice Dalgliesh with exquisitely attuned illustrations by Leonard Weisgard. "This is a true story," the author tells us in an introductory note. "Sarah Noble was a real little girl who came, in 1707, to cook for her father while he built the first house in New Milford, Connecticut. . . . "

She quotes from Samuel Orcutt's "History of the Towns of New Milford and Bridgewater, Connecticut, 1703-1882": "Romance has never painted a picture more perfectly true to the heart of a father, or to the charming bravery of a young daughter only eight years, than is found in the history of the settlement of the first family in the beautiful township of New Milford."

Both the author and artist live in Connecticut towns that are within a few miles of the scene of this story, which perhaps accounts in part for the deeply felt simplicity and the reverence that characterize this quietly told tale—quietly told, yet rich with suspense.

"'Keep up your courage,' her mother had said, fastening the cloak under Sarah's chin. 'Keep up your courage, Sarah Noble!'" And her mother's behest is an echoing refrain throughout the story as Sarah's courage is sorely tried.

Most memorable of many memorable scenes that come to mind is Sarah's first encounter with the lurking Indian children when she draws them to her by reading aloud from her Bible. This is a book unmarred by preachment, piety, or sentimentality—a book without flaw, it seems to me, which must become an American classic.

Frances Lander Spain

SOURCE: A review of *The Courage of Sarah Noble,* in *The Saturday Review,* Vol. XXXVII, No. 20, May 15, 1954, p. 54.

Sarah Noble was only eight years old when she went with her father to claim a homestead in the Connecticut wilderness. Her mother, who must stay behind with a sick baby, bade her keep up her courage, and this loving admonition sustained the little girl through many lonely and perplexing hours.

While her father built their new home, she kept house in a cave across the river. Often Sarah was alone, and one day she was surprised and a little terrified to find herself surrounded by many Indian children. The new settlers had been fair in their dealings with the Indians and so there were good relations between them. Soon Sarah and the Indian children were playing together, learning a bit of each other's language and teaching each other favorite games. Late in the summer the house was finished and Sarah's father made plans to return to Massachusetts for the rest of the family. Sarah was left with the friendly Indians. At first living with an Indian family was strange and Sarah was afraid, but she remembered to keep up her courage and after a few days was very much at home with them. Before winter her father returned bringing her mother, brothers, and sister to the new home.

This is a story of a little girl who often was afraid, but who was brave to face the experiences required of her. Her father told her "to be afraid and to be brave is the best courage of all," and this courage Sarah had. It is based on a real incident that occurred during the settlement of New Mitford, Conn., and is told with directness and understanding.

Leonard Weisgard's brown-and-black illustrations complement the text and add to the attractiveness of the book.

Virginia Kirkus' Bookshop Service

SOURCE: A review of *The Courage of Sarah Noble,* in *Virginia Kirkus' Bookshop Service,* Vol. XXII, No. 10, May 15, 1954, p. 311.

Frontier tales, with the authentic feel of place and time and people, have endless fascination for young and old. This one is unusual in that it harks back to a time when the wooded hills of western Connecticut were frontiers, and when settlers from Massachusetts made the slow trek, on foot and horseback, found friendly Indians, and built their cabins. Here is just such a true story of eight year old Sarah, who took the journey with her father John Noble, cooked for him, and kept house in a cave while he built the home that was to shelter her mother and the children. Then—while he went back to Massachusetts for the family, Sarah lived with the Indians and learned the give and take of kindly people, Indians or whites. It is simply told, with no embroidering of melodrama, but it carries the warmth of sincerity, and the wholesome appeal of true adventure. Charmingly illustrated in stylized, imaginative drawings in black and brown, by Leonard Weisgard.

The Booklist

SOURCE: A review of *The Courage of Sarah Noble*, in *The Booklist*, Vol. 50, No. 20, June 15, 1954, p. 405.

Although many of the details are imagined this is a true story of eight-year-old Sarah Noble who journeyed alone with her father from the Massachusetts Colony to Connecticut to cook for him while he built a home in the wilderness and, when the house was completed, lived with Indians while her father returned for the rest of the family. Charmingly told with an economy of words and with a soberness entirely suited to the situation—a small girl forced into the role of woman, trying desperately to keep up her courage though she is often afraid. Pleasing format.

Virginia Haviland

SOURCE: A review of *The Courage of Sarah Noble*, in *The Horn Book Magazine*, Vol. XXX, No. 4, August, 1954, pp. 246-47.

Here is a remarkable book for younger readers—a true pioneer adventure, written for easy reading but without any sacrifice of literary quality or depth of feeling. Its portrayal of courage in a real little girl is honest and moving. Sarah, though only eight, was her father's companion on a grueling and dangerous journey to build a new home in the Connecticut wilderness of 1707, and she succeeded well in following her mother's advice to "keep up your courage, Sarah Noble." When, however, the log house was finished and her father was leaving her with the Indians while he went back alone to get the rest of the family, Sarah, who had been very brave, confessed that she had lost her courage. To this her father made the discerning and heartening reply, "To be afraid and to be brave is the best courage of all." Leonard Weisgard's warmly alive drawings in brown truly illustrate the story.

B. Clark

SOURCE: A review of *The Courage of Sarah Noble*, in *The Junior Bookshelf*, Vol. 35, No. 2, April, 1971, p. 104.

The story of an eight-year-old girl in the early days of settlers in the U.S.A. Indian territories is published in the usual Antelope format. Yet it is a story of a child whose courage far exceeds her years, and it would seem to be more suitable for the reader of ten and upwards. Young Sarah has a pretty severe time travelling with her father to find a suitable place to build a home for the rest of the family, and cooking for both of them. When her father decides to settle in a certain place, poor Sarah has to stay with an Indian family while her father returns for the other members of her own family. Yet a good idea of the trials of those early days is portrayed in this short story.

THE THANKSGIVING STORY (1954)

Jennie D. Lindquist

SOURCE: A review of *The Thanksgiving Story*, in *The Horn Book Magazine*, Vol. XXX, No. 5, October, 1954, p. 341.

The Horn Book does not ordinarily include in its Booklist any titles that will not have been published by the time the magazine is in the mail. However, as soon as we saw pages for this unusually attractive and much-needed book, we asked for permission to include it although it will not be published until October. Everyone who has anything to do with children will want it in time for Thanksgiving. It is the only really distinguished book we have on that holiday. Miss Dalgliesh has told the Pilgrim story simply from the point of view of the Hopkins family whose little Oceanus was born on the *Mayflower;* and Miss [Helen] Sewell has made wonderful full-color pictures. A beautiful book.

Kirkus Reviews

SOURCE: A review of *The Thanksgiving Story*, in *Kirkus Reviews*, Vol. XXII, No. 20, October 15, 1954, p. 706.

A quiet dignity and a sense of the momentous mark Miss Dalgliesh's story of the first months of the *Mayflower* settlement. In particular, it is the voyage and settlement as seen through the Hopkins, their children—Giles, Constance and Demaris—and Oceanus, the baby born during the voyage. The historical aspects have been well combined with the personal. As the *Mayflower* and the ill fated *Speedwell* set out, there is the religious background of the Pilgrims, the reasons for their sailing and the picture of the many different kinds of travellers—Alden the carpenter, Miles Standish the soldier. Arrival in Massachusetts is filled with relief and hope and as the settlers face their first miserable year there is a sense of immediacy to their problems. And there are the blessings too as friendships are made with the Indians Samoset, Squanto and Massasoit, and as the settlers reap their first harvest and meet for their first Thanksgiving. Helen Sewell's colored pictures have an early American quality and have been excellently matched with the text. Recommended for reading aloud.

Olive Deane Hormel

SOURCE: A review of *The Thanksgiving Story,* in *The Christian Science Monitor,* Vol. XLVI, No. 295, November 11, 1954, p. 12.

There has been a veritable avalanche of books about American history for older boys and girls in recent seasons—but it has remained for Alice Dalgliesh to bring this important subject to the very young in a form both appealing and authentic. Her lovely books, **The Courage of Sarah Noble** was one of the most outstanding of the spring season, and now we have **The Thanksgiving Story** designed to appeal to children of picture-book age as well as the beginning reader group.

The distinctive illustrations in color are in the spirit of the American primitive, by Helen Sewell, well-known author-artist.

The story is centered upon the Hopkins family, Giles, Constance, and Damaris, and the baby brother born in the course of their Mayflower journey who was named Oceanus. Miss Dalgliesh's special distinction is her faithfulness to authenticity. She refrains from the fictional in even a small degree, yet develops the imaginative where it will enhance appeal, while never departing from known facts.

There is simplicity and dignity in **The Thanksgiving Story** both reverent and appealing—as when it concludes the description of the Pilgrims' thanksgiving feast: "Perhaps they sang the hymn they had brought to the New World with them:

> 'Praise God from whom all blessings flow,
> Praise Him all creatures here below . . . '

And if they did, Giles, Constance, and Damaris sang with them."

Bulletin of the Center for Children's Books

SOURCE: A review of *The Thanksgiving Story,* in *Bulletin of the Center for Children's Books,* Vol. 8, No. 11, July, 1955, p. 98.

With great simplicity and dignity the author recounts the events that led to the founding of Plymouth and the celebration of the first Thanksgiving. The account is very slightly fictionalized--just enough to give it interest and reality for young readers. Helen Sewell's colorful, somewhat stylized drawings are a perfect complement for the text and help to make this a distinguished book.

THE COLUMBUS STORY (1955)

Jennie D. Lindquist

SOURCE: A review of *The Columbus Story,* in *The Horn Book Magazine,* Vol. XXXI, No. 5, October, 1955, p. 367.

By far the best telling of the Columbus story I have ever read for younger children, this is distinguished also for its bookmaking and beautiful full-color illustrations [by Leo Politi]. It is a most welcome addition to school and public library collections and a fine choice for a child's personal ownership. It is so well written that it is a joy to read it aloud. A companion volume to the author's **The Thanksgiving Story.**

The Booklist

SOURCE: A review of *The Columbus Story,* in *The Booklist,* Vol. 52, No. 4, October 15, 1955, p. 81.

In the simple, dignified manner of **The Thanksgiving Story** the author presents a bareboned but meaningful account of the explorer which highlights "those events in the life of Columbus which seem to be most interesting to children. The narrative, planned for reading aloud, is historical, with legends omitted . . . "—*Author's note.* Politi's sturdy illustrations convey a feeling for place and time.

Bulletin of the Center for Children's Books

SOURCE: A review of *The Columbus Story,* in *Bulletin of the Center for Children's Books,* Vol. 10, No. 3, November 13, 1956, p. 37.

The story of Columbus told with simple dignity for young readers or listeners. The bare facts of Columbus's early life and first voyage are presented in brief text and colorful, distinctive illustrations to give the child a first acquaintance with the subject, without the introduction of legendary materials that frequently lead to misunderstandings. The style is suitable for reading aloud to young children, and third grade readers will be able to handle the text alone.

THE FOURTH OF JULY STORY (1956)

Virginia Kirkus' Service

SOURCE: A review of *The Fourth of July Story,* in *Virginia Kirkus' Service* Vol. XXIV, No. 13, July 1, 1956, p. 431.

In simplified yet straightforward terms, Miss Dalgliesh has retold the events leading up to the Declaration of Independence and interpreted their meaning for the youngest question askers. Broadly sketched, the material covers the highlights—the thirteen colonies, their wish to govern themselves, Jefferson's writing of the Declaration at the request of the Congressional committee, the carrying of the news and the steps taken, under Washington, to enforce it. A good introduction, in keeping with the author's *The Thanksgiving Story* and *The Columbus Story* and, with its striking color spreads by Marie Nonnast, an attractively presented book.

Frances Lander Spain

SOURCE: A review of *The Fourth of July Story,* in *The Saturday Review,* Vol. XXXIX, No. 29, July 21, 1956, p. 37.

Alice Dalgliesh, who has recently written *The Thanksgiving Story* and *The Columbus Story* here continues her accounts, for younger children, of American history and the days we celebrate with this telling of the origins of the Fourth of July. It is brief and uncluttered, with details and names reduced to a minimum, as it should be for beginning readers, but it gets across the conflicts, the problems, and the satisfactions of the struggle for independence and the ultimate restoration of good relations between Great Britain and her former colonies. The many full-page colored illustrations will help the young child to understand the meaning of this, one of the most colorful and dramatic of our American holidays.

The Booklist and Subscription Books Bulletin

SOURCE: A review of *The Fourth of July Story,* in *The Booklist and Subscription Books Bulletin,* Vol. 53, No. 1, September 1, 1956, p. 28.

Like the author's two earlier books about American holidays, this narrative account of the significance of the Fourth of July holiday is compact, dramatic, and simplified enough to be understandable to younger children. Text and colorful illustrations, effectively explain the American colonies' desire for freedom, the need for the Declaration of Independence, the writing, signing, and adoption of the document, and the proclamation and effect of the news throughout the country.

RIDE ON THE WIND (1956)

Virginia Kirkus' Service

SOURCE: A review of *Ride on the Wind,* in *Virginia Kirkus' Service,* Vol. XXIV, No. 19, October 1, 1956, p. 750.

Miss Dalgliesh's retelling of the Lindbergh story, as it was presented in *The Spirit of Saint Louis* is a fine distillation, capturing as it does the essence of the feelings that went into the flight over the Atlantic. The narrative shows Lindbergh both as a dreamy youth and a practical man who had not forgotten all his dreams and there is a spirit

of immediacy and direct participation in the flight itself and in its triumph. Some soft water colors, in brown and in full color have been done for the text by Georges Schreiber and they too create the atmosphere of the airborne life. Firmly reinforced.

Jennie D. Linquist

SOURCE: A review of *Ride on the Wind,* in *The Horn Book Magazine,* Vol. XXXII, No. 6, December, 1956, p. 456.

'Told . . . from *The Spirit of St. Louis* by Charles A. Lindbergh," this is a remarkable book for in its 32 pages for younger children it really succeeds in giving the very feeling of the original. Miss Dalgliesh touches briefly on Lindbergh's boyhood, his early interest in flying and his work on the mail plane; but the larger part of the book concerns the Paris flight. All the pictures are effective but those of the lone plane above the ocean and the scenes in Paris are particularly so and add immeasurably to the text. Lindbergh himself says that author and artist "bring out beautifully, in writing and in painting, the effect I tried to work into my book during the hours and years I spent on it."

ADAM AND THE GOLDEN COCK (1959)

New York Herald Tribune Book Review

SOURCE: A review of *Adam and the Golden Cock,* in *New York Herald Tribune Book Review,* November 1, 1959, p. 8.

Our favorite historical tale for younger Americana is Alice Dalgliesh's *The Courage of Sarah Noble.* Eight-year-olds can read it easily, love it and learn early to exercise historical imagination as they sense vividly what it would be like to be a little girl in the Connecticut wilderness of 1707. Now Miss Dalgliesh has written a companion piece with a small boy for the central figure. This brief vignette of Adam in the Newtown of 1781, the year General Rochambeau's army camped there for three days, is not as poignant and moving as *Sarah,* but it is a fine piece of Americana. The pictures by Leonard Weisgard in glowing golden tan and black are beautiful, conveying the very essence of summer days in the New England countryside, and Adam's part in the great events is childlike and natural.

Before the coming of the soldiers the boy felt that his life was as monotonous as that of the sheep he tended. He was alone so much he took comfort in pretending to talk to the golden cock on the church steeple. After their arrival everything changed. Every tiny thing was important. In fact, Adam had to make a decision, without help from anybody (even in his dreams of the golden cock he received no aid), a decision that concerned Paul, who had been his dearest friend before it was known that Paul's father was a Tory. No wonder Adam never forgot these extraordinary days when General Rochambeau's army came through and he ceased to talk, even in imagination, with the golden cock.

Zena Sutherland

SOURCE: A review of *Adam and the Golden Cock,* in *Bulletin of the Center for Children's Books,* Vol. 13, No. 5, January, 1960, p. 80.

A Revolutionary War story. Adam used to watch the golden bird that was a weather vane on the church steeple; while he was watching he thought about his friend Paul and wondered what to do about it: Paul's father was a Tory and Adam was not comfortable about Paul's actions when a troop of French soldiers came to town. He dreamed of the cock, and in his dream asked for advice. But Adam had to make his own decision. Good background, and a good description of the two small boys involved in the conflict between maintaining their integrity and holding their friendship. The illustrations are handsome in black, white and gold; the sophisticated colors are adapted with skill to the rural scenes, especially in some of misty and quiet woods.

Virginia Haviland

SOURCE: A review of *Adam and the Golden Cock,* in *The Horn Book Magazine,* Vol. XXXVI, No. 1, February, 1960, p. 32.

Although this story falls short of *The Courage of Sarah Noble,* it maintains a high standard for third-and fourth-grade reading. The author has characterized a boy with realistic emotional pulls and provided a clear sense of history being made. The background is of Newtown, Connecticut, in 1761, with historical facts about General Rochambeau and his French troops who spent three days there on their way to support Washington at Yorktown. The fictional content centers in the boy Adam's interest in the visitors and his problematical friendship with a Tory's son. Richly illustrated in black with golden browns for an effect of sunny autumn days.

Additional coverage of Dalgliesh's life and career is contained in the following sources published by The Gale Group: *Contemporary Authors,* Vols. 73-76; *Major Authors and Illustrators for Children and Young Adults;* and *Something about the Author,* Vols. 17, 21.

Lynley (Stuart) Dodd

1941-

New Zealand illustrator and author of fiction.

Major works include *The Smallest Turtle* (1982; U.S. edition, 1985), *Hairy Maclary of Donaldson's Dairy* (1983; U.S. edition, 1985), *Slinky Malinki* (1990), *The Minister's Cat ABC* (1992; U.S. edition, 1994), *Hairy Maclary, Sit* (1998).

INTRODUCTION

Dodd has been compared to both Beatrix Potter and Dr. Seuss, indicating her ability to create vibrant animal characters and her facility with humorous rhyming stories for preschoolers and early readers. Accompanying the fast-paced text of Dodd's picture books are her colorful illustrations, drawing the reader into the world of the book through line drawings and color washes. Critics have noted the excitement and energy of Dodd's illustrations, especially in her books about the rambunctious dog Hairy Maclary and his animal friends. Ellen Mandel called the illustrations in *Hairy Maclary, Scattercat* "sprightly," and J. Ousbey praised the "lively pictures" accompanying the text of *Slinky Malinki*, a book about a thieving cat. Marcus Crouch praised Dodd's drawings, saying, "Here are strength and exuberance, both firmly under control but by no means lacking in spontaneity." Dodd's illustrations have also been applauded for truly depicting her animal subjects. Margot Hittel, for example, commented on the illustrations in *The Minister's Cat ABC*: "The illustrations are full of movement and many of the cats have wonderful expressions." The cats and dogs and other animals that are the main characters in Dodd's books are true to life, each with their own personality. As Crouch observed, "Lynley Dodd knows cats and knows how to put them into attractive and appropriate settings, knows too how to impart to each a clearly individual character." Each of the dogs in the Hairy Maclary stories, too, are fully formed and recognizable, from Bitzer Maloney "all skinny and bony" to the dachshund Schnitzel von Krumm "with the very low tum."

In addition to comparisons to Potter and Seuss, Dodd received this favorable comparison from an enthusiastic reviewer for *Publishers Weekly*: "With its amusing alliteration, fanciful names . . . and rapid-fire delivery, Dodd's nonsense verse follows quite nicely in the grand tradition of Messrs, Nash and Lear." Although she began her career as an artist and illustrator, Dodd's lively rhymes have also been praised for their contribution to the humor and individuality of her picture books. As Jill Bennett commented in a review of *Hairy Maclary, Scattercat*, Dodd's "rhyme is a delight to read aloud: its rhythm and meter and the choice of words make the verses a pleasure to wrap the tongue around."

While some critics have found that the vocabulary Dodd uses is beyond her intended audience, her writing has generally received positive reviews. Dodd's books frequently have a refrain: a few lines are repeated throughout the story, encouraging readers and listeners to join in and chime along as the story builds. Dodd plays with words not only through the memorable rhymes and the rollicking rhythms that drive her stories, but also through funny names and evocative adjectives. "I don't set out with earnest messages in mind," Dodd told *St. James Guide to Children's Writers*, "I like to have fun with words and characters and I aim to amuse and entertain—if a little learning creeps in occasionally, that's fine."

Biographical Information

Born in Rotorua, New Zealand, Dodd was the daughter of a forester; her early years were spent in isolated areas with, as she told *Something about the Author* (*SATA*), "unlimited space for play, and miles of pine trees in any direction provided plenty of scope for imagination. I have always had and pen and drawing paper ready. . . . " Dodd's early experiments with drawing developed into a lifelong occupation. She graduated from the Elam School of Art in 1962 and, after studying at Auckland Teachers College, she became art mistress at Queen Margaret College in Wellington, New Zealand. She remained in that position until 1968 when she illustrated her first book, *My Cat Likes to Hide in Boxes*, in collaboration with Eve Sutton. "I now write as well as illustrate my own picture books," Dodd told *SATA*, "I find being able to plan the whole book from the outset exiting and rewarding." Her early works were written with her own two children in mind, and her books have been influenced by her pets—*My Cat Likes to Hide in Boxes* was based on Dodd's family cat.

Major Works

Most of Dodd's picture books have been part of the Hairy Maclary series, which began in 1983 with *Hairy Maclary of Donaldson's Dairy*. The book introduces the likeable Hairy, a shaggy black dog who's generally ready for trouble, and his dog friends, including the Dalmation Bottomley Potts, the dachshund Schnitzel von Krumm, and the greyhound Bitzer Maloney. The dogs go on a walk through the neighborhood, but are chased home by Scarface Claw, a fierce cat. Hairy has further adventures with Scarface Claw in *Hairy Maclary, Scattercat* (1985; U.S. edition 1988) and *Hairy Maclary's Caterwaul Caper* (1987; U.S. edition 1988), where the cat gets caught in a tree and Hairy and the other dogs bark uncontrollably at the base until a neighbor hears the noise and rescues the cat. In a later book in the series, *Hairy Maclary, Sit,* Hairy must attend obedience school. True to his character, Hairy leads the other dogs in the class in a rebellion. The pack of high-spirited animals has all kinds of energetic fun until they land in a pond. All of the Hairy Maclary books are written in rhyme, and are filled with Dodd's signature colorful illustrations.

Two of the characters from the Hairy Maclary books have their own titles, Schnitzel von Krumm and Slinky Malinki. Schnitzel's books—*Schnitzel von Krumm's Basketwork* (1994) and *Schnitzel von Krumm Forget-Me-Not* (1998)—find the dog humorously dealing with the exchange of his old, decrepit sleeping basket for a new one, and being accidentally left behind as his family goes on holiday. *Slinky Malinki* is about a sleek black cat who is innocent by day and criminal by night. According to Leone McDermott, Slinky "might have escaped from the pages of *Old Possum's Book of Practical Cats.*" He plays and stretches in the sun during the day, but when night falls Slinky goes about his secret work—stealing things such as pencils, brushes, sausages, biscuits, and slippers. He stashes his booty away, until one night the treasure collapses with a crash. Slinky's family wakes to find him in the midst of all the stolen goods, and in disgrace the cat reforms.

Dodd's books not in the Hairy Maclary series also focus on animals. *The Smallest Turtle* tracks a tiny, newborn turtle (the smallest of the litter, and the last to hatch) as he makes his treacherous way to the sea. Along the way he avoids such dangers as hungry seagulls, a lizard, and the scorching sun. *The Smallest Turtle* is different from Dodd's later books in that it is a realistic depiction of a natural event. *The Minister's Cat ABC,* on the other hand, is about the distinct traits of individual cats. Each letter of the alphabet begins an adjective describing a feline—airborne, huffy, impish, posing, vexed—with an accompanying illustration. Gill Roberts found the illustrations, "full of typical feline majesty and movement [that] match exactly the aptly selected adjectives—which read alphabetically as if, almost, by accident."

Awards

My Cat Likes to Hide in Boxes was awarded the Esther Glen Medal from the New Zealand Library Association in 1975. Dodd won the New Zealand Children's Picture Book of the Year Award for *Hairy Maclary from Donaldson's Dairy* in 1984, *Hairy Maclary, Scattercat* in 1986, and *Hairy Maclary's Caterwaul Caper* in 1988. Dodd received a New Zealand Post Children's Book Award and AIM Children's Picture Book of the Year Award for *Hairy Maclary's Show business,* both in 1992, and the AIM Third Prize for *Hairy Maclary's Rumpus at the Vet* and *Slinky Malinki* in 1990 and 1991, respectively. *Slinky Malinki Catflaps* was named a New Zealand Post Children's Honour Book in 1999.

GENERAL COMMENTARY

Jody Risacher

SOURCE: A review of *Hairy Maclary from Donaldson's Dairy, Hairy Maclary's Bone,* and *The Smallest Turtle,* in *School Library Journal,* Vol. 32, No. 3, November, 1985, pp. 68-9.

Hairy Maclary, a perky Scottish terrier, goes for a walk one day and is joined by his canine companions along the way. On their stroll, they meet Scarface Claw, a fierce tomcat whose fearsome cry causes all to turn tail and run. The last page shows Hairy Maclary peering timidly out from under the blanket that covers his basket. In *Hairy Maclary's Bone,* Hairy finds himself doggedly pursued again after the butcher hands him a tasty bone. In order to elude his pursuers, Hairy leads them on an obstacle course through hedges, signs and a boat yard, and the competition is eliminated one by one. Simply told in cumulative verse opposite each colorful illustration, the stories provide a pleasantly amusing experience for young readers or listeners. *The Smallest Turtle* tells the tale of a sea turtle's instinctive trek to the sea after birth. The dangers of the journey, the hot sun and hungry gulls, are successfully avoided and left behind as the little turtle takes his first ocean swim. Save for the lack of rhyming text, the style and format are the same as in the Hairy Maclary titles. This one will serve as a natural science expedition for the curious young.

Denise M. Wilms and Barbara Elleman

SOURCE: A review of *Hairy Maclary from Donaldson's Dairy* and *Hairy Maclary's Bone,* in *The Booklist,* Vol. 82, No. 6, November 15, 1985, p. 492.

"Out of the gate / and off for a walk / went Hairy Maclary / from Donaldson's dairy," so begins this simple cumulative rhyme in which a small, black, fuzzy-haired dog is joined by a variety of other canines: "Hercules Morse as big as a horse," "Muffin McLay like a bundle of hay," and "Schnitzel von Krumm with a very low tum." Everything goes well until they meet "Scarface Claw / the toughest Tom in town", who, with one loud "EEEEEOW-WWFFTZ," sends them racing back home. In *Hairy Maclary's Bone* the scruffy little terrier gets butcher Stone's tastiest bone. Spying a hoped for treat, Hercules, Muffin, Schnitzel, and some other canines take off in hot pursuit, their eyes on the prize. Hairy's route home isn't the easiest, however, and, at each obstacle, one of the dogs doesn't quite make it through. Hairy does nicely though and, free at last, is completely oblivious to his good luck. Both stories have simple rhythms that trip smoothly along; the first book with its repetitive phrasing will encourage children to chime in. The oral appeal coupled with the sight of the dogs makes this a likely group read-aloud. The caricatures of the animals give individual personalities, and the bright colors add dash.

Nancy A. Gifford

SOURCE: A review of *Hairy Maclary Scattercat* and *Wake Up, Bear,* in *School Library Journal,* Vol. 35, No. 9, June-July, 1988, p. 90.

In *Hairy Maclary Scattercat,* the furry dog "felt bumptious and bustly, bossy and bouncy and frisky and hustly." After scaring off five different cats, along comes Scarface Claw, who chases the dog "ALL the way home." The bouncy rhyming text is often forced with uncommon names and words. Illustrations are colorful, clear, and give a good portrayal of the animals, but Hairy Maclary makes a much better impression in the previous books about him (all Gareth Stevens). *Wake Up, Bear* is set in the spring, and Bear's friends try to awaken him. Lion roars, Squirrel drops a nut, Monkey tickles his toes, etc.—but Bear sleeps on until Bee buzzes around and reminds Bear of honey, causing him to awaken. Clear and colorful illustrations supplement the simple-minded, predictable story. There are also some major flaws. Bear is under a Bulbul tree, which is not listed in a standard encyclopedia or dictionary. (A bulbul is a kind of tropical bird.) Also children will be quick to note that a mixed bag of jungle, forest, and domestic animals, obviously out of their habitats, try to wake Bear. Almost any picture book collection can deliver a more credible animal story that will prove more enjoyable. Although the back of the book lists these books among others as "Gold Star First Readers," they have too many difficult words for beginning readers.

Carol McMichael

SOURCE: A review of *A Dragon in a Wagon* and *Hairy Maclary's Caterwaul Caper,* in *School Library Journal,* Vol. 35, No. 7, March, 1989, p. 160.

Two "first readers" that beginning readers may find difficult. *A Dragon in a Wagon* tells of a little girl's fantasies of her dog as a variety of other creatures, such as a dragon in a wagon or a moose on the loose. For the most part, the slight story skips along in rhyme until readers come to *giraffe* supposedly rhyming with *scarf.* The gnu may throw young readers off entirely since it comes first in the rhyme and the word (and animal) are so unfamiliar. *Hairy Maclary's Caterwaul Caper* is filled with unfamiliar words to beginning readers such as *snippet* and *cacophony,* not to mention the word *caterwaul* in the title. The simplistic story is of a dog, Hairy Maclary, who leads all of the other dogs in the neighborhood toward a terrible noise created by a cat caught up in a tree. Again, this is supposed to be a rhyming tale, although the last lines on most pages do not rhyme—they are more like refrains. Several words in both texts are in bold capital letters—not necessarily as new words nor as words of emphasis. There doesn't seem to be any logical reason. Each title is well illustrated with bright watercolor and pen drawings in a cartoon-like and often humorous fashion. They far exceed the quality of the texts. Other series such as the "Rookie Readers" (Childrens) are much better choices for beginning readers.

Jo Heaton

SOURCE: A review of *Find Me a Tiger* and *The Smallest Turtle,* in *School Librarian,* Vol. 40, No. 1, February, 1992, p. 15.

It is nine years since *The Smallest Turtle* first appeared in hardback, and the arrival of the paperback edition coincides with the publication of *Find Me a Tiger.* The first is the simple story of a turtle who is determined to overcome a range of obstacles to reach the sea. The illustrations of the cute turtle may appeal to some children, but the style of illustration and the quality of the reproduction is somewhat dated now.

Find Me a Tiger is the same size and shape as other books by Lynley Dodd and may get lost among her popular Hairy Maclary books. This would be a pity as it is very different and shows how this author's style has developed. In each picture, an animal is camouflaged by its natural surroundings and children will enjoy finding them all. The text is a simple poem that tells readers what they are looking for, be it a seal on a rock or a bear in the snow. The book can be enjoyed on two levels, as a story in its own right or an introduction to the concept of animal camouflage.

TITLE COMMENTARY

MY CAT LIKES TO HIDE IN BOXES (with Eve Sutton, 1973; U.S. edition, 1974)

Virginia Reese

SOURCE: A review of *My Cat Likes to Hide in Boxes,* in *School Library Journal,* Vol. 21, No. 1, September, 1974, p. 70.

Cumulative verses "catalog" the activities of cats from all over the world and contrast them with the behavior of the narrator's cat who only . . . *Likes To Hide in Boxes.* The stanzas are flat and unimaginative, and Dodd's dull cartoon illustrations are literal portrayals of cats in silly, stereotypic national costumes. Only the pictures of "MY cat" who peers out of an orange crate (forgetting to tuck in his tail) or pops be-hatted from a bandbox, will draw any chuckles from children.

THE NICKLE NACKLE TREE (1976; U.S. edition, 1978)

Margery Fisher

SOURCE: A review of *The Nickle Nackle Tree,* in *Growing Point,* Vol. 15, No. 5, November, 1976, pp. 2991-92.

Lynley Dodd enlivens the inevitable progression in his counting-book, ***The Nickle Nackle Tree,*** by a dégagé text that rather suggests an adult simulating a child's non-sense-improvisation. Whether or not some find the lines a trifle too self-conscious (words like "Four lurking Yuk birds, the sly and smirking kind"), nobody will deny that the alliterative lines are skilfully sustained and that the strong colour and tinted pages help to fix in the mind portraits of fantasy-birds which in an amusingly human way illustrate their definitions. The pictures are admirably composed so that as the numbers accumulate there is no feeling of confusion but a shapely sequence which points up the nonsensical enumerations.

The Junior Bookshelf

SOURCE: A review of *The Nickle Nackle Tree,* in *The Junior Bookshelf,* Vol. 41, No. 1, February, 1977, p. 13.

It is the play on words and the ludicrous invented names that attract in this book. The Nickle Nackle tree provides a home for a variety of odd birds from 'One Ballyhoo bird kicking up a din' to 'Fourteen Fandango birds dancing in the sun'. The 'Seven haughty Huffpuff birds with hoity-toity smiles' are particularly apt.

Publishers Weekly

SOURCE: A review of *The Nickle Nackle Tree,* in *Publishers Weekly,* Vol. 213, No. 4, January 23, 1978, p. 373.

Just the thing to lift the spirits in the bleak, lifeless winter months is Dodd's ridiculous counting book. The spring-time colors in her swirling paintings of a tree and birds that never were delight the eye. The dizzy rhymes do the same for the funny bone. Beginners can go sailing through numbers one through 14 as they tot up the burdens of the nickle nackle tree. First it's "one Ballyboo bird, kicking up a din," then "two squawking Scritchet birds, with legs so twiggy thin" through other noisy flyers, up to the 13 Grudge birds, silently grousing and the proud 14 pink Fandango birds. The kickiest pages show the laden tree dumping her pushy guests, finally.

Kirkus Reviews

SOURCE: A review of *The Nickle Nackle Tree,* in *Kirkus Reviews,* Vol. XLVI, No. 3, February 1, 1978, p. 102.

Mounting up from "One Ballyhoo bird, kicking up a din" to "Fourteen pink fandango birds dancing in the sun," the feathered population with which Dodd over-loads her Nickle Nackle tree includes such alliterated inventions as "Seven haughty Huffpuff birds with hoity-toity smiles" and "Eight cheeky Chizzle birds in cheer-ful chirpy piles." While they don't evoke any strikingly funny or original images, such phrases could serve as starting points for flights of visual nuttiness. But, alas, Dodd's pictures are stock commercial cartoons, ranging downwards from a derivative buzzard type (for "four lurk-ing Yuk birds") to a number of less interesting cookie-cutter shapes.

Gemma DeVinney

SOURCE: A review of *The Nickle Nackle Tree*, in *School Library Journal*, Vol. 24, No. 9, May, 1978, pp. 53-4.

This unexceptional counting-out rhyme introduces young children to the numbers one through 14 as they meet the "jumbly jam of birds" that inhabit *The Nickle Nackle Tree.* The illustrations are bright and colorful and the birds are easily counted, but children reading concept books might find expressions such as "kicking up a din," "hoity-toity smiles," and "grousing at the fun" puzzling. Don't spend a single nickel for this one.

Patricia Jean Cianciolo

SOURCE: A review of *The Nickle Nackle Tree*, in *Picture Books for Children, second edition*, American Library Association, 1981, p. 165.

Nonsense rhymes and superb graphics in clear vital shades dramatize what happens when the tree's twisted branches are overloaded with an assortment of zany birds. A fun-filled countingbook for numbers one through fourteen.

THE SMALLEST TURTLE (1982; U.S. edition, 1985)

Books for Your Children

SOURCE: A review of *The Smallest Turtle*, in *Books for Your Children*, Vol. 18, No. 1, Spring, 1983, p. 9.

Very simple story of how a baby turtle makes his way across a wide beach to the safety of the sea—a true story beautifully told in an easy rhythm that beginning readers will respond to with satisfaction.

Naomi Lewis

SOURCE: A review of *The Smallest Turtle*, in *The Times Educational Supplement*, No. 3492, June 3, 1983, p. 44.

High praise . . . for *The Smallest Turtle* by Lynley Dodd with its direct theme and excellent pictures (assured line,

clear relevant colours—blue sky, white sand, brown shadow). The last of the little turtles to hatch has to find his own way to the sea. It's quite a journey through the hot sand, over stones and tree roots, with beetle, lizard and spider on the route. He begins to crawl in circles. But see him reach at last the reviving sea, and joyfully swim.

A. Thatcher

SOURCE: A review of *The Smallest Turtle*, in *The Junior Bookshelf*, Vol. 47, No. 5, October, 1983, p. 206.

In this delightful story of the life cycle of a baby tur-tle, the smallest turtle has all the appeal of the young-est, the latest to hatch, who has to fight against so many more perils than his brothers and sisters. With his bright eyes, and dark green shell and markings, he is a charming little creature. Each beautifully drawn illustration, in clear bright colour has a few lines of complementary text which tells how, from the time he leaves the egg, he has an overwhelming urge to reach the safety of the sea. He encounters a beetle, a lizard and a spider; the hot sun and a tree with twisty roots confuse him; the gulls threaten him. But, at last, he is safe. A most attractive book.

HAIRY MACLARY FROM DONALDSON'S DIARY (1983; U.S. edition, 1985)

Margery Fisher

SOURCE: A review of *Hairy Maclary from Donaldson's Dairy*, in *Growing Point*, Vol. 22, No. 5, January, 1984, pp. 4200-01.

Neat rattling verses pursue the course of a shaggy dog's walk in a cumulative tale in which rhyme offers a large proportion of the delight; Bitzer Maloney 'all skinny and bony' and Bottomley Potts 'covered in spots' are as in-stantly recognisable as their distinguishing marks are ro-bustly chantable. Ink and paint pictures in a comically grotesque style match the rollicking text perfectly.

Marcus Crouch

SOURCE: A review of *Hairy Maclary from Donaldson's Dairy*, in *The Junior Bookshelf*, Vol. 48, No. 1, February, 1984, p. 12.

. . . *Hairy Maclary* has a perfection which is at once mature and refreshingly new. The text, cut to the bone with masterly economy, builds slowly and inevitably from page to page in a classically cumulative manner. The pictures, for all their generous colour, are equally concerned with basics. Here are strength and exuberance, both firmly under control but by no means lacking in spontaneity. A most notable picture-book in fact, beautifully drawn and constructed, shrewdly observed and above all filled to the brim with genuine humour. (I ought to explain that Hairy Maclary and his dog friends go for a walk and, for the best of reasons, return home at a high speed. Not the most complex of plots but one nevertheless firmly based in doggy behaviour.)

HAIRY MACLARY'S BONE (1984; U.S. edition, 1985)

Jill Bennett

SOURCE: A review of *Hairy Maclary's Bone,* in *Books for Keeps,* No. 40, September, 1986, p. 21.

In this, his second adventure, Hairy Maclary successfully loses all the would-be consumers of his tasty titbit as he makes his way home to Donaldson's dairy. Told in rollicking, rhyming text and humorous pictures, this is another splendid 'shaggy dog' story which will delight both very young listeners and those learning to read who adore getting their tongues round such names as Schnitzel von Krumm and Bitzer Maloney.

HAIRY MACLARY SCATTERCAT (1985; U.S. edition, 1988)

Jill Bennett

SOURCE: A review of *Hairy Maclary Scattercat,* in *Books for Keeps,* No. 46, September, 1987, p. 16.

In this third series of escapades Hairy Maclary terrorises all the cats in the neighbourhood, until he comes upon Scarface Claw that is—then he more than meets his match. As ever the rhyme is a delight to read aloud: its rhythm and meter and the choice of words make the verses a pleasure to wrap the tongue around. Both the feline attitudes and the excitement of the chase are nicely caught in the full-page illustrations. Great fun. Wide appeal.

Margery Fisher

SOURCE: A review of *Hairy Maclary Scattercat,* in *Growing Point,* Vol. 26, No. 3, September, 1987, p. 4866.

A small dog, 'bumptious and bustly, bossy and bouncy', puts to flight Batterball Brown, Pimpernel Pugh (elegantly Siamese), Slinky Malinki and other neighbourhood cats, but is seen off emphatically by sinister black Scarface Claw. In the text the recurrent surprise of lively rhymes, in the pictures dramatically odd, spiky shapes of animals and strongly blocked houses, trees, walls, doors, in a diverting and rumbustious sequel to two previous adventures of impetuous Hairy Maclary from New Zealand.

Ellen Mandel

SOURCE: A review of *Hairy Maclary Scattercat,* in *Booklist,* Vol. 84, No. 16, April 15, 1988, pp. 1428, 1430.

"Bumptious," "bossy," and "hustly" Hairy Maclary is back; this time the dog is out for a chase. His black nose, mischievous eyes, and unkempt dark fur can be spied peeking around a bush, poking through tall grass, or glancing around corners as he sneaks up on a series of unsuspecting felines and sends them scampering to safety. Hairy finally meets his match, however, in defiant Scarface Claw, who chases the bullying pooch all the way home. Youngsters will quickly anticipate the dog's appearances and begin chiming in "but along came Hairy Maclary" with enthusiastic storytellers who can turn this rhythmically phrased and sprightly illustrated cat-and-dog tale into a read-aloud charmer.

WAKE UP, BEAR (1986)

Marcus Crouch

SOURCE: A review of *Wake Up, Bear,* in *The Junior Bookshelf,* Vol. 51, No. 2, April, 1987, p. 74.

By comparison [to Alan Baker's *Benjamin's Portrait*] *Wake Up, Bear* is laboured both in text and in its jokes, but then Lynley Dodd has been unlucky in coming up alongside as mature and skilled a craftsman as Alan Baker. Judged by its own standards *Wake Up, Bear* is an agreeable little book. It deals with the efforts of the wild people to get Bear out of bed after the long winter sleep. Large and small, they all try to wake him, in vain. Only the bee, coming last, rouses the sluggard not with his noise but with a promise of honey to come. Readers-aloud may find that the text, very well printed and laid out, is just a little too long to sustain interest. The pictures are adequate but not perhaps over-brimming with fun.

HAIRY MACLARY'S CATERWAUL CAPER (1987; U.S. edition, 1988)

M. Hobbs

SOURCE: A review of *Hairy Maclary's Caterwaul Caper,* in *The Junior Bookshelf,* Vol. 52, No. 1, February, 1988, pp. 19-20.

New Zealander Lynley Dodd's *Caterwaul Caper* is the fourth adventure of Hairy Maclary, the Cairn dog from Donaldson's Dairy, in catchy Dr. Seuss-like verse. Scarface Claw the cat gets stuck in a tree and his cries bring all the local dogs, of many nationalities and voices, to its foot, till Miss Plum rescues him with a ladder. It is all an excuse for pleasant cartoon-like dog pictures in naturally coloured garden settings, with strawberry bed and passionfruit tree, and much accompanying detail.

Margery Fisher

SOURCE: A review of *Hairy Maclary's Caterwaul Caper,* in *Growing Point,* Vol. 26, No. 6, March, 1988, p. 4952.

Onomatopoeic cat and dog noises break up the rousing, smartly turned verse-story of the day when Scarface Claw was stuck in a tree and the dogs from Donaldson's Dairy went to investigate. Caricature pictures fix the personality of dalmatian Bottomley Potts, mongrel Bitzer Malony and the rest of Hairy's friends, in a cheerful romp purveyed in dashing words and dramatic scenes.

Philis Wilson

SOURCE: A review of *Hairy Maclary's Caterwaul Caper,* in *Booklist,* Vol. 85, No. 7, December 1, 1988, p. 646.

The caper in question involves Scarface Claw, a midnight-colored feline with piercing golden eyes, who gets precariously stuck in a tree. The vociferous cat's wails attract the dog Hairy Maclary's attention. As "wrow-ww-w-w-w-w-w-w" is not easily ignored, other members of the canine crew soon gather, sniffing and bustling around the tree. A chorus of yips, ruffs, woofs, and yaps results in such a din that Miss Plum comes and rescues old Scarface. Dodd's full-page line-and-wash illustrations capture the particular personality of each dog and the humor of Scarface's wounded dignity. Written in rhyme, this will work well in story hour—especially with those who have enjoyed the other Hairy Maclary adventures.

**HAIRY MACLARY'S RUMPUS AT THE VET
(1989; U.S. edition, 1990)**

Marcus Crouch

SOURCE: A review of *Hairy Maclary's Rumpus at the Vet,* in *The Junior Bookshelf,* Vol. 54, No. 1, February, 1990, p. 13.

We have met Hairy Maclary before. This time the raggity-taggity little dog is at the vet's. It is not clear what he is suffering from when he arrives, but very soon he has more to worry about. The inquisitive beak of a cockatoo leads to cumulative disasters, recorded in Lynley Dodd's cheerful drawings and, a little less successfully, in the rhyming text. Only a trifle, this one, but a stylish little book.

Publishers Weekly

SOURCE: A review of *Hairy Maclary's Rumpus at the Vet,* in *Publishers Weekly,* Vol. 237, No. 20, May 18, 1990, p. 84.

Here's a rumpus, indeed: this beleaguered vet's office may never fully recover from the chaos that ensues when Cassie the cockatoo plucks a hair from the hide of Hairy Maclary ("from Donaldson's Dairy"). This mischievous deed sets in motion a rambunctious, rhyming riot, as various ailing pets all decide to forgo their restraints and cavort in grand fashion. And just as some semblance of order is about to be restored, the culprit seems ready to strike again. This extended poem forms the basis for that relatively rare commodity, a book that tickles the funnybones of parents and children alike. With its amusing alliteration, fanciful names (Noodle the poodle; Barnacle Beasley, the sore and sorely vexed beagle; "The Poppadum kittens from Parkinson Place") and rapid-fire delivery, Dodd's nonsense verse follows quite nicely in the grand tradition of Messrs, Nash and Lear. The pictures are amiably animated and suitably silly, but watch those wonderful waggish words.

Denise Wilms

SOURCE: A review of *Hairy Maclary's Rumpus at the Vet,* in *Booklist,* Vol. 86, No. 20, June 15, 1990, p. 1977.

Hairy Maclary, the mischief-prone dog seen most recently in ***Hairy Maclary Scattercat*** is back again, this time creating havoc at the vet's office. The mayhem starts when a cockatoo leans through the bars of its cage and gives Harry a tweak on the tail. Hairy jumps, and a chain reaction ensues, with escaping parakeets, leaping cats, and boisterous dogs skittering, scampering, and tumbling about. The story is told in rhyme, and the watercolor illustrations are as action filled as Hairy fans would expect.

Cynthia Bishop

SOURCE: A review of *Hairy Maclary's Rumpus at the Vet,* in *School Library Journal,* Vol. 36, No. 12, December, 1990, p. 76.

Hairy Maclary, a small black dog, has his tail nipped by a caged cockatoo and, leaping up, precipitates a light-hearted pet riot in the veterinarian's waiting room. Lively watercolor and ink illustrations are carefully coordinated with a brief, rhymed text. Realistic yet simplified paintings completely fill each left-hand page and face a right-hand page devoted exclusively to text. The animated feeling of these paintings is derived more from expressive animal faces than from a sense of motion. The animals are well observed and neatly individualized. The use of language is delightful, being musical, playful, and colorful. The print is large and appropriate for beginning readers, but the vocabulary may prove intimidating to those same readers. This reads aloud well; however, previous books about Hairy Maclary are stronger as this story is a bit muddled. The vet enters to restore peace to her waiting room, but it is never clear that she succeeds before the punchline, which indicates that the rumpus is about to start anew.

Judith Sharmon

SOURCE: A review of *Hairy Maclary's Rumpus at the Vet*, in *Books for Keeps,* No. 73, March, 1992, p. 6.

As an adult I cringe at the thought of yet more of the chaos and mess that somehow dogs (!) Hairy Maclary, but the child in me falls upon it with just as much excitement as everyone in the class. Here Lynley Dodd's irresistible scruffy dog has to visit the vet and as usual he never intends to create difficulties and is always the innocent victim of circumstance, but . . .

SLINKI MALINKI (1990)

M. Hobbs

SOURCE: A review of *Slinky Malinki,* in *The Junior Bookshelf,* Vol. 54, No. 6, December, 1990, p. 268.

Lynley Dodd has forsaken Hairy Maclary for an equally attractive Practical Cat, Slinky Malinky, whose essential feline nature she catches beautifully in her neat jingles. By night he is a thief, but is cured by a noisy discovery resulting from his greed, so that thereafter, "when moon shadows danced over garden and wall", he adjusted his whiskers and stayed at home. The catalogue of his thefts is delightfully inconsequential and funny, and there is a lovely shot of the family (seen from the hip downwards in night attire) discovering him surrounded by the collapsed fruits of his thefts.

Leone McDermott

SOURCE: A review of *Slinky Malinki,* in *Booklist,* Vol. 87, No. 15, April 1, 1991, p. 1578.

This catchy story in rhyme features a mischievous feline who might have escaped from the pages of *Old Possum's Book of Practical Cats.* "Slinky Malinki / was blacker than black / a stalking and lurking / adventurous cat." Though by day he innocently chases leaves and rolls in the sun, at night Slinky Malinki indulges a larcenous streak. "All over town, / from basket and bowl, / he pilfered and pillaged, / he snitched and he stole. / Slippers and sausages, / biscuits, balloons, / brushes and bandages, / pencils and spoons." The furry kleptomaniac hauls home an increasingly unlikely collection of stolen objects, until the whole heap collapses on his head, awakening his family and leaving him in disgrace. He emerges a changed cat. The strong rhyme and rhythm of the verse are inviting, and the pen-and-watercolor illustrations are humorous in depicting Slinky's improbable thefts. New readers will find the vocabulary varied and occasionally challenging but are sure to enjoy the fun.

Christine A. Moesch

SOURCE: A review of *Slinky Malinki,* in *School Library Journal,* Vol. 37, No. 8, August, 1991, p. 144.

Told in rhyme, this is the story of a slinky black cat who prowls at night and becomes a thief. After his loot is discovered, he decides to stay home nights. While there's nothing wrong with this book, there's nothing to recommend it, either. The text is somewhat workmanlike, with very precise rhythm but not much charm. The full-color illustrations lack the personality needed to draw children into the story or to make Slinky an interesting character. Quite simply, the cat steals stuff, then stops. It's hard to imagine many preschoolers who would sit through the whole book. There's just nothing to it.

Gill Roberts

SOURCE: A review of *Slinky Malinki,* in *Books for Keeps,* No. 77, November, 1992, p. 17.

'Cheeky and cheerful, friendly and fun' by day, perfectly named Slinky Malinki turns 'wicked and fiendish and sly' by night. Lynley Dodd creates a rare opportunity to witness cat movements on a moonlit night and Slinky Malinki is a particularly 'rapscallion' cat with superlative characteristics. The full power and aura of feline independence, real humour and night-time magic are evoked by vivid illustrations, simple rhyme and splendid language. This really captivated children of 6 and 7.

J. Ousbey

SOURCE: A review of *Slinky Malinki,* in *Books for Your Children,* Vol. 28, No. 1, Spring, 1993, p. 11.

Slinky Malinky is a 'Jekyll and Hyde' kind of cat—friendly and cheerful by day but a rapscallion at night-time when he pilfers, pillages, and steals anything that catches his eye. How he is caught red handed makes for a most satisfying conclusion.

The jaunty rhythms and neat rhymes, set off beautifully by the lively pictures, make this book a real winner—to be read to 3-5 year olds and by 5 to 7 year olds.

FIND ME A TIGER (1991; U.S. edition, 1992)

Margaret Kelly

SOURCE: A review of *Find Me a Tiger,* in *Magpies,* Vol. 6, No. 5, November, 1991, p. 26.

A departure from Dodd's usual story format, this clever animal camouflage book is written in verse. On each page, an animal camouflaged in both line and colour, waits to be found. The accompanying four line rhyme provides the clue, and always the line: " . . . find me a . . . ".

Having located the animals however, there is much more to see in the wonderfully natural illustrations, evidence of Dodd's great knowledge of and ease with animals.

The book contains a wide variety of animals and a range of habitats—from a lion on an African plain to a bear in the freezing north. The diversity of animals and order of appearance sustains anticipation without allowing excessive predictability. In true Dodd style there is a cat, a sleek black cat, to be found. In so doing, the reader disturbs the cat but completes the book—a neat ending.

The language is descriptive and succinct with some alliteration and a rollicking rhythm: "In a shingle nest by a stony track, find me a chick with a speckled back."

This small form picture book is certainly one to read to the under fives, whilst the challenge of reading the text for themselves would undoubtedly appeal to the five to seven year old readers.

HAIRY MACLARY'S SHOWBUSINESS (1991)

E. Colwell

SOURCE: A review of *Hairy Maclary's Showbusiness,* in *The Junior Bookshelf,* Vol. 56, No. 1, February, 1992, p. 9.

An amusing picture book with gay and spirited illustrations. The story is told in simple rhyming verse and is about a Cat Show: 'There were fat cats / and thin cats / tabbies and greys, / kickup-a-din cats / with boisterous ways. / Cooped up in cages / they practised their wails / while their owners fussed over their teeth and their tails. /'

The atmosphere of the Cat Show is completely destroyed when the disreputable Hairy Maclary slips his lead and breaks into the cats' select quarters, 'prancing and flustering, jumping over chairs, skittering through legs, banging together belongings and bags.' His unkempt and bristling hair is an offence to the carefully combed and scented beauties.

A cat wins a prize for her beauty, another has produced a record number of kittens, but no other cat can beat Hairy Maclary for scruffiness!

A racy story, effectively illustrated, which will please children because of the chaos caused by the undisciplined hero.

The book originated in New Zealand.

Michael Glover

SOURCE: A review of *Hairy Maclary's Showbusiness,* in *School Librarian,* Vol. 40, No. 1, February, 1992, p. 15.

We have met that popular busybody Hairy Maclary many times before; but this time, in **Hairy Maclary's Showbusiness,** we find him kicking up a rumpus at the local cat show: escaping the clutches of human beings; overturning chairs; sliding under tables and, eventually, carrying off first prize for the Scruffiest Cat of the Show. A pleasurable romp for children of six and above—with some brisk, deft versifying to complement the fast-moving artwork.

Judith Sharman

SOURCE: A review of *Hairy Maclary's Showbusiness,* in *Books for Keeps,* No. 83, November, 1993, p. 10.

This latest adventure of Hairy Maclary the dog from Donaldson's Dairy has made him winner of the New Zealand Picture Story Book of the Year Award. It has been read and reread so many times yet is still greeted with gales of laughter at the absurdity of how Hairy Maclary, in his inimitable way, manages to win one of the first prizes in the Cat Show! Lynley Dodd manages to give us the good old rollicking rhythms of Music Hall to match her appealingly zany illustrations. A must for all Hairy fans and a good intro to this style of poetry for any who haven't yet met him.

THE MINISTER'S CAT ABC (1992; U.S. edition, 1994)

Marcus Crouch

SOURCE: A review of *The Minister's Cat ABC,* in *The Junior Bookshelf,* Vol. 56, No. 6, December, 1992, p. 233.

Lynley Dodd has based this ABC on a traditional rhyme to which some attractive variations have been added. This is an adjectival ABC, from which children will derive some choice additions to their vocabulary: huffy, impish, posing, vexed, zooming, all these and the rest accompanied by colourful pictures of action and occasionally repose. Lynley Dodd knows cats and knows how to put them into attractive and appropriate settings, knows too how to impart to each a clearly individual character.

Trevor Dickinson

SOURCE: A review of *The Minister's Cat ABC,* in *School Librarian,* Vol. 41, No. 1, February, 1993, pp. 14-15.

There's plenty to look at and to talk about in this fresh-faced alphabet book. The large, friendly print, with highlighted key letters in different colours, focuses on adjectives rather than on the more usual nouns. The vocabulary properly makes demands which are, in the main, easily overcome through the illustrations. Thus the characteristics of *airborne, impish, keen-eyed, owlish, posing, quarrelsome* and *worrisome* cats are clearly visible. Young children will have further fun with teachers, parents and each other suggesting alternatives.

Margot Hittel

SOURCE: A review of *The Minister's Cat ABC,* in *Magpies,* Vol. 8, No. 2, May, 1993, p. 26.

Have we had enough books about Scarface Claw and all the other cats which have become familiar to us in Lynley Dodd's other work? If the best-selling lists published in daily papers are anything to go on, the answer must be no.

Nevertheless, it is difficult to imagine there can be too many more, as this one definitely seems to have lost the sparkle of Dodd's earlier books. Here is the Minister's cat airborne and busy, the teacher's cat empty and greedy, the postman's cat upside down and vexed, and so on through the alphabet.

The illustrations are full of movement and many of the cats have wonderful expressions. There is, however, a certain monotony in the whole thing, because of the subject matter of the book—every page is dominated by the cat being discussed in that particular letter of the alphabet.

There is, too, another problem with this as an ABC book. It is difficult to convey through illustration for young children, abstract concepts such as "vexed", or ones which tend to be a subjective interpretation of another's behaviour such as "impish". I have found that with a number of

the pages in this book, children simply do not understand the idea which is being portrayed.

The text, which is based on the traditional game The Minister's Cat, has a pleasing rhythm and some pleasant touches of humour.

Gill Roberts

SOURCE: A review of *The Minister's Cat ABC*, in *Books for Keeps*, No. 87, July, 1994, p. 6.

Another cat classic from Lynley Dodd. Children from across the Infant age-range had huge fun being re-introduced to her well-loved, distinctively different cats and their owners. Vivid illustrations full of typical feline majesty and movement match exactly the aptly selected adjectives—which read alphabetically as if, almost, by accident.

Total attention is demanded on every page as the reader/listener meets the Airborne, Busy, Crazy, Dizzy Minister's cat, the Quarrelsome, Rough Farmer's cat and is driven on to a 'Zooming' finale with the Postman's cat. An extremely rich book at many levels.

SCHNITZEL VON KRUMM'S BASKETWORK (1994)

Marcus Crouch

SOURCE: A review of *Schnitzel von Krumm's Basketwork,* in *The Junior Bookshelf,* Vol. 58, No. 5, October, 1994, pp. 163-64.

Schnitzel von Krumm, it hardly needs to say, is a dachshund. Long and hard usage has reduced his basket to a smelly ruin, but when the family banish it and provide stylish new one Schnitzel just can't get it to seem right. So he goes in search of a bed with the right feel and smell, without success. After watching his suffering the family reinstate the old battered basket. The story is told in tolerable rhyme, and the pictures are up to Lynley Dodd's high standard, but somehow the book lacks dynamism.

Carol Woolley

SOURCE: A review of *Schnitzel von Krumm's Basketwork,* in *School Librarian,* Vol. 42, No. 4, November, 1994, p. 145.

A long-time fan of Hairy Maclary, I was delighted to find another of the menagerie in a book of his own. Schnitzel von Krumm goes in search of somewhere 'cosy and comforting' when his tatty old basket is replaced by his owners—but can anywhere live up to his old home? The rhyming text and sing-song rhythm carry the story along swiftly. Readers will enjoy the repetition and there is plenty to talk about in the colourful illustrations. A charming tale for any dog lover and sure to be a hit in story sessions.

SNIFF-SNUFF-SNAP! (1995)

Bette Hansen

SOURCE: A review of *Sniff-Snuff-Snap!,* in *Magpies,* Vol. 10, No. 4, September, 1995, p. 25.

One rather territorially minded African warthog chases away a variety of animals from his watering hole—first two yellow weaver birds, then three shy dikdiks and four old baboons, and so on, up to eight fat elephants. However his guarding skills are less than effective and each time the animals are able to circle around and return to drink their fill until in the final scene when the warthog came back *tired and hot for a long cool drink at his favourite spot . . . BUT what did he see? THICK BROWN MUD.*

Perceptive readers will, on the last page, see the first few drops of rain falling and know that a disaster has been postponed.

Rhythmical verse interspersed with animal noises make for an enjoyable and light-hearted read. The repetitive phrases will have young children joining in with the reader. Sure to be a success.

Frances Ball

SOURCE: A review of *Sniff-Snuff-Snap!,* in *School Librarian,* Vol. 44, No. 1, February, 1996, p. 14.

This latest addition to Lynley Dodd's picture books continues the wildlife theme, this time with a warthog as the central character. He is a bossy creature, and he wants to control the waterhole, but increasing numbers of animals have to be chased away. The two weaver birds are followed by three dik-diks, four baboons, five leopards, and more. The simple rhyming text takes the numbers up to eight, and the waterhole down to a muddy patch. The warthog is a likeable creation with an expressive face and a fallible nature. His dilemma and reactions should appeal to older pre-school children and infants.

SCHNITZEL VON KRUMM FORGET-ME-NOT (1996; U.S. edition, 1998)

Frances Ball

SOURCE: A review of *Schnitzel von Krumm Forget-Me-Not,* in *The Junior Bookshelf,* Vol. 60, No. 5, October, 1996, pp. 182-83.

Schnitzel von Krumm first appeared in Lynley Dodd's 'Hairy Maclary' stories. In this latest story of his own, he makes his entrance in typical style:

> With pattering paws
> and a lolloping tum,
> down the front steps
> galloped Schnitzel von Krumm.

He is pleased to discover that the car and trailer are being loaded, and everyone is cheerful as they prepare for a holiday. But when they are finally ready, they accidentally drive off without Schnitzel. His wails of discontent are heard by a neighbour who sets off with him and finds the rest of the family at the side of the road where they are searching the car and trailer for their missing pet.

The lively verses speed the reader through the story, introducing some memorable rhymes. The illustrations show typical family scenes as the holiday approaches, with Schnitzel having a central role. The book closes with a classic dog picture, showing Schnitzel with his head out of the car window in the wind. Lynley Dodd's books are already popular with many infants and older pre-school children. Having his own books may help Schnitzel become as well-known as Hairy Maclary.

Heide Piehler

SOURCE: A review of *Schnitzel von Krumm Forget-Me-Not,* in *School Library Journal,* Vol. 44, No. 6, June, 1998, p. 103.

Schnitzel von Krumm's family is packing for a camping trip and the little dachshund is definitely in the way. Once on the road, the parents realize they've forgotten one very important thing—Schnitzel von Krumm. A neighbor reunites the neglected pooch with his owners. What could have been a delightful story falls flat. The rhymed verse is lively and rhythmic, but the phrasing is often forced and awkward. The uninspired watercolor illustrations resemble the artwork found in old textbooks. A disappointing effort.

HAIRY MACLARY, SIT (1998)

Trevor Dickinson

SOURCE: A review of *Hairy Maclary, Sit,* in *School Librarian,* Vol. 46, No. 1, Spring, 1998, p. 18.

Lynley Dodd brings Hairy Maclary yet again joyously to life—here setting a marvellously bad example to his canine peers at the Kennel Club's Obedience Class. Each left-hand page, with its comically recalcitrant dogs, has a facing page of vigorously thumping verse—some well-planned repetitions allowing and, indeed, encouraging keen participation by young readers and listeners. It is the kind of excellent book that will enable reading and, more important, encourage and develop lasting readership.

Susan Lissim

SOURCE: A review of *Hairy Maclary, Sit,* in *School Library Journal,* Vol. 44, No. 8, August, 1998, p. 133.

In this latest addition to the series, Hairy scampers away to avoid participating in an obedience class. He is soon followed by the other dogs in the class, as each in turn escapes. The animals are shown running, jumping, and generally having a good time until they all go "splat" in the pond. The full-color illustrations are attractive and simple enough for children to identify the various breeds. However, while the repetitive "galloping here, galloping there, rollicking, frolicking, EVERYWHERE" will please young listeners, the minimal plot offers little else. *Hairy Maclary* lovers will want this one; but if you don't have a current fan club for this pooch, don't start one with this title.

HAIRY MACLARY AND ZACHARY QUACK (1999)

John McKenzie

SOURCE: A review of *Hairy Maclary and Zachary Quack,* in *Reading Time,* Vol. 43, No. 4, November, 1999, p. 41.

No one doubts that Lynley Dodd has a winning 'formula' for creating outstanding picture books where quirky tales, rhythmic language and vibrant pictures combine to entrance the younger readers (as well as the nostalgic adult who revels in the pastoral antics of that inimitable Hairy Maclary). Lynley has done it again!

Zachary Quack is a young duckling that has yet to learn that life is nasty, brutish and short for wayward ducklings. Without an ounce of fear, he espies Hairy Maclary who is dozily dreaming, surrounded by dozens of bees, lazily buzzing. When 'pittery, pattery, skittery scattery, ZIP round the corner came Zachary Quack who wants to frolic and footle and play'. But . . . Well, you will just have to get the book and read what happens next! Like a consummate artist with a wonderful sense of audience, Dodd invites a very slow turning the page (but . . .). This wonderful storyteller knows how to slow down the narrative impulse (what happens next?) to milk the anticipated moment.

An absolute must for the junior school. Any child who loves their pet, who has any sense of a story surrounding their pet (especially a dog and a duckling) will howl with laughter.

Additional coverage of Dodd's life and career is contained in the following sources published by The Gale Group: *Contemporary Authors,* Vol. 107; *Contemporary Authors New Revision Series,* Vols. 25, 51; and *Something about the Author,* Vols. 35, 86.

Mary (Elizabeth) Mapes Dodge

1831(?)-1905

American author of fiction and poetry; editor.

Major works include *The Irvington Stories* (1864); *Hans Brinker; or, The Silver Skates: A Story of Life in Holland* (1865); *Rhymes and Jingles* (1874); *Donald and Dorothy* (1883); *When Life Is Young: A Collection of Verse for Boys and Girls* (1894).

Major works about: *Mary Mapes Dodge of St. Nicholas* (Alice B. Howard, 1943); *Lady of the Silver Skates: The Life and Correspondence of Mary Mapes Dodge* (Catherine Morris Wright, 1979); *Mary Mapes Dodge* (Susan R. Gannon and Ruth Anne Thompson, 1992).

INTRODUCTION

Dodge, known primarily as the author of the children's classic *Hans Brinker; or, The Silver Skates: A Story of Life in Holland* and editor of *St. Nicholas: Scribner's Illustrated Magazine for Boys and Girls*, was a major influence in the shaping of twentieth century children's literature. Although she first began writing and editing for an adult audience, her strong opinions about what children's literature should be made her feel duty bound to give form to her ideals. Children's literature at the time was fraught with didactic stories driven by morals, but *Hans Brinker*, like her succeeding work for children, and much to the satisfaction of its readers, included its moral lessons as part of the plot and character development of the story. Dodge expressed her ideas about writing for children's magazines in an essay published in *Scribner's Monthly*, "the child's magazine needs to be stronger, truer, bolder, more uncompromising than [magazines for adults]. Its cheer must be the cheer of the bird-song, not of condescending editorial babble. If it *mean* freshness and heartiness, and life and joy, and its words are simply, directly, and musically put together, it will trill its own way . . . we must be as little children if we would enter this kingdom." She thought that children's stories should be fun, without sermonizing, and her writing reflected this belief. Dodge was much loved in her own time, and was praised by critics and readers who appreciated her intent and found her stories for children refreshing. Described as natural and straightforward, Dodge's writing was said to exhibit earnestness, wit, vivacity, genial warmth, and a fresh young spirit.

Dodge created *St. Nicholas* magazine in 1873, and it is still considered the best magazine ever published for children. Not only was it immensely popular, it also set the standard of children's literature and illustration for the century to come. Some of its popularity was due to Dodge's early efforts to involve the readers in the magazine. She instituted a Letter Box column to solicit readers' opinions, actively recruited reader contribution, and included games, jingles, and songs. Additionally, she solicited contributions from many prominent artists, novelists, historians, and poets who were among her circle of intimates and believed as she did about writing and drawing for children. Among these were the writers Mark Twain ("Tom Sawyer Abroad"), Louisa May Alcott (*Eight Cousins*), Theodore Roosevelt ("Hero Tales from American History"), and Rudyard Kipling (*Jungle Book* stories), the poets Henry Wadsworth Longfellow, John Greenleaf Whittier, and Alfred Tennyson, and the illustrators Arthur Rackham, N. C. Wyeth, Palmer Cox, and Howard Pyle. After Dodge's death in 1905 William Fayal Clarke wrote in *St. Nicholas,* "It is given to few to exercise so far-reaching an influence upon young minds, and thus upon the future of the nation. [Dodge] left the world not only happier, but better than she found it."

Biographical Information

Dodge was born into a prominent New York family who often hosted the literary and scientific intelligencia of the day, such as Horace Greely and William Cullen Bryant. Schooled at home, she had a liberal education well vested in the arts. At the age of 20 she married a lawyer, William Dodge, who had become her father's business partner, and moved with him to the home of her in-laws where she gave birth to her sons, James in 1852 and Harrington in 1855. By her account, her relationship with her husband was warm and easy going, and her married life a happy one. However, her husband's continued entanglement in her father's complicated business dealings led them into severe financial instability and imminent ruin. To this stressful situation was added the emotional strain of their elder son's serious illness. Both of these factors may have contributed to her husband's suspected suicide in 1858. Dodge remained poised and treated all speculation with a dignified silence, but the loss was agonizing for her and caused her great suffering. Now a widow with two young sons and a shaky financial position, she returned to her parent's home where she made a space for herself and her children in which she could write and educate her sons.

Dodge's writing and editing career began when her father, with whom she was very close, offered her the editorship of a magazine he had purchased titled *The Working Farmer*, used to popularize his own ideas about innovations in farming. After the death of Dodge's husband, her father purchased the *United States Journal*, a publication of cultural enrichment, and made her editor at the age of 28. Besides editing the magazine, Dodge wrote stories, poems, and essays for other leading magazines, and her work was much in demand. Her first book, *The Irvington Stories*, grew from these submissions, and while not a best seller, it received enough critical praise to establish her as a writer of merit. Her next work, *Hans Brinker; or, The Silver Skates: A Story of Life in Holland*, was inspired by Motley's *The Rise of the Dutch Republic* and *The History of the United Netherlands*, and well as by her Dutch neighbors. An instant success, it made publishing history, receiving excellent reviews and becoming an immediate bestseller. After her father died, she took up residence in New York to be near the publishing houses that offered her a career, continued to write and publish, and in 1870 was hired as editor of the home-making department of *Hearth and Home* magazine, a position she held for three years. A letter she wrote to her friend Roswell Smith expressing her strong views about appropriate literature for children was published in *Scribner's Magazine*, inspiring Charles Scribner to offer her the opportunity to create and edit a new magazine for children which she named *St. Nicholas* after the patron saint of children. The definitive magazine for children and enormously popular, its first issue was published in 1873. Dodge remained the editor and a contributor until her death from cancer in 1905.

Major Works

Dodge's first book, *The Irvington Stories*, was based in part on stories she had told to her own children. Although it was never considered a best seller, it went through several editions and established Dodge as a writer with appeal. Lu Runkle, a good friend of Dodge's, claimed, "The stories had just enough of improbability to suit the minds of children, for whom the age of fancy and fable renews itself in every generation." The stories have a strong moral undertone, teaching without stating what is being taught. The book includes two poems, a Hans Anderson style fable, biographical stories, a tall tale, a patriotic song, and several short stories.

Hans Brinker; or, The Silver Skates: A Story of Life in Holland is Dodge's most famous book. It was an immediate best seller, rivaling Charles Dickens' *Our Mutual Friend*, and from 1865 to 1881 received more reviews than any other children's book. She began it as a serial, inspired by her neighbors who had lived in Holland, but turned it into a long book. She intended it to give American children a more realistic picture of Holland than was currently available, and embodied in it what she considered to be an ideal of behavior. It was greeted enthusiastically by both the critics and the public, partly because of the entertaining way it supplied information about the history, customs, and culture of Holland, and partly because it told an interesting story about real people with its morals implied rather than preached. The story is about two poor children, a brother and sister named Hans and Gretel, their experiences as they prepare and participate in a skating race, and the surgery and recovery of their injured father. Caught in conflicts between their own needs and their responsibilities to their family and their society, they grow and mature by making responsible decisions exhibiting their courage, self-reliance, honesty, industry, and generosity toward others. M. E. Dodge wrote, "[Dodge] has produced nothing better than this charming

tale, alive with incident and action, adorned rather than freighted with useful facts, and moral without moralization." *Hans Brinker* has become a children's classic, and has not been out of print since its publication over 100 years ago.

Rhymes and Jingles is a collection of verse for children that was taken from Dodge's earlier writings that appeared in such publications as *Working Farmer*, *Hearth and Home*, and *St. Nicholas*. The book was well received by critics and was republished in various editions for nearly 60 years. A reviewer for *The Nation* noted, "It is full of comical nonsense and the most felicitous absurdities of language."

Donald and Dorothy, which was serialized in *St. Nicholas*, has a complicated and romantic plot full of mystery and suspense and fraught with eccentric characters and amusing episodes. Donald and Dorothy are two children, raised as brother and sister. However, doubt is cast on who Dorothy really is—Dorothy or her cousin, Delia—when Delia's evil guardian appears. Donald frequently saves his sister/cousin from such misadventures as a runaway horse and mad dog, and finally goes to Europe to try to find the truth about her. In the end she is proved to be Dorothy, but only after much anxiety and hard work on the part of the protagonists. Although Dodge appeared to be somewhat critical of the way in which girls were raised, *Donald and Dorothy* generally represented the traditional middle class domestic values of its time, and presented model children who were brave, reverent, and dutiful. Susan R. Gannon and Ruth Anne Thompson wrote, "Although Dodge's novels appear to preach self-sacrifice, discipline, and respect for one's elders, they are not uncritical of the status quo, and their sympathy for young peoples' need to assume responsibility for their own lives endeared them to their young readers."

When Life Is Young: A Collection of Verse for Boys and Girls is a collection of new and reprinted poetry that contains poems about nature, the fairy world, and growing up. It is meant for an older audience than the one intended for *Rhymes and Jingles*. A reviewer for *The Nation* commented "[O]pen *When Life Is Young* wherever you will, the reader's life becomes young also, and the most hardened critic looks round for some child to whom to impart the cheery lay."

Awards

Dodge won the Montyon Prize of the French Academy in 1869 for *Hans Brinker; or, The Silver Skates: A Story of Life in Holland*.

AUTHOR'S COMMENTARY

Mary Mapes Dodge

SOURCE: "Children's Magazines," in *Scribner's Monthly*, Vol. VI, No. 3, July, 1873, pp. 352-54.

Sometimes I feel like rushing through the world with two placards—one held aloft in my right hand, BEWARE OF CHILDREN'S MAGAZINES! the other flourished in my left, CHILD'S MAGAZINE WANTED! A good magazine for little ones was never so much needed, and such harm is done by nearly all that are published. In England, especially, the so-called juvenile periodicals are precisely what they ought not to be. In Germany, though better, they too often distract sensitive little souls with grotesquerie. Our magazines timidly approach the proper standard in some respects, but fall far short in others. We edit for the approval of fathers and mothers, and endeavor to make the child's monthly a milk-and-water variety of the adult's periodical. But, in fact, the child's magazine needs to be stronger, truer, bolder, more uncompromising than the other. Its cheer must be the cheer of the bird-song, not of condescending editorial babble. If it *mean* freshness and heartiness, and life and joy, and its words are simply, directly, and musically put together, it will trill its own way. We must not help it overmuch. In all except skillful handling of methods, we must be as little children if we would enter this kingdom.

If now and then the situation have fun in it, if something tumble unexpectedly, if the child-mind is surprised into an electric recognition of comical incongruity, so that there is a reciprocal "ha, ha!" between the printed page and the little reader, well and good. But, for humanity's sake, let there be no editorial grimacing, no tedious vaulting back and forth over the grim railing that incloses halt and lame old jokes long ago turned in there to die.

Let there be no sermonizing either, no wearisome spinning out of facts, no rattling of the dry bones of history. A child's magazine is its pleasure ground. Grown people go to their periodicals for relaxation, it is true; but they also go for information, for suggestion, and for to-day's fashion in literature. Besides, they begin, now-a-days, to feel that they are behind the age if they fail to know what the April *Jig jig* says about so and so, or if they have not read B——'s much-talked-of poem in the last *Argosy*. Moreover, it is "the thing" to have the *Jig-jig* and *Argosy* on one's drawing-room table. One must read the leading periodicals or one is nobody. But with children the case is different. They take up their monthly or weekly because they wish to, and if they don't like it they throw it down again. Most children of the present civilization attend school. Their little heads are strained and taxed with the day's lessons. They do not want to be bothered nor amused nor taught nor petted. They just want to have their own way over their own magazine. They want to enter the one place where they may come and go as they please, where they are not obliged to mind, or say "yes ma'am" and "yes sir,"—where, in short, they can live a brand-new, free life of their own for a little while, accepting acquaintances as they choose and turning their backs without ceremony upon what does not concern them. Of course they expect to pick up odd bits and treasures, and to now and then "drop in" familiarly at an air castle, or step over to fairy-land. They feel their way, too, very much as we old folk do, toward sweet recognitions of familiar daydreams, secret

goodnesses, and all the glorified classics of the soul. We who have strayed farther from these, thrill even to meet a hint of them in poems and essays. But what delights *us* in Milton, Keats and Tennyson, children often find for themselves in stars, daisies, and such joys and troubles as little ones know. That this comparison holds, is the best we can say of our writers. If they make us reach forth our hands to clutch the star or the good-deed candle-blaze, what more can be done?

Literary skill in its highest is but the subtle thinning of the veil that life and time have thickened. Mrs. Browning paid her utmost tribute to Chaucer when she spoke of

> "——his infantine
> Familiar clasp of things divine."

The *Jig-jig* and *Argosy* may deal with Darwinianism broadly and fairly as they. The upshot of it all will be something like

> "Hickory, dickery dock!
>   The mouse ran up the clock.
>   The clock struck one
>   And down she ran—
> Hickory, dickery dock!"

And whatever Parton or Arthur Helps may say in that stirring article, "Our Country today," its substance is anticipated in

> "Little boy blue!
>   Come, blow your horn!
> The cow's in the meadow
>   Eating the corn."

So we come to the conviction that the perfect magazine for children lies folded at the heart of the ideal best magazine for grown-ups. Yet the coming periodical which is to make the heart of baby-America glad must not be a chip of the old Maga block, but an outgrowth from the old-young heart of Maga itself. Therefore, look to it that it be strong, warm, beautiful, and true. Let the little magazine-readers find what they look for and be able to pick up what they find. Boulders will not go into tiny baskets. If it so happen that the little folks know some one jolly, sympathetic, hand-to-hand personage who is sure to turn up here and there in every number of the magazine or paper, very good: that is, if they happen to like him. If not, beware! It will soon join the ghosts of dead periodicals; or, if it do not, it will live on only in that slow, dragging existence which is worse than death.

A child's periodical must be pictorially illustrated, of course, and the pictures must have the greatest variety consistent with simplicity, beauty and unity. They should be heartily conceived and well executed; and they must be suggestive, attractive and epigrammatic. If it be only the picture of a cat, it must be so like a cat that it will do its own purring, and not sit, a dead, stuffed thing, requiring the editor to purr for it. One of the sins of this age is editorial dribbling over inane pictures. The time to shake up a dull picture is when it is in the hands of the artist and engraver, and not when it lies, a fact accomplished, before the keen eyes of the little folk. Well enough for the editor to stand ready to answer questions that would naturally be put to the flesh-and-blood father, mother, or friend standing by. Well enough, too, for the picture to cause a whole tangle of interrogation-marks in the child's mind. It need not be elaborate, nor exhaust its theme, but what it attempts to do it must do well, and the editor must not over-help nor hinder. He must give just what the child demands, and to do this successfully is a matter of instinct, without which no man should presume to be a child's editor and go unhung.

Doubtless a great deal of instruction and good moral teaching may be inculcated in the pages of a magazine; but it must be by hints dropped incidentally here and there; by a few brisk, hearty statements of the difference between right and wrong; a sharp, clean thrust at falsehood, a sunny recognition of truth, a gracious application of politeness, an unwilling glimpse of the odious doings of the uncharitable and base. In a word, pleasant, breezy things may linger and turn themselves this way and that. Harsh, cruel facts—if they must come, and sometimes its is important that they should—must march forward boldly, say what they have to say, and go. The ideal child's magazine, we must remember, is a pleasure-ground where the butterflies flit gayly hither and thither; where wind and sunshine play freaks of light and shadow; but where toads hop quickly out of sight and snakes dare not show themselves at all. Wells and fountains there may be in the grounds, but water must be drawn from the one in right trim, bright little buckets; and there must be no artificial coloring of the other, nor great show-cards about it, saying, "Behold! a fountain." Let its own flow and sparkle proclaim it.

GENERAL COMMENTARY

Susan R. Gannon and Ruth Anne Thompson

SOURCE: "Play, Games, and Poetry," and "Conclusion," in *Mary Mapes Dodge,* Twayne Publishers, 1992, pp. 74-90, 152-57.

[Jerome Bruner once wrote that] in anyone's "intellectual life there are only a few topics, only a limited set of persistent queries and themes" that in retrospect give continuity to the whole. Widowed under tragic and disturbing circumstances, [Mary Mapes] Dodge was preoccupied by the problem of how best to deal with loss and disappointment. A lover of children, she spent much time and energy writing for them and trying to find literature and art that might teach, amuse, and inspire them. A devoted mother, she sought to share with other parents the methods she had used to make her own sons self-directed and eager learners. An essentially social person, she loved games and play, taking much delight in bringing people together to share their talents and enjoy themselves, whether at one of her evenings at home or through the pages of her periodicals.

In the pursuit of these interests, Dodge adopted a variety of roles that combined, in a curious way, a childlike innocence, spontaneity, and playfulness with [according to Braner,] "the cultivation of competence almost to the point of guile." And gradually she developed around each of these roles a personal mythology. Dodge chose to see herself as the plucky descendant of Dutch forbears whose cheerful optimism, simple religious faith, intelligence, and devotion to duty would carry her through the darkest hours. Her fiction often focused on the virtues symbolized for her in the brave people of Holland and made memorable by her own pictures of Hans Brinker and the little hero of Haarlem. Moreover, she focused some of her more popular poetry for adults specifically on the problem of making the best of difficult situations.

Not surprisingly for the daughter of an agricultural reformer, Dodge came to see herself as a kind of utopian landscape architect. Her favorite metaphor for the ideal children's magazine was the "pleasure ground." She saw the garden she would build for children as a place of their own, where they could have things their own way and learn through free and delighted play. And her poems for both children and adults speak often of what she called in one poem "The Grass World" of an agreeably humanized natural space.

Dodge also played the part of the perfect mother—nurturing and tender, but also an ideal playfellow to her children, a comrade who could enter into their games and studies with zest. Some of the occasional poems she wrote for family birthday celebrations express with more feeling than art the intense, almost-over-whelming affection she felt for her own sons. But her unusual ability to empathize with children more often helped her to avoid such sentimentality. Her "Jack-in-the Pulpit" persona, which gave a human touch to the editorial pieces in *St. Nicholas,* owes much to her image of herself as an idealized parent-teacher-friend.

As the presiding genius of a magazine named for the patron saint of children and embodying the festive spirit, generous sociality, and bounty associated with her favorite holiday, Dodge became a kind of cultural icon: "Mrs. Dodge," the "Conductor" of *St. Nicholas.* In this very public role she was the expert editor, friend of the famous, bringer of good things, mistress of the revels. From the very beginning of her writing career, Christmas was prominent as a theme of stories, articles, and verses; indeed, it became a sort of personal signature theme for Dodge.

In fact, festive occasions of all kinds abound in Dodge's fiction: birthday parties, club meetings, masquerades, holiday celebrations, a house picnic, dolls' tea parties, parlor theatricals. Over and over again, she describes moments when people come together to enjoy themselves, social situations where there are no spectators: all are participants in the happy activity of the occasion, freed from everyday rules and strictures, including etiquette. Individuals are drawn into familiar contact and allowed to express their hidden feelings and ideas, to cross social barriers and forge new relationships. On such occasions there is a delight in absurdity, nonsense, a humorous up-side-down perspective on things. Above all, there is a willingness to look at the world playfully, "as one great communal performance." Dodge's many pieces about parties and games celebrate the value of such experiences. And this openness and sociality are also characteristic of the magazine she created. Though **St. Nicholas** certainly had a didactic agenda, young readers did not find the magazine oppressive, perhaps because at its heart it offered a subversive, imaginative vision of a world open to change. As [Mikhail] Bakhtin says of the carnival spirit in literature, "This sense of the world, liberating one from fear, bringing the world maximally close to a person and bringing one person maximally close to another (everything is drawn into the zone of free familiar contact), with its joy at change and its joyful relativity, is opposed to that one-sided and gloomy official seriousness which is dogmatic and hostile to evolution and change, which seeks to absolutize a given condition of existence or a given social order." Dodge believed with [Friedrich] Froebel that "the organization of childish play should be the first culture of the mind. Growth and learning should slip in among the pleasures the child naturally seeks, and schooling should be an opportunity to extend a process of discovery begun freely through play. Like her friends Louisa May Alcott, Mark Twain, and Robert Louis Stevenson, Dodge often chose to describe children's play in her fiction. Her treatment of imaginative play suggests she saw it as sometimes opening up novel and risky—but ultimately rewarding—lines of action. **"The Hermit of the Hills,"** for example, begins by describing the transgressions committed by a group of playful children on a reclusive old man's privacy. The children are afraid of yet fascinated by him, and their ever-bolder invasion of his space, imaged as a military operation, initiates the story's action. In **"Po-no-kah,"** too, it is an initial period of play in the forest that tempts the Hedden children to explore even more dangerous territory. The central issue in **"Capt. George, the Drummer-Boy"** turns on the difference between pretending to be a soldier and really being one; the story begins with imitative soldier play that projects the young hero into a situation in which he is asked to enlist in an actual war.

Like Twain, Dodge could describe very convincingly the way children interact in play groups. In **"A Garret Adventure"** she has great fun with the story of a mischievous and bored group of children confined to an attic on a snowy day. Their fooling around is realistically described, and the mischief culminates in their decision to build a skating pond there, with predictably comic results as water drips through the ceilings below. Sometimes Dodge seems to suggest that the way a child plays says something about his or her moral nature. In **"The Golden Gate"** the play styles of two little girls define their moral characters. And in **"Cushamee"** it is a refusal of doll play with his sister that brings Tom Laffer a demonic dream-visitation from a doll bent on exacting retribution for his unkindness.

In her novels Dodge sometimes used games metaphorically. Skating in **Hans Brinker** symbolizes the way one lives one's life. In **Donald and Dorothy** the games played at a house party say something about each player's approach to life. Sometimes game-playing represents an individual's attempt to master adverse circumstances: motherless Dorothy Reed in **Donald and Dorothy** dresses up in the old clothes of a beloved aunt and cradles the aunt's doll. Sometimes play is used to find a solution to a vexing problem: Fandy Danby in the same book wants very much to control his friends and his siblings, and so he challenges them to play aggressive games he thinks he can win, and preaches to them make-believe sermons on their misdeeds. Sometimes play tests strength, or prepares a young person for the future: Donald Reed practices his marksmanship until he is expert enough to win a shooting match; the real prize, though, is not the trinket he wins but the skill with which he is able to defend his sister and his friends against a mad dog. . . .

Capitalizing on her knowledge of games, Dodge in 1869 produced an odd and original little book called **A Few Friends and How they Amused Themselves: A Tale in Nine Chapters Containing Descriptions of Twenty Pastimes and Games and a Fancy Dress Party.** At Robert Owen's suggestion, she submitted the manuscript to J. B. Lippincott and Company in Philadelphia, which wanted it for holiday issue. In this work Dodge advocated games to arouse pleasurable excitement and develop cohesiveness in small social groups. Her purpose, acknowledged in the preface, was to "present, in narrative form, a number of pastimes and intellectual games which persons of culture may enjoy, and which may also serve to bring young folk and their seniors together in a common pursuit of pleasure and profit." Although "society in its crude, dressy state is indeed apt to disdain all pastimes of fancy and wit," Dodge asserted that the one human distinguishing trait is the ability to play games. Adopting the persona of a hostess eager to prevent ennui from ruining her social evening, she offered a wry description of guests "enlivened, or rather deadened, by a fell purpose not to enjoy themselves."

In **A Few Friends** all of the wrong people have gathered in little groups "like so many icy stalagmites," and not until the hostess's friend Henry Stykes exerts considerable charm, humor, and ingenuity to organize games does the party succeed. Three guessing games are described in detail, and illustrated through a narrative of the guests at play. The characters of the players are revealed in the ways in which they compete, and the excitement generated saves both the evening and the hostess's sanity.

Delighted with the results of this kind of entertainment, the guests determine to meet every fortnight for the rest of the season to pursue their game plan. Dubbing themselves the Child-again Society, they meet in one another's homes, from mansion to rented room, and engage in varied entertainments: 14 guessing games in the style of Twenty Questions, 5 activities requiring elaborate props and settings (including a fancy dress party), and 5 writing games.

Some of these games involve simple devices, such as attempting to make participants laugh, guessing voices, and using absurd hand gestures; others call on a knowledge of history, art, or literature. "Who Was He?" poses questions about the lives and works of historical figures, such as Michelangelo, Tasso, the Roman matron Arria, John Wilkes, and Mirabeau. "Quotations and Authors" draws on sources ranging from Shakespeare down through many lesser lights, chiefly British, of the nineteenth century. "Charades" necessitates the development of an elaborate dramatic script several pages long, reproduced in toto, the acting of which is described with considerable verve.

The formal code of social behavior sanctioned by the genteel tradition enforced distinctions of class, gender, and age, limiting social interaction at parties; however the right sorts of games and play could free guests from the rigidities of convention. The games Dodge suggests allow participants to escape from prescribed behaviors and to act out in aggressive and competitive ways. They offer challenges to skill and intelligence, a chance to demonstrate physical or intellectual competence, and the satisfaction of winning. Dodge creates a host of characters who reveal hitherto-hidden aspects of their personalities as they enter into the games. For example, Mr. Simmons, a henpecked nouveau riche whose life has been given over to money-making, gets to comment on his wife's garrulity as she mimics a portrait and attempts to refrain from moving or laughing in the face of ingeniously contrived provocation from the other players. The suave Harry Stykes, who appoints himself master of ceremonies and cajoles compliance with the game rules, is driven to uncertainty and anxiety as he falls in love with Mary Glidden and pursues a decorous courtship throughout the biweekly meetings of the Child-again Society.

When the rules of the games have been spelled out, Dodge dramatizes the game-playing with its "lively spirit of good humored rivalry." She stresses the intergenerational suitability of the entertainment by pointing out the ways games can be adapted to children's level, "serving as an incentive to them as well as a delightful vehicle of instruction, and . . . a capital school of discipline for all." She is also concerned that subject matter for the games be not "inappropriately chosen" lest it cause "pain and embarrassment." The entertainment and instructional values of these pastimes must be wedded also to a moral rectitude characterized as both innocent and kind. Competition that permits a spirited one-upmanship is acceptable only when limited by the demands of good taste and the gracious acceptance of both success and defeat. . . .

Dodge wrote verse all her life, with evident ease and delight. Popular in its day, her poetry remains interesting for what it suggests about her own ideas, attitudes, and values and for the way it places her in relation to certain other writers of the time—women poets, poets of the genteel tradition, and writers of verse for children. Many of Dodge's friends and colleagues commented on her ability to write verse on demand, with amazing speed. The knack stood her in good stead when a piece of "filler" was needed and the presses were waiting. But she made distinctions among the rhymes and jingles she turned out for the

enjoyment of the child readers of **Hearth and Home** or **St. Nicholas,** the amusing light verse she wrote for adults, and the relatively fewer serious poems she was able to regard with any special satisfaction.

Dodge received much praise for her poetry from critics like E. C. Stedman, her work was published in prestigious magazines like the *Century,* and one or two of her poems—notably **"The Two Mysteries"** and **"The Minuet"**—became widely popular. But Dodge's head was not easily turned by flattery, and she clearly doubted the real worth of her serious poems. Dodge believed that true poets were rare and that their gift was mysterious and exalted. Her attitude toward poets she truly admired—such as Tennyson, Arnold, Emerson, Longfellow, and Whittier—was one of respect mixed with a sort of religious awe.

When her poem **"The Two Mysteries"** was published, Dodge received a flood of letters about it. **"The Two Mysteries"** is presented in the context of an epigraph describing an incident in the life of Walt Whitman. When his young nephew died, Whitman consoled a little girl who didn't seem to understand what had happened, saying "You don't know what it is, do you my dear?" and adding, "We don't either." In the poem Dodge picks up Whitman's remark and extends it by describing what death looks like and what "this desolate heart-pain," "the dread to take our daily way, and walk in it again" can feel like to the bereaved. She raises some of the questions that arise at such times: Where has the loved one gone? Why are we left behind? Why do we not understand? But the poet takes comfort in reflecting that we can't define life any more than we can define death, and that if one trusts in God it is possible to believe that "as life is to the living, so death is to the dead."

Dodge was pleased at the response of the reading public to her poem but was also somewhat taken aback. She wrote to Longfellow in confidence explaining that she had heard praise of the poem from a number of literary people and—what interested her more—from "persons who had suffered bereavement." She seems to have suspected that these readers were reacting not so much to the poem but to "this treatment of the subject," for she asked him to read the verses and tell her "if they are good or not," adding, "I often write verses, but sometimes I wonder whether it is *right* for me to do so." Dodge's qualms about **"The Two Mysteries"** may be explained by a bit of advice she gave in *St. Nicholas* to a child who had sent in some poetry: "Your verses are quite good considering your age. Beware of being too sentimental. God gives us some thoughts to hold and to live with, not to spin out in labored rhymes. That these thoughts will sometimes flash out, of themselves, in a true poet's verse, makes them all the more sacred. Never start out to write about them." . . .

Much of Dodge's light verse for adults treats manners and social behavior that struck her as amusing. Many verses deal with the relationship between the sexes. She describes flirtation, courtship rituals, marriage proposals—all distanced by a humorous approach. The unspoken assumption of many of these poems is that young men and women leave their deepest feelings unadmitted and unspoken until circumstances surprise them into a recognition of their mutual affection. In **"Snowbound," "At the Picture Gallery,"** and **"A Monday Romance"** Dodge observes the game of flirtation as it was played in her day with a recognition of its absurdities and of the constraints it placed on women, who were conventionally cast in a passive role.

Sometimes Dodge spoke more directly of the frustrations and distortions custom could occasion in women's emotional lives. In **"Miss Flip at the Exposition"** a scatter-brained young belle who gets very little out of a visit to the great Philadelphia Exposition reveals her own superficiality and silliness in her gushing conversation with a friend. But there are hints in some of her asides that she is playing a role dictated to her by the men in her life, whose approval means everything to her. Her frank interest in the dirty, busy workmen at the exposition is disapproved of by them and must be denied. And she wistfully talks of having seen so many people who are doing just what they want to do, something apparently out of the question for her. The hint is that, absurd as she is, she is this way because she is playing an acceptable but unnatural social role that requires she deny her real feelings.

Dodge wrote verses for children readily, often to fill some pressing editorial need. Some of her work is casual to the point of shapelessness—obvious filler that loses in an anthology whatever point it might once have had in the context of an illustration or the theme of a particular issue of *St. Nicholas* or *Hearth and Home.* But the most serious failing of the verses is their occasional sentimentality. When Dodge writes of children as objects of adult affection or when she writes for adults, evoking the charm of children and trying to tug the heartstrings, her tone becomes arch and the effect is cloying and self-indulgent.

The best of Dodge's poems for children are of two sorts. One is the very simple and neatly put didactic sentiment about nature, designed to encourage children to notice and appreciate what they see around them. The other is a kind of updated Mother Goose piece, with clever rhymes, amusing characters with odd-sounding names, and lots of amiable nonsense. As a children's poet, Dodge was certainly not in a league with Edward Lear, Lewis Carroll, or Christina Rossetti; her comic verse at its best was more like that of Laura E. Richards or Tudor Jenks. But Dodge's humor and good-natured sense of fun appealed to her child audience, who enjoyed her witty wordplay, her willingness to be silly, and (since the later poems were usually printed with their *St. Nicholas* illustrations) the often-delightfully-absurd combination of poem and picture she provided for them.

Dodge's poems for children reflect the same ethos as her fiction. Even her youngest readers are urged to accept the trials that come their way without self-pity and to be grateful for their blessings. . . .

For Dodge, it is important to work or play wholeheartedly. Children are told to look at nature to see that constant labor is "the price of . . . thriving." And they are urged to play vigorously in winter, for "Fun is the fuel / For driving off cold." Above all, children in Dodge's nursery world are supposed to be—no matter what the provocation—glad, cheerful, and brave; whining and fretting are mortal sins in Dodge's nursery morality. Dodge seems to envision a family situation in which parents turn to children for hope and love and the courage to go on. Such an attitude puts emotional pressure on the child to provide a cheerful note in a sometimes-cheerless world. In **"Hark! My Children"** Dodge tells children to be like the stars, which, when it is dark, sparkle anyway; the leaves, which keep the flowers warm despite being tossed by storms; and the birds, who sing the gloom of the forest away. Similarly, in **"Fire Flies"** gentle souls "glimmer and glow," "[t]eaching a lesson wherever they go". . . .

Dodge's didactic impulse was sometimes blunted by her awareness of the pleasures of naughtiness. The primary appeal of her poem **"Among the Animals"** is the opportunity it gives for the child reader to empathize with the destructive impulse of a child who frankly enjoys breaking things, jumping and stamping on a new Noah's Ark, and feeling "as grand as would be" until retribution strikes in the form of a parental spanking. . . .

Those verses Dodge wished to acknowledge and keep in print she collected in several volumes. In 1874 *Rhymes and Jingles,* a lively collection of early verse, mostly from her *Hearth and Home* days, was published. Critics described the volume as "full of queer, quaint fancies, abounding with humor, but without much sentiment or pathos," and as "full of comical wise nonsense and the most felicitous absurdities of language." *Along the Way* (1879) included some previously published poems for adults, a few verses from *Rhymes and Jingles* Dodge thought would appeal to adults, and a number of poems published for the first time. The subject matter ranges from simple verses about snowflakes and domestic life to meditations on nature, death, and loss. In 1894 she published *When Life Is Young: A Collection of Verse for Boys and Girls.* Though a few of these verses are first published there, many of them had appeared in *St. Nicholas,* some unsigned, others written under various pen names, and still others signed MMD. Besides a good deal of light, humorous verse for children, this collection includes one of Dodge's most popular poems, **"The Minuet,"** about a grandmother who prefers the stately measures of long ago to "modern . . . rushing, whirling, bumping," as well as Dodge's poem on the death of Hans Christian Andersen and her verses for Fayal Clarke about *Alice in Wonderland,* **"To W.F.C."** In 1904 she published *Poems and Verses* containing some new poems and some chosen by request from among her verses for children.

Edmund C. Stedman, a prominent establishment critic of the time (and an old friend of Dodge's from her Newark days) thought that many of the American women poets of the genteel tradition—people like Dodge's friends Celia Thaxter, Lucy Larcom, and Helen Hunt Jackson—were writing genuine poetry—not terribly original, and sometimes a bit thin, but spontaneous, artistic, knowledgeable, elevating, and pleasantly conventional. He called Dodge a natural singer in her way and said her stanzas were "marked by charming fancy and always tender and sweet." And, he added, she had "a gift" "of seeing into the hearts of children." Altogether, these modest compliments were probably a fair assessment of Dodge's poetic achievement. Her readers may have been a little more enthusiastic, however, for, young and old, they kept her collections of poetry profitably in print during her life-time, and her best-known poems, **"The Two Mysteries"** and **"The Minuet,"** remained popular anthology pieces for some time.

Mary Mapes Dodge's **Hans Brinker** is an acknowledged classic of children's literature. And it is this durable best-seller of 1865 for which she is probably most remembered today. In Dodge's own time her lively essays and amusing light verse appeared in some of America's premier magazines. Her serious poems touched many contemporary readers as an apt expression of their own deepest concerns. And she was revered and loved by three generations of children as the peerless "Conductor" of *St. Nicholas* magazine. Dodge's conception of what the readers of *St. Nicholas* needed and wanted was a major influence on the development of American children's literature in what has justly been called a golden age. The roll call of distinguished authors she persuaded to write for children is impressive, and she had a gift for recognizing and encouraging fledgling talent. Her correspondence reveals the extent to which famous writers like Alcott, Twain, and Kipling deferred to her special knowledge of her audience and to her editorial expertise. It shows the gratitude of young writers like John Bennett, as well as the cordial respect of distinguished figures like Longfellow and Whittier. And a study of manuscripts and interoffice memorandums shows how deftly Dodge and her staff solicited and shaped work they published to fit her idea of what was "right for *St. Nick.*"

Our inquiry into Dodge's personal history has explored the way her mission to children grew out of her own unusual schooling at home and her attempt to provide her sons with a similarly rich experience. For them Dodge created an ambience in which play was indistinguishable from education. The boys were encouraged to observe, experiment, research, and share their findings with an appreciative mother-teacher. Attentive to her sons' real likes and dislikes, Dodge discussed art and literature with them seriously and learned to respect the honesty and shrewdness of their responses. This lesson was to stand her in good stead in both her writing and her editorial work for children.

The pages of the **United States Journal,** which Dodge edited from 1861 to 1862, demonstrate that from the very beginning of her career she possessed the ability to project a strong and pleasing editorial personality. Her commitment to knowing and serving her audience was expressed in an immediate editorial call for reader participation in shaping the magazine's policies. In the **Journal** she began to write about many subjects that were to preoccupy her

throughout her career. She discussed children and their upbringing, the function of play in education, and the value of an active outdoor life for young girls. She wrote thoughtfully and wittily about women's rights and about marriage, and included short profiles of women of achievement who might serve as role models for young girls. She experimented with popular formula fiction and directed the attention of her family audience to the way games, amusements, reading, and art might enrich their lives. . . .

By the end of her long career as an editor, Dodge could look back on accomplishments that would, had her audience been primarily adult, have made her as widely recognized a shaper of intellectual history as any of her colleagues at the *Century, Harper's,* or the *Atlantic Monthly.* She herself had pointed out to Roswell Smith in her famous letter of 1873 that "the perfect magazine for children lies folded at the heart of the ideal best magazine for grown-ups," though the child's magazine had to be, if anything, "stronger, truer, bolder, more uncompromising." Dodge's editorial goals were not, in fact, so very different from those of Holland, Gilder, and Smith. *St. Nicholas* and the *Century* shared more than their offices and printing facilities; they shared a cultural, social, and political program.

Like *Scribner's Monthly* and the *Century,* **St. Nicholas** preached self-reliance, hard work, courage, duty, patriotism, and trust in God. And like its sister periodicals, **St. Nicholas** was reformist in its way. Young readers were reminded from time to time that poverty, disease, and homelessness afflicted innocents no older than they. And they were frequently urged to think of themselves as empowered to change the world for the better, and reminded that the future was theirs to shape. The world that children were shown in **St. Nicholas**—for the most part unrealistically safe and pretty—reflected some "harsh, cruel facts" and an "occasional glimpse of the odious doings of the uncharitable and base,"—when Dodge thought it important to point these out. Of course, a serious limitation of **St. Nicholas** (and of *Scribner's Monthly* and the *Century*) was an uncritical equation of contemporary middle-class American values and assumptions with eternal verities. Looked at a century later, many of the "facts" uncritically acknowledged in its fiction are seen to be harsher and more cruel than they were ever judged to be in the text. Ethnic and racial minorities, for example, were often depicted stereotypically, in painful and degrading terms. Though Dodge did become more sensitive to this issue as time went on, many pages of the magazine during her tenure as editor are marred by an acceptance of the racism, sexism, and ethnic and class prejudice characteristic of her milieu.

Dodge was aware of her own fallibility as an editor. *St. Nicholas* was often praised in extravagant terms, but such flattery made her uneasy, and her correspondence shows that she was often less than satisfied with what she had been able to produce, even when it was well received by the public and the critics. Dodge had said at the outset of her career that it was a heavy responsibility to have the ear of young America once a month, and part of this

responsibility lay in maintaining consistently high standards. She frequently complained of the "trials and disappointments" of being an editor: "fair ideals" she lamented, "get so woefully squeezed under printing and binding presses!" And it was a strain to be personally responsible for keeping a magazine up to the mark. She once told the editor of the *Atlantic Monthly* that she'd often "noticed that the more `new life' there is in a magazine the less there is left in its editor!"

An especially pressing editorial burden was the constant need to accommodate the demands of a divided audience. Adults often saw **St. Nicholas** as a convenient vehicle for inculcating the values of the genteel tradition. Dodge, on the other hand, perceived children as wanting "to have their own way over their own magazine." Her readiness to listen to her young readers, her respect for their views, her orientation toward the future, and her openness to experiment allied her with forces that were changing the very nature of children's literature in her time; even so, she never forgot that she had to please not only the children but their parents. She worked tirelessly to balance the needs of her various constituencies and to meet the demands of her own taste and conscience.

The volumes of **St. Nicholas** published under her direction from 1873 to 1905 prove how well, on balance, she was able to do just that. The editor of a literary periodical needs the ability to attract and keep an effective staff; a flair for business; a sense of audience; the ability to find and cultivate different kinds of contributors; and the skill to select, modify, and arrange

materials effectively. Dodge had all of these. The program that gave **St. Nicholas** its direction reflected her long-term commitment to bringing enlightenment, entertainment, and cultural enrichment to American families. But as Dodge rightly observed, no program, however well devised, can quite make a magazine. It takes something more—an individual vision, a personality whose taste and enthusiasm can give the project life. As we have suggested, Dodge's concept of **St. Nicholas** as a "pleasure-ground" for children had its sources in her experience as a mother, a journalist, a writer of fiction, a lover of games and festivity. In the holiday spirit invoked by its very name, in its earnest but unpreachy morality, in its openness to new things, and in its humor and playfulness **St. Nicholas** reflected its editor's own approach to life. It achieved, brilliantly, her goal—to bring children the very best in literature and art. And it was fun. In Mary Mapes Dodge's "pleasure-ground" the "first culture of the mind" was attended with delight.

TITLE COMMENTARY

THE IRVINGTON STORIES (1864; revised and enlarged 1898)

The North American Review

SOURCE: A review of *The Irvington Stories,* in *The North American Review,* Vol. 100, No. CCVI, January, 1865, p. 304.

Very pleasant little stories, written in good simple English, with just enough improbability in them to suit the minds of children, for whom the age of fancy and fable renews itself in every generation. They are not sermons in words of two syllables, they are not prosy; but what is gracious and lovely in childhood is appealed to indirectly, and with something of motherly tenderness in the tone. Good books for children are so rare, and books to make little spoonies so common, that we are glad to say a word in praise of one so graceful and pleasing.

The Dial

SOURCE: A review of *The Irvington Stories,* in *The Dial* Vol. 25, No. 300, December 16, 1898, p. 468.

A new edition of Mrs. Mary Mapes Dodge's **Irvington Stories** will be welcomed by all those children, now grown gray and dignified, who loved these stories of old, especially with the original illustrations by F. O. C. Darley. Other stories have been added, but Captain George, "Old Pop," and Po-no-kah are still here, and Mrs. Dodge knows how to make them delightful.

Susan R. Gannon and Ruth Anne Thompson

SOURCE: "*The Irvington Stories*," in *Mary Mapes Dodge*, Twayne Publishers, 1992, pp. 42-8, 51-3.

The Irvington Stories, based in part on stories Dodge had told her own sons, appeared in 1865. Though it was not a best-seller, the collection went through several editions quickly enough to establish publisher James O'Kane's confidence in Dodge's ability to appeal to her chosen audience. Dodge's good friend Lu Runkle observed that "the stories had just enough of improbability to suit the minds of children, for whom the age of fancy and fable renews itself in every generation," while the strong moral undertone appealed to their parents. The *Working Farmer,* reflecting the views of those closest to Dodge, commented on Dodge's respect for her young readers: "These stories are not written in the `Harry and Lucy' style, but appeal to the appreciation of children by tacitly recognizing them as on the same plane as the writer. No child likes to be patted on the head while he is reading, but imbibes instruction far more readily if his capacity to comprehend the subject is taken for granted. *The Irvington Stories* aim to please and to invigorate—to teach without stating what is *taught,* and thus convey instruction, improve the moral tone, and inculcate proper principles in the most effectual way."

The warm and reassuring maternal persona that informs the narrative voice of *The Irvington Stories* explicitly supports traditional values parents might see as likely to help their children hold a steady course in a time of great social change and moral confusion: hard work, obedience, religious reverence, patriotism, duty. Yet the best of the stories Dodge told also expressed on a symbolic level many of the unspoken feelings and needs of her child readers.

The Irvington Stories went through four early editions with O'Kane. Thirty-three years later, H. L. Allison, son of an old friend and co-worker of James Jay Mapes, approached Dodge—now a well-established figure in the literary world—with the idea of issuing another edition. Dodge dropped some of the weaker stories and added five more pieces and a preface explaining to a new generation of young readers that the stories had been written long ago and that she had, as the years went by, written "other books that seemed to her better suited to the changing times" but had decided to issue this edition so that it could be enjoyed by the children of her original readers.

The ten items in the 1864 edition of the collection are extremely varied. Dodge uses a number of voices and styles, and attempts different genres. The group includes two didactic poems, a fable in the Hans Christian Andersen mode, a biographical anecdote, a tall tale, a patriotic song, and four ambitious short stories: a weird, *Struwwelpeter*-like dream-vision; a sentimental Christmas story; a timely bit of fiction about the Civil War; and a violent tale about children kidnapped by Indians. In her 1898 revision Dodge dropped the biographical anecdote and the tall tale and added three moral tales and two accounts of family festivities.

Several of the shorter pieces in *The Irvington Stories* are literary experiments, less interesting for their intrinsic merit than for what they can tell us about Dodge's effort to master the craft of writing for children. "**The Golden Gate**" is a fable in the Andersen tradition about a poor child who heeds the Gospel admonition to "love thy neighbor" and a rich one, who doesn't. Three of the stories in the revised 1898 version might also be described as moral fables of one sort or another: "**Dick and the Bantams,**" "**All in a Day,**" and "**Learning by Heart.**"

"**The Artist and the Newsboy,**" the biographical anecdote included in the original edition, concerns the painter Inman, whose picturesquely ragged newsboy model tries to make himself more presentable by washing himself and getting his hair cut. In doing so, he loses the very charm that has made him appealing to the artist. The newsboy is seen from an adult's point of view, and the artist's desire to exploit his colorful raggedness is presented sympathetically. The boy is perceived as an aesthetic object rather than a person, and is considered foolish for having chosen to alter his appearance according to his own taste and, presumably, that of his social class. Dodge's treatment of the newsboy is mawkish, and the story is likely to seem sentimental and patronizing to modern tastes. The author here may be writing about a child, but she is not speaking effectively to a child audience. Dodge herself probably sensed that this was not her best work, for it is one of those she dropped in the revised edition, along with an even weaker sketch called "**Brave Robbie and the Skeleton.**"

Two of the pieces added to the 1898 edition are slight accounts of family festivities. One, "**The Wonderful Well: A Christmas Sketch from Life,**" is a reminiscence of one of Dodge's own dazzling childhood Christmases at her Grandmother Mapes's house in New York, a party attended by Lizzie, Louise, Sophie, and all the cousins and relations. The event is recalled through a child's eyes, and the mystifications of a family Christmas surprise are presented so that observant young readers can guess for themselves how Lizzie's cousins made a magic well, a fairy, and an outsize monkey appear in the grandmother's back parlor. This evocation of a warm family celebration with lots of games and an elaborate gift-giving ritual explores a situation that appears frequently in Dodge's fiction. Here, the party games and music are described so carefully as to make the piece almost a how-to article.

Another, similar description, "**A Doll's Party: A Sketch from Real Life,**" presents a picture of a party for girls "under eleven," but the event sounds more appropriate for quite young children. What point the piece has in the telling seems to come from the narrator's choosing to treat the little girls as the "mothers" of their dolls, and the children's social event appears to be a solemn imitation of an elaborate adult party with a good deal of conspicuous consumption. The appeal to children might be like the appeal of an animated Christmas window in a fashionable toy store: everything is miniature, pretty, elaborate, expensive—fascinating to look at, if a little out of reach of the average child.

Dodge's more ambitious pieces, **"The Hermit of the Hills," "Cushamee; or, The Boy's Walk," "Po-No-Kah: An Indian Tale,"** and **"Captain George, the Drummer-Boy: A Story of the Rebellion,"** offer variations on themes and story patterns that were to preoccupy her throughout her career. Among them are three basic formulas that R. Gordon Kelly identifies as prominent in the sort of fiction that was later to appear in *St. Nicholas:* the "ordeal," the "change of heart," and the "gentry mission."

The ordeal involves isolation; the need to respond quickly and decisively to some challenge, trial, or temptation; and the return to the adult world of the family, where there will be a reward for the performance. Kelly compares the pattern with Arnold Van Gennep's rite-of-passage paradigm involving separation, isolation, and transition and incorporation into a new social world or reintegration with an older world. This pattern is especially clear in a story like **"Capt. George."**

The change-of-heart formula often follows a similar basic plot pattern but involves the protagonist's conversion, "a dramatic shift in perception which combines a conscious recognition of the erroneous nature of the individual's former behavior with a conscious resolution to do better." Although a number of change-of-heart stories are found in *The Irvington Stories,* probably the most striking is the story of Tom Laffer, in **"Cushamee,"** who learns not to torment dumb animals or tease his little sister.

The gentry mission involves a "figure who embodies the moral values of gentility and whose moral force brings about a change in the values of others." (It is not unusual for such values to be carried forward by a very young person.) Dodge's drummer boy, George, teaches a young comrade how to write and opens up a new world to him; the kindness of young Elsie to the unsociable old hermit she befriends in **"The Hermit of the Hills"** restores him to his family, to his community, and to an active social role in bringing happiness to the children of the town.

In Dodge's practice, the ordeal, the change of heart, and the gentry mission are often incorporated in a story pattern that might be termed Dodge's own personal myth of the fractured family. Over and over in her stories, families are parted by some sudden disaster (accident, shipwreck, war, kidnapping) and can be reunited only through the generosity and faithfulness of some member of the group who effects a healing. Frequently, though not always, the initial rupture of the family unit occurs because a father figure refuses—or is unable—to play his traditional role as guardian, guide, and protector. The story then dramatizes what the father's failure means to the family: a painful separation, followed by some providential intervention and the coming together of the group again—healed and whole. . . .

"The Hermit of the Hills" is a sentimental Christmas story in which a child's kindness restores an old man to the family he had long ago rejected. The hermit, a seemingly stern, cold, and lonely man, had cut himself off from his daughter when she married against his wishes. A little girl—who turns out to be his granddaughter—offers him an act of kindness, and he is transformed into a benevolent figure who gives a Christmas party for the children of the town and is reunited with his family. . . .

"Captain George, the Drummer-Boy: A Story of the Rebellion" is Dodge's answer to her father's request that she write a story for boys about the Civil War. Dodge herself felt that **"George"** was the best piece in *The Irvington Stories* and was pleased when General McClellan, after reading it in manuscript form, told her it was "the finest and most accurate war story for boys that he had seen." The young protagonist's father has died during the war, and at 14, much to his widowed mother's regret, he enlists in the Union Army as a drummer boy. He finds soon enough that the reality of a soldier's life is very different from that depicted in the war stories he has read in books. George becomes a hero, but the warm family reunion that ends the story is somewhat shadowed by Dodge's realistic depiction of the war's real cost in human suffering. . . .

"Po-no-kah: An Indian Tale" is modeled to some extent on a popular literary form, the Indian captivity narrative. Beginning in the seventeenth century, tales of settlers' experiences at the hands of Indian captors in the wilderness were widely read by children as well as adults. The early narratives were cast in an allegorical mode and thematically showed young people "the horrors of captivity in Biblical terms that reaffirmed their dependence upon a parental God. Both captives and readers were, after all, the children of Israel; and the slaughters of innocent children were vividly portrayed."[3] But the narratives also satisfied their young readers' taste for "excitement, suspense, and terror.". . .

The story begins with an evocation of the difference between the safe, comfortable, upper-middle-class home of the implied readers and the narrator (complete with references to napkin rings and silver saltcellars) and the precarious life of the frontier settler, who "after cheerfully leaving home in the morning for a day's hunt" would "return at night to find his family murdered or captured, and his cabin a mass of smoking ruins." Although it relies on stereotyped characterization and formulaic action, the story depicts quite frankly the subversive appeal of both the wilderness and Indian life to its young protagonists. . . .

When *The Irvington Stories* was reissued in 1898, Dodge expressed a concern in her preface to the collection that the picture of Indian life presented in this story might give a distorted view of it to her readers, to whom "the tale of `Po-no-kah' will be tempered by what they may have read or heard of the present condition of tribes of American Indians, who with the help of noble workers in their behalf, have made good progress towards civilization and education." She added, "Po-no-kah is but one example out of many, showing how certain men of his race have been distinguished by high traits of character even under the most savage conditions."

Although the parents who purchased *The Irvington Stories* might well have been attracted by the educational program presented in the didactic verses that frame the volume, the children who read and loved the stories in the book were presented with a much more mixed—and more interesting—message. Dodge saw these children as responsible moral agents with the future in their hands, and since "The heritage of noble work / Descends from sire to son," she urged on them the virtues she felt they needed: courage, truth, honor, learning, civility, loyalty, and generosity. But she also peopled her stories with very human boys and girls and set them in a complex world where choices are difficult and being good is not easy. This honesty to children's experience may explain something of Dodge's ability to engage the sympathy of younger readers as well as the confidence of their parents. . . .

HANS BRINKER; OR, THE SILVER SKATES: A STORY OF LIFE IN HOLLAND

M. E. Dodge

SOURCE: A review of *Hans Brinker; or, The Silver Skates: A Story of Life in Holland,* in *The Nation,* Vol. 2, No. 30, January 25, 1866, pp. 119-20.

Though a little late for the holidays, this boys' and girls' book is appropriate to the season and yet quite independent of it. To be sure the plot is woven about a skating match, and there is a grand tour on skates undertaken by a band of clever Dutch youngsters. But this is really incidental to most agreeable descriptions of Amsterdam, Haarlem, and Leyden, and the Hague; to scraps of Dutch history; to pictures of the general scenery, position, popular life, and manners of Holland; and to the instructive development of character in the hero and heroine: just as good reading, every bit, for midsummer as for midwinter. The authoress has shown in her former works for the young a very rare ability to meet their wants, but she has produced nothing better than this charming tale, alive with incident and action, adorned rather than freighted with useful facts, and moral without moralization.

The Nation

SOURCE: A review of *Hans Brinker; or, The Silver Skates: A Story of Life in Holland,* in *The Nation,* Vol. 17, No. 441, December 11, 1873, p. 389.

It is eight years since *Hans Brinker* was first published, and there is no good reason why it should not be in active circulation eight years hence. The story is, as we remarked at the time of its appearance, appropriate to the holiday season, yet independent of it. It will always furnish wholesome reading to the young, who will find in the skilful and natural development of character something to admire and to imitate, and for whom the descriptions of scenery and manners in Holland, and the tales from heroic

Dutch history, will have an abiding charm. We should be troubled, indeed, to name any child's book written in this country which better deserves to be counted a classic. For this reason we make bold to reproach the publishers with putting at the front so bloodthirsty an illustration as that representing the capture by the boys of the robber at the *Red Lion* inn. It relates, of course, to one of the incidents of the narrative, but precisely the one which least needed illustration; and as frontispiece it conveys a false impression of the character of the story. And if we may grumble a little more about the pictures, we would point out how inferior they are in value (and would be, even if intrinsically of far greater artistic merit) to as many photographic illustrations of life in Holland. We hope that the success of *Hans Brinker* under its new imprint will be such as to justify the publishers in preparing next year an edition somewhat more attractive typographically, and adorned with autotype views of dykes, and canals, and windmills, and skaters, and town-halls, and perhaps a portrait or two of the old-time Dutch worthies whose deeds are recounted by Mrs. Dodge.

The New York Times Book Review

SOURCE: A review of *Hans Brinker; or, The Silver Skates: A Story of Life in Holland,* in *The New York Times Book Review,* Vol. 63, No. 1641, December 10, 1896, p. 444.

The new edition of Mrs. Mary Mapes Dodge's well-approved and standard children's story, *Hans Brinker,* is furnished with an unusually full and harmonious set of illustrations and vignettes, which really illustrate, at once adorning the book and instructing the reader. The artist, Mr. Allen B. Doggett, made an especial trip to Holland for the purpose of having his work sound and consistent; and he has reason to be satisfied, for his pictures not only are correct and full of local spirit, but have an illuminating relation to the text too often wholly wanting in books of like character.

Susan R. Gannon and Ruth Anne Thompson

SOURCE: "Dodge and Motley: History in Hans Brinker," in *The Lion and the Unicorn: A Critical Journal of Children's Literature,* Vol. 15, No. 1, 1991, pp. 43-56.

Nineteenth-century America found the Dutch fascinating. Washington Irving's whimsical *Diedrich Knickerbocker's A History of New York* (1809) so caught the public fancy that it shaped the popular view of many Americans about their own past, and his other folklore-like stories about the American Dutch were widely admired. Influential members of the New York Historical Society and Irving's own St. Nicholas Society kept interest in New York's Dutch heritage very much alive. Even Santa Claus—in the nineteenth century still noticeably Dutch and often depicted puffing on a clay pipe—was an effective ambassador for his homeland. Popular histories of Spain and England by William H. Prescott and Thomas Babington Macaulay focused attention on the Dutch, who figured prominently in them. And by mid-century "forgotten links heightened the discovery of identification with the Dutch: Dutch alliance with the Americans against Britain, with the British against Napoleon." The scene was set for the extraordinary public response to two remarkable—and related—best-sellers: historian John Lothrop Motley's three-volume *The Rise of the Dutch Republic* (1856) and Mary Mapes Dodge's **Hans Brinker; or, The Silver Skates.**

We will suggest here that in **Hans Brinker** Dodge interpreted Motley for young America. She approached her audience, of course, in ways appropriate to its special needs, and modified the materials she borrowed as necessary. And she had her own cultural program in mind for America's youth. But **Hans Brinker** owes much to *The Rise of the Dutch Republic*. Motley's conception of Dutch history and character as exemplary for nineteenth-century Americans is a central premise of Dodge's novel, which is, to a degree, a work of speculative fiction in the utopian mode. Motley's ideal of heroism and his stress on communal responsibility are central preoccupations of **Hans Brinker.** And the novel's theme, the heroism required of ordinary young people as they struggle toward their own independence, echoes the central theme of *The Rise of the Dutch Republic*. . . .

Mary Mapes Dodge, "like the rest of the reading world," "had been thrilled and fascinated by the . . . histories of Motley," *The Rise of the Dutch Republic,* and the then-appearing *History of the United Netherlands.* A young widow with two sons to support, she had already made a modest literary success with her **Irvington Stories** for children, and in 1865, inspired by reading Motley, "resolved to make Holland the scene of a juvenile tale, and give the youngsters so much of the history of that wonderful country as should tell itself, naturally, through the evolution of the story." She intended **Hans Brinker** "to combine the instructive features of a book of travels with the interest of a domestic tale" and insisted that "the descriptions of Dutch localities, customs, and general characteristics" would be "given with scrupulous care."

Like Motley, Dodge had a definite moral and cultural program to impart to her readers. Unlike Motley—who was extremely anti-Catholic—Dodge was determinedly nonsectarian, but she claimed a religious purpose for writing the book:

> Should it cause even one heart to feel a deeper trust in God's goodness and love, or aid any in weaving a life wherein, through knots and entanglements, the golden thread shall never be tarnished or broken, the prayer with which it was begun and ended will have been answered.

In **Hans Brinker,** Dodge also presented a picture of Dutch history and culture designed to teach her audience of middle-class children what she believed they needed to know to live productively in late nineteenth-century America. In the tradition of speculative fiction, Dodge used her readers' desire for novelty, their curiosity about an alien

way of life, to give them a fresh perspective on their own lives. Like the eighteenth-century satirists who exploited the image of the Chinese as technologically backward yet—paradoxically—wise and virtuous, Dodge made shrewd use of the image of the Dutch current in her own time.

The popular view of the Dutch character, influenced by Washington Irving, stressed stolidity, sleepiness, love of comfort, and ferocious cleanliness. Holland was thought to be quaint and a bit old-fashioned, some windmills seeming "sadly in need of Yankee `improvements.'" Dodge noted regretfully that some contemporary Americans found the Dutch funny and called them "human beavers," hinting "that their country . . . [might] float off any day at high tide." . . .

Dodge intended **Hans Brinker** to give American children a juster picture of Holland, and to "free them from certain current prejudices concerning that noble and enterprising people." The Dutch in Dodge's novel embodied an ideal of behavior she thought worth setting before American youth. It combined courage, patience, self-reliance, industry, willingness to work and to sacrifice for the common good, with a reverence for democratic traditions. It stressed the importance of the arts, commerce, and technology, and envisioned cultural progress as calling for its own special kind of heroism. . . .

In **Hans Brinker** Dodge created something new, a realistic story for children with believable young people caught in conflict between their own needs and their familial and social responsibilities. Though to modern readers the didacticism of the novel may seem intrusive, Dodge's control of the narrator-reader relationship, the novelty and charm of the Dutch background, and the holiday atmosphere of the book seem to have persuaded her contemporaries that they were being well entertained rather than preached to.

Parents concerned that their children learn to live responsibly in a rapidly changing and "turbulent" world helped to make the book a best-seller. The courage, self-reliance, honesty, industry, generous concern for others, and firm (if unsectarian) religious faith urged upon children by Dodge—and other general writers of the literary establishment of the sixties and seventies—reflected the deep anxiety of nineteenth-century adults "about the contemporary state of their society and about its future, even about its survival." Parents and critics admired Dodge's ability to convey what they considered "wholesome influences on the young heart and mind" without seeming overly preachy. *The Atlantic Monthly* was pleased to notice that in **Hans Brinker** "There is no formal moral, obtruding itself in set phrase. The lessons inculcated, elevated in tone, are in the action of the story and the feelings and aspirations of the actors." A number of reviews lauded the book for the naturalness of its characterization, which set it apart from other children's books of the time.

But the critics also praised the book for the authenticity of the background and local color, despite the fact that at that time Dodge had not yet been to Holland. Though it is a commonplace of recent criticism that *Hans Brinker* is overloaded with information on Dutch history, geography, and popular culture, the response of early critics and readers to the story's heavy cargo of information about Dutch history and customs was positive. Indeed, one review, in *The Nation,* noted that the plot "is really incidental to most agreeable descriptions of Amsterdam, Haarlem, and Leyden, and the Hague; to scraps of Dutch history; to pictures of the general scenery, position, popular life, and manners of Holland; and to the instructive development of character in the hero and heroine." Commenting on Dodge's reputation for appealing to the real interests of young readers, this reviewer asserted that she had produced "nothing better than this charming tale, alive with incident and action, adorned rather than freighted with useful facts, and moral without moralization.". . .

In *Hans Brinker* problems of growth and maturation are explored playfully for young readers in terms of quests to be carried out, games to be won, puzzles to be solved. The ability to skate becomes a metaphor for young people's growing readiness to assume responsibility for their own lives. The often painful story of the Brinker family is supplemented by the stories of other parents and children whose experience is presented in a more detached way. In particular, Dodge uses wealthy young Peter van Holp as a kind of double, an alter ego for Hans. While the brave, self-sacrificing young hero of the novel goes about his business, Peter and a group of his friends enjoy a skating journey during which they explore the history, geography, and culture of their homeland. . . .

Visitors to Holland today can raise a glass in a student bar decked with silver skates like the ones Gretel won or visit a statue of the fictional little boy who thrust his finger in the dyke to save his country. The fable featuring this child is the best-loved set piece in *Hans Brinker.* The story is a simple, but affecting one. A "gentle," "sunny-haired" boy, son of a dykeman, coming home late, notices a leak in the dyke. The boy understands the danger at once and thrusts his finger in the hole. His first reaction is delight that he has stopped the "angry waters." But soon other feelings come: cold, dread, fear, numbness, pain. The boy prays for help, and resolves—despite his terror and his feeling that he might not survive the night—to trust in God and stay at his post till the morning, when, indeed, help does come. . . .

The little Hero of Haarlem's story is so perfectly adapted to Dodge's purposes that it might easily be supposed she created it herself. But though the story has been attributed to Dodge by scholars, it is not original. Dodge never discussed its provenance, perhaps because she believed it in the public domain, like the historical anecdotes she retold. Its appearance in a school reader within the text and the insistence on its historicity by the Dutch characters in the story suggest that Dodge was not trying to claim any special originality for it. What is original is the "emblematic" way she used it.

Within the novel many exemplary stories are presented to model audiences of varied age, background, and experience. . . .

One of Dodge's great gifts as an editor and as a writer was her ability to adapt material from the world of adult literature to the needs of her own special audience. Clearly, *Hans Brinker* could not have been written without the inspiration of Motley's *Rise of the Dutch Republic.* But when Dodge undertook to give the young readers of her novel "so much of the history" of Holland "as should tell itself naturally, through the evolution of the story," she wove the material she borrowed into a dramatic novel that could readily engage the minds and sympathies of young people. She translated the struggle for independence into personal terms with which children and adolescents could identify. She modified the historical vignettes she used so that they supported her message of hope, encouragement, reform. So successful was she in creating an appealing and enduring work that today—while Motley's heavy volumes molder on library shelves—*Hans Brinker* flourishes in a variety of editions and in many languages. It has been the subject of plays, television films, even an ice-drama. And the little Hero of Haarlem she made so famous has long since entered popular culture as an emblem of the courage, endurance, and moral autonomy Dodge admired in the Dutch and urged on young Americans of her day.

Susan R. Gannon and Ruth Anne Thompson

SOURCE: "Hans Brinker," in *Mary Mapes Dodge,* Twayne Publishers, 1992, pp. 54-73.

For most readers, it is *Hans Brinker; or, The Silver Skates* for which Mary Mapes Dodge is remembered today. The title brings to mind quaint Dutch backgrounds, a fresh holiday atmosphere, skating races on the canal, the appealing boy and girl protagonists, and the unforgettable story of the little boy with his finger in the dyke. Even those who haven't read the book may be familiar with it through one or more of the films and plays it has inspired. Over 100 editions have been printed in many languages, and in the century and a quarter since it was originally published the book has won critical acclaim and become a children's classic. It remains available today in formats ranging from elaborately bound and illustrated editions to inexpensive paperbacks.

In 1865 Dodge began to write a short children's serial for Tilton's *Independent.* She had already read Motley's *The Rise of the Dutch Republic,* a long, detailed historical work that had been recommended to readers of the *Working Farmer.* And she plunged so enthusiastically into more research on the subject that her short serial soon grew into quite a long book. Her New Jersey neighbors the Scharffs, who had lived in Holland, generously supplied her not only with information on the Dutch background but also with the story of Raff Brinker. Dodge took care to thank "these kind Holland friends" as she acknowledged in her preface other "obligations to many well known writers on Dutch history, literature, and art."

Since the *Independent* now found the story too long, Dodge submitted it to O'Kane, the publisher of her *Irvington*

Stories, to whom she was committed for another book. O'Kane didn't want *Hans Brinker,* but Dodge, with sure judgment, pressed him to take it. The public was delighted with the book, and it became an immediate best-seller. In fact, in 1865 the only book with comparable sale figures was Charles Dickens's *Our Mutual Friend,* and in the years 1865-81 *Hans Brinker* received more reviews than any other children's book in the United States. Many of these reviews were the results of new editions of the novel; still, the number of those editions also attests to the book's reputation and genuine popularity.

In *Hans Brinker* Dodge created something new, a realistic story for children that broke with the heavy-handed didacticism of the earlier part of the nineteenth century. Its publishing history indicates that Dodge's story of young people caught in conflict between their duties to themselves and their familial and social responsibilities has a perennial appeal. A number of the early reviews praised the book for the naturalness of its characterization, an aspect that set it apart from other children's books of the time. Richard Darling has observed that "if Hans seems almost too good to be true to the modern reader," he must nevertheless have seemed real to a generation brought up on the Rollo books and he "paved the way for even more natural boys to come."

Most early reviewers regarded the story's heavy cargo of information about Dutch history and customs as an attractive feature. Indeed, one review, in the *Nation,* noted that the plot "is really incidental to most agreeable descriptions of Amsterdam, Haarlem, and Leyden, and the Hague; to scraps of Dutch history; to pictures of the general scenery, position, popular life, and manners of Holland; and to the instructive development of character in the hero and heroine." This reviewer thought the novel "good reading" and, commenting on Dodge's reputation for appealing to the real interests of young readers, asserted that she had produced "nothing better than this charming tale, alive with incident and action, adorned rather than freighted with useful facts, and moral without moralization."

Critics commented on the wide audience for the book, the *Atlantic Monthly* claiming that while it was addressed to children, it might be read "with pleasure and profit by their elders." One critic even expressed the opinion that should Dodge wish to write a "strictly legitimate novel" for adults, she would certainly be successful at it.

The *Atlantic Monthly* praised Dodge's ability to convey "wholesome influences on the young heart and mind" without being overly preachy: "there is no formal moral, obtruding itself in set phrase. The lessons inculcated, elevated in tone, are in the action of the story and the feelings and aspirations of the actors."

The considerable attention given to the book from the very first was especially impressive because it was originally published by a relatively obscure New York firm. But the book's popularity grew steadily, particularly after more attractive, illustrated editions were published by

Scribner, Armstrong and by Charles Scribner's Sons. A reviewer for *Scribner's Monthly,* commenting on the 1873 edition with illustrations by Darley, Nast, and other well-known artists of the day, was highly complimentary and (not surprisingly, since *Scribner's Monthly* shared staff with **St. Nicholas Magazine,** then edited by Dodge) seemed to know a good deal about Dodge's philosophy of writing for children. This reviewer noted that "one of the charms of *Hans Brinker* is that it seems to be written by an author who has no ideal child in her mind; whom she seeks to interest and instruct; not even an ideal Real Child—that precious creature who is the bane of much of the finer sort of juvenile literature of our day." The book was in fact praised for qualities close friends like Frank Stockton and Fayal Clarke frequently saw in Dodge herself: a natural, straightforward earnestness; unaffectedness; wit; vivacity; a genial warmth; and a fresh young spirit.

In 1979 Catharine Morris Wright saw the appeal of Dodge's novel this way: "Long, lively, informative, it was full of color and personalities and action. It was a catalogue of Dutch art and architecture, of daily habits, points of view, politics; it was guidebook, romance, tragedy. Above all, it was people—real, live, and close by—part of its readers' own world, an amazing mixture of intent and theme with hardly a facet left wanting." Jerome Griswold in 1984 stressed the story's thematic concern with the danger of being carried away by turbulent emotion, especially anger. Unmistakable parallels exist between Dodge's own experience as the widow of a man presumed to have drowned himself in the stormy Atlantic and the plot of "a novel involving a mother that townspeople call `Widow Brinker' and her two children who lost their father during an oceanic storm but later recovered him." Griswold suggests that in *Hans Brinker* Dodge has written a story that invites a strong emotional response from its young readers and yet condemns giving way to such a response: "She provides abundant temptations to test her readers' resolve and seduces them to abandon it, thereby creating the juvenile version of the romance novel."

Marilyn Kaye hailed *Hans Brinker* as a remarkable book for its time, citing Dodge's lack of dogmatism and her "open-minded, realistic approach to the human condition, and especially the state of childhood." And Harriet Christy in 1988 agreed with Wright that though Dodge was much concerned with the Dutch background, on another level the story is "a straightforward, earnest, and simple account of ordinary people, without regard to nationality.". . .

"On a bright December morning long ago, two thinly clad children were kneeling upon the bank of a frozen canal in Holland." So begins *Hans Brinker; or, The Silver Skates.* Here in the opening pages of the novel, Hans and Gretel Brinker find they can't skate very far or very well on their crude, homemade wooden skates. Their ability to skate becomes a metaphor for their growing readiness to assume responsibility for their own lives. The novel, which begins with two half-frozen children adjusting skates that cannot take them far, is designed to show young readers how courage and endurance can win them the freedom of action they desire.

and to the slow-moving, psychologically realistic story of Hans and Gretel Brinker she adds mythic, illustrative, and symbolic elements that clarify the meaning of their struggle toward autonomy. In particular, she makes interesting use of the history of Holland itself, the "land of pluck," whose people have traditionally embodied the kind of Spartan courage needed to bring her young protagonists safely through their period of trial and danger. . . .

Hans Brinker presents three related stories, all of them involving families. The first tells of Dr. Boekman, the great Dutch surgeon whose unhappy son Laurens, acting reluctantly as his father's assistant, makes an error in compounding a drug for a patient. Ten years before the novel begins, Laurens flees the Netherlands, believing himself a murderer. He gives his silver watch and a farewell message for his father to the kind peasant who helps him on his way.

The second story is that of the family of Raff Brinker, the peasant who helps Laurens. Brinker suffers an accident while working on the dykes the night Laurens meets him. A severe head injury leaves him a helpless amnesiac, unable to communicate with his family and given to fits of violence. Dame Brinker cares for him tenderly, but without the family's savings—which Raff has hidden—she is forced to work very hard to make ends meet. For 10 years the Brinkers struggle along, hoping for some improvement in Raff's condition. Raff's daughter, Gretel, has to leave school and work tending geese, while his son, Hans, takes on a variety of odd jobs and tries his best to take his father's place. The family suffers not only from real poverty but from social rejection by many of their neighbors.

The part of the Brinker story that most grips young readers tells of the coming-of-age of the Brinker children, Gretel and Hans. When the novel begins, she is 12 and he is 15. It is time for them to begin to take an active role in determining the direction in which their lives will go. Hans decides, against his mother's advice, to seek further medical help for the father he has been told is a hopeless case. Gretel faces her very mixed feelings toward her father, the pain of being a social outcast, and her own deep desire to achieve, and she begins to dream of winning the skating race that has caught the imagination of all the young people in Broek. Hans's generosity and self-sacrifice impress Dr. Boekman, who is persuaded to treat Raff's head injury. Once cured, Raff remembers where he hid the family fortune and—conveniently—is able to deliver the message Laurens Boekman had left for his father 10 years before. Because Gretel has had the courage to reach out for what she wants, Dr. Boekman can be reunited with his son, whose address is inscribed on the case of the silver skates she wins.

Hans Brinker may be experienced by young readers as a relatively accessible and unthreatening text. But Dodge's interest in themes of doubleness and the divided self and her refusal to underrate the risks and real costs of interpersonal commitment lend the novel a subversive moral ambiguity. Dodge does not ignore the dark side of the

Dodge's lifelong concern with the shaping role of imagination and play in the moral and social development of children led her to create in her novels—as she did in *St. Nicholas Magazine*—what she called a "pleasure-ground," in which problems of growth and maturation could be explored in terms of quests to be undertaken, games to be played, races to be won, and puzzles and mysteries to be solved. Dodge used these ritual contests to symbolize the hazardous process of growing up—a process requiring that children disengage themselves from their parents, achieve a certain self-realization, establish new relationships with their peers, and integrate themselves within the larger society.

There comes a moment when children ready to assume the freedom that goes with adult responsibility must begin to see their parents' protective attitudes as constricting and oppressive. There is much that is painful for both children and parents in this situation, and it can be difficult to present to young readers whose experience of life is yet limited.

Dodge meets the needs of such readers in several imaginative and effective ways. The often sad and frightening story of the young Brinkers is contrasted with the experience of other children and their parents, whose stories are told in a more detached and stylized way. Dodge adopts a narrative style well calculated to appeal to her audience, psyche, but she handles potentially traumatic situations with sufficient detachment to make them bearable for young readers. Like many authors of the late nineteenth century, she uses literary doubles to explore the conflict laden emotional situation of growing up.

If Hans Brinker is a somewhat idealized caregiver whose choices are unfailingly noble and selfless, Gretel is a repository of many of the inadmissible feelings young people may have as they struggle to free themselves from the domination of even the most loving parents. Gretel is allowed to feel weakness, resentment, fear, anger, hatred of a father she thinks she should love, anxiety that she won't be able to achieve what others achieve, and a great deal of guilt. In exploring the responses of both the disciplined Hans and the more volatile and sensitive Gretel as they struggle through their inevitable rites of passage, Dodge gives her young readers the comfort of catharsis together with the consolation of a happy ending.

Dodge's third story concerns a whole group of young people from the Brinkers' hometown of Broek who, like Hans and Gretel, face the challenges of adolescent life but whose experience—viewed in a more detached way—can more readily demonstrate the causal connection between right action and its consequences demanded by the moral economy of the novel. These young people are from more fortunate families than the Brinkers. They include the wealthy Peter van Holp and Hilda van Gleck (who intervene significantly in the Brinker story), as well as the prosperous peasant girl Annie Bauman, stout Jacob Poot, handsome Carl Schummel, and the English boy, Benjamin Dobbs.

The novel begins with the two Brinker children playing ice tag on squeaky wooden skates, "clumsy pieces of wood narrowed and smoothed at their lower edge, and pierced with holes, through which were threaded strings of rawhide." Those rawhide strings can hurt, and the children can't skate for very long before the damp wooden skates begin to trip them up. As Hans and Gretel begin to make significant choices for themselves—Hans deciding to ask Dr. Boekman's help and Gretel setting her heart on winning the race—they acquire better skates and move more effectively among the peers who have rejected them. Young readers may not appreciate exactly why Hans makes a series of difficult, selfless choices, culminating in his decision to become a surgeon. But the cost of a life of service to others will be brought home to them, vividly, when Hans sells his skates to buy medicine for his father or lends a skate strap to Peter at a crucial moment in the race. And they will appreciate why Peter, the winner, feeling that Hans has won a moral victory of sorts, attempts to give him the silver skates Peter himself has won—a gesture Hans, of course, refuses.

Though Gretel is the best skater among the young girls of Broek, she shivers in a thin jacket and stumbles on homemade skates. But Gretel is empowered by Hilda van Gleck, who generously gives her a warm jacket and good skates, and invites her to compete in the great race. The effect of Hilda on Gretel's life is pointed up in a significant incident.

Closed out of the family discussions about the operation to be performed on her father, Gretel understands little of what is happening and looks on in terror as the doctor begins his work. She flees the cottage in tears, and when Hilda finds Gretel asleep outside in the cold, she shakes her awake and, by forcing her to move, saves her from freezing to death. Later, encouraged by Hilda, Gretel wins the race and is crowned "Queen of the Skaters."

It is not surprising to find, by the conclusion of the novel, that Gretel has begun to model her own life on that of the girl who has befriended her, becoming not only "the finest singer, the loveliest woman in Amsterdam," "the dearest sister ever known," "the brightest, sweetest little wife in Holland" but also a woman whose kindness to the poor makes the air "fill with blessings." Lest the reader forget the depths of despair from which Gretel rose to attain this full self-realization, however, the very last image in the book is an evocation of "a tiny form trembling and sobbing on the mound before the Brinker cottage," "the darling little girl who won the silver skates."

Peter and Hans are of an age, and, like Gretel, Peter serves as a double for Hans. Both boys are intelligent, generous, and brave, but Peter is a free agent, unconstrained by poverty and misfortune. In the middle of the novel the narrative of the Brinkers' story breaks off—for 21 chapters—while the reader is told in great detail of the skating trip taken by Peter and his friends to The Hague. Dodge uses this trip to introduce many stories from Dutch history that serve as parables to teach the virtues needed to survive in a dangerous world. But the events of the skating trip are also a kind of miniature quest in which "Captain Peter" proves his leadership and his heroism. Significantly, when Peter loses the travel money entrusted to him, it is Hans Brinker, skating to Leyden to find Dr. Boekman, who returns it and makes it possible for the trip to be finished. In turn, it is Peter who volunteers to complete Hans's mission so that he can return to help his mother and sister with the now-seriously-ill Raff Brinker.

The skating trip has often been seen by critics as "disruptive" to the story and essentially nothing more than a "travelogue" in which "every sight becomes an excuse for conversations in which accounts of historical events, noted personages in Dutch history, and significant aspects of Dutch culture are discussed in great detail." Aside from its other rhetorical and dramatic functions, however, the skating trip offers an opportunity for the young boys (and especially Hans's alter ego, Peter) to play out the familiar fairy-tale drama in which the young separate from the family, go out into the world, face and overcome symbolic obstacles to their growth, and achieve the wisdom necessary to their final happiness.

Unlike the overbearing Dr. Boekman, who failed to respect his son's need to find his own way in life, or the violent and unreasoning Raff Brinker, whose brutal moods threaten to destroy his family, the parents of Peter and his friends are warm, supportive figures who have encouraged their sons to skate to Leyden and have paid their travel expenses. Peter and the boys easily meet the dangers and challenges of their symbolic journey to autonomy, for in the fairy-tale world of the skating trip their every effort is blessed with providential good fortune.

The incidents of the journey test Peter's prudence, generosity, and courage, as he must deal with a lost purse, the sickness of a friend, and a murderous thief (perhaps suggestive of the dark side of his own father) who threatens the boys as they sleep. Having met these challenges and having been instructed in the brave and responsible traditions of his people, Peter is rewarded by being able to stay for two days at The Hague in the home of his sister and her husband, Mevrouw and Mynheer van Gend. The van Gends' home is described as "a royal resting place," and as Peter approaches it he is like "a knight, an adventurer, travel-soiled and weary, a Hop-o'-my Thumb grown large, a Fortunatus approaching the enchanted castle." A spell of quiet hangs over the house; the servants are described as genies, Peter's sister as a sleeping beauty, and her conservatory as a "Garden of Delight." Each boy has his heart's desire and is provided with a private room, a space of his own. "Every boy his own chrysalis" is their motto, suggesting that this stay at the van Gends will be an occasion for growth and transformation, the boys' well-earned rest a participation in the restorative magic of the place.

The young couple are idealized quasi-parental figures who can support, amuse, and entertain the boys without pressure or coercion. After a stay in their home, the boys are refreshed and ready to return to Broek. It is perhaps significant that their journey home is without untoward incident. They skate like champions and return in triumph. Far from being a distracting digression, the journey to The Hague is an effective device to bring home to the younger reader the essential message of *Hans Brinker:* that the adolescent crisis of separation from the family can, when negotiated successfully, lead to a reconciliation with the family that renders both parents and children capable of living a fuller life. . . .

Hans Brinker is in a sense a travel book, but it is also a piece of speculative fiction in which Holland offers an alternative moral landscape designed to make readers think critically about their own ethical world. The Dutch national character is presented as an ideal to which Americans might aspire. These passive-looking folk are described as braver than anyone else in their ability to achieve ultimate victory—not by being aggressive and warlike but through their patient, principled resistance to the oppressor and their unrelenting struggle against the angry waters of the sea. They are praised for their art, music, and literature; their intellectual and technical achievements; and their "important discoveries and inventions," "learning" and "science." But they are also notable for the industry and flair for business that has made them excel at commerce and for the curiosity and sense of adventure that have made them famous navigators. Their "promotion of education and public charities" and "the money and labor" they expend on public works are described as noble examples to the rest of the world. . . .

One of the best-loved set pieces in *Hans Brinker* is the fable about the little boy who saved Holland from a flood. The story is a simple but affecting one. A gentle, sunny-haired boy, son of a dykeman, comes home late and notices a leak in the dyke. The boy understands the danger at once and thrusts his finger in the hole. His first reaction is delight that he has stopped the "angry waters." But soon other feelings come: cold, dread, fear, numbness, pain. The boy prays for help and resolves—despite his terror and his feeling that he might not survive the night—to stay at his post until morning, when indeed help does come.

The story is imbedded in a chapter of the novel that raises the questions, Are people really brave and noble? and What is an appropriate response to semi-legendary stories of selfless heroism? The members of Peter's skating party discuss and debate these issues while they are skating "beside the Holland dyke" at Haarlem. The group includes an English boy, Benjamin Dobbs, to whom Dutch history, language, and culture are new and strange. Ben's little brother and sister, Robby and Jenny, have not visited Holland, but by a feat of authorial sleight of hand, Dodge arranges matters so that at the very moment Ben is skating through Haarlem, Robby and Jenny, back in England, stand "ready to join in the duties of their reading class," which is about to read the story of the little Dutch hero. The children in the English schoolroom are required to roar out "at schoolroom pitch" "Lesson 62. THE HERO OF HAARLEM." Jenny Dobbs takes her turn in reading the story aloud, and as the hero's situation becomes more painful and dangerous, her voice begins to falter with emotion. She is told by a stern and unsympathetic schoolmaster, "[If] you cannot control your feelings so as to read distinctly, we will wait until you recover yourself."

Jenny's unquestioning belief in the possibility of human nobility and her emotional response to the story of the little hero of Haarlem are confirmed as appropriate in a conversation the skaters have (coincidentally, at the same moment the children in England are reading the tale). Ben says he has heard the story before but only now realizes it is true. Lambert insists it is known to be true all over Holland, and reaffirms the lesson of the piece by adding, "[T]hat little boy represents the spirit of the whole country. Not a leak can show itself anywhere either in its politics, honor, or public safety, that a million fingers are not ready to stop it at any cost."

The little hero of Haarlem is in essence very like Hans and Peter, and his story is so perfectly adapted to Dodge's purpose that it might easily be supposed she created it herself. But though the story has been attributed to Dodge by scholars it is not original. In 1855 Beeton's *Boy's Own Magazine* presented a story called "The Little Dutch Hero" that, paragraph for paragraph and sometimes phrase for phrase, tells the same story. No author is listed for this version, which predates Dodge's by 10 years. But in 1871 there appeared in *Old Merry's Annual* a similar piece, called "The Little Dykeman," said to be translated from the French of Madame Eugénie Foa. It would seem likely, from a comparative reading, that the

Boy's Own Magazine version and the Dodge version stem from the same original source as "The Little Dykeman."

Dodge never discussed the provenance of this little story, perhaps because she believed it to be in the public domain, as were the historical anecdotes she retold. Its appearance in a school reader within the text and the insistence on its historicity by the Dutch characters in the story suggest Dodge was not trying to claim any special originality for it. What is original, however, is the way she uses it. Within the novel many exemplary stories are presented to model audiences of varied ages, backgrounds, and experiences. The privileged older boys of the skating party hear (and debate) stories from Motley that teach them what they need to know: what it means to be good, brave, and dutiful. Hans and Gretel, who already possess these virtues and who need hope, hear instead the legend of St. Nicholas, giver of second chances at life, of largesse and of happy endings. Ben's little brother and sister read a story that reduces the heroic tales from Motley to childsize, for they—and the youngest readers of Dodge's novel, who will identify with them—need to know that they, too, can in their everyday life be brave—like its nameless young hero.

The courage needed by ordinary children to meet the challenges of ordinary life is a recurrent theme in Dodge's work. Dodge felt that children's fiction should cultivate the child's imagination, should give pleasure, and should stimulate ambition, but she also believed that it should prepare children for life as it is. And life, as Dodge had come to know through tragic personal experience, is not always easy. The happy ending of **Hans Brinker** is bitterly hard won, and many of her characters sustain real—and irrevocable—losses.

The full title of Dodge's novel, **Hans Brinker; or, The Silver Skates,** epitomizes the ambiguity of the experience Dodge explores in it. The adolescent quest for independence and self-realization can be painful. Hans does not win the silver skates but sacrifices his chance in much the same way he has sacrificed many opportunities to practice for the race. And Gretel's victory is hard won, the symbolic reward of a difficult inner journey toward maturity and reconciliation with her father. Yet, without denying the reality of pain and loss in the lives of her protagonists, Dodge suggests that the adolescent struggle for autonomy can be successfully achieved and can bring precious rewards. She supplements the Brinker's story with illustrative and symbolic elements that clarify the meaning of their struggle and bring home effectively to the younger reader that personal myth of endurance rewarded by victory which is her essential message.

RHYMES AND JINGLES (1874; new edition, 1904)

The Nation

SOURCE: A review of *Rhymes and Jingles,* in *The Nation,* Vol. 19, No. 492, December 3, 1874, p. 369.

Parents will have only to read a short way into **Rhymes and Jingles** to want it, and to read it all through to determine to keep it as a volume of unequalled entertainment for small fry if scarcely less for themselves. It is full of comical wise nonsense and the most felicitous absurdities of language. It can speak best for itself in the following extracts taken at random; for almost everything is good, and only a few out of the 270 pages really inferior or commonplace.

> Baby Nell had ten little toes,
> Baby Nell had two little hose,
> She always stared when the hose went on,
> And thought her ten little toes were gone.

The verses to a picture of a very new duckling looking at a broken egg-shell, though a trifle disrespectful, will also bear quoting:

> Well, I'm out after all!
>   And I'll say, on my word,
> That's a pretty mean house
>   For a duck of a bird!
> Why, I couldn't stand up,
>   And I couldn't sit down,
> But I lay in a cramp
>   From my toes to my crown.
> My good mammy and dad
>   May have thought me a spoon,
> But they'll not get me back
>   In that thing very soon.

The Dial

SOURCE: A review of *Rhymes and Jingles,* in *The Dial,* Vol. 37, No. 444, December 16, 1904, p. 432.

There is not much poetry, as distinguished from mere jingle, among the children's books this year, but the little that there is deserves prominent mention. Mrs. Mary Mapes Dodge has prepared a new and enlarged edition of her **Rhymes and Jingles,** known to younger readers for thirty years past. The pieces newly included show no trace of their author's more than three score years, but are as fresh and youthful as their predecessors of a long generation ago. The book has been beautifully illustrated and decorated by Miss Sarah S. Stilwell.

THEOPHILUS AND OTHERS (1876)

The Nation

SOURCE: A review of Theophilus and Others, in *The Nation,* Vol. 123, No. 594, November 16, 1876, p. 304.

Mrs. Dodge's **Theophilus and Others** is not fairly a novel; it is a collection of short sketches, and it is, by far the most amusing book of our whole list. It is full of humor, and, although there are at times signs of watering the jokes, there is hardly one of the sketches which is not entertaining. The first and longest one, **'Dobbs's Horse,'** is a fair sample of Mrs. Dodge's humor in its derision of the seeker after pleasure in the country. But perhaps the best is 'Miss Malony on the Chinese Question,' which first appeared, if we are not mistaken, in *St. Nicholas.* 'Our Debating Society Skeleton' also shows how a good story can be well told. The book is not one of great importance, and the humor is of an irresponsible kind which does not strike very deep, but it is always innocent and agreeable.

The Spectator

SOURCE: A review of *Theophilus and Others,* in *The Spectator,* Vol. 50, No. 2532, January 6, 1877, p. 23.

One of those clever books of essays which we now get so frequently from the other side of the Atlantic,—essays about husbands, about "helps," and about things in general, we may almost say. They are always sensible, and almost always bright and amusing, sometimes, when the writer chooses to work that vein, not a little pathetic. Such, for instance, is the story of the brave old seamstress, who is cheered under the load of many sorrows by Adelaide Proctor's beautiful little poem, "One by One." But the humorous is the more common kind. Such is the first essay in the volume, an adventure in horse-buying, "Dobbs's Horse;" and such, too, the last, "United Ages." Who has not been provoked by those idiotic paragraphs with which the *Times* occasionally fills up a corner about the "united ages" of old ladies and gentlemen whose names have appeared in the obituary of the day before?

ALONG THE WAY (1879; revised edition published as *Verses*, 1904)

The Nation

SOURCE: A review of *Along the Way* in *The Nation,* Vol. 30, No. 757, January 1, 1880, p. 15.

Mrs. Mary Mapes Dodge has made a book of a number of her poems that have already appeared in various magazines, supplemented by enough that are now for the first time published to make a little volume of 135 pages, called *Along the Way.* They are of a "homely" character, it may be said, if by that somewhat vague term be understood that which is not only domestic, but in any way familiar, intimate, sensible, and, though not wholly superficial, at least the reverse of recondite. Some of them recount little incidents of a pathetic or other nature, such as that entitled "Motherless," in which his little girl first brings the tears to her father's eyes by allusion to her dead mother, and then kisses them dry with many childish endearments— an incident which, if told in rhythm, cannot but be touching however ill done, and here it is well done. Others are short poems on such subjects as "Faith," "Trust," "Death in Life," "Long Ago," "Once Before," the character of which will not be inferred amiss from the several titles. Each was undoubtedly the result of a genuine impulse, is entirely straightforward and unaffected, and displays a good ear and practised hand at rhyme and metre.

THE LAND OF PLUCK: STORIES AND SKETCHES FOR YOUNG FOLK (1894)

The Nation

SOURCE: A review of *The Land of Pluck: Stories and Sketches for Young Folk,* in *The Nation,* Vol. 59, No. 1534, November 22, 1894, p. 387.

The Land of Pluck is the apt name which Mrs. Mary Mapes Dodge has given to Holland: and the chapters on Dutch life and Dutch history which appeared some time ago in *St. Nicholas* make up the first part of the book so entitled. They are written in the bright, entertaining style which Mrs. Dodge always commands, and are well fitted to rouse an interest in the manners and history of this admirable people. In the second part of the book are gathered a number of short stories of all sorts. Perhaps the most amusing of these is **"A Garret Adventure,"** in which some good, obedient children *thought* they had their mother's permission to make a skating-pond by freezing water on the garret floor. Naturally, the pond refused to "stay put" long enough to freeze, and its appearance below stairs surprised no one more than the mother.

The Dial

SOURCE: A review of *The Land of Pluck: Stories and Sketches for Young Folk,* in *The Dial,* No. 17, No. 203, December 1, 1894, p. 340.

Of books about foreign countries, *The Land of Pluck,* in its dress of "Dutch pink," is one of the most attractive. An idea of life in Holland, and of the determination and patience of that brave little country, is given with much picturesqueness, and with that simplicity of style which contributes so greatly to the success of its author, Mrs. Mary Mapes Dodge, in writing for children. The text is ably supported by the pictures, which, in addition to several by Mr. George Wharton Edwards, number several reproductions of the old Dutch masters, chiefly pictures of children. The series of Dutch sketches is an amplified form of an article which appeared in *St. Nicholas* some years ago; but the short stories that make up the second part of the volume, though not entirely new, have never before been published in book form. They are very sweet and wholesome in tone, in every way suitable for children.

WHEN LIFE IS YOUNG: A COLLECTION OF VERSE FOR BOYS AND GIRLS (1894)

The Dial

SOURCE: A review of *When Life Is Young: A Collection of Verse for Boys and Girls,* in *The Dial,* Vol. 17, No. 204, December 16, 1894, pp. 389-90.

Very little boys and girls will enjoy with equal relish the text and pictures in Mrs. Dodge's collection of rhymes and jingles, *When Life Is Young.* Some of them have already appeared in *St. Nicholas,* but they bear repetition, as they are full of humor and sweetness, and are now collected in a dainty and serviceable form.

The Nation

SOURCE: A review of *When Life Is Young: A Collection of Verse for Boys and Girls,* in *The Nation,* Vol. 59, No. 1538, December 20, 1894, p. 469.

Mrs. Dodge . . . send[s] forth [a] volume. . . for children. . . —*When Life Is Young: A Collection of Verse for Boys and Girls.* . . . Mrs. Dodge is the natural singer for children, trained and developed. . . by long practice. . . . [O]pen *When Life Is Young* wherever you will, the reader's life becomes young also, and the most hardened critic looks round for some child to whom to impart the cheery lay.

Additional coverage of Dodge's life and career is contained in the following sources published by The Gale Group: *Contemporary Authors,* **Vols. 109, 137;** *Dictionary of Literary Biography,* **Vols. 42, 79;** *Dictionary of Literary Biography Documentary Series,* **Vol. 13;** *Major Authors and Illustrators for Children and Young Adults;* **and** *Something about the Author,* **Vols.**

Ernest J(ames) Gaines

1933-

American author of fiction.

Major works include *Catherine Carmier* (1964), *Bloodline* (1968), *The Autobiography of Miss Jane Pittman* (1971), *A Gathering of Old Men* (1983), *A Lesson before Dying* (1993).

INTRODUCTION

Gaines, one of the most prominent contemporary adult writers also read widely by young adults, is best known for bringing to life the history, culture, and people of the South. A distinguishing feature of much of his work is the victimization of the poor and what Craig W. Barrow describes in *Twentieth Century Young Adult Writers* as the "constant struggle [that] exists between the demands of survival and the desire for dignity and self-respect." Gaines draws upon his deeply rooted experiences and storytelling traditions from his childhood in Louisiana to develop the setting for much of his work. He is praised for his convincing and authentic characterization and powerful themes with narratives that cut through and expose the rural life of the South. In all of his works, Gaines shows the strength and dignity of his black characters in the face of numerous struggles such as racism, the breakdown of relationships due to social pressures, and the conflict between traditions and the radical measures needed to bring about social change.

Critics have found Gaines's fiction to be subtle, realistic, and convincing. Larry McMurtry commented that "it is the force of Mr. Gaines's character and intelligence, operating through this deceptively quiet style, that makes his fiction compelling." Melvin Maddocks called Gaines "a patient artist," adding, "Gaines sets down a story as if he were planting, spreading the roots deep, wide and firm. His stories grow organically, at their own rhythm. When they ripen at last, they do so inevitably, arriving at a climax with the absolute rightness of a folk tale." Gaines has said that he sees no end to the inspiration he finds in his Louisiana heritage, and he likely will continue to write about the American South. "Before Alex Haley called it *Roots*, I was trying to do something like that, to write about our past, where we come from," Gaines told Mary Ellen Doyle in *Melus*. He further explained, "I'm trying to write about a people I feel are worth writing about, to make the world aware of them, make them aware of themselves." In addition, the author revealed that "my aim in literature is to develop character, not only the character in the book, but my character as well as yours, so that if you pick up the book, you will see something you feel is true, something not seen before, that will help develop your character from that day forward."

Biographical Information

Gaines was born on a sugar cane plantation in Louisiana. He began contributing to his family's welfare at the early age of nine by working in the fields digging potatoes. Gaines has said that his happiest times were spent with his great-aunt Augusteen Jefferson, who cared for him and his siblings despite her disability. "Anytime someone asks me who had the greatest influence on me as an artist or a man, I say she had," Gaines said in an *Essence* interview. She later became the inspiration for the title character for his best known novel, *The Autobiography of Miss Jane Pittman*. Gaines's family worked hard to escape the poverty of the Great Depression. They moved to Vallejo, California, when Gaines was fifteen, where he spent much of his time in the library looking for books about the South and his heritage. The library opened up a whole new world for Gaines—he had not visited a library in Louisiana since libraries were off-limits to African Americans living in the South. He was fascinated with the various works of Chekhov, Turgenev, and Gogol.

Gaines began his college education at the Vallejo Junior College in California and soon thereafter he joined the army. This did not deter him from his passion for literature. While in the army, he read widely and began writing. He used the works of Russian novelists Ivan Turgenev and Leo Tolstoy to help give him inspiration and teach him how to write about the people he knew and cared about. Before graduating from San Francisco State College with a Bachelor of Arts degree in 1957, Gaines had published his first story which won him a creative writing fellowship to Stanford University where he did his graduate work. While completing his graduate studies, he found a literary agent on the advice of a critic and began work on his first novel *Catherine Carmier,* which was published in 1964.

Major Works

Gaines's first novel, *Catherine Carmier,* was not a critical or financial success. "[It] took me five years to finish and gave me a lot of trouble," Gaines told Bernard Magnier of the *UNESCO Courier,* "But all the time I was learning how to write." The novel is about a young man, Jackson Bradley, who returns to his Southern home town from California to find himself changed. His education has alienated him from his rural community and his heritage. Jackson struggles with the thought of leaving due to the love he has for Catherine, a black Creole woman. Catherine is torn between her love for Jackson and her deep love and loyalty to her father Raoul, who has forbidden his daughter from seeing Jackson because he is not of Creole heritage. Gaines spends much time with Catherine's fluctuating loyalties and Jackson's uncertainty about their future. They see each other in private without her father's knowing until Jackson and Raoul eventually confront each other in a fistfight. Although Jackson defeats Raoul, he must continue to wait for Catherine as she insists that she must nurse her father back to health. The ending is ambiguous; as Keith Byerman noted in the *Concise Dictionary of American Literary Biography:* "The reader is left in a state of uncertainty. . . . Either [Jackson] has lost Catherine or, the deepest irony, he has succeeded in his quest, but at the price of his freedom."

Bloodline is a collection of five stories. Each takes place on a single day in Louisiana and examines the relationships between the younger and older generations. *Bloodline* begins with "A Long Day in November," which was also published separately as a children's book in 1971. The story is narrated by a six-year-old boy named Sonny who is describing the day-long conflict between his father and mother. The center of their argument revolves around his mother's feeling that his father loves his car more than his family—his mother ends up leaving and his father spends the day searching for a way to win her back. Sonny narrates the tale of his difficult day, which includes an embarrassing incident at school. In "The Sky is Gray" an eight year old learns about the social rules of race relations and personal integrity. The final story, "Just Like a Tree," tells the story of Aunt Fe who is moving from her home because she fears retribution from whites, who have been bombing black homes, due to her grand-nephew's involvement in the civil rights movement. She is visited by family and friends the night before she is to leave, and the story is narrated by these visitors. Before the night is over, however, Aunt Fe dies. In the *Concise Dictionary of American Literary Biography,* Keith Byerman commented "[Aunt Fe's] death, which seems willed, signifies that life for her is sustained by a time, place, and community that contain the richness of her experience. To leave all of that is to die spiritually, and for her physical life is nothing without the spirit."

The Autobiography of Miss Jane Pittman is described in Jack Hicks's *In the Singer's Temple: Prose Fictions of Barthelme, Gaines, Brautigan, Piercy, Kesey, and Kosinski* as "fiction masquerading as autobiography, but mostly, it is a powerful folk history of Afro-American life from the Civil War to the mid-1960s." Miss Jane, the 110-year-old former slave who is the title character, was inspired by Gaines's beloved aunt Augusteen. In recollections taped by a historian, Miss Jane tells of the arrival of Union troops to her home, her trip to the North and her emancipation, her marriage, the adoption of the orphan Ned, Ned's return home after being educated in the north, his assassination for challenging white racism, and her experiences in the modern civil rights movement. These experiences, according to Gaines, echo the history of African Americans in the South. Gaines tells the his tale in a restrained manner and keeps the story fresh and interesting. Jerry H. Bryant commented in the *Iowa Review,* "in other novels dealing with blacks in an oppressive white society, Jane's resigned decision to stay in Louisiana would be the signal for either the pessimistic ending of the story, or the beginning of a detailed account of further outrages committed against the black by the white. . . . The absence of this familiar note in Jane's narrative is one of the things that make *The Autobiography* such a milestone in American fiction." The novel became a highly successful television movie in 1974.

Gaines continued to write about the theme of racism in *A Gathering of Old Men.* In this novel, Gaines tells the story of a Cajun work boss, Beau Boutan, who is found shot in the yard of Mathu, one of the black plantation workers. Mathu is accused of the murder due to his history of confrontations with the Boutan family. However, as Sheriff Mapes finds when he arrives at the scene, the case is not as clear cut as expected. Nineteen elderly black men and a young white woman, Candy Marshall, all claim responsibility for the murder in an attempt to foil the lynch mob. Candy's purpose for confession is to protect the old man who essentially raised her. With multiple confessions, Sheriff Mapes is compelled to listen to each story which serves as the emotional center for the novel. One of the strengths of the book, according to Penny Parker, is that the reader is brought into the story through the minds of the characters "without losing interest in the events, nor even suspecting what will occur." Keith E. Byerman in the *Concise Dictionary of American Literary Biography* explains the psychological impact of the confessions of the old men by saying that they "serve as ritual purgings of all the hostility and self-hatred built up over the years," adding that, "through their stories they face their self-hatred and enter, at least metaphorically, their manhood."

A Lesson before Dying tells the story of a black field worker named Jefferson who is an unwitting participant in and the only survivor of a robbery of a white grocery store owner. Jefferson, who panics, takes the cash from the register, and leaves the store as two white men enter and see him, is arrested and charged as a co-conspirator in the robbery and sent to trial for murder. Despite his defense attorney's claims that executing Jefferson for the murder would be inhumane, since it would be tantamount to killing a "hog," he is condemned to death. Outraged by the portrayal of her godson as an animal, Miss Emma convinces Grant Wiggin's, a schoolteacher, to prepare Jefferson to die like a man. Although reluctant to do so, Wiggins inspires Jefferson to succeed by writing his thoughts in a journal. Charles L. Larson noted, "More than any other novel about African American life in the United States, *A Lesson Before Dying* is about standing tall and being a man in the face of overwhelming adversity. And, equally important, Gaines's masterpiece is about what Ralph Ellison and William Faulkner would call the morality of connectedness, of each individual's responsibility to his community, to the brotherhood beyond his self. This majestic, moving novel is an instant classic, a book that will be read, discussed and taught beyond the rest of our lives."

Awards

Gaines has received many awards. *The Autobiography of Miss Jane Pittman* won the Commonwealth Club of California fiction gold medal and the Louisiana Literature Award from the Louisiana Library Association, both in 1972. *A Gathering of Old Men* received the Commonwealth Club of California fiction gold medal in 1984. *A Lesson before Dying* received the National Book Critics Circle Award for fiction in 1994. In 1999, Gaines received an Honorary degree of Doctor of Letters from the University of Miami for his important contribution to American literature.

AUTHOR'S COMMENTARY

Ruth Laney

SOURCE: "A Conversation with Ernest Gaines," in *The Southern Review*, Vol. X, No. 1, January, 1974, pp. 1-14.

LANEY: Your moving introduction to ***The Autobiography of Miss Jane Pittman*** reads in part, "to the memory of my beloved aunt, Miss Augusteen Jefferson, who did not walk a day in her life but who taught me the importance of standing." Could you tell me something about her?

GAINES: She was my great-aunt, and she never walked a day in her life. She'd crawl over the floor as a child six or seven months old might crawl over the floor. But her arms were very strong. She'd cook for us—we'd bring the things to the stove for her and set it on a little table in front of her, and she'd mix the things up. She could make bread, bake our bread—we had the old wood stoves then. She could wash our clothes: she sat on a bench and leaned over the tub and used the washboard, you know those old tin things. She could sew our clothes. She used to use the sewing machine. She could not use her feet, but she could use her hands—how she ever did this I really don't know. You know those old things with the pedal down here—she would reach down and do this with her hands, because there was no other way to run it. It was one of these old machines, probably one of the oldest ones. I wish I knew where it was today—if I could find it, I'd keep it forever. Besides that, she used to go into the little garden to work among her vegetables. She'd crawl over the floor, out of the house, down the steps into the yard, into the garden. Other times, she would crawl into our back yard to pick up pecans.

LANEY: She must have been a courageous woman.

GAINES: Well, this is the kind of courage that I tried to give Miss Jane in the book. Many of my characters have tremendous courage and I think it is basically because of her. She never felt sorry for herself a day in her life. I never heard her complaining about her problems. And as a result nobody felt sorry for her.

LANEY: When you were growing up in Louisiana did you ever think about writing?

GAINES: Oh, yes. When I was about twelve or thirteen, I put on a little play in church, and I'd act as writer and director and make-up man and everything else. It was really a lot of fun doing. Miss Jane talks about Jimmy doing that once, he puts on this play and everybody laughs. She talks about that just after he gets religion. They want him to be a minister or something, and he doesn't want to, but he puts on this play and entertains everybody for one night. That happened, I did that.

LANEY: Did you go through the experience of "getting religion" as Jimmy does in ***Miss Jane Pittman?***

GAINES: Yes, I went through all that. You've seen these baptisms, haven't you, where you have to go through all of that before you get dumped in the water? It was in False River, I was baptized in False River. I think now they might use a lake or something; some of them are such high-class they have the things in churches now, you know. But mine was in the river. I was about twelve.

LANEY: Were you reading many books at this time in your life?

GAINES: No, I was not reading. I doubt that I read two novels before I went to California. But I come from a long line of storytellers. I come from a plantation, where people told stories by the fireplace at night, people told stories on the ditch bank—especially this time of year, when you have the sugar cane shuck that you can burn, mix it with some firewood. People sat around telling stories. I think in my immediate family there were tremendous storytellers or liars or whatever you want to call them. My aunt was not a storyteller, she was more of a recorder; she could tell about what happened in the past. She remembered quite well. Since Auntie could not go to their place, the old people used to come to ours. They would talk and talk and talk, and I listened to them. *Miss Jane Pittman,* before it became an autobiography of Miss Jane Pittman, was a short biography of Miss Jane Pittman—that is, a group of people telling about her. Because originally she had just died and they'd come together at someone's house, much like my aunt's. They would do the same thing now. Say there was a funeral today, or a wedding, the old people would sort of gather in a little room and they would talk about things, you know. They might start with the wedding, or they might start with that particular funeral, but by the time they end up, they've talked about everything that happened the last twenty years.

LANEY: You moved to California when you were fifteen. How did that come about?

GAINES: My stepfather was in the Merchant Marine, and my mother followed him to California. I had finished the little eighth grade school, and I did not have any high school that they wanted to send me to nearby. I did not have close enough relatives in the town with whom I could stay. So I went to California. I flagged down a Trailways bus. You know, you take out your handkerchief and stand on the river and wave it down and get on it. I went as far as New Orleans by bus and caught a train out of New Orleans and went on to a place called Crockett, California, just across the Bay from Vallejo. That's where we were living at the time, Vallejo—it's about thirty miles out of San Francisco. We lived in the projects, a government project, and I had a lot of friends there. There was a mixture in the projects at that time of whites, blacks, Chicanos, Filipinos, Japanese, Chinese. So things were okay for a while. But then we moved from there to downtown Vallejo and I got caught up with some pretty rough guys. And my stepfather told me, none of that. These guys would go into movies without paying, or pick up comic books, or just stand on the corner and make noise—as any boys would do. But my stepfather didn't want me to be part of it. He was a very strict person with me. Very strong. A very handsome man, a big man. Most of my strong characters, I think, are built around him. When I first left here, I was lonely for my friends, my family. Then my stepfather in Vallejo told me to get off the block, get off the street, you know, and do something else. I went into the library in Vallejo and started reading—I read a lot. But I wanted to read about the South, and I wanted to read about the *rural* South. But at that time you had very few people writing anything that was in any way complimentary about blacks or the rural South. So I decided to write a novel myself. I wrote it in one summer, the summer

I was sixteen. (*Laughs*) It was probably the worst novel, the worst number of pages that anyone could possibly call a novel. I'm sure it was. I sent it to a publisher in New York and they sent it right back. I knew nothing though. I had not read anything, I had not had any kind of help or any kind of direction toward the proper way of reading. I had nothing like that.

LANEY: Did you talk to anyone about it?

GAINES: Oh, I think my mother, or my stepfather when he'd come in from the sea. But he thought I was crazy because I was spending like twelve, thirteen, maybe fifteen hours a day doing that. I first wrote the whole thing out in longhand, then I got a typewriter—one finger here, one finger there. At any rate, I went through high school and then junior college, and then I did not have a penny in the world to finish college. Junior college was free if you lived in the town—Vallejo—but it was not top education, just an extension of high school, really. Then I was drafted and spent two years in the army. When I came out, I got the G.I. bill, $110 a month. I finished college in that way. And that's when I really got into studying writing. When I came out of the army, I moved to San Francisco and went to San Francisco State, and graduated in two years. And I worked a year after that. And then I got a fellowship to Stanford, and that's about the education I've had.

LANEY: The fellowship was the Wallace Stegner award?

GAINES: Yes. I was at State from '55 to '57, and I wrote some stories while I was at San Francisco State College which were published in the college magazine. I had heard about the creative writing fellowship at Stanford, so when I got out in '57 I went to work for one year. While I was working, I submitted the two stories that I had written at State, plus another one. I think you had to submit three stories or part of a novel, something like that. So I wrote another story and submitted those three stories to Stanford and I heard that I'd won a fellowship.

LANEY: You mentioned at the lecture you gave yesterday that you had based your first novel, *Catherine Carmier,* on *Fathers and Sons.* When did you discover Turgenev?

GAINES: I discovered Turgenev at State. I mentioned that I had been trying to find books about the South. Then I began to read anybody who would write about the earth—Steinbeck, Willa Cather. For some reason, reading these writers led me into discovering the writers of other countries who wrote about the same sort of thing. I think in this way I discovered Turgenev's *A Sportsman's Sketches.* That was about hunting and meeting people in rural life. And then, the clarity and the beauty of his writing, even in translation. Then I discovered *Fathers and Sons.* It was a simple, small book—I know I could never write a big book. And this small book had just about everything that a small book can have. And, too, at the time I discovered Turgenev I could almost see myself in Bazarov's position, you know? When you go back, *what?* Not that I'd become a nihilist, but I could understand the nihilistic attitude after someone had been away awhile. But I think the major thing I liked about him was the structure of his small novels. My *Catherine Carmier* is almost written on the structure of *Fathers and Sons*. As a matter of fact, that was my Bible. I used it on my desk every day. It was the same novel I had written when I was sixteen in the library that summer. I started writing it again when I was at Stanford. This time it took me five years because I did not know how to really write.

LANEY: Did you ever have times during this period when you felt you'd never be any good at all, you might as well give up?

GAINES: Yes, yes. But then I'd feel, I can't do anything else, I don't want to do anything else with my life. I mean, right now I don't know what I would do—I'd probably be teaching. And I would hate to teach because I couldn't do anything else. If I were to teach, I'd want to teach simply because this is what I want more than anything else, you know? When I graduated from State in '57, I gave myself ten years. I said, in ten years I must be a writer or I don't know what else I'll do with my life. I didn't know what I'd do—become a farmer? *Catherine Carmier* was published seven years after I made this decision, it was published in '64, but nobody ever heard of the book, nobody ever read it. But exactly ten years later, in '67, I published *Of Love and Dust,* which was rather successful; it began to get some notice. And during that time I published three stories, **"A Long Day in November," "Just Like a Tree,"** and **"The Sky is Gray."** I had published these stories by the time my second novel came out. Then I published the collection of stories, *Bloodline.* I always knew my stories were better than anything else I had written. When *Of Love and Dust* was published I told the publishing house, give me a two-book contract because these stories are going to make it for me. They might not make money, but they will make my name. So they gave me a two-book contract. And they have been successful. **"The Sky is Gray"** has been anthologized twelve to fifteen times. . . .

LANEY: Do you ever start thinking a lot about a character and let a story evolve from the character?

GAINES: Not really. *The Autobiography of Miss Jane Pittman* was supposed to be just a series of conversations after Miss Jane has died. But those conversations would have had a wide range of many subjects, and Miss Jane would have been just part of it, to give it some kind of order. The book was not begun as a book about just a single person, a character. But the events around her life and her interpretation of them is what I wanted— a folk autobiography.

LANEY: I'm interested in how you feel about the character Tee Bob in the *Autobiography,* as the white man who falls in love with a black woman.

GAINES: I've always considered Tee Bob as being one of the men in Miss Jane's life. Whenever they talk about the

men in her life, they would mention Ned, of course, Joe Pittman, and Jimmy—the three. And very seldom did they mention Tee Bob, but I think Tee Bob is very, very important as one of the men in her life. I'm very sympathetic toward Tee Bob, as that innocent person caught up in something he has no control over. His problem and Mary Agnes Le Fabre's problem are no worse than, say, Miss Jane's problem and the old man—what's his name, Tee Bob's *parrain*—Jules Raynard—in that, I'm pretty sure if Miss Jane were white, she and Jules Raynard would be much closer than just two older people who sat back in the kitchen. They might live together, you know, they might be—not lovers, but people so close that they would depend on each other all their lives. Tee Bob was a victim. He had no strength, he was not tough and hard. He *loved,* you know, but hell, you just can't make it on love. You got to be able to do other things. . . .

[W]hen I first started writing, one of the things that impressed me most about *Fathers and Sons* was Bazarov's feeling toward things. But I think I'm a mixture of all these things. I cannot write only about Miss Jane and man surviving. And I cannot write only about man failing. I write about both. I try to write about both of them. I don't know exactly what my philosophy is. My only philosophy is to write truly, as well as I can, for as long as I can, and about things that I care about. And of course I care about people, their failures, and their accomplishments. My philosophy, in a way, is that you must stand individually in order to stand with the crowd. Or in order to be able to lead, you must be an individual. I like Miss Jane because she's small, she has fantastic courage, and she is an individual. She's not orthodox religious at all—she'd rather listen to a baseball game any day. Well, she'd go to church, but not when the Giants are playing the Dodgers, you know. She isn't going to church; she'll stay home and listen. But I can understand the guys who fail and the guys who doubt. But there's no change in philosophy, no change in philosophy at all.

LANEY: Could you tell me a little about your new book?

GAINES: I don't like talking about anything that I'm working on. But it's called *In My Father's House.* The old proverbial battle between father and son. A theme I play around with in almost everything I write. In the case of the black man, he and his son were separated in slavery and they have been trying to reach each other since then. That is the central theme in this particular book. It's a novel, and it takes place in Louisiana. Everything—all of my work—takes place in Louisiana.

LANEY: Have you ever written any nonfiction?

GAINES: No, no. I write little talks, now and then, to give to a class. I don't have that talent and, as of right now, I don't have the interest in that sort of thing. As long as I can make it in fiction, as long as there's something that I feel is truly worthwhile to write about, as long as I feel that what I'm doing is honest work, I'm more concerned with fiction, the novel, and the short story.

LANEY: Many people tend to look up to artists as having some kind of inside track on things. Do you have any sort of precept or code that you try to live by?

GAINES: I keep writing these codes down, but I keep forgetting them. People are always asking me these things, and I keep forgetting. I just try to live well, I want to write and write honestly, as I've said. I want to be a man toward my family, toward my woman, toward my friends. I wish I could help some other children, black or white, become writers—and better writers than myself.

LANEY: What would you tell someone who came to you and said, I want to write?

GAINES: Well, first I'd tell him to do a lot of reading, a lot of reading and a lot of writing. And I'd try to prepare him in that I'd tell him that it's a very lonely job, terribly lonely job, he has to sacrifice much. If he's poor, he's gonna have much, much to sacrifice, and be hungry a long time. But if he really wants to write, there's nothing in the world I feel would be greater for him than to write. If that's what he wants. But I'll try to show him what he has to face. But the number one thing I'd tell him is to read as much as he can and especially read the classic things, the things that have stood so long. Those are things you must read. But then, you tell him, read other things, too, much of other things—everything. . . .

LANEY: Do you ever resent being lumped in a class with other black writers?

GAINES: Oh, no, no. I never take them seriously. They put me where they want. I know *Time* magazine and a couple of others have said that Ernie Gaines is the best, quote, black writer, unquote, in this country today. But that doesn't mean a thing in the world to me. Even if they said I was the best *writer* in this country today, it wouldn't mean anything. It wouldn't mean anything if everyone said it. I don't know who the top critic is in the country today, but if he said, "You're the best writer there is," it wouldn't mean anything to me. It would mean just that I gotta work harder the next day to maintain that top thing, which I don't believe in doing. I believe in doing my work as well as I can do it. Now, you can say I'm the worst writer. I think I feel good when people—just the average person—say, "I love that." I was down by the Parlanges', who own probably the oldest house in Louisiana, the house is over two hundred years old. On False River. I was there just yesterday. And Mr. Walter Parlange, Jr., who owns the place now, he and I were talking in the living room—one of the front rooms—and he was saying that—we're so proud that you come from this kind of background, and what you've done. And he said, I read that book, and Lucy, his wife, had read it. No, I think he said he read half and Lucy read half—and they talked about it. And he says, I really love that book. And I had met his mother when I was there at the place about a week earlier, and she had read it and she loved it. Now, for people like that to say this to me means so much. Or for people who don't read much, say like many of my people, to say I read that

and I liked it. That's what does make me feel much better. I mean, of course, you want the New York critics to say, this is it, you are that good. But if they say it, and your family and your friends say that it isn't anything—that hurts, that hurts. . . .

LANEY: How politically involved do you think a writer should be?

GAINES: Well, it depends on the writer, whoever he is. I'm very objective in these things—I don't know if that's the right word. I can be quite involved, but I'm not really totally involved in politics. But I can get quite moved by these things. There are certain governors and senators and a few other people I think should be shot tomorrow morning. But when it comes down to writing, I feel that it has to work into a form of art. Now, if you can go out and shoot everybody and make it a form of art, it's okay with me. But I think I have a lot of protest in, for example, the story **"Just Like a Tree."** After all, a woman dies because she is moved out of her home. It's nothing more than that. But she's uprooted. The bombings going on—well, you could go into a long, long dialogue about things like that. But I think one gets the message, one gets the *feeling* from it. And if I cannot move you by dramatizing a situation like that, then I'm not going to try to move you by all the rhetoric in the world. I just am not that kind of person.

LANEY: Do you feel, as a writer who does have influence, that you have a certain responsibility as far as ever taking a stand or using that influence to some social purpose?

GAINES: Well, people have been trying to make me do it, but I never thought about doing it. I feel that I'm going to write and write well, and I think if I write well and truly about, you know, the human condition, I think I'll leave the politicking to someone else. I'll say yes to certain things, and no to certain things, but as far as my writing, I'm gonna write what I want to write. Nobody's gonna tell me what to write. But there are some magazines that, because I don't take their particular stand, ignore me. . . .

LANEY: What is the thing in your life that you're proudest of?

GAINES: Being able to work, do my work—that I'm proud of. I think one of the greatest things that has happened to me, as a writer and as a human being, is that I was born in the South, that I was born in Louisiana. Because when I grew up on a plantation in the late thirties and the forties, I'm pretty sure it was not too much different from the way things could have been when my ancestors were in slavery. Oh, we could do a few little things more. But that I went through that kind of experience—there's a direct connection between the past and what is happening today. I'm very fortunate to have had that kind of background. I think that Louisiana's probably the most romantic and interesting of all southern states—the land, the language, the colors, the bayous, the fields—all these things together, the combination of all these things, I think, make it an extremely interesting place. If I were to come from any southern state, I think Louisiana is the one that I would choose. And I'm glad I came from here. I'm glad I came from here.

Paul Desruisseaux

SOURCE: "Ernest Gaines: A Conversation," in *The New York Times Book Review,* June 11, 1978, pp. 13, 44-5.

When prosperity came around the corner, Ernest Gaines moved two doors up the street. The success of his novel *The Autobiography of Miss Jane Pittman* changed the size of his living accommodations—from three rooms to six—but not their location. Mr. Gaines has lived in California since he was 15, and the last half of those 30 years has been spent on Divisadero Street in San Francisco.

"This is where I've done all my work," he says. "This is considered the ghetto, but most of the people here are just hard-working, middle-class folks. They'd be *embarrassed* if they ever saw a rat."

The living room of Mr. Gaines's second-floor flat overlooks the street. His office, however, is at the back of the house, where it's quieter and, with an only slightly obstructed view of downtown San Francisco and the bay, more scenic. The walls are papered with maps that stake out the author's personal geography: Louisiana, California, the United States and Africa. . . .

There are books in every room of this house, and there seem to be just as many records. Mr. Gaines says his writing has been influenced by music—jazz, blues, Negro spirituals and other kinds—almost as much as it has by literature. And this house always has music: when I arrive it's Rubinstein and Beethoven and, when I leave, B. B. King and the blues. . . .

Q. [Paul Desruisseaux] Where did the idea for *In My Father's House* come from?

A. [Ernest Gaines] In my books there always seem to be fathers and sons searching for each other. That's a theme I've worked with since I started writing. Even when the father was not in the story. I've dealt with his absence and its effects on his children. And that is the theme of this book.

It just seemed time—after five books—to write a book about that. And if I've failed, then I've failed; but it's something I've wanted to do for a long while, long before I did *The Autobiography of Miss Jane Pittman,* or even the *Bloodline* stories. It just happened that I didn't do it until now.

Q. It's your smallest book, but it took you longer to write than any other. Special problems?

A. I knew what I wanted to write; it was a question of bringing it off, a technical problem. Usually, once I develop

a character and "hear" his voice, I can let him tell the story. My writing is strongest when I do that. In most cases when my books are giving me a hard time I am not using *that* voice but my own, the omniscient narrator, the voice of God looking down on things. Which is what I did in this book. It was necessary because so much of the story is due to what Phillip Martin is thinking. He does not tell anyone what's on his mind, so it would have been almost impossible for another character to tell the story without it sounding false.

Q. To what would you liken the experience of writing a novel?

A. When I start writing a book I never know exactly all the things that will happen in it, but I know certain things. It's like taking a train to Louisiana: I know I'm going to go through Texas, and that I will arrive by a certain day, but I don't know how the weather is going to be, who will sit next to me, what the conductor's going to look like. These are the little details you don't know when you start writing. Of course, there are some *major* details you probably won't know either!

Q. Is writing a novel essentially coming up with a story?

A. Oh no, no. Content is probably only 40 percent of it, no more than 50 percent, as far as I'm concerned. If a book doesn't have *form,* then damn, it ain't no novel. We can go down the block right now and find a guy on the next corner who'll tell the biggest and truest story you can ever hear. Now, putting that story down on paper so that a million people can read, and feel, and hear it like you on that street corner, that's going to take form. That's *writing.*

Q. What do you look for in a novel?

A. I must find immediate action. I look for something going on right from the beginning. I believe what Poe said, that if you don't grab the reader right at the start, you've already lost him. It must touch me. Look at how Pushkin starts his novels; that's how novels should begin.

Q. What part of writing do you most enjoy?

A. When I deal with dialogue. Once I develop my characters I can hear their voices quite easily. Not that it's easy writing, but for me it's easier than writing straight narrative, or descriptions, or anything else. When it's going well, I just love hearing those voices. Of course, when it's *not* going well I don't like hearing them at all. . . .

Q. In your books there's a high price attached to bravery.

A. You must understand that the blacks who were brought here as slaves were prevented from becoming the men that they could be. They were to be servants of the whites, nothing more. A *man* can speak up, he can do things to protect himself, his home and his family, but the slaves could never do that. If the white said the slave was wrong, he was wrong. These things happened even after slavery, in the South and here, too.

So eventually the blacks started stepping over the line. They said, "Damn what *you* think I'm supposed to be—I will be what I ought to be. And if I must die to do it, I'll die." And for a long time they did get killed. Once they stepped over that line there was always that possibility, and quite a few of my characters step over that line.

Q. You list Hemingway among your influences. To what extent?

A. I think he influenced everyone who was trying to write in the 50's. I've always liked the way he understated things, and I admire his writing style, which told me I did not have to use adjectives and adverbs, and that's the damn truth. Also, he wrote about people who always came through gracefully under pressure. Now *nobody* has experienced as much pressure as the black in this country, and nobody has come through more gracefully. I'm afraid I give most of my characters a heavy burden to carry, and then expect them to come through with dignity. This is why I admire Hemingway: he showed me how to write that kind of thing. . . .

Q. Do you consider yourself a Southern writer?

A. Southerners consider me a Southern writer, blacks consider me a black writer, I don't know. My Southern experience certainly made the greatest impact on my life, that's what I draw on in my writing, so maybe that makes me a Southern writer, even though I've lived in California twice as long. I really don't think about it.

Q. What is the job of the black writer in America?

A. I don't believe in telling anyone what he or she ought to write; the job of any writer is to write truly about what he knows and feels. But I do think—and I've been criticized for saying so—that too many blacks have been writing to tell whites all about "the problems," instead of writing something that all people, including their own, could find interesting, could enjoy. And in so many cases they leave out the humanity of their characters. Black writers have to do more than work out their anger on paper.

I like pride in people, I try to show the strength of black people, but I was criticized when I was writing *Miss Jane Pittman* because blacks were expected to write novels of protest, it was your "duty" as a black writer. I stuck to my guns and wrote what was true to me, and if you read that book you'll see that there *is* protest in it. Every novel has its own protests—if you're not commenting on the human condition then what are you doing but playing with words, shuffling paper?

Q. All your books have been set in this fictional locale you've created along the St. Charles River. Are you going to write only about Louisiana?

A. I could be happy doing that. Everything I've published has been set there, but I've probably written as many books about California that have been unpublishable. I

find a closeness with Southern characters, their language, their habits. When I try to write about California it just doesn't ring true.

Many writers have done their best work when dealing with things that impressed them early in their lives. There's something about those early impressions that pulls you back. And if the place you come from is rich with tradition, stories, myths, superstitions, that's more of an attraction. Louisiana, of course, is rich in these things; it also has a very romantic history. But all of this may be incidental—it's still the place that I come from.

Q. You left there when you were a boy. How had you learned these things?

A. Working in the fields, going fishing in the swamps with the older people, and, especially, listening to the people who came to my aunt's house, the aunt who raised me. She was a cripple and could not go visiting, so people came to visit her. I'd be there to serve them icewater, or coffee. There was no radio, no television, so people *talked* about everything, even things that had happened 70 years earlier. I learned about storytelling by listening to these people talk. The idea behind *Miss Jane Pittman* was based on things I'd heard as a child, and from the life I come from, the plantation.

Q. Do you think a book defining the black experience in America should be set in the South?

A. Yes, of course. No period in this country's history can better depict it—good and bad—than the decade between 1958 and 1968 in the South. More people from more levels of society were involved in what was going on in this country during that time than at any other. Not necessarily more people, but more kinds of people, from the lowliest black peasant who could not read his name in box-car letters to the President. And I think that period in the South has the makings of a great American novel. Of course it would take someone with the talent of Tolstoy, and a 1,000-page book. And, I've always said, a black.

Q. Is this a book you're planning to write?

A. I will write parts of such a book, slices of it, but not *that* book and maybe no others; it would take all the energy I have. I think I have the imagination for it, but you'd need to do a tremendous amount of research. . . .

Q. How do you feel when you finish a book?

A. Great. Whether the book is going to be accepted by people who read it is not as important, and does not make you feel as good, as actually finishing it. Because you always feel that you've failed, that you did not say in this book what you wanted to say, and you're happy the damn thing is done so you can move on to some other book to try to say in it the things you want to say, and maybe do a little better. You're forever going to that next book, and you're forever happy when it's over with.

That's how I've felt after every book I've written. Hell, if I'd have put everything I wanted to into *Miss Jane Pittman* there would have been no point in writing *In My Father's House*. Faulkner said that once you're satisfied with everything you've done, you might as well break the pencil and cut your throat. I mean, the whole damn thing is over with. So you never really finish. Not if you are a writer. And it never gets any easier.

Marcia Gaudet and Carl Wooton

SOURCE: "Oral Tradition and Literature," in *Porch Talk with Ernest Gaines: Conversations on the Writer's Craft,* Louisiana State University Press, 1990, pp. 7-21.

CW [Carl Wooton]: You've said before that you write for your stories to be read aloud, that you more or less think your stories are being told in that kind of way. Do you have some sense of yourself as being the storyteller and the performer at the same time, the way Reese [Spooner] does when he's sitting on that porch talking to us?

GAINES: If you're saying entertaining through words is also performing, well, yeah. I have a sense somebody's going to read it, but I don't have a particular audience out there. I don't have any faces of anybody in mind when I'm writing it, but I feel that I'm writing to entertain, whether it's a comic scene or a tragic scene.

I must bring in some kind of reality to what my narrator is talking about. For example, if Reese is telling me a story and I want to repeat something he said, I have to do some research. If he's going to talk about the event of Huey Long's death—for example, I had to bring that in *The Autobiography of Miss Jane Pittman*—I cannot just write what he says, because I'm not absolutely sure about what he says. So what I do is I go back and read something on this stuff. I've been listening to blacks talk about Long's death all my life, but I don't want to look like a damned fool by putting down what they said in a book. They might be telling me anything.

This is a very important thing when you write about Louisiana. You can mess up on Long's death—because everybody has messed up on Long's death. I can talk to everybody around here, and they're all going to tell me a different story about Long's death, why he died and how he died and all that sort of thing. So, after listening to everything these people had to say, I thought when I got ready to write that chapter, I'd better do some research. So I read T. Harry Williams' biography and I read *All the King's Men*—Robert Penn Warren's book—and Long's book, *Every Man a King*. I read newspaper clippings. I did all kinds of things. Then I went to the Louisiana Room at the LSU library and I went through page after page, manila folder after manila folder of things. Then I said, OK, I've got all this information, and now I must go back and give it to this little old lady back here, Miss Jane. I've got to give her all this information, but I can't give her this information as I got it. I can't give her this information as

a trained historian. I must in some way—and that's how we come back to the voice thing—give her all this information and let her tell this thing the way she would tell it, as an illiterate black woman a hundred years old talking about these things.

I must let *her* do it. It's like getting pork and putting it in the machine and grinding it up and grinding it up and grinding it up and letting it come out a different way from what it was when it was obtained. At the same time that I give her that information, I have to keep her in character. I cannot just give her hunks of history and throw them to her and have her describe, "It was Sunday, at seven o'clock and Huey Long was going from New Orleans to such and such a place, and the guy, [Carl A.] Weiss, comes from behind this pillar and shoots Long." I don't need all that because she never would have spoken that way. I would have been the one speaking that way. The historian would have been the one speaking that way. But I have to give her that information as if she were just holding a regular conversation with her friends sitting out on the porch. She doesn't know. She has heard this information from third or fourth or fifth persons. She's never read it in a book or a newspaper. She has just heard about it, and this is what she talks about.

So when you say what Reese is doing, I must have some idea of what Reese is talking about. He cannot just tell me anything. I must know what he's talking about. I, the writer, must know what he's talking about. See, my character Reese and Reese are two different people. Reese is a real man. My character is going to say what I want my character to say, but he's going to say it in the way that you think Reese would've said it. He's a character and he has to do what I want him to do, give you the information I want him to give you.

MG [Marcia Gaudet]: Do you have a sense that that work is going to depend on how much you involve the reader, just as the oral storyteller has to involve the listener?

GAINES: Well, yes. I have to do something that can be understood. I have to do something that can be recognized. I have to write the proper kind of dialogue. I try to write dialogue in short sentences so you can grasp it. I try to make things as clear as possible. An actor or performer can make gestures or throw his voice out, and cry and weep and do all sorts of things like that. What I have to do is use those twenty-six letters that tell you these things.

CW: When the actor weeps or laughs, he's often trying to make his audience weep or laugh with him. Do you have a sense of trying to do that?

GAINES: I never think about making someone weep. I never think about making someone laugh. If I laugh at something I'm writing, I try to write it until I stop laughing, because I think then you'll get all the fun. You'll get the point of it. I don't try to make people weep or go out and act. If I write about a murder scene, I don't want anyone else to pick up a gun and go out and shoot somebody, but I try to make you feel it, and make you think, well, I would not want to be this kind of person, I don't want to be that, I want to be this.

CW: Do you want to involve the audience emotionally?

GAINES: I want the audience to see himself. I want the audience to see himself intellectually as well as emotionally.

CW: Are you also trying to disappear?

GAINES: I'm disappearing if I am writing from that first-person point of view. I'm totally disappearing because I must put everything into that character. That character has to be the entire person.

CW: What about in *Catherine Carmier* and *In My Father's House?* Were you trying to get the same kind of distance? Is the third-person voice as clear and separate, as distinct from you, as a first-person voice is?

GAINES: I don't think that it is, and that's why it's much more difficult for me to do. And I think it's much more difficult for American writers. I tell my students that what we've done with the first person is as great in literature as anything else we have done—any of our characters that we have created, any of the stories we have told, or anything else. I know that I'm not nearly as in control in the third-person omniscient as I am in the first person. If I get a character too close to me, I can't work with him. I'm having to deal with a character in this book I'm working on now. He's too damned close to me, and I'm having all kinds of problems. He's one of the reasons I'm not working as fast. He's too much like me. He's cynical at times. He hates things. He wants to say, "Goddamn it all. The hell with this stuff." . . .

When I write, I try to write well. I think that's the only way one should write. One should be proud enough to write well. If I were a painter, I would paint well, so someone could see the thing. I take more pride in what I do well than I care for what anyone else appreciates, takes from my work. Sometimes, really, I say, OK, I've done this. You like it? OK, good. You don't like it? I don't give a damn, because I do it well. That's all I want to do, just do my work well. I'd want my friends to read it. I'd read a chapter, say, to Carl, and say, "OK, man, what do you think of this?" Carl might say, "Well, it's the shits." Well, so what? I think it's good. Really, I never think of an audience. I just think of getting something down that is good and then having it published. I want someone to buy it, of course, because that's how I support myself. Friendship or whatever, I do as well as I possibly can, and that's it. And if I can get along with you by doing it well, good. If I can't get along with you by doing it well, I don't care anymore.

MG: You wouldn't change your writing to make people buy it.

GAINES: No way! No way will I change, no! People have asked me quite often, "Who do you write for?" I say I don't write for any particular group. But if there's a gun put to my head and someone says, "OK, name somebody you write for," I'd say, "I write for the black youth of the South." And if there are two groups, I'd say, "I write for the black and white youth of the South." Those are the people I would write for.

Number one, I would want the black youth to say, "Hey, I am somebody." And I'd want the white youth to say, "Hey, that is part of me out there, and I can only understand myself truly if I can understand my neighbor." That's the only way one can understand himself, if he can understand other things around him. We live—you know, Donne's "No man is an island" and "Don't ask for whom the bell tolls"—Every little piece of things around us makes us a little bit whole. We can go through the world being half people, and most of us do that most of our lives. But in order to understand more about ourselves and the world, we must understand what's around. So that's what I'd want: the white kids to understand what the black kid is, and the black kid to understand who he is, if I had to write for any group. *Jane Pittman* has been translated into Chinese. I did not write for the Chinese. *Miss Jane Pittman* has been translated into Japanese, Russian, German, and two or three other languages. *A Gathering of Old Men* just came out in German, and it will come out in Russian next year. I'm not writing for them, but I try to write as well as I possibly can and just hope the readers come from wherever they come from.

MG: What you say reminds me of Faulkner's statement that what he's really concerned about are the concerns of the human heart. You're just interested in writing well, and you hope that what you write will appeal to anyone who is concerned about humanity.

GAINES: True! And if you write well and true enough, you're going to find that a little old lady in China, a little lady in Russia or in Japan, will see that and say, "Oh, you know, yeah." Not all of the little things that happened to Miss Jane, but one of the little things or two of the little things that happened, that person can see herself in it. So you try to write as truly and as deeply and understandably about the human condition as you possibly can. That's all you can do. There's nothing else to do. . . .

MG: We know that you have a large collection of jazz albums, and you have commented before that you usually play music when you're writing. Do you still do that?

GAINES: Oh, yes. Whether I'm playing jazz or classical music, or just listening to the radio, I usually have music in the background, but soft, so it does not disturb me. I have to keep music. It relaxes me, and at the same time it gives me a sense of rhythm, of beat.

MG: Do you think maybe it gives you the atmosphere, or the kind of feeling, you want?

GAINES: I don't know that it sets a mood or anything like that. I think I have to sort of build myself to the mood myself before I begin to write. And yet, at times, it can. It's possible that when I was writing *The Autobiography of Miss Jane Pittman,* because I played *Pictures at an Exhibition* just about every day while I was writing it—two years, I guess—maybe I needed that to get started. But sometimes I play music just for the background, but soft in the background. I don't play Beethoven's Fifth because that's too disturbing. I play some sort of soft music, violin or cello or whatever, as sort of the background. It's just like you need water or coffee around the place, you know. You have some music in the background to keep you going that day, I guess.

CW: How was music present in your world as you were growing up?

GAINES: Well, of course, I came from a plantation. There was a church not very far from our house. I could hear the people singing all the time. I had to go to Sunday school and church as a child, and, of course, the people sang. I could never carry a tune myself, but the old ones did. And my mother sang, and my aunt. I didn't hear classical music or anything like that. I don't think the radio worked half the time, but there was always music, somebody doing something.

MG: And was it typical of people to be singing—for your mother to be singing?

GAINES: Yes, while they were working. People sang when they were working.

CW: So far you've described the indirect importance music has had in your writing. Do you ever see it creeping in more directly, through musical language or musical references?

GAINES: Oh, no. I don't think I ever use music, really, like that. In *Of Love and Dust,* Jim has a guitar. I think in **"The Sky Is Gray,"** the young kid, James, thinks back on the old man who plays a guitar around the house. When I was a small child, we did have a man like that who played the guitar around the place. But I don't know anything about music. I can't read music at all. I remember when I had to do the reading of the *Portrait of Lincoln* with the USL orchestra, I explained to the conductor, "I don't know one note of music, so whenever you want me to start reading, you just nod your head." We had a record of Carl Sandburg reading it, so I could figure out the rhythm and speed, the way the thing should be read. But I couldn't follow the notes and all on paper. I don't know a thing about music.

Marcia Gaudet and Carl Wooton

SOURCE: "Fictional Characters and Real People," in *Porch Talk with Ernest Gaines: Conversations on the Writer's Craft,* Louisiana State University Press, 1990, pp. 38-63.

MG [Marcia Gaudet]: The common concept is that when older people get eccentric, it's because of old age, when quite often they were like that all their lives. It also seems true of your characters that they are not stereotyped, that there are older characters who do change, and there are other characters who never change.

[ERNEST] GAINES: Oh, yes, I have stereotypes in my books. For example, Bishop in *Of Love and Dust* is a stereotyped character, but then I have someone to counter it, like in Marcus. Marcus is going to counter Bishop; he's just the opposite of whatever you think when you say [about Bishop], "There's a stereotype black." You get somebody like Marcus who'll say, "Wait a minute, pardner. We're not all like this guy, and before I'll be like this guy, I'll be dead. I'll die first."

MG: That's what I was trying to get to. I wanted something to characterize the older people, and they're very, very different, like the mother-in-law in **"A Long Day in November."**

GAINES: Oh, yeah. I wanted a comic figure. That's what I wanted all the time in her.

MG: This all seems connected to how you portray men and women in general, and to how you show the black man in relation to women, and how other writers—for example, Alice Walker and Ntozake Shange—show that relationship. Some critics have criticized you for being too kind to the black man, and in some other writers' works, especially some black female writers, there are no redeeming qualities in the black male character. There is such a contrast, in fact, between your portrayal of these man-woman relationships and the way we see them in other black writers' works, that there is a question about how you verify that your portrayal is an accurate one—the one that some people say is too kind to the black male character.

GAINES: Those same kind of people have said I'm too kind to white characters, and others have said I make my black heroes too nice, too. But I've lived with and seen the actions of these men. I think I know more about the black male because I'm male myself. I know something about his dreams. I listened to them when I was a kid growing up, I've drunk with him, I've been in the army and in athletics—I know what men dream about. All men dream about certain things. All men have hopes, and all men brutalize other things near them, at home, when they cannot fulfill those hopes. I read Joyce's Dublin stories, and I see the same sort of thing. I read this story, "The Informer," that was made into a great film about how these men are afraid of the Black and Tan—the British—and how they treated other people around them. You'll find that, among men, the more brutalized they are, the more they brutalize other people. I remember reading Faulkner's "Dry September," where they come from this lynch mob and this guy comes home to his wife. His wife says something to him, and he wants to beat her up. It's just continual brutalization of one thing after another. The lynching was not even enough for him to get rid of all the aggressiveness or hatred or whatever it was that drove him to participate in the lynching. He comes back to the house and he continues it at home.

But then there's the other side of things as well. It's not only one side. I never look at things just one way. In my writing about black males, I've known the cowards, I've known the men who would take chances—men who, if they were given the equal chance, would be as brave as any man. We can see that in athletics. We can see that in reading about soldiers, guys fighting in Vietnam or the Second World War: that men, given an equal chance, will say, "OK, I'm a man," and he does his job as well as anyone else does. This is complicated stuff.

Marcia Gaudet and Carl Wooton

SOURCE: "Folklore and Ethnicity," in *Porch Talk with Ernest Gaines: Conversations on the Writer's Craft,* Louisiana State University Press, 1990, pp. 77-86.

MG [Marcia Gaudet]: You often use folk beliefs, folk practices or traditions, folk medicine, and so on, in your writing. For example, in **"A Long Day in November,"** there is the hoodoo lady; in *Miss Jane,* there is the reference to jumping over the broom for marriage; and in *Of Love and Dust,* Charlie Jordan uses a piece of salt meat on his foot to draw out the soreness after he stepped on a nail. How do you choose the specific items of folklore or folklife to include when you're writing?

[ERNEST] GAINES: I don't know. I don't know, in that it depends on what the situation is. I know as a kid growing up—and it had happened to me—-that in cutting your foot or sticking a thorn or a splinter in your foot, after drawing out the stick or whatever, you had this piece of salt meat tied on your foot. I don't know where they got the idea from. I know damn well I wouldn't do it today. But for the characters I'm writing about, there's nothing else for that character to do. That character would use that at that particular time, in the thirties or forties.

For example, in **"The Sky Is Gray,"** there is the kid with a toothache. They have this guy praying over his tooth and pressing on his tooth. Of course it fails. I think it fails because they were saying two different prayers, but the damn thing fails. So they end up by going to a dentist to have the tooth extracted. If they had not gone to town, maybe I would have had something else happen. Maybe it would have been cured by the praying. I had that done to my tooth when I was a child. I also had something stuck in my foot, and salt meat was put on it. Luckily for me, I survived. Another kid died.

MG: Was all of the folklore you use in your writing learned directly from the culture, or did you get some from books?

GAINES: I didn't learn any of this from books. The only thing I learned from books was about the slave thing. Now, that I *did* learn from reading, because no one ever told me. I didn't know anyone that old to tell me that. But the salt meat thing and the praying on the tooth, I learned that from direct experience. To me, if you've been accustomed to it, it's not folklore. It's just part of your life.

MG: I think that's what makes folklore such an integral part of your work, because these things come naturally. These are the things the people would do and say and believe. When writers study a book of folklore and say, yes, I'll have them do this or that, then it becomes superimposed on the narrative. When you were growing up, did you know people who were recognized as having the power to heal or other special powers?

GAINES: At that particular time, yes. That's what **"A Long Day in November"** is all about. When everything else fails, you go back to the tradition, even to the point of superstition. When everything else fails, we go back to the old things and become almost primitive again. . . .

MG: Often in black folklore, when the situation is hard to handle and when there are so many negative things about it, the only way to deal with it is to see the humorous side and to have the underdog use trickster behavior to triumph over the person who is oppressing him. You seldom, if ever, use the trickster.

GAINES: I did this type of thing with Marcus in an early version of *Of Love and Dust.* I was playing games with that. It was not based on any mythical characters like Br'er Rabbit, but on real characters. It wasn't working out, though.

MG: In your fiction, there are no tricksters who triumph. The survivors are those who deal with situations with dignity, pride, and integrity, and you've often said that one of your themes is survival with dignity. Robert Hemenway has said [in *Zora Neale Hurston: A Literary Biography*], "Folk traditions enabled black people to survive with strength and dignity." Do you think that folk beliefs and customs help people to survive with dignity?

GAINES: Yes, I would agree there, as long as they live in a certain environment, such as a plantation. If they have no access to anything else, these things do help them to survive. Chekhov said of the peasants that they would not trust anyone else, not even a doctor. They survived on their own. I went through it, and I heard about that stuff. When I began to write about it, I'd think, "Good Lord, how could they do this?" But as a child, I knew people who did these things. You say, "You're writing about folklore," but it's not folklore to me. I think damned near everything that's folklore has been done a hundred years ago and has become "folklore" to "civilized" people. But it's not folklore to the people it's happening to at the time. Hell, it's reality to the people it's happening to at the time.

MG: You're using the term *folklore* to mean only things in the past. It's used in a much broader sense by folklorists; it includes what the people believe traditionally and continue to do.

GAINES: Right. I agree with that, but when I use it in my writing, it's not that I believe it, but that my characters believe it.

MG: Through his folklore we can define the person. If we know what he believed traditionally, then we know who he is.

GAINES: Yes, and if a man has no past, he has no future.

MG: I think that's the crucial thing, when you show what the past is for these people.

GAINES: Not that you live in the past, but we must recognize it, even if we reject it. If you don't have a base, there's nothing to go on to.

MG: In your article in *Callaloo,* "Miss Jane and I," you say: "Truth to Miss Jane is what she remembers. Truth to me is what people like Miss Jane remember."

GAINES: Yes, because it's all in what you remember and in what you want to say, what's important to you. Here is this little old lady, Miss Jane. She believes in what she's saying, and she's as good as anybody else. What she says is as good and true as what anyone else says.

MG: Her perspective is equally valid.

GAINES: Yes.

MG: Do you think that the South Louisiana setting, with that sort of unique mixture of French and Cajun and black, makes your writing different from that of other southern writers? Or do you see yourself basically as a southern writer or a Louisiana writer?

GAINES: I see myself as a writer, and I happen to have been born here. I was born black. I was born on a plantation. I've lived in that interracial, or ethnic, mixture of the Cajun, and the big house owned by the Creoles—not Cajuns, but Creoles—and the blacks. I was associated very early with the Baptist church; I was christened as a Baptist. But I went to Catholic school, a little school in New Roads, my last three years in Louisiana. I had to go through their kind of discipline. I had to go to mass. I didn't go to confession or anything like that. I didn't take the Holy Sacrament. I had to go through all these kinds of things. My aunt who raised me and who was crippled spoke Creole. Some of the old ladies on the plantation and some of the old men spoke Creole. I traveled around with another aunt of mine who sold the little cosmetic things all over Pointe Coupée and West Baton Rouge parishes, and I met all these people who put these things on their faces and made themselves smell sweet, and they spoke French because my aunt spoke Creole.

I am a different writer from, say, Faulkner, and I'm a different writer from a lot of black writers. A writer from North Louisiana would not have had the same experiences I had in South Louisiana. One who came from Mississippi or Alabama or Georgia or Texas would not have had the same experience. I never think of myself as, number one, a black writer, quote "black," or "Louisiana black," but as a writer who happens to draw from his environment what his life is, what his heritage is. I try to put that down on paper.

I think my work is unique in that, I think, I come from a place that is quite unique, certainly very different from all the rest of the southern states. Louisiana has a tremendous romantic history about it, the Spanish and the French and all those things. We're just a different group, and we have problems maybe others don't have or don't pay so much attention to. I think we have a big problem among the darker-skinned and the fairer-skinned black people in this state, more than in any other state in the Union. I see it all the time, and I live it. I saw it in New Orleans just this last week, and I've seen it in areas around Lafayette and Baton Rouge. I've experienced that. This guy was talking to me about our African ancestry, and he looks as African as I look Japanese. I'm pretty sure that, deep down inside, they don't look at themselves as being "black" as I look at myself being black.

MG: That's the kind of thing you handle in *Catherine Carmier.* It's an identity problem, because, obviously, they have not identified themselves as white either.

GAINES: Right. That's one of the things about Lillian. Lillian says: "Hey, listen, wait awhile. I cannot live in this middle-of-the-road kind of situation. I cannot cross this fence anymore. I'm white enough to go over there, and I'm going to make this choice. I'm going over there because I can't live across this fence anymore, the way I've been trained to do." And I saw a lot of people at the museum in New Orleans the other night who could have gone one way or the other. And yet they're saying they are black. But they don't feel that way—they don't feel that they are.

MG: In Louisiana it's always been something more like an ethnic identity, linked to the idea of the Creole of color. This group of fair-skinned people of black and Creole descent were at one time, if not almost a separate race, at least a separate ethnic group, who prided themselves on being neither black nor white.

GAINES: That's what all the Creole stuff is about right now, because if you think about it, there's no such thing as a Creole with mixed blood. There's no such thing as a Creole with African ancestry. But that is the one identity they could use: "I'm not black, I'm not white, I'm Creole." That is a falseness in itself, because the Creoles were either French or Spanish. . . .

MG: Of course, right now *Creole* is usually used to mean "mixed-blood."

GAINES: Well, this is what I mean. You can easily say that: "I'm not black, but I'm Creole." And most of them hide behind this until it becomes necessary, in politics or whatever, in order to get what you need to accomplish, [to] say, "I'm black." But I think that, deep down inside, they know they haven't paid their dues. Too many black people got murdered and bled to change this thing in the South while these people hung back. Yet because they were closer in their features to the Caucasians, closer to the whites in power, they were the ones who could get in much easier than the black ones who had to die for it. They were not black when they had to go out there and die in the streets and suffer in the streets as the blacks had to do.

I think it was your [CW's] class I was in, and this kid sat in the back—a dark-skinned kid, almost as dark as I am—and he said that he never heard of anything like that in his family. I didn't want to call the kid a liar. He said that his ancestry were those people that I talked about. I cannot imagine a family made up of a mixture of darker people and fairer people who have not had these problems. I had it in my family.

MG: Your portrayals of Cajuns seldom show their positive characteristics and values as strong, hard-working, congenial, family-oriented people. What does the word *Cajun* mean to you?

GAINES: I don't know. It depends on—I think I could ask the same question, as what does *black* or *Negro* mean to you? And I think it depends on your education, your intelligence, your knowledge of people. I think I have a different interpretation of what Cajun means than what my stepfather's interpretation of Cajun was. Now, to my stepfather and people of his generation, Cajun meant a white who would give them hell on False River, because it's been known that this would happen since the time a Cajun killed this man in 1903. And anytime there was a problem on the river, and because so many of the whites there were Cajun, it would always be "that Cajun," whether one of them was involved or not. This is what the whole Fix thing in *A Gathering of Old Men* is about; it's what Mapes is talking about.

Now, that does not mean the same thing to me, because I'm quite aware of the difference. . . . I think I was aware of the difference between mine and my stepfather's interpretation even when I was a child growing up. I never did face what he faced as a young man growing up, probably in the early twenties or in the late teens. It's a different world. . . .

GENERAL COMMENTARY

Jack Hicks

SOURCE: "To Make These Bones Live: History and Community in Ernest Gaines's Fiction," in *Black American Literature Forum*, Vol. 11, No. 1, Spring, 1977, pp. 9-19.

With *The Autobiography of Miss Jane Pittman,* Ernest Gaines has become one of our most highly regarded Afro-

American writers. While *Miss Jane Pittman* is his signal achievement, the world of the novel is identical to that of his three earlier books—*Catherine Carmier, Of Love and Dust,* and *Bloodline.* All of Gaines's work is seeded in a basic land derived from his native Pointe Coupee Parish in Louisiana: extending chronologically from 1865 to the mid-1950s; geographically, from the winding bayous and tablelands to the decaying plantations and slave quarters northwest of Baton Rouge, along his fictive St. Charles River. Upriver, beyond the corn and cotton and cane fields, lies the small town he calls Bayonne. His characters are ordinary people, black, white, and "in-between." This last group of mixed bloods and cultures is important, for Ernest Gaines's special interest is indeed in those who are "in-between": races or ethnic groups (poor Blacks, Cajuns, Creoles, "'Mericans"); traditions and institutions (slavery, religion, share-cropping, the great web of folkways and unwritten laws that bind and separate all Southerners).

While his lands and subjects are consistent, there is an evolution of Ernest Gaines's vision through his four works, as he becomes increasingly concerned with black history and black community. The movement from *Catherine Carmier* to *Miss Jane Pittman* is from personal and racial history rendered as a kind of bondage, a solitary existential nightmare of dead ends and blasted families, toward history sensed as a natural cycle, wheeling slowly through the rebirth of a *people,* toward their inevitable collective liberation. As his vision matures, there is an accompanying shift in Gaines's use of materials and fictional techniques. He moves away from a personal version of the white "existential" novel, later assimilating and adapting folk forms—popular sermons, slave narratives, folk tales, oral histories—re-making the long fictional forms to his own unique ends. . . .

While most of Jackson Bradley's trials in *Catherine Carmier* are conducted off-stage, the social disintegrations one can read in his state are far too dim and summary to fully engage us. Gaines's second novel, *Of Love and Dust,* shares the same time and locale, but the conflicts and divisions are concretely dramatized for us, rendered as functions of the lives of fully developed characters. . . .

With *Bloodline,* Ernest Gaines sounds a very different emphasis on black history and community. The vision of history as fate, as a cycle from which one cannot escape, is expanded. As the title *Bloodline* suggests, the book is concerned with the living, the organic, and Gaines is writing with a vision of the natural history of a people. The dominant concern through these five stories is with natural patterns of growth and decay, the evolution from childhood to maturity to old age as seen in the lives of people, races, generations, eras. In the shapes of these stories, and in the recurrent images and metaphors, the past, present and future are all of a piece; history is part of a natural process, and humans who live within it find their lives infused with significance. . . .

The dust that drifts through *Catherine Carmier* is what remains of a dead past, stifling Jackson Bradley. But for

Miss Jane Pittman, the dust is alive, a viable reminder of the price paid by her black ancestors for her own meager freedom—and of the price paid by those younger than her, such as her adopted son Ned Douglass, shot down by a hired white murderer. The headnote for this section [History Is Your People's Bones] is taken from Ned's last sermon on the St. Charles River, and lest we overlook his message, Jane drives it home at his graveside: "I remember my old mistress, when she saw the young Secesh soldiers, saying: `The precious blood of the South, the precious blood of the South.' Well, there on that river bank is the precious dust of this South. And he is there for all to see."

The Autobiography of Miss Jane Pittman is fiction masquerading as autobiography, but mostly, it is a powerful folk history of Afro-American life from the Civil War to the mid-1960s. If such comparisons are helpful, it is a novel and a racial repository as well, *sui generis* like W. E. B. DuBois's *The Souls of Black Folk* and Jean Toomer's *Cane*. Jane Pittman's life is a framing metaphor, complex and vibrant, like Toomer's sugar cane. Her life and his field are poetically imagined, specific and concrete; people go in and out of them, they can be sweet and raw, can harbor love and lust, spawn tragedy and hatred. And like DuBois and Toomer, Ernest Gaines taps the languages and forms and powers of black folk-rooted art forms. The bones of his book are communal, oral and rhetorical: spirituals, black folk sermons, slave narratives, biblical parables, folk tables, and primitive myths. These are spoken, declaimed forms, issuing from a collective human voice. As the putative "editor" tells us in his "Introduction," the novel is built on a series of interviews with Miss Jane Pittman, a one hundred-ten-year-old former slave, and many of her friends. The "friends" is important, for her being is truly a repository of Southern black life since the Civil War. As our editor notes of those "wonderful people" and their relation to Miss Jane, "Miss Jane's story is all of their stories, and their stories are Miss Jane's.". . .

As I suggest earlier, the power of *The Autobiography of Miss Jane Pittman* does not lie in the patterns and motifs of recurring characters, actions, themes. There are familiar patterns, to be sure: black leaders are consistently thrust up, only to be slain and dash the hopes they inspired; and again and again, Jane and her people take to the road on still another exodus, in search of still another homeland. But there is less of a concern with shoring-up the structure of the novel, and a much greater willingness on Gaines's part to allow his material its own natural course—indeed the richness of the fiction lies in the momentary eddies and pools into which the narrative stream is deflected. When Gaines speaks of Richard Wright's decline, he attributes it to an inability to continue writing from a black "American soil, not out of a European library." In his own writing, he demonstrates his strong suspicion that the traditional techniques of the novel are too analytical, schematic, do not properly define his materials or express his vision of the natural history of black people. Gaines seems to agree with his contemporary William Melvin Kelley's assessment that "to carry the weight of our ideas, the novel

has got to be changed. We are trying to tap some new things in a form which is not our form."

That power lies in Gaines's careful assimilation of Afro-American folk materials, particularly those of the South, in which his historical vision is absorbed and vivified. His debt is to the rich fund of customs and folkways of black American pasts, to the unique forms grown out of them—to the spirituals, determination songs, church music like Jane's "Done Got Over," urging a rock-like perseverance even as "they tell," heard by W. E. B. DuBois, "of death and suffering and unvoiced longing toward a truer world, of misty wanderings and hidden ways." From the church he also draws on folk sermons and church talks, adapting them to his own more secular uses; to these, a debt for the compelling rhetorical power running through Ned Douglass and Jimmy Aaron, and a broad, historical apology for pain and suffering. And to slave narratives—like that of Frederick Douglass—testifying to the moral diseases incipient in human bondage, and to the psychic devastations resulting in both Black (Black Harriet) and White (Cluveau and Tee Bob). A more regional Louisiana folk heritage is spun out in the presence of hoo-doo Madame Eloise Gautier and the many webs of prophecies bound in dreams, visions, superstitions. Their presences suggest a world more alive and mysterious beyond our own, and are borne earlier in the folk tale, as in the remarkable account of Albert Cluveau's suffering and death, "The Chariot of Hell." Many of Gaines's figures are familiar to black myth: Singalee Black Harriet and her return to the shelter of her homeland via insanity; the hunter in search of his mother, pausing in the swamps to trap food for Ticey and Ned. To this rich stream, played through Gaines's own shaping contemporary imagination, we owe the spectrum of Afro-American life and language set loose in *Miss Jane Pittman.*

His direct concern with history and those who record it is apparent from the start. The putative "editor" is a teacher of history, and explains to Jane and her friends that her life will help students to better learn their lessons. "'What's wrong with them books you already got?'" her friend asks. "'Miss Jane is not in them,'" is his reply. Teachers are important throughout Jane's story, and good ones such as Ned Douglass and Mary LeFabre are treasures; the lessers, like Miss Lilly and Joe Hardy, are quietly indicted—and damned simply—as being among "the worst human beings I've ever met."

But it is not easy to teach: we are often reminded of the difficulty of knowing a truth, of daring a vision of history. Jane is first made aware of this painful fact by a riddling old man in whom a world of mystery was refracted. Discouraging her trek to Ohio in search of a kind "Yankee soldier name Brown," he images a detailed and exhausting account of her fruitless travels, concluding: "'And the only white Brown people can remember that ever went to Luzana to fight in the war died of whiskey ten years ago. They don't think he was the same person you was looking for because this Brown wasn't kind to nobody. He was coarse and vulgar; he cussed man, God, and nature every day of his life.'" And as long as man can speak it and shape it, history can deceive, can be a weapon against one's foes. Remembering Herbert Aptheker's adage that "History is mighty," especially for the oppressor, we listen to Jules Raynard's account of Robert Samson's suicide. His reading of the past is historically myopic, consciously blurring the pattern of cause and effect. In his account of slavery, for example, the lion and the lamb lie down together, and each is equally guilty and helpless before the fated retribution for the sins of a common past. Raynard drives Jane home from the plantation to the old slave quarters, and she listens quietly from a back seat, suspicious of his version of "the gospel truth." For all his decency, Raynard is still another white man whose dream of the past makes those in the present impotent; history is a wall for him, before which master and serf can do little but surrender.

For Ernest J. Gaines, like his creation Jimmy Aaron, there is immense power in language, and its use is a sacred trust. And like Aaron, he assumes his obligations cautiously and naturally. Aaron's simple skills to read and write family letters and papers, and his rhetorical talents that serve him later; Gaines's powers to create fiction: each is a way a people are preserved, a heritage passed on. Ned Douglass's last text is a popular folk sermon, adapted from the "Vision of Dry Bones," in Ezekiel, in which it is taught that words can bring a past to life, put flesh on bones and a seed in the soil. "Son of man, these bones are the whole house of Israel: behold, they say. Our bones are dried up, and our hope is lost; we are clean cut off" (Ezekiel 37:11). Ernest Gaines writes from this lament, and *The Autobiography of Miss Jane Pittman,* his finest work, is his mighty attempt to open the graves, make these bones live, and re-unite a people.

John W. Roberts

SOURCE: "The Individual and the Community in Two Short Stories by Ernest J. Gaines," in *Black American Literature Forum,* Vol. 18, No. 3, Fall, 1984, pp. 110-13.

The interaction between the community and the individual, along with its role in the shaping of human personality, is a primary concern of Ernest J. Gaines in much of his fiction. It is in probing the underlying community attitudes, values, and beliefs to discover the way in which they determine what an individual will or has become that Gaines gives poignancy to the pieces in his short-story collection *Bloodline.* Because his fiction focuses on the peculiar plight of black Americans in the South, Gaines must consider an additional level of significance—the strong communal bonds characteristic of Southern black folk culture. In these stories, black folk culture, with its emphasis on community-defined values and behaviors, shows signs of deterioration, while Western individualism and the development of more personally-defined values appear as catalysts in the demise of the black folk world view. In such a cultural climate, the spiritual and emotional well-being of both the community and the individual is threatened. Faced with the necessity to act and finding

traditional solutions no longer viable, the characters in Gaines's stories struggle desperately to restore some semblance of normalcy to their worlds. The dramatic conflict endemic to the stories in *Bloodline* arises out of the efforts of various characters to reconcile their individual needs with community prerequisites. Two of the stories in *Bloodline,* "A Long Day in November" and "The Sky Is Gray," are particularly illustrative of the conflict between community perspective and individual needs. The conflict in these two stories further illustrates the importance of the changes taking place within Southern black culture to the development of the social consciousness of children. While the action of the stories revolves around two young boys, the resolution of the conflict resides with their parents.

In "A Long Day in November," the friction in the story arises over a conflict between Amy's and Eddie's definition of manhood and male responsibility. At the outset of the story, Amy decides to abandon her marriage to Eddie and, with her young son, Sonny, returns home to her mother. Her dissatisfaction stems from her conviction that Eddie spends far too much time with his car and not enough time with his family. Eddie, however, is unable to understand Amy's objections. Although he is not very attentive to his family and household, he works to support them, a traditionally acceptable means of fulfilling his male responsibility. In this conflict of values, it becomes clear that Eddie's concept of the male's responsibility to his family is based on more traditional considerations than Amy's. While Eddie is comfortable with the traditional definition of the black male's familial role, he fails to realize that the circumstances which gave rise to it do not necessarily continue to exist for him. The inability of the black male to provide for and protect his family has traditionally forced him to find alternative means of demonstrating his manhood. Through his car, a traditional symbol of masculinity and male independence in American culture, Eddie attempts to define his manhood outside of his family. Amy, however, refuses to accept either Eddie's attachment to his car as a demonstration of his masculinity or his staying out until the early morning hours as a definition of his familial responsibility. By leaving him she forces him to seek a new way of conceptualizing his role as father and husband.

The action of the story is filtered through the consciousness of the couple's young son, Sonny. The use of Sonny as narrator suggests that this story is more than a simple narrative of male/female conflict. The centrality of the disagreement between Amy and Eddie to the development of Sonny's emerging social consciousness is implied from the very beginning of the story. From his being awakened in the early morning hours to face the "cold" realities of a new day until his return to those covers in the evening, Sonny is an initiate/observer in a long day's manhood ritual. Eddie, who, up to this point, has defined his manhood in terms of what he has perceived as community standards, suddenly discovers after Amy's departure that the old communal consensus on male behavior no longer exists. Consequently, the lessons learned from the day's events become as important, if not more so, for Sonny's father as they do for the boy. Through conversations with other male community members, both Eddie and Sonny discover that the traditional definitions of manhood and male responsibility have also proved inadequate for others. For Eddie, the changing perspectives on manhood mean a reevaluation of his conscious knowledge of the world, and for Sonny, they precipitate the development of a consciousness based on different preconceptions than those of his father's time. . . .

The symbolic act of burning his car is performed in view of the entire community, illustrating the strong communal bonds still in existence. Because of Rachael's involvement in the dispute between Amy and Eddie and Eddie's own ineptness in handling his problem, the disagreement between the couple has become a community concern. Consequently, the ritual of burning his car to placate Amy no longer harbingers simply individual significance for Eddie but also acts to restore community equilibrium. Eddie must not only demonstrate his recognition of a need for change in his relationship with his family to Amy but also offer the community a symbol sufficient to atone for the chaos that he has brought to it. Even Rachael, who has maintained throughout the story that Eddie is incapable of change, is sufficiently moved by Eddie's action to exclaim: "'I must be dreaming. He's a man after all.'" And it has been Amy's goal all along to force Eddie to accept his manhood. . . .

Throughout **"A Long Day in November,"** the sense of a unified folk community with a vested interest in its members looms in the background. Values and behaviors more indicative of an individualistic world view, however, also exist. They are evident in the conflict between Eddie and Amy over appropriate male behavior toward the family, and they are evident in the disagreement between Rachael and Amy on a generational level. Amy's refusal to condemn Eddie on the same grounds that her mother does, as well as her willingness to accept change in Eddie's character as a possibility, represents a move toward the acceptance of more personally-defined values. The recognition of individual needs is also salient in Eddie's search for a solution to his marital crisis. His failure to find Madame Toussaint's advice to the other men in the community applicable to himself is illustrative of the changes taking place. Ultimately, Sonny becomes a passive recipient of this cultural change. The story suggests that he, too, will be faced with the task of sorting out his own individual needs within a communal framework. He, however, will not only have the example of his parents but also the support of a concerned community.

The feeling of community which permeates **"A Long Day in November"**—that sense that whatever happens to Amy and Eddie is everybody's concern—is conspicuously absent from the second story in *Bloodline,* **"The Sky Is Gray."** James, the eight-year-old narrator of this story, struggles to understand his mother and her conceptions of manhood and dignity without aid from the community. With the exception of Auntie and Mr. Bayonne,

who attempt to explain his mother's cold, dispassionate treatment of him on one occasion, James is alienated in his effort to come to grips with both the social and personal forces governing his life. The source of James' isolation is his mother Octavia, who moves through the world of the story with a calm and control which always seem on the verge of eruption. She has cut herself completely off from the community which conceivably could have provided her with support while her husband does his tour of duty in the army. Although her relationship with this absent husband is only briefly mentioned, one senses in her attitude and behavior that his departure left her vulnerable. As a result, she has made protecting James from becoming vulnerable her primary goal in life. The problem in the story arises not so much from her efforts to make James a "man" as from her approach to and definition of manhood.

In her efforts to make James a "man," Octavia apparently believes that she has only her own behavior and attitude toward life to offer as a model. To project an image of invulnerability for James, she alienates herself from the community and deals with her world on an individualistic level. The community, presumably, offers no such model. Taking what she has—her pride and her poverty—, she moves toward her goal of inculcating in James a sense of independence and dignity in self undeterred by offers of kindness and generosity. However, because she never explains her motives to him, she presents James with a world filled with extremes which endangers his realization of the manhood she attempts to force prematurely on him. The "gray" of the sky which hangs threateningly over the action of the story symbolizes the dangers inherent in the extremes which James must reconcile. While "gray" literally represents the harmonious blending of black and white, its use in the story to describe the sky before a brewing storm symbolizes a potentially destructive force. The force implicit in the story is Octavia's individualism, which threatens to deprive James of membership in the human community. . . .

In both **"A Long Day in November"** and **"The Sky Is Gray,"** Gaines involves the reader in the dilemma faced by individuals who find traditional folk values inadequate to meet their needs. In both cases, the situation is presented as a puzzle to the young who must attempt to resolve the conflicts that come about as a result of this realization. For Eddie in **"A Long Day in November,"** the ability to solve the enigma created by Amy's decision to leave him is compounded by his already established communal world view. However, his indirect discovery that the community is no longer capable of defining his individual responsibility to his family is potentially important both for him and for Sonny. Furthermore, the story implies that the community can continue to provide the individual with emotional support in his efforts to fulfill his individual needs. On the other hand, James in **"The Sky Is Gray"** will never know the values of communal bonds if Octavia has her way. Although the point is never explicitly stated, it is apparent that Octavia finds the values of her community inadequate to make James the kind of man that she feels he must become. Her personal situation can be seen as a metaphor for the plight of blacks. Dependency on the philanthropy and good will of others leads to vulnerability when that support is no longer forthcoming. Her alternative, however, creates an atmosphere which, for James, is potentially equal in the dangers it poses. The fact that neither story offers a resolution to the underlying conflict apparent in the situations is indicative of the contemporary nature of the issue which Gaines raises.

John F. Callahan

SOURCE: A Moveable Form: The Loose End Blues of *The Autobiography of Miss Jane Pittman*," in *In the African-American Grain: The Pursuit of Voice in Twentieth-Century Black Fiction,* University of Illinois Press, 1988, pp. 189-216.

As a writer, Gaines feels the burden of imbuing his fiction with the immediacy of the spoken word. "Now maybe what I need to do," he tells one interviewer, "is sit in a chair on a stage and just tell people stories rather than try to write them. I wish I could do that. I wish I could be paid just to sit around and tell stories, and forget the writing stuff." Yet he knows that Charles Dickens, Mark Twain, and other platform storytellers first reached their audience through the written word. "But, unfortunately, I am a writer," Gaines continues in tones recalling [Ralph] Ellison's phrase for the demands of craft—"that same pain, that same pleasure"—"and I must communicate with the written word." As Gaines talks about writing, you hear the arduous, self-wrenching, self-creating transition he has made to the writer's vocation. You feel the pull of the past (and present) oral tradition of the old folks whose voices and stories Gaines heard and absorbed as a boy in Louisiana, and, after he arrived in California as a teenager in the late 1940s, vowed he would get on paper.

Clearly, he prefers to give up little or nothing of the heritage he remembers so vividly: "Sometimes they would sew on quilts and mattresses *while they talked;* other times they would shell peas and beans *while they talked.* Sometimes they would just sit there smoking pipes, chewing pompee, or drinking coffee *while they talked.* I, being the oldest child, was made to stay close by and serve them coffee or water or whatever else they needed. In winter, they moved from the porch and sat beside the fireplace and drank coffee—and sometimes a little homemade brew—*while they talked.*" "One gets the flow," Michael S. Harper has written [in "Gains," *Images of Kin: New and Selected Poems*] of Gaines's work, and it is not surprising to hear Gaines say that "once I develop a character and hear his voice, I can let him tell the story." Speech is Gaines's gift, and he reoralizes the written word with the old immediacy of oral storytelling.

"Usually," he repeats, "I think of myself as a storyteller. I would like for readers to look at a person telling the story from the first person point of view as someone actually telling them a story at that time." In his fiction "that

time" is often a condition similar to Gertrude Stein's continuing present, a double conscious time of things happening and perceived happening, simultaneously. This sense of present time derives from the oral tradition and the immediate contact that existed between accomplished storytellers and their audience. For Gaines, the stories he has heard and those he creates revivify a world of kinship ties based as much on reciprocal speaking and listening as on blood. This is why his stories are often told from the perspective and in the voice of someone who participates in or initiates the action as well as tells it. As Gaines develops a character, conventions of seeing and knowing yield to a prior necessity. For although Gaines writes words on the page, he changes seeing-is-believing into hearing-is-believing. According to his speech-driven *donnée* of fiction, for the writer to be free, his characters must be free, and an independent, individual voice is the first test of freedom.

For Gaines and his characters, writing and storytelling are acts of remembrance, creation, and performance that sometimes lead to acts of change. His characters witness, experience, and sometimes promote change, yet their idiom changes little. Speech stabilizes their lives and helps them find the courage to participate in the changes coming in what one of them calls "the scheme of things." Gaines's time in Louisiana—1933-48—precedes the turning point in southern experience when a social order, defined and sustained by the officially sanctioned relations between blacks and whites, was about to be disturbed. His fiction mediates two complementary facts of life: first, that very little changes in his remote parish between the Civil War and his departure after World War II; and, second, that even rural Louisiana could not resist the racial upheaval of the 1950s and 1960s. But a social, political, and economic order as powerful and long-lived as the deep South's peonage system does not crumble overnight.

"The past ain't dead," Gaines is fond of paraphrasing William Faulkner, "it ain't even passed." So, too, the voices of the living and the dead from Gaines's past possess and quicken his memory. In oral performances of the kind he witnessed down in the quarters, people presented themselves and their stories as their ancestors did in slavery days. But only through the artifice of the written word can Gaines introduce strangers to his Louisiana world. Paradoxically, he shifts from speech to print, from oral storytelling to fiction so that readers may hear his people's voices and experience imaginatively their oral culture. But writing involves performance, too, although the action is of a different, more interior kind. Writing is a solitary struggle, sometimes painful, sometimes exhilarating. With luck and skill, you move from talking to yourself to conversation with your characters and, later perhaps, with readers. In writing as well as speech, voice articulates the self and the self's capacity for form and eloquence. The link between form and voice explains why Gaines listens until he hears and recognizes his character's voice, then, convinced of the character's individuality, allows him to tell the story.

"My writing is strongest when I do that," Gaines says referring to the flash point when he yields the storytelling voice to his character. He seeks what Kate Chopin, whose fiction is also full of the sensuous feel of Louisiana sun, sky, and speech, calls that point of moral awareness when one is "beginning to realize her position in the universe as a human being, and to recognize her relations as an individual to the world within and about her." Gaines's first-person narrators come into possession of storytelling voices, but in *The Autobiography of Miss Jane Pittman* Gaines discovers his form in the oral tradition of call-and-response between storyteller and audience. Until then, his narrators, though audible to readers, and other characters, lack the immediate audience enjoyed by oral storytellers. Jim Kelly, narrator in *Of Love and Dust,* and the narrators of the *Bloodline* stories, including the ten successive individual voices in **"Just Like a Tree,"** tell Gaines's stories in interior voices. In an interview Gaines compares Kelly with Nick Carraway, F. Scott Fitzgerald's participant-narrator in *The Great Gatsby.* "I needed a guy who could communicate with different people. I needed a guy who could communicate with Bon Bon, the white overseer, with Aunt Margaret, with Marcus." Like Carraway, Kelly hears parts of the story from other characters and incorporates them into his narrative. Yet Kelly has no audience directly in mind and, unlike Carraway, does not tell of writing down his words.

Likewise, the stories in *Bloodline* are not told in a dramatic context. No one appears to be present except the character, and the stories seem to unfold entirely inside the narrator's mind. But they are told with an accuracy of idiom, an authenticity of voice, and an economy of form worthy of Gaines's approving phrase—*"That's writing."* . . .

Telling your story is a way of shaping your life, and therefore a struggle with the form of experience and imagination. *Bloodline* prepares for change in the social order through personal changes. Its narrators bide their time and intensify the possibilities of their lives as individuals in a threatened black community. Gaines follows *Bloodline's* limited, immediate, temporal and social scale with *The Autobiography of Miss Jane Pittman* whose voice and story lines work back to the Civil War and forward to the continuing present where, before her death, Jane Pittman puts her eloquence to work for change—a small heroic action, perhaps unanticipated when she begins to tell her story, but an act that her mastery over storytelling and experience makes her ready to perform. *The Autobiography of Miss Jane Pittman* begins with a call for storytelling. Jane responds, and before she is done, history and circumstance also call. Here, too, she responds and changes storytelling from a secondary to a primary act. Her voice, her life, her story, and her last civil rights action fuse with her people; individually and together, they influence "the scheme of things" in the quarters and, through the history teacher's good offices, the world beyond. . . .

In *The Autobiography of Miss Jane Pittman* Gaines wanted more than the feel of voices. He wanted the novel's *donnée* to be a complex performance of oral storytelling. Like the characters whose voices he puts on paper, especially the young history teacher, Gaines arrives at his eventual form only after a long hard struggle. "I wanted to continue from `**Just Like a Tree'**—where a group of people tell the life story of a single woman," Gaines characterizes his original intention. "The story was to begin on the day that she was buried—the old people who had followed her body to the cemetery would later gather on the porch of a lady who had never walked in her life, and there they would start talking." Everyone would be a storyteller, and from the start the audience would be a congregation performing the essential community work of culture. "At first," Gaines notes, "a group of people were going to tell about this one person's life, and through telling of this one person's life, they were going to cover a hundred years of history, superstitions, religion, philosophy, folk tales, lies." But after a year Gaines discarded this form of multiple voices, multiple points of view. "I had fallen in love with my little character," he admits, telling a little of his story, "and I thought she could tell the story of her life much better than anyone else." As a craftsman, Gaines questions the authenticity of his initial multiple-voice storytelling. "After I'd written it like that one time, it was untrue, so I broke it down to one person telling the story, the individual herself telling the story." Thus, *A Short Biography of Miss Jane Pittman* becomes *The Autobiography of Miss Jane Pittman.*

"All I could do was act as her editor," Gaines says playfully of his relationship with Miss Jane Pittman, "never her advisor." But he turns over the editorial function to the history teacher. In the introduction *the editor* tells how Jane Pittman's story becomes the community's before and after her death. His account reenacts complexities of African-American storytelling going back to the time when slave tales were told on request to outsiders—whites like Joel Chandler Harris and blacks with some claim to membership in the community but who, like Zora Neale Hurston, had a professional interest in having the stories told. Because the young teacher apparently has grown up in or near the quarters, he understands the old slave saying: "Everything I tells you am the truth, but they's plenty I can't tell you." There is plenty missing from the books he uses to teach history, so he is determined to expand what is told and the audience it is told to. So the history teacher takes the lead and tells his story. He tells of his sometimes blundering struggle for Miss Jane's story. His account reinforces oral storytelling as a vital, functional everyday habit and also as a ritual occasionally of sacred significance in African-American culture. . . .

[Gaines commented:]

> I wanted to smell that Louisiana earth, feel that Louisiana sun, sit under the shade of one of those Louisiana oaks, search for pecans in that Louisiana grass in one of those Louisiana yards next to one of those Louisiana bayous, not far from a Louisiana river. *I wanted to see on paper* those Louisiana black children walking to school on cold days while yellow Louisiana busses passed them by. *I wanted to see on paper* those black parents going to work before the sun came up and coming back home to look after their children after the sun went down. *I wanted to see on paper* the

true reason why those black fathers left home—not because they were trifling or shiftless—but because they were tired of putting up with certain conditions. *I wanted to see on paper* the small country churches (schools during the week), and I wanted to hear those simple religious songs, those simple prayers—that devotion. (It was Faulkner, I think, who said that if God were to stay alive in the country, the blacks would have to keep Him so.) And I wanted to hear that Louisiana dialect—that combination of English, Creole, Cajun, Black. For me there's no more beautiful sound anywhere—unless, of course—you take exceptional pride in "proper" French or "proper" English. I wanted to read about the true relationship between whites and blacks—about the people that I had known.

When Ernest Gaines confesses his love for the Louisiana of his experience, he simultaneously declares his craft. He brings into existence the world of his fiction, and creates his characters from the Louisiana dust. Through the act of writing Gaines reexperiences the landscape on a primary sensuous level. His repeated incantations of the word Louisiana transport him to the place; once there, he puts on paper the historical but alterable society that exists in the midst of nature's abiding reality. And the instrument behind the passage of the spoken word to the page is the writer's healing human voice. Like his storyteller, Miss Jane Pittman, and his editor, the young history teacher, Gaines breaks down the barriers between his voice and the voices of his people, his characters. He has heard them all and, writing, hears them still, talking, living their lives, and telling their stories. As a writer for his people, Gaines keeps faith with the oral tradition—a tradition of responsibility and change, and, despite violent opposition, a tradition of citizenship. In turn, his novel's spirit of call-and-response invites readers to pick up the loose ends, join in the storytelling, and, like Miss Jane Pittman, come home.

Anne K. Simpson

SOURCE: "Writing Style: Influences and Characteristics," in *A Gathering of Gaines: The Man and the Writer,* University of Southwestern Louisiana, 1991, pp. 105-36.

Ernest J. Gaines could be called a philosopher as well as a novelist, though in his works he does not preach, nor judge, nor does he try to inflict his personal views on the reader. He does not need to. The reader immediately senses the feelings of the author's finely drawn characters, convinced from the first sentence that Gaines' sinner man is present. . . .

Since Gaines had read almost no black writers at the time he began writing, he does not consider that any particular one has consciously influenced him. Though he admires many of them, he deplores the fact that some of them deny having learned anything from preceding writers. Gaines has been especially impressed by Jean Toomer (1894-1967), and he has mentioned the works of writer/ethnomusicologist Zora Neale Hurston (1891-1960) as peripheral influences. Of Toomer's poetic novel *Cane,* published in 1923 and reissued in 1975, Gaines says, "To *me* that's

the Black American novel. That *is* my novel." He was particularly taken with Toomer's structuring of *Cane,* in which he combined short chapters of poems and short sketches, mostly about women. . . .

Gaines has repeatedly admitted the profound influence of Tolstoy, Dostoevsky, Turgenev, Chekhov, Faulkner, Hemingway, Joyce, Shakespeare, Twain, and the dramatists of ancient Greece upon his own writing style, a fact almost belabored by analysts of Gaines. Though of different locale, generation, and race, the Russian writers, in particular, addressed themselves to the peasantry and its struggle for dignity, a theme also pervading most of Gaines's works, for Gaines knows that the black man *is* America's peasantry.

In a speech in 1969 in Chapel Hill, North Carolina, where he was invited by Professor Joe Ritok, Gaines defined the American peasant, asking

> But why this fear [of other writers] to write truly about the American peasant? Is there no such thing as a peasant in America? Then what do we call the man who works the land and does not own it? The man who lives in a one room shack and works and works and barely makes enough to eat? If you don't want to call him a peasant, call him something else—the name does not matter—that he exists does, and that he has not been properly described is true. In Hollywood, as in our novels, he is either ignored or romanticized. Today if Hollywood wants to make a movie about peasants, they must go to Mexico or to some oriental or European country. Never Mississippi, Alabama, or Louisiana. They can find the most peasant of peasants a hundred miles out of Hollywood, but they prefer moving their millions of dollars of equipment to film peasants in Mexico, Europe, or the orient.

He considered *The Grapes of Wrath* the only good movie that Hollywood made about American peasants,

> and the only time you can see that is on the late, late show—as if they were afraid that it might shock the more sensitive. I doubt that it would, but I do think it would make them think and ask questions. . . . Once you start asking questions about the Joads, you might ask questions about the conditions of the blacks.

In Baton Rouge at Southern University in 1971 Gaines expanded on the Russians' expertise in writing about the peasantry.

> Their peasants were not caricatures or clowns. They did not make fun of them. They were people—they were good, they were bad. They could be as brutal as any man, they could be as kind. The American writers in general, the Southern writer in particular, never saw peasantry, especially black peasantry, in this way; blacks were either caricatures of human beings or they were problems. They needed to be saved, or they were saviors. They were either children, or they were seers. But they were very seldom what the average human being was. There were exceptions, of course, but I'm talking about a total body of writers, the conscience of a people.

Gaines continued by pointing out some of the Russian contrasts to his own culture which were fascinating but confusing to him, such as their icons and religious worship, their four and five syllable names, their greetings, their food and customs.

> I had eaten steamed cabbage, boiled cabbage, but not cabbage soup. I had drunk clabber, but never kvass. I had never slept on a stove, and I still don't know how anyone can. I knew the distance of a mile—never have I learned the distance of a verst. The Russian steppes sounded interesting, but they were not the swamps of Louisiana. Siberia could be just as cruel, but still it was not Angola State Prison. So even here, those whom I thought were nearest to the way I felt still were not close enough.

Of the American writers Gaines especially champions Hemingway's understatement of things, which he considers as profound as Count Basie's musical understatements. Hemingway's style, which is relatively free of adjectives and adverbs, and the stoicism of many of his characters who always "came through gracefully under pressure" have provided a bible for Gaines. For who knows better than Gaines that *no* one has experienced as much pressure as the black in America, and managed to come through more gracefully? In each of Gaines's works, a black person is given a heavy burden and is expected to "come through." He always shows the strength and pride of his race. He feels that the job of black writers is not to tell whites of black racial problems, that they should do more than work out their anger on paper. He prefers to show strength, pride, and humanity in his characters. *Miss Jane Pittman* has been criticized as being a novel of protest. If so, it is one of subtle protest. . . .

In expressing the concept of manhood, perhaps Gaines's most persistent theme, he mentions the Greek influence again. The black man's status as a man has been denied by the white race since he was brought to America as a slave in chains. Tradition demands that his attempts to be a man should be dangerous. Gaines says,

> The hoodoo lady and Joe Pittman [in *Miss Jane*] both say that man has come here to die. So whenever my men decide that they will be men regardless of how anyone else feels, they know that they will eventually die. But it's impossible for them to turn around. This is the sense of Greek tragedy that keeps coming back in my writing, that men are destined to do things and they cannot do anything but that one thing. Whatever that one thing is, it is to be done as well as the man can do it. . . .

He has often been asked if the works of Ralph Ellison, author of *The Invisible Man,* influenced him. He has considered Ellison, along with James Baldwin, better essayists than writers of fiction. In an interview with Gregory Fitzgerald for The *New Orleans Review* Gaines said:

> No. . . . I didn't read anything at all by Ralph Ellison until I had formed my own style of writing. . . . I knew very early what it was I wanted to write about. I just had to find a way to do it, and the white writers

> . . . showed me this way better. I looked at Hemingway as a man who can really construct paragraphs; when I want to construct a good paragraph, I read a little Hemingway. You can look at Turgenev's structure of his *Fathers and Sons* for a perfectly constructed little novel, or at F. Scott Fitzgerald's construction of *The Great Gatsby.*

> You look at everything in Tolstoy, who I think is the greatest of them all, the greatest man to write a novel. So you learn from all these people; I've learned from all of them. I learned how to get what was in me onto the paper. As I said about the story **'A Long Day in November,'** I had to get it from Faulkner and from Joyce, but not from Richard Wright or Ellison or Baldwin, or anybody like that. They showed me how to get it much better than the black writers had done because so many of them really dealt with style, whereas I think the black writers are much more interested in content—you know, putting it down like it is—and the style is sort of secondary. . . .

In Gaines's address to the Modern Language Association in 1981 he recalled German philosopher Nietzsche's remark, "Without music life would be a mistake," and elaborated further.

> Well, music makes my writing go, and I know that for sure. The most wonderful musical instrument is the human voice. My characters must speak musically. My narrator must have a sense of rhythm. The great thing about listening to a story teller is not only what he says, but the way that he says it. In writing, I try to make you hear that story teller. Not only read descriptions, or dialogue, or follow the narrative, but hear it. People have asked me was it hard to write **The Autobiography of Miss Jane Pittman.** No, it was not, once I caught the rhythm of her speech. . . .

He continued,

> Music is as much an assistant in my writing as anything else is. Lester Young with his saxophone teaches as much about understanding as does Hemingway on his typewriter. Lester, or Prez, shows you how to play round the note of the ballad, rather than the note itself, and still tell the story as truly as if he was playing the ballad word for word. . . .

> I think jazz is basically folk music. Originally it was, though I'm not sure what they're doing with it now. And folk music is a very simple thing. All folk music is very, very simple. Listening to jazz I find simple rhythms, simple repetitions. In order to communicate jazz to the layman it has to be simple, and of course these musicians were playing to people just like themselves, uneducated people. I wish to reach the same sort of thing in my fiction, to use the simplest terms in the world, you know, terms like 'Jesus wept;' I think that's. . . . the most beautiful two-word sentence that has ever been written. It has all the meanings in the world in it. Another thing about jazz is that to be impressive it has to be repetitive. You get hooked upon a phrase and you stay with that phrase until you have really convinced the people. . . .

Gaines's previously mentioned record collection includes not only jazz, blues, spirituals, European classics, but

African and American Indian folk music as well. In the speech at Southern University Gaines said:

> I think I have learned as much about writing about my people by listening to blues and jazz and spirituals as I have learned by reading novels. The songs of Billie Holiday and Bessie Smith I find superior to the poetry of Gwendolyn Brooks and Nikki Giovanni. The blues of Leadbelly, Muddy Waters, B. B. King, and spirituals of Paul Robeson and Marian Anderson, I find far superior to the writing of Don L. Lee and the rest of that Chicago crowd. The understatements in the tenor saxophone of Lester Young, the crying, haunting, forever searching sounds of Coltrane, and the softness and violence of Basie's big band, all have fired my imagination as much as anything in literature. But the rural blues, maybe because of my background, is my choice in music. . . .

The most profound influence on Gaines's writing has been neither the literary nor the musical one. The contour of his works may in larger part be attributed to his early life in South Louisiana. Without this particular background, backlog, there would be no Ernest J. Gaines as we know him.

Probably the strongest recurring theme which emerges in Gaines's works, as well as in Hemingway's, is the struggle of his characters to live with grace, courage and dignity under social and racial stress. Without detracting from Hemingway's influence on the subject, it is obvious that Gaines's South Louisiana background has heavily contributed to his need to probe this theme so thoroughly. After the publication of *Miss Jane Pittman* in 1971 Gaines said:

> That [grace under pressure] might be a good description of my work. I hope it is; it is such a beautiful description that any writer should be proud of it. I know that my characters are usually poor, mostly uneducated, and almost always very independent. The conflict in which they usually find themselves is *how to live as a man* in that short period of time.

Speaking of his native Louisiana as a writing source Gaines said:

> It is something I have never tried to forget. I never hated things so much that I tried to blank them out. I love my people and I love the land. I don't love the politics, of course. If you had that hate you couldn't be a receptacle. You couldn't be open to do things. My use of narrative and dialogue are the strongest parts of my writing and I can bring in things because I am open. I can bring in the smells, the weeds, the roads, the houses, the trees. There are people who write about an oak tree and when you read it you feel they don't really know about it. They don't know an oak can be used for shade; can be used for shelter; that the old people used its moss to stuff their mattresses. My receptacles get out and capture things—old women complaining, men talking about dreams, even what my characters are thinking. I ask myself, how would they say, what they *don't* say?

Gaines avoids using a heavy-handed pen because there is something he *likes* in all of his characters, both black and white, no matter their imperfections. If he does happen to write with hatred of a character, he realizes that he has lost control, and ultimately deletes such passages. Comparing the artist to a heart surgeon, Gaines says that both must have sympathy, but stay removed enough to achieve perfection. . . .

Most of Gaines's stronger male characters are built around his step-father, Mr. Colar. Understandably, one of Gaines's strongest recurring themes is the search of the young man for the missing father, or the absence of the father, since his own father remained on the plantation only a few years after he was born. Gaines expressed his use of the theme in *Black Creation,* joking in **"A Long Day in November"** about the father's involvement with mechanical things and other diversions, not pertinent to a real education of his son. As a symbol of the mechanized world, the father seeks changes in ridiculous ways to regain his wife and child's affections. The search for a father is evident as well in **"The Sky Is Gray,"** and clearly things would be better if the father were there. The agony of the painful tooth forces the boy to become a man in the father's place. . . .

Another of Gaines's themes is the control of life within a framework of society, one often entwined with the law; the concept of slow change and the black person's reaction to it and his role in it—change in society, in attitudes, and in material and emotional values. He is saddened that today's children would value an expensive Christmas gift more than the old-time apple, some marbles, and firecrackers that he used to receive, which at the time were given with love and respect. "I wish children could put the feeling before the gift," he told a *San Francisco Chronicle* reporter in 1978. . . .

Gaines does not actually commit himself to saying that his noblest, most dignified characters are on the right track, that they can definitely better themselves and make the world better. But in all the writings there seems to be one character who tries. Gaines's more dramatic scenes seem to culminate in the slow confrontations of two groups, precipitated by the actions of two individuals, for example Creole and white (Robert Carmier and Marc Grover in *Catherine Carmier*), between convict and foreman (Marcus and Bonbon in *Of Love and Dust*), between young black and planter (Marcus and Hebert in *Of Love and Dust,* and Cooper and Frank in **"Bloodline"**). Blacks have largely asserted their maleness with rebellion. Movement in Gaines's works is carried by those who stand for change and openness, but critics wonder if he truly believes there is potential for real change.

A strong theme in Gaines's writing is the inability, especially for the artist, to escape the past, though living in the past and trying to escape it are different things.

> If you do nothing but worship the past you are quite dead, I believe. But if you start running and trying to get away from the past you will, I think, eventually run yourself out of whatever it does to you. It will run you mad, or kill you in some way or the other. So you really don't get away. It's there, and you live it.

This conflict between change and stasis is evident in many of Gaines's characters. Some are victims of the past who are willing to change but who cannot overcome their racial and cultural past. Others sacrifice integrity by allowing the past to control them (Tee Bob in *Miss Jane Pittman* and Jackson in *Catherine Carmier*). Gaines says this problem will always be present in his writing, because one person alone cannot endure the burden of cleanly breaking away from the past. Each hands it on to another. He has no answer for resolving the conflict. . . .

Asked if he has any bitterness, Gaines says he is concerned about humanity rather than bitterness. He does not like racism, bigotry, or war. He wants his works to be considered the best art that he can produce, and above all to show that it is possible for an individual, black or white, to face a given situation alone, bravely. Gaines especially appreciates praise from Louisianians, because then he knows that they recognize him for being himself, for writing about them without florid language, and because they are proud to see themselves in his writings.

Of his respect for Louisiana ties, he told interviewer Ruth Laney that he feels good when people he has known at False River compliment his work. He mentioned, in particular, the Parlange family, owners of the oldest house in Louisiana, several of whom had read his work and commented favorably upon it. Appreciation from such people means more to him than compliments from the New York critics. He expressed a desire to Laney to be buried on River Lake Plantation.

In September of 1983 Gaines told a Lafayette interviewer:

> I believe in form and language—not only content—and that's what makes writing an art. Most of my characters have a dialect. But I create the dialect through syntax and the placement of words, not through misspelling. I also want my characters to be psychologically true so they'll be as real as real people.

Gaines has an uncanny ability to string out a story with dialogue, and make use of repeated words or phrases within the dialogue, typical of black storytellers and words in blues tunes. He usually builds small incidents with it, using description sparingly. Drawing generously from his memories of radio shows, such as one favorite, "Gunsmoke," he likens conversation heard through a wall to radio talk. As an unseen voice, radio talk resembles somebody listening through a wall to someone else talking whom he cannot see.

Gaines feels that in conversational situations people understate things by leaving out words. Though he has no problem with dialogue, his best weapon, he always has a need to refine it, rewrite it, and add a little description. In recent years he has preferred to refine it as he goes, rather than fill in the whole story and then redo it. . . .

Gaines told interviewer Paul Desruisseaux that writing a novel is like taking a train somewhere—you know the general route, but not all the major happenings which might occur, such as "What the conductor's going to look like." If a book has no *form,* "then damn, it ain't no novel," Gaines said. The content should make up forty percent. When a story takes form, "that's writing." This desire for form is immediately evident when one notices that Gaines's books are in small sections, sometimes designated as chapters, usually grouped to form three or four large parts. Plot, Gaines says, is what makes readers turn the page. His basic requirements are plot, characters, and action. . . .

Gaines continues to hope that his books will gain a following from children and adults in foreign countries, but perhaps more importantly, from both black and white American youth, since he feels that in recent years the two groups have intermingled with a growing understanding.

> I think I have some things to say that not every one else says. I want everyone to read it, especially the Black kids in the South, because I think so much of the stuff being written today doesn't touch the Black kids' life in the South. You never read a book on the black ghetto in a Southern city. You always read about Chicago, New York, Watts, or Detroit. Many of your black writers are in the North now and they usually don't write about the South.

Speaking of the advantage black writers writing about the white have over white writers writing about the black Gaines said in the same lecture:

> When the white man is writing about the black, he's always sort of looking down . . . he doesn't have to fit into the black man's world . . . he can just pass by . . . look at it objectively and write about it. Whereas the black, since he is the minority in this country, he must always try to fit into something. . . . So I think I'm in a [better] position to write about the white man than, say, Truman Capote or William Styron is to write about the black man, because I've always had to be on guard, you know, a thing Baldwin always talked about. Whereas, the white doesn't have to do these things. He can look down on things where I must not look up to things, because there's not a thing in the world that I, Ernie Gaines, has to look up to, because I think I'm in a competitive world.

> You have to write as honestly as you can, as truthfully as you can, [with] all kinds of pressure on you . . . by one group who says that every damn thing must lead toward the revolution . . . [by] those who don't want to say anything bad about Blacks, and I, Ernie Gaines, say that Blacks do awful things too. Now if you can stand up under that pressure then you can be a writer. My world is as tough as anybody's world to compete in and I think I'm doing a pretty decent job as of right now.

Most readers and critics agree that the job Gaines is doing is more than decently. Some interesting comments were found in an unsigned term paper which discussed Gaines's works frankly. The writer described a typical Gaines work as having

> an attractive antique quality, as if it descended from the classical epic or medieval romance rather than the modern novel. . . . Gaines seems to view everything

from the outside, and to present it with the detachment of the traditional folk singer or old minstrel. His narratives, therefore, have a kind of remoteness, and move with a slow, colloquial dignity, externalized and intense, but cool, controlled, austere. Sometimes the slowness turns to blandness, and the austerity leads to washed out characters. And sometimes the remoteness short-circuits the passions that are so important to him. But on the whole, when we read even his weakest material, we know that we're in the hands of a skilled writer and an acutely sensitive human being. . . .

In a novel Gaines sets up immediate action which grabs the reader from the start. Rather than description, he most enjoys writing dialogue, when he has begun to "hear" his characters. "Of course when it's not going well, I don't like hearing them at all," he said. but he is always eager to write, even when things do not go easily. He is able to discipline himself to sit, waiting until something comes to him.

He has said numerous times that he does not lose sleep over the critics' favorable or unfavorable remarks about his writing. *Time,* May 10, 1971, commented: "He [Gaines] sets down a story as if he were planting, spreading the roots deep, wide and firm. His stories grow organically, at their own rhythm. When they ripen at last, they do so inevitably, arriving at a climax with the absolute rightness of a folk tale."

Time has called Gaines the "best black writer in the United States." But Gaines told journalist Ruth Laney this was almost meaningless to him, even if *Time* had called him the best *writer,* regardless of race. Rather than maintain a peak, his philosophy is to do his work as well as possible.

He usually feels good after completing a work, while also feeling like he has not said everything he meant to say, a state of mind leading to the next book. Recalling Faulkner's philosophy on the subject, he told interviewer Desruisseaux, "Once you're satisfied with everything you've done, you might as well break the pencil and cut your throat . . . the whole damn thing is over with. So you never really finish. Not if you're a writer. And it never gets any easier."

Gaines is interested only in writing fiction, as long as he considers it "honest work." One interviewer asked him why he had not written more short stories. Gaines replied that once he finished a novel, he always seemed to have another in mind, but that usually no interesting short stories had taken shape. In an undated, unnamed news item in Gaines files he addressed the situation frankly: "The problem isn't creating a story. It's getting it published." He constantly collects fragments from everyday experiences and lets them simmer and shift until he can use them. In the same news item he said, "I saw a lady in a bar, a small lady with a plump mouth, and she would sort of squint her eyes when she smiled and she would smile all the time. Watching her, I knew I'd use that smile in a story sometime."

David C. Estes

SOURCE: "Gaines's Humor: Race and Laughter," in *Critical Reflections on the Fiction of Ernest J. Gaines,* edited by David C. Estes, The University of Georgia Press, 1994, pp. 228-49.

When an interviewer asked Ernest J. Gaines if he saw himself as a humorist, he replied, "I don't tell jokes. Whenever I do tell a joke, no one laughs. . . . I think I am more of a listener, really. . . . I like to listen to the way that people talk, and I like to listen to their stories. Then when I get into a little room some place, I try to write them down." Despite the self-deprecating modesty, his short stories and novels abound with funny characters and incidents. Only in *Catherine Carmier, In My Father's House,* and *A Lesson before Dying* does he counterpose no laughter against the disappointment and pain that overwhelm the central characters and their families. When humor appears in Gaines's fiction, it is intrinsic to the narrative. He does not elicit laughter by embellishing stories with superfluous scenes and characters intended merely to shift attention away from the bitter legacy of racial injustice that his characters face. Rather, the humor directly foregrounds issues of racism, so that through incongruities and ironic reversals, Gaines uses laughter as a weapon to retrieve the dignity of African Americans. In particular, his fiction repeatedly depicts the amusing qualities in people's behavior at times of crisis and also the more profoundly ironic reversal of the established racial hierarchy by the long-suffering oppressed. His two most widely acclaimed works, *The Autobiography of Miss Jane Pittman* and *A Gathering of Old Men,* reflect an essentially optimistic, comic view of the future in spite of the history of discrimination and racial tensions they portray. . . .

[L]aughter is integral to Gaines's dramatization of the deep ironies in race relations. He has said that "humor and joking are part of change." Thus the laughter that occurs throughout his novels does not deny the intensity of racial conflict but rather provokes people to see each other, and themselves, differently. It is a weapon against racist misperceptions of weakness and power, of foolishness and dignity.

Nathan Huggins has argued that in the early twentieth century Negro ethnic theater was crippled because black-face minstrelsy had so strongly influenced the popular American imagination that writers were unable to deviate from the "Negro theatrical type" it had established. Gaines's fiction exhibits a creative surpassing of this barrier, erected by white popular culture, to a full, realistic representation of the complexities of African-American life in art. He has found ways of taking some of the stock characters and humorous situations that are part of minstrelsy's legacy and incorporating them with integrity into fiction with a social message that critiques the racist notions out of which that popular art form grew and which it in turn perpetuated. Gaines's humor originates in a double vision that ridicules conventional stereotypes of African Americans by revealing their complex humanity. His comic spirit holds forth the promise that, by possessing such a liberating double vision of themselves, they will become effective agents of change in society.

Marcia Gaudet

SOURCE: "Black Women: Race, Gender, and Culture in Gaines's Fiction," in *Critical Reflections on the Fiction of Ernest J. Gaines,* edited by David C. Estes, The University of Georgia Press, 1994, pp. 139-57.

Ernest J. Gaines portrays some of the central experiences and concerns of women in his fiction. In particular, he shows how black women shape their identities and deal with social relationships in a rural folk community. Elizabeth Fox-Genovese says that "race and gender lie at the core of any sense of self." While race and gender are dominant, culture often defines or determines how they affect identity. This dynamic is particularly true for rural black women rooted in a place, knowing only one set of cultural rules. . . .

Gaines says of his early reading of fiction about the South, "I did not care for the way black characters were drawn. . . . Whenever a black person was mentioned in these novels, either she was a mammy, or he was a Tom; and if he was young, he was a potential Tom, a good nigger; or he was not a potential Tom, a bad nigger. When a black woman character was young, she was either a potential mammy or a nigger wench. For most of these writers, choosing something between was unheard of" ("Miss Jane and I"). Gaines's women characters show not only "something between" but also something more complex, both as individuals and as character types. Frank Shelton notes that "women are a preserving, conserving element in Gaines's world" (*In My Father's House*), certainly characteristic of the aunt and grandmother figures, yet there is also a diverse range of women characters. Portraits of black women in Gaines's fiction reveal individuality and a compelling sense of strength in dealing with the world. They possess devotion to their family and a commitment to the culture in which they live, despite the need to question or negotiate cultural rules. Three issues Gaines deals with concerning women—the influence women have over men, violence toward women, and women's communities—reveal that he creates female characters with an awareness of the complexity of attitudes toward gender and culture.

Certainly the most popular, positive, and pervasive women in Gaines's fiction are the elderly aunts or aunt figures. They have positions of power and respect within the community, and they seem to combine strength, humanity, and an assured wisdom about life. The "auntie" who raises her nieces and nephews, or more often her great-nieces and great-nephews, is a common figure in black fiction and in black culture, and Gaines himself was reared by a great-aunt. The title "aunt" is usually used for an older woman even by those who are not really related to her, especially if they have known her all their lives. Though generally identifying themselves in terms of relationships to men, these women in Gaines's works are not passive servants but are influential in the development of these men. The aunt figures are often sources of strength and wisdom, but they can also be a stifling influence, especially when trying to protect the boys or men from danger, real or imagined. The older women generally seem to have a confidence and sense of place within their community that the men lack. They create a sense of continuity and cohesiveness among their people. Nevertheless, there are important limitations, in Gaines's view, in what they can offer. . . .

A second category of female characters Gaines portrays is the mother. His mothers are strong, mature women concerned with young children and their needs. They sacrifice for their children, who almost always are boys. Amy, the mother in **"A Long Day in November,"** is unusual in Gaines's fiction because she is not on her own but is raising her family along with her husband. She is presented through the consciousness and narrative voice of her young son, Sonny. She cares for and protects him, though at the same time she is trying to cope with her own marital problems. Amy shows tenderness for Sonny by smiling at him and calling him her "baby." He says, "She hugs me real hard and rubs her face against my face."

Octavia in **"The Sky Is Gray"** is perhaps the fullest development of the strong mother figure, intent on teaching her children how to survive with dignity. She is unsentimental and harsh because survival and manhood for her son are her goals. In addition, she is raising her children alone, since the father is in the army. Octavia has strength and dignity, but she lacks warmth and the ability to show love openly to her children. She is so determined to teach them how to survive that she will not allow them to cry or to be afraid, nor does she condone tenderness or open displays of affection. In spite of her harshness, James (the eight-year-old narrator) understands that she loves them and they love her. James says he loves her and wants to buy her a red coat. Gaines has said that in the rural black culture of the late 1940s, the first duty of a mother who loved her children was "To show us how to live, to show us how to survive." Octavia does this by forcing her son to kill animals for food and by defending herself from a pimp by pulling a knife on him. . . .

[W]omen as mothers in Gaines's fiction seem to have the ability to make decisions, to protect and provide for themselves and their children, and to deal with the realities of life. Their strength, wisdom, and dignity come through confronting the hardships of their lives in a racist culture that shows little, if any, compassion for them and their children.

Gaines's fiction has many portraits of women at work. They earn a living, not only for themselves but often for their family, as hoodoo ladies, boardinghouse keepers, fieldworkers, domestics, waitresses, and schoolteachers. . . .

Because Gaines portrays black women firmly rooted in a definite historical and geographic place, we must look at the culture's mores regarding gender roles in order to understand more fully the foregoing character types. To date, the subject of fathers and sons has received almost all the attention of scholars focusing on gender roles in Gaines's works. Indeed, he has spoken about this theme repeatedly in published interviews. Nevertheless, the influence of women on men, violence toward women, and women's communities are important gender issues in Gaines's fiction.

The most important aspect of relationships between the genders in Gaines's fiction is the attempts of black women to influence the black male in his quest for manhood. Rather than having their paths in life determined by men, women in Gaines's fiction are more likely to try to help determine the paths for their boys and men. The image of the boy or young man achieving direction is almost always connected to his mother's or aunt's strength and teaching. . . .

Gaines's fiction presents black women in relation to a rural folk community unique in the South because of the Louisiana French Creole culture. Race, gender, class, and culture are inexorably bound to questions of identity, just as a sense of place is tied to pursuit of individual needs. While there are varieties of adaptations, it is clear in Gaines's fiction that despite being black, female, and poor, the women gain strength and wisdom from life experiences. Moreover, survival with dignity leads in old age to a secure position of prominence within the community.

TITLE COMMENTARY

OF LOVE AND DUST (1967)

Publishers Weekly

SOURCE: A review of *Of Love and Dust,* in *Publishers Weekly,* Vol. 192, No. 8, August 28, 1967, p. 275.

A shocking, disturbing novel, beautifully told in simple but dramatic terms. The narrator is a Negro field hand working on a large Louisiana plantation under virtual slave conditions in the 1940's. He and the other Negroes in "the quarter" passively accept all the brutality handed out by the white man. The Cajun field boss, Sidney Bonbon, has a mistress in the quarter and mulatto sons and an unhappy white wife. Then along comes Marcus, a far from passive young Negro who has killed a man in a barroom brawl and been bonded out to work on the plantation while he awaits trial. Unwilling to accept his fate as the other Negroes have, he plots a clever scheme to help the white plantation owner get rid of Bonbon, who has been blackmailing him. It involves the seduction of Bonbon's lonely wife. But the plan backfires when Marcus falls in love with the woman and dreams of taking her away with him after he has been freed in a rigged trial the plantation owner arranges in exchange for his destroying Bonbon. This will never be possible, however, and the breathless reader knows it as surely and fatalistically as the field hands of the quarter. The Louisiana-born author has worked as a field hand. His first book, *Catherine Carmier,* received excellent reviews, and so should this one.

Kirkus Service

SOURCE: A review of *Of Love and Dust,* in *Kirkus Service,* Vol. XXXV, No. 17, September 1, 1967, pp. 1073-74.

This second novel by a young Negro writer has an honest simplicity and tremendously involving, complicated characterizations. It's contemporary Louisiana and down on the plantation we find Jim Kelly, narrator, easy going, handy with machinery, who is put in charge of "Playboy Marcus," Baton Rouge boy bonded to plantation owner Marshall Hebert after he had killed another Negro in a brawl. Seems Hebert owed Marcus' granny a little favor for forty years of service and a certain little incident in the past. Hebert is also indebted, mysteriously to Bonbon his white overseer who pushes Marcus to the limit in the fields. When Marcus seeks revenge, first with Bonbon's black mistress Pauline (whom he loves) and then with his willing wife who bears the marks from a Bijou past and present shame, the plantation people see trouble like a slow storm, waiting to engulf them all. The build-up in meticulous scenes from the scorching fields at noon to the cool nights with the intricate relationships between Bonbon and Pauline, Marcus and Louise have an abiding realism. Mr. Gaines sees people as pawns, caught up in a slip-stream of circumstance and his sympathetic story transcends the Negro-white motif.

The Booklist and Subscription Books Bulletin

SOURCE: A review of *Of Love and Dust,* in *The Booklist and Subscription Books Bulletin,* Vol. 64, No. 8, December 15, 1967, p. 490.

Troublemaker Marcus, who has killed a fellow Negro, is a young man whose violence expresses conscious and unconscious rebellion against the indignities of his existence in present-day Louisiana. He carries rebellion even to the point of defying the South's double standard which sanctions a love relationship between a white man and Negro woman, providing it is not dignified by marriage, but does not tolerate the reverse. Effective characterization and sensitive handling of his theme allow the author of *Catherine Carmier* to develop his story and to reveal the tragic stature of wild, troubled, and troublesome Marcus convincingly.

The Times Literary Supplement

SOURCE: A review of *Of Love and Dust,* in *The Times Literary Supplement,* No. 3466, August 1, 1968, p. 817.

Young Negro murderer is farmed out to a Louisiana plantation and makes total conquest of the sad little white wife of his Cajun overseer who has a flourishing, long-standing liaison with a black girl from the estate. The violence, perversity and end of the set-up are, of course, implicit in detail from the start. But the tale is so cunningly nurtured and the tenacious, diseased social network so richly dimensioned that even a much-tried story-line feels genuinely original.

A LONG DAY IN NOVEMBER (1971; originally published in *Bloodline*, 1968)

Kirkus Reviews

SOURCE: A review of *A Long Day in November*, in *Kirkus Reviews*, Vol. XXXIX, No. 15, August 1, 1971, pp. 815-16.

An affectionate and genuinely funny story, set in the black "quarter" of a Southern sugar cane plantation around 1940 and told by Eddie, a first grader who is mildly bemused when his mother abruptly leaves her husband and his father endeavors to get her back. Mama's grievance is Daddy's preoccupation with his car, which Daddy in the end sorrowfully burns to the ground on the advice of Madame Toussaint, a voodoo woman cast here as a sort of shrewd and earthy Dear Abby. The brief novel is expanded from an adult short story in Gaines's *Bloodline,* and one wonders if it really works as a juvenile. It's perfectly wholesome, with no problematic sex episodes or any questionable language (unless you object to "nigger," used repeatedly by Gran'mon about her "no good, gap-toothed, yellow" son-in-law). But the crises and concerns are of essentially adult interest, and the action, even though it's seen through Eddie's eyes, is filtered through an adult sensibility. Still, for whoever does tune in, it's warming and refreshing fun.

Zena Sutherland

SOURCE: A review of *A Long Day in November,* in *Bulletin of the Center for Children's Books,* Vol. 25, No. 6, February, 1972, p. 91.

Set in the rural South in the 1940s, a story of a day in which marital discord threatens his security is told by a small black boy. His mother, angry because his father has been out driving his beloved car until late in the night, goes off to her mother's. The boy goes to school unprepared and, nervous because he doesn't know the lesson, wets his pants and is teased. When he comes back to his grandmother's, Sonny finds his mother's old suitor there, encouraging her to leave her husband, a plan the grandmother approves, since she has a low opinion of Sonny's father. Father comes, takes the boy, runs from the grandmother's gun (she says, "I shot two miles over that nigger's head.") and visits a friend, a minister, and a voodoo woman in turn. The latter's advice is to burn his car. He does, his wife realizes that he loves her enough to sacrifice

his dearest possession, and the story ends with Sonny snuggled in bed listening to the comforting sound of his parents' voices. Since the author was born on a Louisiana plantation in the 1930s, this may well be a reflection of his own childhood, if not in a personal way at least in the characterization of the people in the story. The book is written with flair and sensitivity, but it seems more an adult short novel than a children's story.

Mary M. Burns

SOURCE: A review of *A Long Day in November,* in *The Horn Book Magazine,* Vol. XLVIII, No. 2, April, 1972, p. 153.

The life style of a cane-plantation worker in the early 1940's is vividly re-created through the eyes of a child, Sonny, who recounts the events of that momentous day when his parents quarreled, separated, and were finally reconciled through the aid of Madame Touissant, an old woman skilled in the arts of voodoo. Because children's books generally include young people as important characters, distinguishing between a book about children and a book for children is not always an easy task: Henry James's *The Turn of the Screw* is not necessarily a work for children in spite of the important roles assigned to the brother and sister. *A Long Day in November* calls for a reader sufficiently sophisticated to appreciate the subtle nuances of characterization, the skilled uses of contrast, and the superbly realized setting of the rural, black Southland. Indeed, rather than a story about a child, it is about adult relationships and emotions as chronicled by a child observer who is sensitive to, and yet confused by, events which are beyond his level of experience. Thus, his reactions to the quarrel between his parents are of the most elemental nature—an ego-centered response, where his own bodily functions and needs are documented with as much attention as his mother's decision to leave his father. Consequently, what makes the book succeed from the adult's point of view may tend to limit its appeal for children: first, because the child narrator, a first-grader, is too young to interest the average adolescent; second, because he is acted upon rather than being the prime mover; third, because he senses the problems but plays no real part in their solution. Listing these points for consideration is not intended to discourage, but rather to encourage, those working with young people to find the right audience for a well-wrought story which is very real and touchingly human.

THE AUTOBIOGRAPHY OF MISS JANE PITTMAN (1971)

Kirkus Reviews

SOURCE: A review of *The Autobiography of Miss Jane Pittman,* in *Kirkus Reviews,* Vol. XXXIX, No. 4, February 15, 1971, p. 190.

Gaines's Miss Jane is an invented character roughly in the standard mammy mold, but with such strong personal presence that readers may still have to remind themselves this is fiction. Born a slave on a Louisiana plantation, she was not yet in her teens when emancipation came and she began her journey toward freedom as a literal walk overland to Ohio. When her narrative ends she is still moving out to join the freedom marchers though she is well over one hundred and has made precious little progress geographically or legally. To that extent her story is that of the southern Negro, particularly the southern Negro woman, and its private incidents reflect matters of public record. What distinguishes this account is the sustained, gritty characterization and its definitely personal slant on representative people and events. Miss Jane has been persuaded to reminisce by a young historian hoping to find "material" he can "use." The difference between material and a life is quietly brought home, but that is finally the point that dominates all others just as it is Miss Jane who seems strangely to have the upper hand with circumstances beyond her control. Artless art with a strong cumulative effect.

Melvin Maddocks

SOURCE: A review of *The Autobiography of Miss Jane Pittman,* in *Time,* Vol. 97, No. 19, May 10, 1971, p. 97.

Ernest J. Gaines has not received anything like the attention he deserves, for he may just be the best black writer in America. He is so good, in fact, that he makes the category seem meaningless, though one of his principal subjects has been slavery—past and present.

Born on a Louisiana plantation 38 years ago, Gaines is first and last a country-boy writer. He sets down a story as if he were planting, spreading the roots deep, wide and firm. His stories grow organically, at their own rhythm. When they ripen at last, they do so inevitably, arriving at a climax with the absolute rightness of a folk tale. **"Just Like a Tree,"** the final story in his fine 1968 collection, *Bloodline,* could serve as the description for all Gaines's work. Making a slow concentric dance around the life and death of a matriarch named Aunt Fe, the story also anticipated Gaines's new novel.

Jane Pittman is the ancient of ancients, nearly 110 years old, on a Louisiana plantation. Recollecting her life for a tape recorder, she remembers herself first as a slave child, fetching water for Confederate soldiers in retreat, then for Yankees in pursuit. A Yank corporal named Brown tells her to look him up in Ohio. After the Emancipation Proclamation, she sets out to do just that. Most of the ex-slaves impulsively migrating north with her are killed by white-trash patrollers. The moral is fundamental to Gaines's temperament: the more things change, the more they seem to stay the same.

Jane never gets out of Louisiana. But she has begun a pilgrimage of the soul, at first so creepingly tentative that she seems to be motionless. She marries a broncobuster

who is killed by a black stallion. An orphaned boy she has adopted grows up to be a school-teacher. For his premature ideas about civil rights ("Don't run and do fight"), a hired gun shoots him down.

Still Jane's life goes on, apparently as before, such moments of violence surrounded by uneventful years. Accepting her humiliations the old-fashioned way—pretending not to notice them—she takes pride in sanctioned achievements like cotton chopping. She gets religion, and she takes to Huey Long. When Jackie Robinson comes along, she turns into a Dodger fan. In the 1960s Jane's new surrogate son rises up to make an issue of segregated drinking fountains. He too is killed, but this time, almost 100 years after she tried her first step out of slavery, Jane continues that march.

Obviously this is not hot-and-breathless, burn-baby-burn writing. Unlike apocalyptic novelists, Gaines does not make the revolution happen by surreal rhetoric. He simply watches, a patient artist, a patient man, and it happens for him. When Jane, disobedient at last, walks past her plantation owner to take part in a demonstration, a code goes crack, as surely, as naturally as a root pushing up through concrete.

Alice Walker

SOURCE: A review of *The Autobiography of Miss Jane Pittman,* in *The New York Times Book Review,* May 23, 1971, pp. 6, 12.

In the beginning of Ernest J. Gaines's third novel the narrator-historian approaches Jane Pittman for an interview:

"I had been trying to get Miss Jane Pittman to tell me the story of her life for several years now, but each time I asked her she told me there was no story to tell. I told her she was over a hundred years old, she had been a slave in this country, so there had to be a story. When school closed for the summer in 1962 I went back to the plantation where she lived. I told her I wanted her story before school opened in September, and I would not take no for an answer.

"'You won't,' she said.

"'No ma'am.'

"'Then I reckoned I better say something,' she said."

And say something she does in this grand, robust, most valuable novel that is impossible to dismiss or to put down.

Miss Jane's story begins when she is 10 or 11 years old; at that time her name was not Jane, but Ticey. A Yankee corporal renamed her Jane Brown (after his daughter in Ohio) when he led his troops across the plantation of Ticey's master. Freed about a year later, Jane and a group of former slaves leave for Ohio; among them are Big Laura—"tough as any man I ever seen," Jane says—and her son Ned. But a day later their group is set upon by a gang of rebel troops and Klansmen, and Big Laura is killed. Jane and Ned then head South again and, meeting a group of wandering former slaves, are told that they are in Louisiana.

They remain there, and Jane finally finds work on a plantation. She adopts Ned, and he becomes perhaps the most important person in her long life. Later she meets Joe Pittman, a strong, sensitive cowboy who breaks horses for a trader on the Louisiana-Texas border, and they are married.

Ned grows up to be a freedom fighter and a believer in education and Frederick Douglass. After studying in the North and fighting in the war in Cuba, he returns to Louisiana to build a school near the plantation where Jane lived. What he decided to teach was unpopular:

"America is for all of us," he said, "and all of America is for all of us. . . . I left from here when I was a young man. . . . But I say to you now, don't run and do fight. Fight white and black for all of this place. . . . Fight for all, not just a corner. The black man or white man who tell you to stay in a corner want to keep your mind in a corner, too."

It was as unlikely following Reconstruction as it is now for a black man to teach blacks in this fashion in America and live in peace. Shortly after Ned laid the foundation for his school, he was assassinated by a hired killer, a garrulous old Creole who had often fished along the river with Miss Jane.

After Ned's death Miss Jane joined the church. Gaines's handling of her religious belief, her faith in God is marked by humility before the reality of Miss Jane's spiritual experience and physical endurance, before the living *result* of her belief in God. For Miss Jane leaned on a God who, in turn, supported her; whether He was dead or had never existed was a question she did not need to raise.

Near the end of Miss Jane's narrative another young man, similar to her son, Ned, rises up to do battle for his people. Like Ned he is gunned down. And it is at his death, when Miss Jane is 109 or 110 years old, that she joins the civil-rights movement, going off to demonstrate against segregated water fountains.

Because politics are strung throughout this rich and very big novel, it will no doubt be said that Gaines's book is about politics. But he is too skilled a writer to be stuck in so sordid, so small a category.

Certain of his preoccupations have emerged before in *Bloodline,* a collection of excellent short stories, and in *Of Love and Dust,* an earlier novel. One is that although politics are, for the black Southern writer, an inevitable consideration—if only because blacks in the South are often the only *real* political issue—they must never be allowed to obscure the stoical dignity and worth of the people they have largely been used against. Nor must they be more than an underscoring of what is most obvious about the people they represent.

Gaines somehow manages to show that there is more even to a redneck than his racism. Racists are dangerous, unstable, vicious individuals, but never that alone. They are people, fully realized in Gaines's fiction, and have a haggard futility, a pale and shrieking dullness, a pained unsatisfiedness that makes them appear wounded and deficient and far less complete than the blacks they attempt to intimidate.

Gaines's people are never completely wiped out by whites, even when they are killed by them. They are too large and the whites around them too small. His heroes would fight to walk upright through a hurricane. They do no less when confronted with a white world intent on grinding them down. They fight to maintain small human pleasures and large human principles in a hostile and morally degenerate world. They have seen the level to which humankind can sink and have managed to remain standing all these many years.

Gaines is much closer to Charles Dickens, W. E. B. DuBois, Jean Toomer and Langston Hughes than he is to Richard Wright or Ralph Ellison. There is nothing in Gaines that is not open—to love or to interpretation. He also claims and revels in the rich heritage of Southern black people and their customs; the community he feels with them is unmistakable and goes deeper even than pride. Like the beautifully vivid, sturdy and serviceable language of the black, white and Creole people of Louisiana, Gaines is mellow with historical reflection, supple with wit, relaxed and expansive because he does not equate his people with failure.

The Booklist

SOURCE: A review of *The Autobiography of Miss Jane Pittman,* in *The Booklist,* Vol. 67, No. 22, July 15, 1971, p. 930.

Authentic dialog and characterizations mark a well-written fictional autobiography told in the vernacular by an over-one-hundred-year-old black woman who started life as a slave on a Louisiana plantation. Freed at the age of eight or nine at the end of the Civil War the narrator becomes one of two survivors when the group she is traveling north with is massacred by whites. The novel follows her as she settles in Louisiana to raise a young boy— the other survivor who is killed when he tries to teach his fellow Negroes about their civil rights—works in a variety of positions, loves, gets religion, grows old, and survives to take part in a modern-day demonstration for freedom. Having the ring of veracity of an actual slave narrative this is a highly moving saga of the Negro in America in terms of one person's life. Gaines also wrote **Bloodline,** short stories portraying Negro life in the contemporary rural South.

Bede M. Ssensalo

SOURCE: "The Black Pseudo-Autobiographical Novel: *Miss Jane Pittman* and *Houseboy*," in *African Literature Today: 14 Insiders and Outsiders,* edited by Eldred Durosimi Jones, Heinemann, 1984, pp. 93-110.

It is generally agreed that an extremely large proportion of the finest literature from Black authors all over the world has been written in the form of autobiography. The autobiographical mode has continued to flourish as a basic instrument for Black literary expression. Through it the Black author has articulated, defined and responded to the Black experience. . . .

The pseudo-autobiographical novel is not to be confused with the autobiographical novel. The latter is simply a novel which, whether written in the first person narrative style or otherwise, presents a character who is a mask of the author and lives within the writer's own experience. . . .

The prime characteristic of the pseudo-autobiographical novel, however, is the author's deliberate attempt to convince the reader that the events described actually occurred. The pseudo-autobiographical novel employs all the elements of the autobiography. It reads as an autobiography and is often presented as such. In Ernest Gaines's book, for example, the word 'autobiography' even occurs in the title. Indeed, unless the reader knows facts to the contrary, there is very little to indicate that such a work is not a verifiable autobiography. Surely this is a deliberate strategy adopted by the author. . . .

As in all autobiographies, *The Autobiography of Miss Jane Pittman* has one main character. Miss Jane, the narrator, is the central figure around which the story evolves. All the other characters are minor and are seen through her eyes. They are important to the story only to the extent that they illuminate Miss Jane's character. As a consequence, the facts or historical events of the story are related through the context of her experience.

Another link between this novel and the autobiography as a genre is that Miss Jane's tale covers a very significant segment of her life: from the age of five to eight months before her death, one hundred and ten years later. This in itself elevates her story and enhances its significance and validity. Further, since Miss Jane tells her story from memory, the novel acquires an added depth. . . . Miss Jane attaches a new meaning to each event in retrospect because, like the autobiographer, she is dealing with a *fait accompli*.

The book is written in the form of a series of tape-recorded interviews of a Black woman who was once a slave. In his attempt to simulate the autobiographical form, Ernest Gaines went out of his way to demonstrate Miss Jane's dependence upon . . . memory. Due to her age, however, many times her memory fails her. The narrative is full of statements to illustrate this point. . . .

In fact, in the introduction to the book, the school teacher who 'conducted' the interviews talks about the difficulties caused by the lapses in Miss Jane's memory; at some points she was said to forget everything.

Another strategy Ernest Gaines employed to make his book look like a real autobiography was to model it after a major sub-genre of the Afro-American autobiography, the slave narrative. In the tradition of this mode, the ex-slave would risk recounting his life only after he was safely out of the slave states. Similarly, the fictional Miss Jane tells her story from a position of relative impunity. When she agrees to talk to the school teacher, she is already over a hundred years old. Her life has run its course and is only a few months from its glorious end. The incidents she narrates, including the bold and militant act of drinking from a fountain marked FOR WHITES ONLY, are of no consequence to her future life. . . .

The final theme of the slave narrative that Ernest Gaines employs so effectively is that of naming. Most slave narratives make reference to the fact that after the Africans had been brought to the New World against their will, every effort was made to strip them of their language and traditions. In their place they were forced to learn what the slave holders deemed safe for them to learn. To symbolize and to emphasize their westernization, slaves were denied the use of African names and given others. These names were first names only. The slaves were denied a last name, one which is associated with family history, and thus, respectability. Or if the slave had two names, one would be the master's name, either first in possessive form, as Brown's William, or simply, William Brown. Such naming practice symbolized the slave's essential nature: mere property. Upon gaining freedom, therefore, the first thing most ex-slaves did was to name themselves anew. In so doing, the ex-bondsman rejected an identity forced upon him by society and asserted his new-found freedom. The rite of naming was thus a central experience in the life of the ex-slave, symbolizing the act of liberation.

True to the slave narrative mode, *The Autobiography of Miss Jane Pittman* addresses itself to the question of naming. The topic is first mentioned in the first chapter of the novel. During the civil war the Yankees came to Miss Jane's plantation. Her master went into hiding and Miss Jane, then Ticey, was asked by her mistress to give them water to drink. One of the Yankees struck up a conversation with the young girl concerning slavery. By the time the conversation was through, he had convinced Ticey of the evils of slavery (if any convincing was necessary) and had given her another name not associated with slavery— two names in fact: Jane Brown. After being offered respectability (by the only member of society that accepts her) as a human being, Jane, at the age of eleven, was willing to die in defence of what her new name symbolized. . . .

Two other elements unique to the black autobiography are also found in Ernest Gaines's novel. One of these is the theme of violence; the other is the tendency on the part of the author to regard his life as a microcosm of the race. Regarding the first, it seems that one of the functions of black autobiography is to portray in realistic and convincing terms the violence to which Blacks have been subjected and the contradictions and absurdity of racism. . . . Gaines has employed the character of Miss Jane as a vehicle for the exposure of the inhumanity and irony of American racism. Her low-key, matter-of-fact reportage neither detracts from nor diminishes the violence and injustice of the facts described. If anything, the author has given Miss Jane a style much more effective in portraying her rage than a more melodramatic stance might have been. . . .

In the introduction to **Miss Jane Pittman,** the interviewer, a young white schoolteacher, expresses his belief that the story of this one Black woman will give him some insight into the lives of other Blacks, confident that 'her life's story can help (me) explain things to my students'.

Gaines further demonstrates his skill as a novelist by involving other characters in the interviews. . . .

It is natural and plausible that at her age, Miss Jane has lapses of memory or occasionally tires of talking. Aside from adding to the realism of her portrayal, her silences also provide an opportunity for her friends and companions to recount events and experiences that are not only part of Miss Jane's life, but shared by them all. By the end of the project, the young teacher is convinced more than ever that what has been captured on tape is not just Miss Jane's story, but rather the story of a whole race.

Thus, the reader comes away from the novel with the conviction that *The Autobiography of Miss Jane Pittman* is centred not around a solitary heroine but around a people whose collective deeds border upon the heroic. Though Miss Jane is the dominant personality of the narrative, the autobiography itself is that of a people. It recounts the life and death struggles of slaves and freedmen alike. As the novel progresses, all these people, together with Miss Jane, come together in the historic march towards dignity and freedom. That final march in Sampson is only a symbol of the march that has been going on for centuries. . . .

Miss Jane Pittman embodies the spirit of the truly proud and defiant. Her acceptance of death after her long life puts her beyond the threat of retribution. She leads the march against the Jim Crow laws in the hope that this action will prevent her successors from going through the same humiliating experiences she has endured. After years of quietly accepting the racist indignities and physical abuse which have so characterized her life, she decides to act in sheer defiance.

Furthermore, the events in a pseudo-autobiography need little corroboration by other characters or authorities because they are presented by the person who lived them. This is the advantage the autobiographer possesses over the novelist. Closely connected with this is the fact that in the pseudo-autobiography realism is created through the use of the first person account of events. This is especially true of those experiences of the narrator which are based on historic facts that are well-known and accepted. Dramatic tension and suspense are decreased and uncertainty removed because the reader knows that the narrator must survive each crisis in order to be able to record. . . .

The pseudo-autobiography, taking over from where the Black autobiography leaves off, represents the attempt of Black writers to establish within the realm of fiction a realistic, sensitive, and dynamic recreation of the Black experience with emotions and events that transcend the stereotyped images often depicted in White literature and media. The pseudo-autobiography as a genre satisfies a need to validate an experience in a form that is less subject to question than most fictional forms.

IN MY FATHER'S HOUSE (1978)

Kirkus Reviews

SOURCE: A review of *In My Father's House,* in *Kirkus Reviews,* Vol. XLVI, No. 7, April 1, 1978, pp. 386-7.

The quietly repressed tension in the opening chapters here—a dead-eyed young stranger appears in the black section of St. Adrienne, Louisiana—seems to be revving up a subtly gripping and artfully shaped narrative. What Gaines actually delivers turns out to be neither subtle nor shapely, nor especially original, but on every page there's an authentic moment, or a dead-right knot of conversation, or a truer-than-true turn of phrase—enough of them to carry you through to the overly theatrical finale. That wine-drinking, street-walking, gun-toting stranger calls himself Robert X, but he is really Etienne Martin, come to town to kill the father who abandoned him 21 years ago: Rev. Phillip J. Martin, the Martin Luther King of St. Adrienne. Phillip is 60 now, a loving (second) family man and Christian, but when he recognizes yet can't remember the name of his denied son—at a civil rights soirée—he falls to the floor, swamped with guilt for the sins that no amount of good works has really made up for. Desperate for a reconciliation, Phillip betrays the movement (to get his son out of jail he promises that an upcoming demonstration will be scrapped), but his son scorns him, the movement leaders vote him out, and all he can do is try to reach his son indirectly—by learning all he can about the common-law wife and children he deserted. The father's journey-search for his son (reminiscent of everybody from Alan Paton to Toni Morrison) takes him into the back streets of Baton Rouge, where an old friend fills him in on Etienne's tortured life, where he debates with a burn-baby-burn black guerrilla, and where he receives the news that Etienne has drowned himself back in St. Adrienne. Despair and loss of faith ("How come He stood by me all those years, but not today?"), followed by growth—the ability to turn to his wife for help—and renewal: "We just go'n to have to start again." Since we hardly get to know Phillip before his great trauma, this novel doesn't really work as a character study; nor does it quite click as a parable of generation gaps in the post-King (the action is set in 1970) civil rights movement. But Gaines's people talk real talk and walk real streets—and these bedrock strengths of observation can survive even the most blatant or uncoordinated twirling of themes.

Larry McMurtry

SOURCE: A review of *In My Father's House,* in *The New York Times Book Review,* June 11, 1978, p. 13.

Ernest Gaines's fiction has been characterized from the first by its quiet force. The characters in his several fine books often raise their voices, but the author declines to raise his. These characters are mainly poor, and mostly black; their lives are seldom far removed from the threat of violence, physical or emotional or both. Sooner or later the violence arrives, and the characters cry out at one another, or to the heavens. Their pain, struggle, bewilderment, joys and agonies are registered with precision and sympathy, but the strong prose that carries their stories is not affected by the fevers or the biases of those it describes.

A swimmer cannot influence the flow of a river, and the characters of Ernest Gaines's fiction—from Catherine Carmier to Miss Jane Pittman, and from Miss Jane to the Rev. Phillip Martin of *In My Father's House*—are propelled by a prose that is serene, considered and unexcited. It is the force of Mr. Gaines's character and intelligence, operating through this deceptively quiet style, that makes his fiction compelling. He is, pre-eminently, a writer who takes his own good time, and in this case the result of his taking it is a mature and muscular novel.

The Rev. Phillip Martin is a pillar of the black community in the little town of St. Adrienne, La., in the country near Baton Rouge. He is at the height of his influence as a civil-rights leader and is about to lead his forces in an assault on one of the most hated remaining bastions of white supremacy in the town, an unrepentantly racist department-store owner. Then, before the assault can be launched, the Reverend Martin's past abruptly catches up with him. A stranger arrives in the town: a deeply uncommunicative, desperately lonely young man who calls himself Robert X.

Robert X, as it happens, is Phillip Martin's son, one of three children of a liaison formed in Reverend Martin's wild early years, long before he got the call. He has neither seen nor sought his first family in more than 20 years, during which a combination of poverty, neglect and profound outrage have broken it. Robert X himself is in the last stages of terminal self-hatred when he comes to St. Adrienne, intending to confront and possibly kill the father who never claimed him, before he finishes himself off.

The sudden appearance of this tortured, dying boy forces Phillip Martin to—if one might put it mildly—reassess his life. He is a vital man, and though he flinches at first sight of his son, he does go on and make the reassessment. Because this of necessity involves those people he is living his current life with—his wife, his friends, his constituency—the scope of this book is more comprehensive than a summary might suggest. We have revealed to us an individual, a marriage, a community and a region, but with such an unobtrusive marshaling of detail that we never lose sight of the book's central thematic concern: the profoundly destructive consequences of the breakdown of parentage, of a father's abandonment of his children and the terrible and irrevocable consequences of such an abandonment.

Not the least of the book's virtues is the variety and richness of its minor characters. Phillip Martin's guilty search into his past takes him, internally, down a long road of memory. Externally it brings him into contact with a number of people—his godmother, an old girlfriend, a former gambling buddy and an embittered young black guerrilla—whose portraits are done with Flaubertian economy but equally Flaubertian vividness. The dialogue is spare, but unerring, and humor will keep slipping in subtly, despite the tragedies behind these lives. The tone of the book is determined by Mr. Gaines's decision—a brilliant one—to set the novel not in the expected context of a sweaty, dripping Louisiana summer, but in the miserable, frigid, sunless Louisiana winter. The sun never shines on this story, and the metaphors that describe the doom of Robert X are, appropriately, metaphors of chill.

There are few blemishes on the book. Now and then a character strays into polemic; once or twice the tone breaks. Perhaps Robert X should not have been allowed to speak at all, for his condemnatory silence is far more eloquent than the little that he eventually says. But these are small blemishes indeed on a book that attempts a large theme, and is fully adequate to it.

Ellen Lippmann

SOURCE: A review of *In My Father's House*, in *School Library Journal*, Vol. 25, No. 3, November, 1978, p. 81.

Reverend Phillip Martin is suddenly pulled from a secure existence as minister, civil rights leader, and family man by an unexpected visit from the illegitimate son he has never met. The mysterious appearance of Robert X (or Etienne, the son's given name), who has come to kill Martin for having wronged his mother by his 30-year absence, causes quite a stir in St. Adrienne, Louisiana. Martin returns to Baton Rouge for a night spent revisiting old haunts, reliving his long-buried youth, and re-examining his life's values. The book explores the connections and conflicts between older, cautious Blacks and young Black activists, touched upon in Gaines's *The Autobiography of Miss Jane Pittman*, and will attract both fans of the earlier book and those readers interested in the nonviolent vs. violent activism question. Gaines's pace is a little slow, however, and, unfortunately, neither Martin's developing urgency nor Etienne's desperation rings true.

Frank W. Shelton

SOURCE: "*In My Father's House:* Ernest Gaines after Jane Pittman," in *The Southern Review*, Vol. 17, No. 2, April, 1981, pp. 340-45.

Ernest J. Gaines's most recent novel, *In My Father's House*, published in 1978, was not widely reviewed. The notices that did appear were respectful but a bit gingerly and unenthusiastic in tone, as if the reviewers did not quite know how to respond to the book. The relative neglect of the work, in comparison to the more compelling *Autobiography of Miss Jane Pittman,* is understandable. But it is unfortunate in view of the fact that *In My Father's House* is an important work, showing significant development in Gaines's art and thought, especially in light of his depiction of and reaction to the 1970s.

One reason for the lukewarm response to *In My Father's House* is the voice Gaines uses. In fact, according to his own testimony, he had trouble completing the novel because it employs an omniscient narrator, while he wrote most of his earlier works in the first person. His use of omniscient narration led to a phenomenon much noted by reviewers—a severe detachment, a distance between story and narrator. The reader does not get as personally involved with Philip Martin as he does with Miss Jane or Jim Kelly or the narrators of the stories in *Bloodline.* Yet are not detachment and the consequent irony precisely what Gaines aimed to create in *In My Father's House?* He does not intend for the reader to become intimately involved either with the characters or with the story.

Gaines's distancing of his readers—and himself—from this novel may not indicate a change in his philosophy, but it does, I think, reflect a change in his attitude toward his characters' potential development. Considered in sequence, Gaines's first three novels show a gradual development in his characters' ability to grow, change, and prevail. All the characters in *Catherine Carmier,* his first novel, are victims of social or environmental forces, while in *Of Love and Dust* Jim Kelly and Marcus Payne achieve growth through fighting the inertia of southern black life and, within limits at least, gain the capacity to shape their lives. Gaines's sense of this power on the part of his characters culminates in the depiction of Jane Pittman, who prevails over seriously adverse circumstances. The *Autobiography* reconciles the dichotomies of the earlier novels: past and present, young and old, man and woman. In *In My Father's House* the reconciliation falls apart. Discussing the novel while he was still writing it, Gaines contended that it does not reflect a change in his views: "I cannot write only about Miss Jane and man surviving. And I cannot write only about man failing. I write about both." Certainly his works do portray both survival and failure, but I think *In My Father's House* questions the emphasis on black progress reflected in the *Autobiography,* and, in the perspective of developments in America during the late 1960s and the 1970s, suggests that Gaines feels that a modification of the positive conclusion of the *Autobiography* is in order.

Another reason for the relative neglect of *In My Father's House* is, I think, the absence of elements we tend to associate with Gaines, an absence which reinforces his purposes. When we think of Gaines's earlier novels, we think of lovingly depicted rural settings and common people, but *In My Father's House* is set in a town, and many of the characters are teachers, ministers, or businessmen. Emphasizing leaders in conflict over who speaks for the people and stressing the inherent danger of leaders' forgetting just whom they are leading, the novel rarely presents the people who are affected by the actions of the leaders and thus lacks the sense of a community rooted in the soil which was so powerful in Gaines's other novels.

This change in emphasis is in part a result of the setting of the novel. It takes place in early 1970, when the black community, having seemed on the verge of success in its fight with the white power structure, was beginning to experience disillusionment as national support for the civil rights movement waned. The *Autobiography* ended very hopefully, with the unity of the black community appearing to be assured, but Gaines suggests that such unity was, if not illusory, at least only temporary. His latest novel shows both personal and political confusion and disunion. Especially clear is the picture of the relationship between the generations. In the earlier novels, the younger characters lead in the fight for change, while their elders are conservative and traditional, save for Miss Jane, who unites young and old. In *In My Father's House* the older characters lead, while the young hang back. If, as Gaines suggests in the *Autobiography,* the hope of a people is in the union of young and old, that union has disappeared. The young seem either disillusioned, having retreated into drink, cynicism, and indifference, or committed to violent, suicidal revolution. Thus Gaines questions the possibility of the political success of the movement which so hopefully ended the *Autobiography.*

Surely every appreciative reader of Gaines's works recognizes that he is not primarily a political writer, that his themes are really the timeless ones which transcend particular time and place. This is illustrated by the depiction of his main character, Philip Martin. A leader in the community, he is both a personal and political success, a man who has carried on the work of Ned and Jimmy in the *Autobiography.* But the story of *In My Father's House* reveals that the hero has feet of clay. This becomes evident as his past, in the person of his son, catches up with him. Martin has believed that he has made up for his past neglect of his illegitimate children and their mother by his devotion to religion and to the social advancement of his people. Like numerous American literary characters, he has wanted to wipe out the past and start over again. But his success in doing so is illusory.

In *In My Father's House* Gaines again focuses on two themes implicit in all his earlier works: the nature of black manhood and the relationship of fathers and sons. He includes his familiar deterministic explanation of why black men cannot assume their responsibilities and be men. Martin tells his illegitimate son, "'It took a man to do these things, and I wasn't a man. I was just some other brutish animal who could cheat, steal, rob, kill—but not stand. Not be responsible. Not protect you or your mother. They had branded that in us from the time of slavery. [To have acted any differently would have been] to break the rules, rules we had lived by for so long, and I wasn't strong enough to break them then.'" Like some other Gaines male characters, Martin moves toward manhood and indeed does assume responsibility for family, church, and community. But when encountering the virtually wordless accusations of his son, he is forced to wonder if he has truly escaped his past. . . .

The novel ends *we just go'n have to start again.* It will be interesting and illuminating to see where Gaines goes from here, whether his future vision will emphasize triumph or tragedy, whether in the context of the 1970s and the 1980s he can find the possibility of hope and reconciliation for humanity.

A GATHERING OF OLD MEN (1983)

Kirkus Reviews

SOURCE: A review of *A Gathering of Old Men,* in *Kirkus Reviews,* Vol. LI, No. 13, July 1, 1983, p. 716.

In the first half of this short novel, Gaines makes something poetic out of a melodramatic moment in Southern race relations; in the second half the melodrama more or less takes over, as does a slightly muddled web of themes. Candy Marshall, 30-year-old heir to the rundown Marshall place in 1970s Louisiana farm-country, discovers the dead body of neighboring Cajun farmer Beau Boutan— and standing nearby with a gun in his hands is old Mathu, the proud black family-retainer who raised Candy, and her Daddy before her. Determined to protect Mathu, Candy quickly announces that *she* shot Beau; furthermore, Candy sends out the word that all the old black men in the area should join her at the murder-site, bringing shotguns identical to Mathu's. So, as the dialect-wise narration shifts from voice to voice around the neighborhood, a dozen old men respond to Candy's call—fearful, eager, skeptical: "We wait till now? Now, when we're old men, we get to be brave?" They gather near Beau's body, each of them (as well as Mathu and Candy) confessing to the killing, with their proclaimed motives becoming a whimsical yet powerful litany of long-standing grievances. (One old man says he did it because of the overgrown, neglected black cemetery: "I did it for every last one back there under them trees. And I did it for every four-o'-clock, every rosebush, every palm-of-Christian ever growed on this place.") And they stubbornly, effectively stand up to the rough, savvy local sheriff—while they all wait for the inevitable arrival of the much-feared Fix, Beau's Klan-ish father. Then, however, as the novel slips from fable-like intensity to more conventional storytelling, there are a series of plot-turns, each reflecting an aspect of the South-in-transition: Fix will wearily decide *not* to play vigilante (two of his sons, for largely selfish reasons, argue that lynching days are over); Mathu will reject Candy's paternalistic protection; the *real* killer will surface, brave enough to confess as well as to fight back against white abuse; and when local rednecks demand instant justice, the redneck sheriff will oppose them—with death coming to the most violent men on both sides in the shootout that follows. As usual, Gaines offers spare atmosphere, keen-eared dialogue, and quietly taut confrontations. But the novel's second half tries to compress too much socio-symbolic action into

a small-scale story; and it's the book's simple, eloquent, inspired opening that stays—hauntingly—in the mind.

Gregory Maguire

SOURCE: A review of *A Gathering of Old Men,* in *The Horn Book Magazine,* Vol. LIX, No. 6, December, 1983, pp. 739-40.

The author of ***The Autobiography of Miss Jane Pittman*** tells a story of a single day in the lives of a number of people associated with the fictional Marshall plantation in Louisiana. A white man has been shot and killed in the front yard of a poor elderly black man. To save him from the law and from the lynch mob, the young white female owner of the plantation claims to have committed the murder; furthermore, she gathers around her some eighteen elderly black men, all with shotguns capable of having delivered the bullet, all with honest motives for killing the white man. The white sheriff is caught between his duty to justice and his fear of the arrival of the murdered man's vengeful brothers, father, and friends. Almost as if delivering testimony in a court of law, the characters, both significant and minor, take turns reporting on the day's events, slowly drawing back the curtains of conjecture and suspicion which hide the truth from the law and from the reader. The author tells a tale of pity and strength; his portraits of the aged men taking a stand against their oppressors—some of them for the first time in their long lives—are beautiful and painful. Mathu, the old man suspected of the killing, is "built like a picket—no, more like a post. A old post in the ground—narrow but still strong, and not leaning, and not trembling, either." Some of the characters, white as well as black, are recognizable types— the paunchy sheriff, the ringleader of the lynch mob, the super-muscular black laborer. But the shifting perspectives give a fuller portrait of each of the players in the drama, a technique used not to dazzle but to illuminate. And the suspense is unrelenting.

Mary Helen Washington

SOURCE: "The House Slavery Built," in *The Nation,* Vol. 238, No. 1, January 14, 1984, pp. 22-4.

Ernest J. Gaines's fifth novel, ***A Gathering of Old Men,*** is set in the black rural Louisiana parish where all his stories take place—in the cotton and cane fields northwest of Baton Rouge, near the bayous. It is the land where Gaines was born and where he spent the first fourteen years of his life. City people and Northerners may have a hard time understanding the codes of this place, for, in many ways, its inhabitants still live in the house slavery built. They work, usually as sharecroppers, on plantations; the "quarters," as they call the black housing area, look very much like a scene from slavery days—rows of rickety log cabins lined up on a flat, treeless plot of ground; nearby is the "big house," surrounded by magnolias, where the plantation owner lives. On the way to the little nightclub in town, one passes long, gray, lonely cane fields, almost as isolated as the little cemetery where Gaines says "many, many of my people are buried." These images, from a photo essay called "Home" which Gaines compiled between 1963 and 1969, show the bleakest existence, and yet one can see in them all the themes that motivate Gaines's fiction and from which he has created such powerful books as *Catherine Carmier, Of Love and Dust, Bloodline, In My Father's House,* and the beautiful folk novel *The Autobiography of Miss Jane Pittman.*

Change happens very slowly in this world; codes of behavior are rigidly observed; people live near one another for a lifetime and their kinship networks, like nothing else in their lives, are lasting and dependable. It's not an easy world for readers to enter. I imagine that many will share the impatience of the fast-talking city slicker named James in *Bloodline,* who says of these backwoods people, "All they know is talk, talk, talk. . . . They do these little bitty things, and they feel like they've really done something. Well, back in these sticks, I guess there just isn't nothing big to do."

Yet these little bitty things James has dismissed—the living with violence, the patient refusal to give up one's dignity, the "bearing witness calmly against the predator"—are the very things which Adrienne Rich says have the power "to reconstitute the world." *A Gathering of Old Men* asks us to read the lives of black peasants as Rich reads women's lives: with attention to "the enormity of the simplest things."

When twelve old men from those Louisiana backwoods gather with shotguns to prevent a lynching, it is the most courageous and meaningful act they have ever performed. They have lived in continuous submission to the white power structure. Now in their 70s and 80s, they gather to confront the power that has humiliated and degraded them. When Beau Boutan, a vicious Cajun farmer, is found shot, the young white owner of the Marshall plantation, Candy Marshall, calls these aging black men to bring their guns and gather at the plantation before the whites demand "a nigger's blood." The story is told in a succession of voices, as each man explains the complex web of circumstances that drives him to take part in this ritual of resistance. The past weighs heavily on these men because each in his own way feels he has submitted to oppression. "We had all done the same thing sometime or another; we had all seen our brother, sister, mama, daddy insulted once and didn't do a thing about it."

The most powerful moment in the novel occurs when the old men, each claiming to be the murderer almost as though he wants to assert that right, stand up to recite the wrong done to them, to acknowledge their complicity in a system of oppression and, in a sense, to reverse that history of themselves as failed men. Gable tells how they electrocuted his retarded 16-year-old son for allegedly raping a white woman: "Called us and told us we could have him at 'leven, 'cause they was go'n kill him at ten." Tucker tells how a white mob beat his brother Silas to the ground for

defeating them in a contest between his mules and their tractor. Silas knew he was a nigger and was supposed to lose, and Tucker says he sold him out because he was afraid of the power of white men: "Out of fear of a little pain to my own body, I beat my own brother with a stalk of cane as much as the white folks did." Jacob Aguillard recalls: "It was me. . . . I remember what that crowd did to my sister." Another testifies: "I kilt him. . . . Me. What they did to my sister's little girl." A wall of old black men, each speaking his piece of history, a generation of black men living in the Jim Crow South, where the prerequisite for manhood was to break the law and where the price of one's dignity literally meant the willingness to offer one's life. Finally, these old men are prepared to stand against the white men's laws, to make history instead of lying passively beneath its flow.

I have often wondered how black people survived under Jim Crow in the years before the civil rights movement, when it seemed that they were constantly assaulted by laws, written and unwritten, which governed every aspect of their lives from how they were supposed to address a white person to where they could sit on a public bus. Richard Wright's "The Ethics of Living Jim Crow" suggests that many blacks internalized the submissiveness necessary to accommodate this system and stay alive. Black fiction writers have written about the Jim Crow South in two ways. They have written from the point of view of blacks who were trying to survive and who, in the process, created traditions that sustained and nurtured; or they have written, like Wright, of the power of whites not only to menace blacks but to define them.

Which viewpoint a writer selects is a critical esthetic and political decision. It is a tricky and complex issue, for blacks have always lived, as Du Bois pointed out, with that dubious gift of double consciousness, "this sense of always looking at one's self through the eyes of others." And in the South, where the brutality of whites was palpable, the question of viewpoint is all the more difficult. That artistic dilemma is posed in one of Alice Walker's stories of the South, "A Sudden Trip Home in the Spring." In it a young black artist is unable to paint the faces of black men until she resolves the question of who has the power to define. . . .

Gaines is most in touch with that black sensibility in *The Autobiography of Miss Jane Pittman* and in *Bloodline.* Jane Pittman's relationships to her husband, to her adopted son, Ned, and to the other people who live that hundred-year history with her are what establish her courage, her character and her identity. With his women characters Gaines seems freer to make those connections between character and community. But when Gaines considers the question of manhood (as he does in nearly all his stories), the arbiter of character is no longer the black community. In order to prove manhood, black men must stand up against white men, and the proof of their manhood is their ability to wrest respect from white men. All the passionate revelations in *A Gathering of Old Men* are made to the white sheriff, Mapes, and although the men are making their confessions to one another, the call and response is between the men and the sheriff.

What is even more disturbing than the white sheriff's dominant role is the subordination of women in this novel. The one woman who has a strong role is dismissed like a child. The white woman, Candy Marshall, the person responsible for the men assembling in the first place, is finally shown as just another threat to manhood. Women leading men is another form of slavery, so Candy must be eliminated. First she is warned by her black friend Mathu: "'I want you to go home,' he said. Not loud. Quiet. Soft. The way he used to talk to her when she was a little girl." That mild warning doesn't take because Candy is determined to retain her place of power in the men's world. In an act of public humiliation, she is carried off under her boyfriend's arm—at the sheriff's insistence and with the approval of all the black men—and is thrown, kicking and screaming, into her car. We are left at the end of this scene with a strange coalition: these elderly black men and a brutal white sheriff—bitter lifetime enemies—suddenly united in their antipathy for a strong woman.

Black women are just as effectively silenced. Of the fifteen voices joined to tell this story, only one is that of a black woman, Janey, and she is too hysterical to do anything but pray. No women are called to be a part of the resistance movement. The wives of the men involved play out the stereotype of the saboteur of the male quest for danger and glory. Failing to understand their men, they turn into distant and bitter shrews. Old Mat looks at his wife as he prepares to join his buddies and sees for the first time a stranger:

> I looked at that woman I had been living with all these years like I didn't even know who she was. My chest heaving, and me just looking at her like I didn't know who she was. . . . "All these years we been living together, woman, you still don't know what's the matter with me?"

Mat bitterly recounts the life they have lived under a system that has made him poor, cruel, angry and hopeless. But his anger and resentment are directed at her. Like the other old men, he leaves behind a confused, ignorant wife, cowed by this exhibition of manhood and unable to share in his political act.

These portraits of women leave me with a question I will not try to answer here. In exploring this vital issue of how black people can exert control over their history, why does Gaines so thoroughly deny the power of the women who contributed equally to that history? This disempowering of women compromises the novel's greatest strength—its recreation of the past through language. These communal voices constitute a kind of collective revision of history, giving proof in their own words of the existence of ordinary people whom the world noticed only briefly in the long-gone era of the civil rights movement. But in that revision, women are denied the right to suffer or to be heroic or even to claim the power of language.

Someone comes upon this strange scene of old men with shotguns and thinks how much like a Bruegel painting it seems—as weird as the painting of Icarus falling out of the sky and disappearing into the sea while people who may have heard the splash continue with their everyday work. As W. H. Auden suggested in "Musée des Beaux Arts," suffering takes place while the rest of us are busy with our own lives—out having dinner or at a film festival. Ernest Gaines makes us witness the lives and suffering of people whose small acts of courage make up the history of the race. I only wish that *A Gathering of Old Men* acknowledged that half of those people were women.

Penny Parker

SOURCE: A review of *A Gathering of Old Men,* in *Voice of Youth Advocates,* Vol. 7, No. 1, April, 1984, p. 30.

A Gathering of Old Men begins with a murder. Beau Boutan, Cajun farmer and son of Fix Boutan, who long terrorized the Black community in this little bayou setting, is found dead. Candy Marshall, a feisty, young, white woman who is the plantation owner, though not a slave owner, immediately begins circulating the story that it is she who has killed Beau. Candy was reared by several of the Black people in Marshall and is especially protective of 80ish year old Mathu. It is Mathu whom the reader believes shot Beau; what a surprise is in store when we discover the actual murderer.

Gaines's ability to draw complex characters and enable the reader to gain insight into the whys and hows of his/her actions is much evident here. Like *The Autobiography of Miss Jane Pittman,* we are privy to the private musing, hatreds, fears and motivations of a very diversified group of people. Gaines has many strengths as a writer, not the least of which is his ability to draw us into the story and evoke memories—both pleasant and unpleasant—without losing interest in the events, nor even suspecting what will occur. His writing is tight; his storytelling unique and interesting; his characters are multi-dimensional. . . .

A Gathering of Old Men takes place now, but as we see the reasons these old, old men surround the murderer and finally gain the courage to stand up to white folks, we are swept into a maelstrom that began many, many years before. This *Gathering of Old Men* were a courageous bunch.

A LESSON BEFORE DYING (1993)

R. Z. Sheppard

SOURCE: A review of *A Lesson before Dying,* in *Time,* Vol. 141, No. 13, March 29, 1993, pp. 65-6.

A lesson before Dying is, like Earnest Gaines's best-known novel, *The Autobiography of Miss Jane Pittman,* set in rural Louisiana. The year is 1948, and the particulars have a familiar ring. A young, black male is convicted of murder and sentenced to death on inconclusive evidence. The youth, called Jefferson, had the bad luck to be in a white man's store at the same time that two acquaintances attempted a robbery. They shoot the owner, but not before he fires effectively at them. Left with three dead men on the floor, Jefferson panics and helps himself to a bottle of whiskey and the contents of the cash register as two customers walk through the door.

The impulsive action ensures Jefferson a date with Gruesome Gerty, the state's portable electric chair, even though his lawyer argues that the accused is incapable of premeditating a murder. "No, gentlemen, this skull here holds no plans," the defense claims. "What you see here is a thing . . . to hold the handle of a plow, a thing to load your bales of cotton, a thing to dig your ditches, to chop your wood, to pull your corn." In effect, Jefferson is not condemned to die like a man but be destroyed like a beast. Worse still, he believes that he is no better than a dumb animal.

The job of persuading him otherwise falls to the local schoolteacher, Grant Wiggins, who has seen something of the world before returning south to teach at the black grammar school. Burdened with his own frustrations, not the least of which is downplaying his intelligence and college education when dealing with whites, Wiggins reluctantly undertakes to instruct Jefferson in his humanity. In short, to teach him how to die.

The lesson succeeds appropriately through an act of language. Wiggins gets the young man to write his thoughts in a journal, nine pages of semiliterate dialect that should not work in 20th century fiction but does because Gaines delivers a written equivalent of authentic oral expression, not a romanticized rendering of black English.

That is not all the author gets just right. The year may be 1948, but the plantation manners are circa 1848. There is an ominous courtesy between the races. The whites are soft-spoken and patronizing. The blacks reply with exaggerated deference and little eye contact. Few writers have caught this routine indignity as well as Gaines. Fewer still have his dramatic instinct for conveying the malevolence of racism and injustice without the usual accompanying self-righteousness.

Charles R. Larson

SOURCE: "End as a Man," in *Chicago Tribune Books,* May 9, 1993, p. 5.

The incident that propels the narrative of Ernest J. Gaines's rich new novel is deceptively simple. Shortly after World War II, in a Cajun Louisiana town, a 21-year-old black man who is barely literate finds himself in the wrong place at the wrong time, an innocent bystander during the robbery of a liquor store. The white store owner is killed, as are the two black men who attempt to rob the store;

Jefferson—who is just standing there—panics. He grabs a bottle of liquor and starts drinking it. Then he looks at the phone, knowing he should call someone, but he's never used a dial phone in his life. Flight seems the only option, but as he leaves the store, two white customers enter.

That event takes place at the beginning of *A Lesson before Dying,* Gaines's most rewarding novel to date, and it's followed by a brief summary of Jefferson's trial. The 12 white jurors find him guilty, assuming he's an accomplice of the two other black men, and the judge sentences Jefferson to death by electrocution. Much of what follows in this often mesmerizing story focuses on Jefferson's slow rise to dignity and manhood.

The obstacle to be overcome is a derogatory remark made by the defense during the trial, supposedly to save Jefferson from the death sentence. The lawyer asks the jurors,

> "Do you see a man sitting here? Look at the shape of this skull, this face as flat as the palm of my hand. . . . Do you see a modicum of intelligence? Do you see anyone here who could plan a murder, a robbery . . . can plan anything? A cornered animal to strike quickly out of fear, a trait inherited from his ancestors in the deepest jungle of blackest Africa—yes, yes, that he can do—but to plan?. . . No, gentlemen, this skull here holds no plans. What you see here is a thing that acts on command."

Finally, wrapping up his plea, the lawyer concludes, "What justice would there be to take his life? Justice, gentlemen. Why, I would just as soon put a hog in the electric chair as this."

The fallout from the lawyer's defense is devastating. In his cell, after receiving the death sentence, Jefferson is close to catatonia. As his aged godmother Emma and her friends try to make contact with him, he withdraws further into himself. In one wrenching scene when they bring him home-cooked food, he gets down on all fours and ruts around in the food without using his hands.

The complexity of this painful story is richly enhanced by Gaines's ironic narrator, Grant Wiggins. Only a few years older than Jefferson, Grant is college educated and a parish school teacher. Bitter in his own way and aloof from the community he has come to loathe, Grant is initially uninvolved, until his aunt (Miss Emma's friend) asks that he try to make Jefferson into a man. This quest for manhood becomes the emotional center of the story and a challenge for Grant himself to become reconnected to his people.

Assuming he will fail, Grant articulates his feelings to his mistress: "We black men have failed to protect our women since the time of slavery. We stay here in the South and are broken, or we run away and leave them alone to look after the children and themselves. So each time a male child is born, they hope he will be the one to change this vicious circle—which he never does. Because even though he wants to change it, and maybe even tries to change it, it is too heavy a burden because of all the others who have run away and left their burdens behind. So he, too, must run away if he is to hold on to his sanity and have a life of his own. . . . What she wants is for him, Jefferson, and me to change everything that has been going on for three hundred years."

Grant's task is further complicated by the local minister, who believes that saving Jefferson's soul is more important than making him into a man. The tensions between the teacher and the preacher add still another complex dimension to Gaines's formidable narrative.

Nowhere is the story mere moving than in the scenes in which Grant and Jefferson are together in Jefferson's cell, agonizing over his horrific past—for Jefferson has been shaped not only by the animalistic designation thrust upon him in his 21st year but also by the deprivations of the previous 20.

When Grant can finally mention the unspeakable—the last day of Jefferson's life—Jefferson tells him, "I never got nothing I wanted in my whole life." When asked what he wants to eat that last day, Jefferson responds, "I want me a whole gallon of ice cream. . . . Ain't never had enough ice cream. Never had more than a nickel cone. Used to . . . hand the ice cream man my nickel, and he give me a little scoop on a cone. But now I'm go'n get me a whole gallon. That's what I want—a whole gallon. Eat it with a pot spoon."

More than any other novel about African American life in the United States, *A Lesson Before Dying* is about standing tall and being a man in the face of overwhelming adversity. And, equally important, Gaines's masterpiece is about what Ralph Ellison and William Faulkner would call the morality of connectedness, of each individual's responsibility to his community, to the brotherhood beyond his self. This majestic, moving novel is an instant classic, a book that will be read, discussed and taught beyond the rest of our lives.

Carl Senna

SOURCE: A review of *A Lesson before Dying,* in *The New York Times Book Review,* August 8, 1993, p. 21.

Near the end of Ernest J. Gaines's novel *A Lesson before Dying,* set in the fictional town of Bayonne, La., in 1948, a white sheriff tells a condemned black man to write in his diary that he has been fairly treated. Although the prisoner assents, nothing could be farther from the truth in that squalid segregated jail, which is an extension of the oppressive Jim Crow world outside.

A black primary school teacher, Grant Wiggins, narrates the story of Jefferson, the prisoner, whose resignation to his execution lends credence to the lesson of Grant's own teacher, Matthew Antoine: the system of Jim Crow will break down educated men like Grant and prisoners like Jefferson to "the nigger you were born to be."

Grant struggles, at first without success, to restore a sense of human dignity to Jefferson, a semiliterate, cynical and bitter 21-year-old man, who accepts his own lawyer's depiction of him as "a hog" not worthy of the court's expense. The social distance between the college-educated Grant and Jefferson appears as great as that between the races, and class differences often frustrate their ability to communicate. It does not help that Grant has intervened only reluctantly, prompted by his aunt, a moralizing scold and a nag, and by Jefferson's godmother, Miss Emma.

Mr. Gaines, whose previous novels include *A Gathering of Old Men* and *The Autobiography of Miss Jane Pittman,* admirably manages to sustain the somber tone of the issues confronting the black citizens of Bayonne. What is at stake becomes clear. We find Grant vicariously sharing in the triumphs of Joe Louis and Jackie Robinson. The larger-than-life achievements of these black heroes make it intolerable to the black folks that Jefferson die ignobly. For that reason, Grant, who makes no secret of his disdain for Jefferson, reluctantly becomes their instrument in trying to save him from disgrace. Justice, or Jefferson's innocence, becomes secondary to the cause of racial image building—no trifling matter.

With the day of Jefferson's execution approaching, Grant begins to despair. Jefferson himself dismisses appeals from Grant and the blacks of Bayonne that he die with dignity—like a man, not like a hog.

To complicate the plot further, Grant must overcome another racial divide, crossing the color line to love a divorced Creole woman, Vivian Baptiste. She becomes yet another reason why Grant must save Jefferson's dignity, if not save him from execution. By rejecting Creole prejudice against blacks, Vivian must accept that she too has a stake in how Jefferson confronts the electric chair. She crosses the black-brown line, to the horror of other Creoles and the subtle animosity of Grant's black relatives.

It is a tribute to Mr. Gaines's skill that he makes the conflicts convincing. Jefferson, chained and securely behind bars, still has one freedom left, and that is the freedom to choose how he accepts death.

Despite the novel's gallows humor and an atmosphere of pervasively harsh racism, the characters, black and white, are humanly complex and have some redeeming quality. At the end, Jefferson's white jailer, in a moving epiphany, is so changed that he suggests the white-black alliance that will emerge a generation later to smash Jim Crow to bits.

The New England abolitionist preacher William Ellery Channing observed just before the Civil War that "there are seasons, in human affairs, of inward and outward revolution, when new depths seem to be broken up in the soul, when new wants are unfolded in multitudes, and a new and undefined good is thirsted for." *A Lesson before Dying,* though it suffers an occasional stylistic lapse, powerfully evokes in its understated tone the "new wants" in the 1940s that created the revolution of the 1960s. Ernest J. Gaines has written a moving and truthful work of fiction.

Jane Chandra

SOURCE: A review of *A Lesson before Dying,* in *Voice of Youth Advocates,* Vol. 16, No. 4, October, 1993, p. 216.

A young black man is likened to a hog and condemned to die in the electric chair for his part in (presence at) the shooting of a white store owner in a small Louisiana plantation community in the late 1940s. Grant Wiggins, the college-educated teacher in the plantation school, is implored by his aunt and Jefferson's godmother to visit Jefferson in jail, to instill dignity in him and make a man of him. Wiggins understands his place in society: "I tried to decide just how I should respond to them [white officials]. Whether I should act like the teacher that I was, or like the nigger that I was supposed to be." Through Wiggins's visits to Jefferson, Gaines explores the agonizing role of the educated black caught between his own desires, the way of life in the black quarter, the ties of family, and the strength of religion. The prisoner is at first unresponsive but gradually gains the strength to walk to his execution like a man.

Gaines is the author of **The Autobiography of Miss Jane Pittman** and **A Gathering of Old Men.** With his straightforward prose and appropriate dialect, he draws the reader into the characters' lives and proves without a doubt that it is possible to write an absorbing novel without the use of profanity. A fine story to bring about awareness of time, place, and racial inequalities and prejudices, this adult trade novel is good leisure reading and will enhance the social studies curriculum.

Chris E. Crowe

SOURCE: A review of *A Lesson before Dying,* in *Kliatt,* Vol. 28, No. 6, November, 1994, pp. 8-9.

This story shows how noble and horrible an execution can be. This is not a graphic portrayal of a man's death but a sensitive representation of how a young man's execution deeply affects those who know and love him, and how it affects the victim himself. Grant Wiggins, the plantation school teacher in a small Louisiana town in the 1940s, is coerced by his aunt to educate and remake Jefferson, a young man convicted of murder, so he can go to the electric chair as a man, not a "hog." Neither Wiggins nor Jefferson believes the transformation is possible and neither is willing to make any effort to bring it to pass. However, despite their combined reluctance, the metamorphosis, for which Wiggins is the catalyst, gradually takes place. At Wiggins' persistence and prompting, Jefferson begins to think for himself, to keep a journal, to realize his own worth as a human being. Wiggins also undergoes a change; ever since his return from college to his small town, he believed his future would be—should be—somewhere away from the poor plantation town where he had grown up. His college education had expanded his horizons, prepared him for grander things than a plantation school and poor, ignorant children. However, after his experience with Jefferson, Wiggins begins to realize that he has something to offer his community, that his future could still be bright and satisfying in this poor Cajun town.

Gaines writes liquid prose; his words and story flow as smoothly as a mountain stream. His portrayal of a poor Cajun town and its people in the 1940s when prejudice was an unhappy but accepted way of life is realistic and moving. This is a fine novel of character; both Wiggins and Jefferson are changed for the better. It's also a good historical novel, providing an intimate view of life in the South in that era. For readers young and old, it provides an education about how terrible racial prejudice is and prompts thought about such basic questions as the essence of humanity and the purpose of life. This book would work well in high school classes studying mid-20th century American history, African-American history, or literature of the South. It's a sad but inspiring tale, well told.

Additional coverage of Gaines's life and career is contained in the following sources published by The Gale Group: *Authors and Artists for Young Adults,* **Vol. 18;** *Black Writers,* **Vol. 2;** *Contemporary Authors,* **Vols. 9-12R;** *Contemporary Authors New Revision Series,* **Vols. 6, 24, 42, 75;** *Contemporary Literature Criticism,* **Vols. 3, 11, 18, 86;** *Dictionary of Literary Biography,* **Vols. 2, 33, 152;** *Major Authors and Illustrators for Children and Young Adults;* **and** *Something about the Author,* **Vol. 86.**

Constance Clarke Greene

1924-

American author of middle-grade and young adult fiction.

Major works include *A Girl Called Al* (1969), *I Know You Al* (1975), *Leo the Lioness* (1970), *Beat the Turtle Drum* (1976), *The Love Letters of J. Timothy Owen* (1986), *Just Plain Al* (1986).

INTRODUCTION

With more than 20 books to her credit, Greene is highly acclaimed for her witty and realistic portrayals of relationships between her characters including mothers and children, friends, and sisters. Publisher's weekly notes that "[t]he author's hallmarks are genuine humor, believable and attractive characters and (most significantly) skillful control of her prose." Greene has a sense of humor and it carries through her stories.

Greene writes primarily for middle grade children with two novels for young adult and one adult novel to her credit. She has paid attention to the lives of her five children as they have grown up and successfully uses these experiences in her novels. In *Something About the Author* Greene states that she writes "to amuse and entertain children, but also to teach them to laugh at themselves and at the vagaries of life." She feels that "[b]ooks extend their knowledge, expose them to thoughts, ideas, emotions they might not otherwise explore."

To acquire fresh material, Greene enjoys listening to young people. In *Authors and Artists for Young Adults* Greene calls this "eavesdropping—in the nicest possible way..." and remembers a time when she was window-shopping and heard one young person tell a friend to "have a weird day". She was intrigued by the phrase and used it in the later books of her Al series. Some young fans even sign off their letters with "Have a weird day". Greene further commented that "life is not a bowl of cherries, but in my books for younger readers, I'd really prefer to make them laugh." She does write about divorce often because "it seems to be here to stay", but chooses not to write about drug abuse, alcoholism, or terminal illness because these subjects have been written about so often. She also avoids graphic sex in her novels as she doesn't want one of her books to be used as a "textbook for kids about contraception" after a librarian said she uses Judy Blume's book *Forever* in this way.

One of her best known works is titled *Beat the Turtle Drum.* It is based on the death of her older sister when Greene was eleven and her sister was thirteen. While choosing to write it after the death of her parents, she found that many of the details of that awful time in her life were

unclear, but writing the book did make her feel a little better. Greene is also well known for her Al book series which contains six books and begins with *A Girl Called Al.* These stories follow a fourteen year old girl through various relationships, predicaments, and trials of growing up.

Barbara Elleman states that Greene's writing contains "[w]armth, vitality, and wit..." and that she has the "ability to draw believable characters, identifiable to the boy or girl next door..." Elleman goes on to note that "the underlying theme in Greene's work is self-adjustment" as many of her characters are experiencing growing pains and self awareness.

Biographical Information

Greene was born October 27, 1924, in New York, NY the daughter of Richard W, a newspaper editor, and Mabel (McElliott) Clarke, a journalist. In *Something about the Author* Greene comments that "[s]ince both of her parents worked for the New York *Daily News* (Greene) was born with the 'tools' of her trade readily accessible." In *Authors and Artists for Young Adults* she is certain that ". . . while it wasn't inevitable that I'd become a writer, that background certainly, influenced me." She did always want to be a writer and it was her mother that influenced Greene's love for short stories as Mabel Clarke wrote and published short stories in magazines. After attending Skidmore College for two years Greene quite as she felt she was wasting her time and her father's money. What she really wanted to do was work for a newspaper. Her newspaper career began as a mailroom clerk at the Associated Press in New York City. She enjoyed her time in the mailroom and especially liked delivering AP wire photos to other newspapers in the city. She would hitch rides from the AP motorcycle drivers who wore leather and zipped in and out of traffic. "What a thrill it was to breeze into the city room (at the *Daily News)*, toss the packet of photos down, say 'Hi Dad', and waltz out, never missing a beat" remembers Greene in *Something about the Author Autobiography Series*. Since many men were at war, and because Greene worked hard, she was able to become a reporter fairly quickly. Working at the Associated Press taught Greene how to write tight sentences and tight leads to get the reader's attention from the beginning. She quit the Associated Press when she married Philip M. Greene, a radio station owner on June 8, 1946. They had five children together and currently live in Long Island, N.Y. Greene found the children distracting to her writing, so she chose small projects such as short stories because she could finish those in one sitting. Her mother suggested she write children's stories, and Greene had a series of short stories published in the *Daily News*. During a short-story writing group session, her teacher suggested that she write a book for the juvenile market. Greene then wrote her first book *A Girl Called Al*.

Major Works

In the first of a series of Al novels, *A Girl Called Al* is narrated by Al's nameless best friend, who lives down the hall in the same apartment building. Al (short for Alexandra) is the thirteen year old daughter of divorced parents who comes home to an empty house every day because her mother works. Al is a smart, self proclaimed nonconformist, but doesn't always strive to reach her potential. She has been to many places which the narrator's family of a mother, father and little brother cannot afford to visit. Greene doesn't choose a happy ending for this story as she notes that life doesn't always work that way. The next Al novel, *I Know You Al*, which Carolyn Johnson calls "[a] welcome follow-up . . ." in the Al series, deals with Al not getting her period, meeting her father after not seeing him for eight years, not caring for her mother's boyfriend, and feeling too heavy. Zena Sutherland finds that "[b]oth these stories are entertaining, warm, and perceptive." *Your Old Pal Al* finds Al unhappily wondering why she hasn't received letters from her recently married father and step-mother, or from the boy named Brian that she met at the wedding. Al is struggling to decide if she should write to Brian first and wonders if "Your old pal, Al" is the best closure to the note. Al has a spat with the

still unnamed narrator over jealousy towards her best friends's houseguest. The girls make up and discuss what happened which causes them to be closer than ever. Barbara Elleman exclaims that "[t]he witty dialogue is right on target", while Christine McDonnell feels that "[t]he plot is less substantial than *A Girl Called Al*, but the characters have vitality." In *Al(exandra) the Great,* Al is almost fourteen years old and is still best friends with the unnamed narrator of the Al books. After planning a trip to her father's farm in Ohio where she will be able to spend time with Brian, Al's mother gets sick with pneumonia. Al decides to cancel her trip to take care of her mother, even though everyone encourages her to go anyway as her mother is improving. In *Just Plain Al*, she is anticipating her fourteenth birthday and deciding what her new name should be as she is tired of being "just plain Al". Rebecah Ray notes that in typical Greene style, the "relationships in the book unify the story". Ray also finds that "Greene has a delightful talent for believable, hilarious dialogue." *Al's Blind Date* deals with Al's concerns about whether or not to go on a blind date with her best friend and two boys. While the girls are making their decision, they help a lonely teacher and almost get killed from a fire bomb at a new Mafia gym. The story ends just as the girls are about to go on their date, so readers will have to wait until the next in the series to find out what happens. *Al's Blind Date* is found to be ". . . a disappointing addition to the popular series featuring Al(exandra)" states Ilene Cooper, but does note that "[f]ans of the series won't want to miss this one, since . . . there is enough witty dialogue to elicit some chuckles." Eleanor MacDonald agrees that this story line is inferior to previous Al books stating that "while this book will not attract new readers, it will be enjoyed by old acquaintances."

Leo the Lioness is told in first person by a 13 year old girl named Tibb who enjoys astrology and the fact that she is a Leo. Based on facts taken from her own children's lives, Greene writes in a style that is ". . . convincingly that of a teenager . . . " finds Zena Sutherland, who compliments the story by saying ". . . the dialogue is excellent and the relationships are drawn with sympathetic understanding." Tibb believes that Leos are the strongest sign in the Zodiac. Her older sister and best friend have become obsessed with boys and Tibb is irritated by this and by what she feels are her inadequacies. When a former baby-sitter who Tibb idolizes becomes pregnant and is forced to marry, Tibb's mother helps her deal with her feelings of betrayal in a real life way. Mary M. Burns believes this story to be a ". . . brisk, contemporary narrative which is both poignant and funny". Tibb finds that she has matured and changed during her thirteenth summer and also discovers that she is a "sadder and wiser person" for it.

While Greene has looked to members of her family, including her own children and grandchildren, for inspiration *Beat the Turtle Drum* is the only book taken from Greene's own personal life. It is based on the story of her older sister's death at age 13 when Greene was 11. The book is narrated by older sister Kate and tells the story of Joss's final weeks of life. Joss and Kate combine their birthday money to rent a horse for a week. This proves to be the happiest week of their lives. Then Joss dies an accidental, tragic death and each person whose life she touches deals with their loss in a different way. *Publishers Weekly* believes that Greene ". . . has succeeded so well in bringing all her characters to life, especially 11-year-old Joss, that the death of the lovable child means bereavement to readers as well as to those in the book." In *Something about the Author Autobiography Series* Greene states that she wrote *Beat the Turtle Drum* as "an attempt to bring back those terrible days, to put them in perspective, to sort out my thoughts and feelings." Many of the items in the book are made up, but the main story line is autobiographical. Children often ask Greene about this novel who says she doesn't want this to be the only thing she is known for. In 1976, the successful story was turned into an *ABC Afterschool Special* titled "Very Good Friends".

Publisher's Weekly writes that Greene's book *Star Shine* ". . . may be deemed the topper of all the funny, moving unpredictable stories that have won her awards and devout fans." The story follows twelve year old tomboy Jenny as she is chosen for a small part by a company that is shooting a movie in her town. This happens after her amateur actress mother leaves to try out for the summer theater. Judie Porter feels that "[t]he stars don't shine because this book lacks both the plot and zaniness that typifies Greene's work." While the main character Jenny is "well defined", but the other characters are not and much of the story is "lacks depth". Where Greene does shine is through the relationships of the characters and by showing that there is more happening than what shows at first sight.

Monday I Love You, which deals with a girl's low self-esteem, and *The Love letters of J. Timothy Owen,* a story about a boy's problems growing up, are the two novels that Greene has written for young adults. *Monday I Love You* is a suspenseful story of a 15 year old overweight girl named Grace who wears a size 38D bra. She travels from her friendless, dreary life into fantasy and happy memories. One memory that she savors is when she became blood brothers, at age six, with a boy named William. While she is babysitting a knife-wielding criminal breaks into the home and threatens her. She talks to him and shows him the scar. When he kisses her and leaves peacefully she suspects that this may have been William. A teacher is sympathetic and helps Grace feel better about herself, but also supports Grace's decision to not tell the police about the incident even when an innocent man is jailed. The break-in is the turning point for Grace who does begin to gain confidence and feel better about herself. Susan F. Marcus believes that readers will be uncomfortable with the ending of this story and that the "absence of a closure creates an unpleasant note and makes it difficult to recommend the book for its intended audience." In *The Love letters of J. Timothy Owen* a sixteen year old boy named Tim who, in an effort to win over a girl he secretly admires named Sophie, copies world famous love letters and sends them anonymously to her. He resorts to the letters when he is rebuffed after offering to help her babysit the children next door to his home. The

letters backfire and Tim eventually turns his attentions elsewhere. "Pleasant, amusing, and realistic, this is more impressive for its humor and smooth narrative flow than for depth of characterization or strong plot development" states Zena Sutherland.

Awards

A Girl Called Al was named a *Washington Post Book World* Spring Book Festival Honor Book, 1969, and listed as an American Institute of Graphic Arts Children's Book, 1970. *A Girl Called Al, Beat the Turtle Drum* and *The Love Letters of J. Timothy Owen* were all named American Library Association Notable Books.

AUTHOR'S COMMENTARY

Constance C. Greene

SOURCE: "What You Can Make Live," in *The Writer,* August, 1982, pp. 23-6.

Write about what you know. Time-honored and good advice. Flannery O'Connor says it another way: "You are always bounded by what you can make live."

Since we all have been children, *ipso facto,* writing for children should be simple, like falling off a log. Not necessarily. You'd be surprised, however, how many people think they can write for children. Many more than think they can write for adults.

Ideas come from everywhere; your children, your neighbor's kids, the newspaper. Eavesdropping—in the nicest possible way—can be very productive. I was hanging around upper Madison Avenue in New York, window-shopping, when I heard a kid say to a friend, "Have a weird day." I filed that one away for future use. The switch on the ubiquitous "have a good day" appealed to me. I used it in my *I Know You, Al,* and in subsequent *Al* books. Kids write to me and use the phrase to sign off in their letters.

Children are not emotional beggars. They share the same emotions adults experience, and perhaps with more intensity. Many children are very sharp, very aware, very hard nosed. They know more than grown-ups give them credit for. Don't talk down to them. Books extend their knowledge, expose them to thoughts, ideas, emotions they might not otherwise explore.

Try to capture the sensations, as well as the emotions, of childhood . . . the smells, the taste of things, and the feelings of a child. Do you remember what it was to be left out? To be the last chosen for a team? To lose at everything, never to come in first? Or always to come in last? To fail spelling, to be the tallest, shortest, thinnest, fattest kid around? Total recall isn't important in writing for children; a lively imagination and a good ear are. Dialogue is as important in children's books as it is in adult books. Maybe more so. Children love dialogue. And it's a fine and telling way to reveal character. It pays to listen to how people talk, what they say and leave unsaid. The nuances of dialogue are enormous.

Children like books with problems, sometimes the heavier the better. Conflict is essential. It's up to you as the writer to decide how severe the problem, how intense the conflict will be. I don't choose to write books about homosexuality, anorexia nervosa, teen-age pregnancy. Not because I'm not aware that they exist, but because that sort of thing isn't my bag. Instead, I choose to write *Isabelle the Itch.* She has problems, the main one being that she's an itch. How shall she control her itchiness so that her mother will be saved from a nervous breakdown? How will she channel her energy, win the fifty-yard dash at school? Isabelle is not hyperactive. She's an itch, pure and simple. There's a big difference. I met Isabelle in church. She had bright brown eyes and brown hair, and she was looking for trouble: pinching, poking, agitating. Her father shot her frosty looks, which she ignored. I came away from the service elevated in mind and spirit from the knowledge that I'd found a perfect heroine when I was least expecting one. It was marvelous, like winning a lottery.

I write to amuse and entertain children, not to instruct or educate them, which I am not qualified to do. I am not an educator, I am a writer. It gives me great pleasure to say that: I am a writer. I've been at it a long time, since I was ten years old. My ambition was to write short stories. The idea of writing a book had never occurred to me until, thoroughly discouraged by many rejection slips from short story editors, I began writing *A Girl Called Al.* At that time I was a member of a writing group in Connecticut. Our instructor took a look at the first few chapters of *Al* and said, "This is good. This is what you should do." Inflamed by these words, I forgot short stories and worked on *Al* until it was finished, or semi-finished.

The first editor who saw my book liked it, but the changes she suggested were so many and so varied I became discouraged and decided against attempting them. The second time out, the book went to Viking Press. The editor called me in and said, "You have the bones. Now all you have to do is flesh them out." That did it. I fleshed out the bones, and Viking bought it. There is no thrill that I know of greater than that of selling your first book. Absolutely none. It's the most marvelous feeling in the world, and I hope that all of you experience it someday.

I want to make children laugh—at themselves, at others, at life. I laugh in order that I may not cry, someone once said. "A good laugh is good for the soul, Mr. Richards," one of my favorite characters says in *A Girl Called Al.* Laughter wakes up the mind, Vladimir Nabokov has said. I believe these things to be true. It's the basic premise

from which I start when I write my books. But children agonize, so there should be agonies. Children cry, so there must be tears. There should be some unhappiness in books for children; otherwise how will we or they appreciate happiness when it arrives? As it surely must.

"The book was funny and sad," a young reader wrote me. "It was like real life. I felt you wrote it for me. There was so much feeling and understanding." I cherish the knowledge that I sometimes reach children, make them feel. If a book leaves the reader cold, the writer has failed. My goal is to write books that are both funny and sad. Life is full of deep emotions and rejections. Hurt can and does come in many sizes, many guises. Loneliness abounds. More laughter is needed. Laughter is an antidote against life's ills. Today's children are expected to cope with a great deal, things they may not be equipped to handle. They learn about evil sooner than they used to; and about brutality, hatred, sex, violence. All tough things to understand, to explain.

A writer of humor isn't taken as seriously as a serious writer. Humor connotes fluff, humor means lightweight, which in turn can mean mindless, frivolous, insignificant. Lamentable but true. The writer of humor must try harder. If, on the other hand, humor and laughter are your aim, as they are mine, then the only thing to do is go ahead, write it. Never mind if you're regarded as light in weight. It beats heavy.

Hyperbole is also a useful tool for the writer. Children love and appreciate exaggeration. They invented it, as a matter of fact. Use hyperbole whenever indicated. Just don't overdo. A sense of the ridiculous is good, if not invaluable. A sense of fun helps.

Contrast is the name of the game. There must be ups and downs, good people, bad people, happy times, sad times, if you strive to reflect real life.

"Why do you write about death?" I am asked by someone who has read *Beat the Turtle Drum,* a story of two sisters, one of whom dies. Because, I reply, it's part of life. "Why do you put bullies in your books?" a boy wants to know. Because bullies, like it or not, are here to stay. Why do you have so much divorce in your stories? Because divorce is an actuality that is widespread.

A terrible story in our local newspaper led me to write *Getting Nowhere.* A fourteen-year-old boy took the family car out for a spin while his mother and father were away. He demolished the car but was unhurt himself. He then went home and committed suicide. A true story. I tried to imagine what had driven this real boy to such a tragic act. Of course, he had done something bad, but not something that demanded such retribution. I tried to reconstruct in my mind his relationships with his parents, his siblings, his peers. What had this boy been like in life? What went on inside his head? What had made him take his own life?

In *Getting Nowhere,* Mark Johnson, also fourteen years old, takes the car out while his father and his stepmother are out for the evening. He has two passengers, his younger brother and a friend. He totals the car, and his passengers are injured, but Mark walks away, unhurt. And here the story veers from the original facts in the newspaper and becomes fiction, because I didn't choose to write a tragedy. Mark and his father have long been at odds: Mark's mother died some time ago, and his father has recently remarried. Mark hates his stepmother for no reason other than that in the manner of fourteen-year-olds he's angry at the world and is trying to come to grips with his own newly discovered sexuality. Mark's father and stepmother are obviously deeply in love. The stepmother, a nice woman, tries very hard to win Mark over. The ending of *Getting Nowhere* is not happy, nor is it conclusive. How could it be? But it is not without hope. I try to leave a promise of better things to come, a taste of hope.

A happy ending is nice if it fits, but not if it's dragged in by the heels, kicking and screaming. I am an optimist. I like happy endings. A satisfying ending doesn't have to be happy; the ending must fit. If I'd given *Getting Nowhere* a happy ending, it would have jarred the reader. And also me. Whenever possible, I try to write happy endings. But there's no sense in trying to squeeze the foot into a too-small shoe. My favorite ending of all is in *I Know You, Al.* It makes me laugh every time I read it.

Dotty's Suitcase is a story that takes place during the Depression. It's about Dotty Fickett, whose dream is to own her own suitcase. The ending suits me, but not, I understand, everyone. Dotty visits her friend Olive, who has moved away. Olive and her mother are destitute after her father dies. On her journey to reach Olive, Dotty finds a suitcase filled with money from a bank robbery. When she and Olive part, Dotty leaves the money under Olive's pillow. Olive's mother has made it clear that under no circumstances will she keep the money. Of course this was wrong of Dotty. She should have returned the money to the bank. But she chose to give it to someone who needs it far more than she thinks either she or the bank does. An immoral ending, some say. I think it's right. It fits Dotty. As far as I'm concerned, Dotty did the right thing.

Beware of writers who say "Every word of this is true. It all happened, just the way I wrote it." As if this were a recommendation. Truth doesn't necessarily lead to lively or interesting fiction. Veracity doesn't always lead to vivacity. In fact, truth can lead to tedium. Remember this when you write. Don't be afraid to use bits and pieces of anything you have lying around in your head. A pinch of this, a pinch of that, never mind whether it really happened or not. It *could* have happened.

The same applies to creating characters. One of my best and, I think, most satisfactory characters is Gran in *The Unmaking of Rabbit*. I took a pinch of this, a dab of that, and fleshed out the bones of my mother-in-law, of all people, and *voilà!*—there was Gran. Gran, who likes her gin and ginger ale at night to help her sleep; Gran, who burns holes in table tops with her cigarettes, which she smokes in an exotic holder. Gran, a lady of great strength, great eccentricity, a woman with a mind of her own.

The Unmaking of Rabbit is a story of a boy who lives with his grandmother because his mother can't cope and his father has flown the coop. A boy who wrote to tell me how he felt after reading the book said, "I liked how you showed people's feelings. I wondered how you thought of this boy's life. This boy was very lonely. I was wondering if you were once as lonely or almost as lonely as this boy, or did you just think of a very touching book."

A very touching book. Beautiful words. The boy who wrote that letter didn't know it, but he had given me a rare gift. Those words hold everything a writer hopes for. I had touched him, and he, in turn, had touched me.

If you want to write books for children, make fast tracks to your local library, have the librarian give you a list of the most popular books for children, and read them. Some of you will undoubtedly say, "I can do as well as that," about some of those widely read books. Go to it.

GENERAL COMMENTARY

Zena Sutherland

SOURCE: "Constance Green: *A Girl Called Al, I Know You, Al*, in *Children and Books*, Scott, Foresman and Company, 1986, pp. 353-54.

There is poignant sympathy for the girl in Constance Greene's *A Girl Called Al*. Plump and caustic, Al is a nonconformist who is won over by the understanding friendship of the building superintendent and who is catapulted into maturity by his death. *I Know You, Al* tells us more about Al as she faces the problems in her life: being the only girl in the class who hasn't yet begun to menstruate, being too plump, not liking her mother's suitor, and meeting the father she hasn't seen for eight years. Both these stories are entertaining, warm, and perceptive, as are their sequels, *Your Old Pal Al* and *Al(exandra) the Great*. Perhaps Greene's most dramatic story, *Dotty's Suitcase* is set in the Depression era, and its young protagonist is off on a series of adventures when she finds a suitcase that has been thrown out of a car by bank robbers; the book is exciting yet wholly credible.

Greene turns to boys and their problems in *The Unmaking of Rabbit*. Paul is shorter than the other boys in his class and has large ears that stick out. Paul gathers his courage, reads a paper in class about refusing to join a gang for break-ins, and is invited to join another group for sleep-outs. He firmly renounces the name Rabbit. In *Ask Anybody* an uneasy friendship ends when Ned's feckless family hastily leaves town. Both stories are realistic and written with ease and humor, with sympathetic characters who have believable problems.

TITLE COMMENTARY

A GIRL CALLED AL (1969)

Kirkus Reviews

SOURCE: A review of *A Girl Called Al,* in *Kirkus Reviews,* Vol. XXXVII, No. 8, April 15, 1969, p. 441.

A sparkler. . . . My friend Al the nonconformist says she has a high I.Q. but doesn't work to capacity. She comes to our house for dinner a lot, especially when her mother (who's divorced) goes out. "I don't always know what she is talking about" even though we're both in the seventh grade but we're best friends and we like the same people—like Mr. Keogh at school (who doesn't call her *Alexandra,* which she hates) and Mr. Richards, assistant superintendent in our building. I introduced them and when Al wasn't allowed to take shop at school Mr. Richards taught us how to build a bookcase. And when Al was really getting fat he substituted carrot sticks for bread and sugar (and said nothing, which was nice). When he died was the only time I saw Al cry and her mother even broke a date to stay with her that night—I guess she understood how special Mr. Richards was to us. . . . *A Girl Called Al* has some of the precocious sting and the benefit of a contemporary happy-family girl (forever nameless) to put it into perspective. Quite convincing, with live laughter, and thin-line illustrations that seize on the essentials.

The Booklist and Subscription Books Bulletin

SOURCE: A review of *A Girl Called Al,* in *The Booklist and Subscription Books Bulletin,* Vol. 75, No. 22, July 15, 1969, p. 1274.

On the fat side and wearing pigtails and glasses, Al, short for Alexandra, is a nonconformist with a high I.Q. whose divorced mother leaves her alone in the apartment most of the time and whose father remembers to send her presents now and then. She becomes best friends with the girl down the hall, also a seventh grader, who is the narrator of this story. The warm and completely believable account of their friendship is written in a spare, scintillating style which underlines both the humorous and sober aspects of the story, and perceptively reveals Al's insecurity and loneliness in contrast to the other girl's normal happy family life.

Ethel L. Heins

SOURCE: A review of *A Girl Called Al,* in *The Horn Book Magazine,* Vol. XLV, No. 4, August, 1969, pp. 411-12.

Told in the first person in a disarmingly casual, amusing style, the story deals with a few months in the lives of two seventh-grade girls. The narrator (never actually named) is a forthright, good-humored child whose family life is stable and secure. Her best friend Al (short for Alexandra), whose parents are divorced, lives in an apartment down the hall with her busy, distracted working mother. Al—a bright, overfat girl—proudly tries to be a "nonconformist" to hide the hurt and loneliness. Their unconventional friendship with Mr. Richards, an elderly ex-bartender who works as assistant superintendent of the building, draws the girls together. His detached, folksy wisdom gives them self-confidence while they instinctively perceive his own basic loneliness. Al's growing acceptance of her father's neglect ("' . . . I feel sorry for him. I am the only daughter he's got and he'll never really know me.'") and Mr. Richards' sudden, quiet death help both girls to mature a little. A story that implies more than it tells about two girls on the edge of adolescence.

Zena Sutherland

SOURCE: A review of *A Girl Called Al,* in *Bulletin of the Center for Children's Books,* Vol. 23, No. 1, September, 1969, p. 9.

"There's a new girl moved down the hall from us," and we meet Al, who does not wish to be addressed as Alexandra. Al is plump, intelligent, caustic, and—she says it herself—a nonconformist. Living alone with her divorced mother, Al is slow to relax her guard. Taken by the old resident (the author, who is another seventh-grade girl and never named) to visit the building superintendent, Mr. Richards, Al finds a friend. The book ends on a poignant note with Mr. Richards' death, and the two girls beginning to move into adolescence—part of the relationship missing with Mr. Richards gone, part of the change due to the inevitability of time. The first person telling is most convincing, the characterization and dialogue sharply observant, and style permeated not with humor but with the awareness of a sense of humor.

LEO THE LIONESS (1970)

The Booklist

SOURCE: A review of *Leo the Lioness,* in *The Booklist,* Vol. 67, No. 9, January 1, 1971, p. 372.

Tibb describes the emotional upheavals of her thirteenth summer in a breezy, modern first-person narrative that portrays with frankness and humor the frustrations and heartaches of a young adolescent girl's adjustment to the realities of an imperfect world. Discomfited by her own seeming inadequacies and irritated by the boy-crazy antics of an older sister and a former close friend, Tibb, hipped on astrology, takes comfort in being a Leo because Leos are forceful, steadfast persons. When an older girl whom Tibb idolizes is forced to marry because of pregnancy, Tibb feels betrayed, but her understanding mother helps her face the crisis realistically and at summer's end Tibb realizes she has become a more mature and wiser person.

Mary M. Burns

SOURCE: A review of *Leo the Lioness,* in *The Horn Book Magazine,* Vol. XLVII, No. 1, February, 1971, p. 50.

"I think I have changed a lot this summer. I have grown and matured and I am also a sadder and wiser person. This comes with age." Aging, as Tibb learned, is not a comfortable process at best—particularly when one is thirteen-going-on-fourteen. But there is some relief in having been born under Leo, the strongest sign in the zodiac. And one needs every possible support to cope with the fluctuating moods of an older sister and a former friend who have become interested solely in boys, dates, clothes, and cosmetics; or with the discovery that one's ideal young woman suddenly has to leave college to be married. Tibb's chronicle of her growing awareness during the summer before her fourteenth birthday is a perceptive re-creation of that painful moment when one becomes acutely conscious of the gulf separating the world as it is from the world as one wants it to be. The author has believably delineated the bewilderment of a sensitive adolescent trying to understand social and personal values, sex, parents, siblings—and herself—in a brisk, contemporary narrative which is both poignant and funny.

Zena Sutherland

SOURCE: A review of *Leo of Lioness,* in *Bulletin of the Center for Children's Books,* Vol. 24, No. 8, April, 1971, p. 124.

There is a point in every young person's life at which he discovers, as Tibb does in her thirteenth summer, that "people and things are not always what they seem. I know that people you think are strong sometimes turn out to be weak . . . when the chips are down, I turned out to be mean and small and almost didn't go to Carla's wedding." Carla was the girl who had been Tibb's adored baby-sitter, and it had come as a real blow to learn that she was pregnant. It had been a traumatic summer. When your older sister and your best friend can think of nothing but boys, it is hard to be flat-chested and have big feet. Tibb's only consolation is that she was born under the sign of Leo, and is therefore strong, forceful, steadfast "and practically everything good." Not an unusual theme, the adolescent girl who grows into a more mature person, but it is handled unusually well here. The writing is convincingly that of a teen-ager, the problems are universal and imbued with a humor that does not lessen their importance, the dialogue is excellent and the relationships are drawn with sympathetic understanding.

THE GOOD-LUCK BOGIE HAT (1971)

Kirkus Reviews

SOURCE: A review of *The Good-Luck Bogie Hat,* in *Kirkus Reviews,* Vol. XXXIX, No. 21, November 1, 1971, p. 1155.

In this disappointing trifle from the author of *A Girl Called Al,* a disgruntled younger brother comments from the sidelines as 16-year-old Ben, a spiffy dresser in deliberately outre secondhand duds, falls for a girl who influences him to dress straight, but reverts after she rejects him to his former outasight regalia. The tone is consciously up to the minute, but just what minute, year or decade it reflects is difficult to pin down. The boys banter in a social and political vacuum, and their preoccupation with clothes (of whatever style) and cars (especially one girl's Mustang) seems oddly out of tune with phrases like "right on" and "uptight." But most of the diction is less specifically "now" ("It's dutch treat or no soap," for example) and much falls short of any target (Ben's friend Ack Ack, discussing a double date, asks "if we have to take these cats out and tie on the old feed bag after the concert"). There are other failures too: the ungrammatical, poetry-quoting old-clothes dealer remains a deliberately invented "character," never convincing like the assistant superintendent in *A Girl Called Al,* and the boys are just ragtag bits of outer wrapping, fashioned in no particular mode.

THE UNMAKING OF RABBIT (1972)

Kirkus Reviews

SOURCE: A review of *The Unmaking of Rabbit,* in *Kirkus Reviews,* Vol. XL, No. 21, November 1, 1972, p. 1239.

"Once there was a boy who had no friends. He got a chance to make some, to be a member of a gang and go on a sleep-out and everything, but first he had to do something bad, namely steal. . . . At the last minute he chickened out and said he was going to puke all over everybody. He still doesn't have any friends, but at least he has a clear conscience." Paul's autobiographical composition does not of course tell the whole story; there is also Gram who has raised him, his mother who keeps postponing the day when he can go and live with her, and an out-of-town visitor who becomes Paul's first real friend. After an abortive Sunday visit, Paul finally stops kidding himself about his mother, and when reading his composition in class yields not the beating he expected from the gang but a no-strings invitation to the sleep-out, he accomplishes *The Unmaking of Rabbit:* "'One thing.' He prayed to God, asking Him not to let him stutter. 'One thing, my name is Paul. It's not Rabbit. It's Paul. And don't you forget it. Just don't you forget it.'" Readers will share Paul's final elation just as they've shared his tensions and disappointments and semi-hysterical laughter, for Constance Greene's brisk, unsentimental telling is studded with the sharp spontaneous observations that brought *A Girl Called Al* and *Leo the Lioness* to life.

Mary M. Burns

SOURCE: A review of *The Unmaking of Rabbit,* in *The Horn Book Magazine,* Vol. XLIX, No. 2, April, 1973, p. 143.

For most eleven-year-olds, life is a state of perpetual anticipation; for Paul it was a monotonous stretch of waiting for a friend, for his mother to settle down, for a real home (perhaps with his mother and a stepfather), and for his schoolmates to stop calling him "Rabbit." True, he had his Grandmother, but she was no substitute for a father who could share the delights of sports, camping out, or the small pangs of daily life. Yet, eleven also means growing up and realizing that adults can be appreciated in spite of their quirks, that life ultimately demands positive action rather than meek acceptance, and that even a "rabbit" has a respectable kick when he chooses. In comparison with the heroines of *A Girl Called Al* or *Leo the Lioness,* Paul seems less real, his problems more contrived, his ultimate resolution almost predictable. The reader becomes a bystander rather than an active participant in his progress possibly because the young hero is thoroughly upstaged by his Grandmother, a scene-stealing golden-ager—marching into old age gallantly rather than tranquilly—who drinks gin and ginger ale as a bedtime soporific, never smokes without using her long, thin, black cigarette holder, and delivers caustic commentary with the aplomb of a W. C. Fields. A positive antidote to the stereotyped grandmother image, she deserves a book of her own; on second thought, perhaps she already has it—if unintentionally.

Zena Sutherland

SOURCE: A review of *The Unmaking of Rabbit,* in *Bulletin of the Center for Children's Books,* Vol. 26, No. 9, May, 1973, p. 138.

Paul was shorter than the other boys in his class, he had large ears that stuck out, and his skin, Gran said, was wasted on a boy. Shy, lonely, Paul hated being called "Rabbit" by the other boys; he lived with Gran and he dreamed of the day his mother would ask him to join her—but there always seemed some reason why it just wouldn't work out—yet. When his mother remarried, Paul was sure there would be a home for him, but his week-end visit was so disastrous he cut it short. The only things that gave him confidence were a friend, Gordon, who occasionally visited his grandmother (a neighbor) and an elderly storekeeper who treated Paul like a friend. After he reads a paper in class that divulges the truth about his one encounter with a peer group (invited to participate in a break-in, he had rebelled) Paul finds that his courage has achieved what he'd hoped for, an invitation to be one of the group that goes on sleep-outs. Staunchly he requests that he no longer be called "Rabbit"—and it works. The story is told with deft ease, the problems and solutions are realistic, and the characters are distinctive.

ISABELLE THE ITCH (1973)

Kirkus Reviews

SOURCE: A review of *Isabelle the Itch,* in *Kirkus Reviews,* Vol. XLI, No. 19, October 1, 1973, pp. 1095-96.

Isabelle's story is funny and true and itchy enough to give to girls who don't like to read; the hyperactive ten year-old acts out unsanctioned impulses and suffers the parent-teacher flak that make her a real sister to them. Isabelle's mother, a master of contradictory orders (slow down and hurry up), fears that Isabelle will drive her crazy and, after a few minutes in the examining room, the doctor extends his sympathy—to the mother. Her teacher, when Isabelle fails a spelling test, tells her she could do better (how maddeningly familiar that will sound) and hateful Mary Eliza, a girl in her class, has a talent for making her feel ignorant and unwanted. Isabelle's father, however, assures her that when she sets her mind to it she can scale mountains, and at last her best friend Herbie with whom she fights on schedule each day after school, the new girl Jane who beats her in the field day race, and old Mrs. Stern whom she meets when subbing on her older brother's paper route all help her to see that it might be true.

Pamela D. Pollack

SOURCE: A review of *Isabelle the Itch,* in *Library Journal,* Vol. 98, No. 20, November 15, 1973, p. 3452.

Isabelle's not an itch, she's just a pain. Presumably her problem's an excess of unchanneled energy, but it seems more like lack of consideration—for the mother of the baby whose ugliness she loudly announces in the doctor's office, for transferee Jane Malone who's not yet aware that handbags aren't *de rigueur* at her new school ("'How come you carry that big dumb pocketbook everywhere?'"), and for her unbelievably tolerant parents. There's not enough cause for Isabelle's contentiousness: she gets an "F" and then a "D" in spelling ("'You're gaining,'" her mother says); she's not invited to a slumber party attended by her nemesis, Mary Eliza Schook; she gets a few mild chewing outs. As was the formula in Greene's earlier novels, at this point a savvy Senior Citizen steps in to straighten out the situation and provides the story's moral. Here it's eccentric Mrs. Stern, encountered while Isabelle's taking over her brother's paper route, who believes that annoyance in the form of galling companions is necessary to keep people on their toes. This dubious if not ulcerative philosophy somehow helps Isabelle to tolerate Mary Eliza and be a sport about losing a race to newcomer Jane. Characterization stops at attributing a quirk—some credible, some not—to each protagonist (Dad bakes bread, Mom has half-baked ideas about constipation); this bland brand of humor will suffice for kids itching for an easy laugh, but the book's not up to scratch.

Publishers Weekly

SOURCE: A review of *Isabelle the Itch,* in *Publishers Weekly,* Vol. 204, No. 21, November 19, 1973, p. 60.

Stories about *real* girls who aren't too good to be true are mightily appreciated by the real girls who read them. Isabelle likes to fight with her neighbor Herbie, wears Adida track shoes on her great big feet, hopes that she'll win the 50-yard dash, writes hate messages on her blackboard, and is so full of energy that her mother has to ask the doctor just why Isabelle is such an itch. Isabelle gets to use some of that energy taking over her brother's paper route and making friends with Mrs. Stern who likes to paint the rooms of her big house different colors. But she also begins to realize that, though LIFE ISN'T EASY, as her blackboard says, all that energy *channeled,* instead of just used for driving people crazy, could really get her somewhere. Ms. [Greene] makes her kids talk just like kids, and doesn't belabor any morals either.

The Booklist

SOURCE: A review of *Isabelle the Itch,* in *The Booklist,* Vol. 70, No. 7, December 1, 1973, p. 386.

A refreshing book in many ways: it's good clean fun with no redeeming social value; the ten-year-old heroine is in perpetual motion, running, fighting, and talking, while her father bakes bread on Saturdays—both break a mold without being "counter-culture." Isabelle's mother is an honestly normal blend of impatience and loving warmth. None of the children are brooding introverts but react to each other with natural spontaneity ranging from mean teasing to kindness. Low-key and somewhat episodic—though it moves Isabelle, through her paper route and track meet, toward channeling her energy—this is fun to read alone or aloud.

THE EARS OF LOUIS (1974)

Kirkus Reviews

SOURCE: A review of *The Ears of Louis,* in *Kirkus Reviews,* Vol. XLII, No. 21, November 1, 1974, p. 1151.

Fifth grader Louis wishes desperately that his ears were smaller and his muscles bigger—until a neighbor lady he plays poker with gives him an amulet, and an old man at a garageless garage sale gives him some bar bells, and before long he's playing football with the big kids who call him "ears" as if they like him. An unpromising outline, but Greene makes affecting human encounters out of the poker games with the old lady, the reverse bargaining with the henpecked old man, and the exchanges in the school hall and lunch room with teasing sixth graders. In addition, Louis has a couple of friends who are nicely individualized, as well as honestly supportive. All in all, though Louis's ears remain his most prominent characteristic, he is still an acquaintance worth making.

The Booklist

SOURCE: A review of *The Ears of Louis,* in *The Booklist,* Vol. 71, No. 8, December 15, 1974, p. 425.

The ears from the title are large and belong to a fifth-grade boy who reacts to proverbial name-calling with passive resistance until his good friend and poker partner Mrs. Beeble gives him a silver talisman and explains that big ears are a sign of character. Confidence doesn't come easily to Louis, but he has received just enough moral support to begin a campaign that includes weight-lifting and being prepared for when the "big guys" may need a football sub during recess. Louis's touchdown and a closing scene in which he gracefully turns the tables on his enemies are predictable but not inconceivable. This has none of the gritty kind of realism used so often in today's "character molding" books. Rather, its strength lies in a low-key approach, complete with unique but understated characters and a great deal of humor and empathy. The black-and-white drawings [by Nola Langer], of which there are few, charmingly reflect the story. By the author of *Isabelle the Itch.*

Zena Sutherland

SOURCE: A review of *The Ears of Louis,* in *Bulletin of the Center for Children's Books,* Vol. 28, No. 8, April, 1975, p. 130.

It was no consolation to Louis, whose big ears made the boys at school tease him, when his mother said Clark Gable had big ears and always got the girl. Louis didn't want to get the girl, he wanted to play football even through he was small. One person who didn't care was his friend Matthew, who *liked* Louis's ears because they were all pink when the sun shone through them, another was his friend Mrs. Beeble next door, with whom he played poker. Louis finally realizes that some of the teasing is just standard operating procedure—and as for the bullies, they stop calling him "Sugar Bowl" when they find that Louis is a buddy of the older football players. The problem/solution aspect of the story is firmly realistic and satisfying, but it's the sympathetic characterization, the ease and humor of the writing style, the perception shown in relationships (particularly between Louis and Mrs. Beeble), and the felicitous dialogue that make the book enjoyable.

Virginia Haviland

SOURCE: A review of *The Ears of Louis,* in *The Horn Book Magazine,* Vol. LI, No. 2, April, 1975, p. 149.

The author has a clear understanding of and a humorous point of view towards the candor and teasing of fifth- and sixth-grade schoolboys. Louis, the central figure in a plotless series of incidents, is blessed with small muscles and big ears, and he is full of determination to play football with the bigger boys. He has a sympathetic and happy relationship with Matthew, one schoolmate who doesn't tease, and with Mrs. Beeble, an elderly neighbor who makes light of his afflictions. She gives him an amulet, a carved figure with great ears, which he secretly hangs around his neck for good luck. One great day, however, the big boys look for him—"'that kid who made the run the day before yesterday'"; and at last he can forget "Dumbo," "Elephant Ears," and "Sugar Bowl."

I KNOW YOU, AL (1975)

Publishers Weekly

SOURCE: A review of *I Know You, Al,* in *Publishers Weekly,* Vol. 208, No. 7, August 18, 1975, p. 68.

The author's hallmarks are genuine humor, believable and attractive characters and (most significantly) skillful control of her prose. In a sequel to the story of *A Girl Named Al* which was highly praised, the narrator tells what befalls the two friends as they advance into adolescence. Al (Alexandra) suffers the usual and some unusual anxieties. Her divorced mother has a boy friend who uses (ugh!) pungent shaving lotion; neither Al nor pal has experienced her first period (why don't they call it an exclamation mark? Al wonders), which is like getting a driving license, a sign of growing up. Al is afraid her mother will marry the square boy friend and she doesn't know how to react when her father, after years of absence, shows up and invites her to his wedding. The story is not only witty entertainment, it's a kind of reassurance to other adolescents.

Carolyn Johnson

SOURCE: A review of *I Know You, Al,* in *School Library Journal,* October, 1975, pp. 98-9.

A welcome follow-up to the already popular *A Girl Called Al,* nonconformist Al is concerned with getting her period, meeting her father whom she has not seen for eight years, and keeping a close eye on her mother's new boyfriend. The wry humor of the earlier book prevails, and readers catch a funny, and sometimes embarrassingly truthful, look at contemporary love, sex, and marriage (Friend Polly's liberal parents who doubt the value of formal marriage; a grandfather who is still involved in the male-female game). Greene is right on target here; preteens will enjoy this lively go-around.

M. R. Hewitt

SOURCE: A review of *I Know You, Al,* in *The Junior Bookshelf,* Vol. 42, No. 1, February, 1978, p. 55.

This is one of the most difficult books I have received for review. I have never been an advocate of the 'social problem' story, so many of them seem to be written to a formula lacking any real story interest. After the first few references to the late onset of menstruation and artificial insemination my main thought was 'Oh, not again'.

The story then develops to the reappearance of a long divorced father, his new marriage, Mum's new boyfriend,

a girl friend with a very liberal family and an elder sister 'sleeping around'. My mind would have boggled but for the skill and humour with which this story is told.

The heroine, Al, is a very well balanced girl, as is her nameless friend, the narrator of the story. Al of the broken family and late starting period has a style of dialogue which would not shame the best American quick fire comedian. Her friend, of the secure home—albeit with a young brother given to reciting rude verse in public—is the anchor man of the plot.

Both girls are totally believable, feeling their way into a confusing adult world, protecting themselves with catch-phrases but developing a tolerance and sympathy for their elders. They are growing up and one feels that they will be responsible and caring adults—they give more hope for the new generation than the present adult one might sometimes expect.

Not a book for the under twelve plus age group, and a book of which some parents may not approve. (As most librarians I am cowardly towards public opinion.) But this is a book I thought extremely funny, and sensitive in its awareness of troubled adolescence. As a parent myself, I applaud it, as one concerned with the reading interest of teenagers, I applaud it equally.

It is relevant to present day life and whether or not we like what is happening, an author who can relate this to younger readers in a form with which they can identify, and still suggest standards of humanity, is to be much admired for her skill and compassion—and not least her sense of humour.

After all the parent generation is the one which sets them most of their problems, why should we be embarrassed when someone writes about them? A guilty conscience?

BEAT THE TURTLE DRUM (1976)

Publishers Weekly

SOURCE: A review of *Beat the Turtle Drum,* in *Publishers Weekly,* Vol. 210, No. 6, August 9, 1976, pp. 78-9.

Seldom has Constance C. Greene put a foot wrong since she began writing for young people. She is an author with rare insights, an acute eye and ear. In her new novel, she has succeeded so well in bringing all her characters to life, especially 11-year-old Joss, that the death of the lovable child means a bereavement to readers as well as to those in the book. The title comes from Serraillier's poem, "O dance along the silver sand,/ And beat the turtle drum,/ That youth may last for ever/ And sorrow never come." Joss spends her birthday money to rent a horse for a heavenly week of summer. Her sister Kate tells about the good times, the girls' friends who share the fun (and those who don't), their neighbors and their loving, understanding parents. At the end of the horse's visit, the girls are up in a tree and reliving the joys when Joss falls and is killed instantly. Here is a book to read and remember.

Barbara Elleman

SOURCE: A review of *Beat the Turtle Drum,* in *The Booklist,* Vol. 73, No. 6, November 15, 1976, p. 472.

The way 12-year-old Kate tells it, her younger sister Joss is affectionate, lively, and completely devoted to horses. The two share confidences, neighborhood companions, an occasional sibling tiff, and are, in Kate's words, unusually good friends. Joss is currently looking for gift money from her upcoming birthday to finance a week's rental of a horse; she spends her days calculating her cash and visiting Prince at Mr. Essig's farm. Kate's glib, offhand chatter about the weeks prior to Joss' birthday and her expectations for Prince's visit enforces the impact of Joss's sudden, accidental death. The tone of the book dramatically changes as Kate, struggling to cope with and understand her loss, fluctuates between numbness, anger, and a quiet sorting out of her own feelings. Greene, author of *I Know You, Al,* successfully brings Kate and the book through the difficult transition, resulting in a touching, poignant story.

Virginia Haviland

SOURCE: A review of *Beat the Turtle Drum,* in *The Horn Book Magazine,* Vol. LII, No. 6, December, 1976, pp. 624-25.

Kate, at twelve, tells with sisterly love the story of a few weeks in the life of eleven-year-old Joss who longed to own a horse. With her birthday money added to her own Joss was able to rent a horse for a week; the book is about her anticipation and devotion and the sudden tragedy that changed the family's world. Picture books and stories for older readers today often deal with death, and the author is successful in the genre. The closing chapters handle sensitively the effect of Joss's death on members of her family and neighbors: Kate says of their father, "I had never seen my father pray before. He was not a religious man." And from one of the girls' teachers comes a letter to Kate assuring her that "in years to come you'll remember Joss and the things you did together and you'll get pleasure from your memories.'" Built on a sharp characterization of Joss, so loved by everyone, the story makes a sure impact.

Gale K. Shonkwiler

SOURCE: A review of *Beat the Turtle Drum,* in *School Library Journal,* Vol. 23, No. 6, February, 1977, p. 64.

Joss saves money for her 11th birthday so that she can rent a horse for a week. She and her older sister, who narrates the story, have the happiest week of their lives until Joss falls from the apple tree and breaks her neck.

Joss's death stuns the family: Mother lies in bed sedated by tranquilizers, Dad takes to drink, and 13-year-old Kate is left to her own resources. Slowly she gathers strength from her older cousin Mona, the wife of the man who rented the horse and a former teacher. Although this does not focus on grief as closely as *A Taste of Blackberries* by Doris Buchanan Smith nor is the story as finely distilled as Greene's *A Girl Called Al,* the characterization is sensitive and readers will empathize with Kate's feelings of loss.

Zena Sutherland

SOURCE: A review of *Beat the Turtle Drum,* in *Bulletin of the Center for Children's Books,* Vol. 30, No. 8, April, 1977, p. 124.

This is Kate's story, but it is about her younger sister Joss. Joss has a loving heart, a gift for friendship; she and Kate are close friends even though Kate knows Joss is their parents' favorite. Joss is almost everyone's favorite. Her dream comes true on her eleventh birthday when she gets a horse, and one day she and Kate tie the horse to a tree and climb another tree to picnic; Joss falls from the tree and breaks her neck. Because the author has so powerfully drawn the special quality Joss has, especially as seen through Kate's eyes, the conclusion of the story has tremendous impact. Kate lives through the period of numbness, the pain of her own and her parents' grief, the service, and the ambivalent reaction to condolences in a daze. She knows things will get better, but ends, "It's the now that hurts."

Fred Inglis

SOURCE: "Love and Death in Children's Novels," in *The Promise of Happiness: Value and Meaning in Children's Fiction,* Cambridge University Press, 1981, p. 285.

Loss is, we say, like something being cut off. It is an amputation. This is not true for children (and for the essential childishness of all good men and women) who relish fiercely present joy because they know it will soon be lost: this afternoon on a summery beach, this birthday picnic, this Christmas Day. The loss by death in these novels is abrupt and arbitrary. In our times, perhaps this is the best a novelist can do. In a novel which addresses itself directly to a now-rare experience, the death of a child, the novelist can do little, though she does it beautifully, but write of the loss as a sudden severance.

The novel in question is Constance Greene's *Beat the Turtle Drum,* which tells of two sisters through the voice of the elder, thirteen years old, and of the sudden death of the enchanting eleven-year-old Joss who breaks her neck as she falls while tree-climbing. The shock hits suddenly and solidly, as it would in life. The plainness of the prose, having established Joss and her sister as the merry, alert, exquisite little girls they are, is well up to recording the plain facts, the simple pain, of seeing Joss in her coffin, and thereafter the flat, unrumpled sheets and pillows of her still-made-up bed. The reading is as painful as the living would be. The loss is terrible. And, these secular days, that is probably what it would be for a child.

GETTING NOWHERE (1977)

Peggy Sullivan

SOURCE: A review of *Getting Nowhere,* in *School Library Journal,* Vol. 24, No. 2, October, 1977, p. 124.

Occasionally earthy conversations tell most of this story of 14-year-old Mark Johnson, who deeply resents his new stepmother. Teasing at school, uncertainty and curiosity about his own sexual development, and attempts to keep his outgoing younger brother from going over to the enemy keep Mark occupied and closed in on himself. The crucial incident comes when, in a mood of elation, he takes his brother and friend for a ride in his stepmother's old car, crashes into a tree, and must bear the guilt for his friend's serious injuries and his brother's minor ones. Family members and friends are portrayed concisely and credibly, and, as in life, no one is right or wrong all the time. (Mark's understanding and supportive father, for example, is enraged at being unable to reach his older son, strikes him and, after the accident, will not even consider psychiatric care for him.) In spite of strengths in the writing and development of characters, however, the story offers little satisfaction, and Mark is left chastened but still detached from his family, concluding: "Do you know where you are? The words keep coming at me. . . . If I did answer, it might be different today from tomorrow. So. No answer at all."

Barbara Elleman

SOURCE: A review of *Getting Nowhere,* in *The Booklist,* Vol. 74, No. 3, October 1, 1977, p. 290.

Mark's resentment toward his stepmother of a year is relentless and manifests itself in spiteful remarks punctuated with four-letter words. And knowing his father is happy and his brother Tony wholeheartedly accepts Pat does nothing to soothe his groundless anger. An invitation from a couple of pranksters to a nonexistent party at the home of a girl he idolizes embarrasses Mark and furthers his growing turmoil. His only solace is a friendship with elderly Mrs. Baumgartner, who provides understanding and offers providential remarks. It takes a tragic accident (in a car "borrowed" for a joyride around the block), which leaves Tony in a coma and a friend with serious facial injuries, for Mark to finally face himself. Although Greene, author of **Beat the Turtle Drum,** uses her familiar ingredients—troubled young protagonist in a family situation, elderly comforting friend, and somewhat kookie sidekick—she again fashions them into a sensitive, probing story that is natural and believable. The character of the father could be stronger, but the portrayal of Mark as a 14-year-old pulled in a thousand directions reaches directly into the mind and heart.

Ethel L. Heins

SOURCE: A review of *Getting Nowhere,* in *The Horn Book Magazine,* Vol. LIII, No. 6, December, 1977, p. 662.

Part of Mark Johnson's difficulty was simply a matter of temperament; a negligible provocation would often call forth a burst of indignation. But the fourteen-year-old boy's fury over his father's remarriage seemed totally irrational: His mother had been dead for several years, his attractive stepmother went out of her way to be kind and understanding, and both his father and his amiable younger brother were obviously happy with the new arrangement. To add to his rage, Mark unwittingly let himself become the target of a heartless practical joke, and pride forced him to be silent. He should have heeded the warning when even his best friend Jeff was shocked at the insolence and sarcasm Mark leveled against the family; but by the time his anger and misery turned into self-loathing, it was too late, and he had brought them all—including Jeff—to the brink of catastrophe. "'It was almost like a Greek tragedy. . . . Inevitable. Something terrible had to happen. . . . So much rage inside a person eventually corrodes.'" His father's words carry no ring of melodrama, for conviction and verisimilitude are written into the direct, well-told story.

Zena Sutherland

SOURCE: A review of *Getting Nowhere,* in *Bulletin of the Center for Children's Books,* Vol. 31, No. 7, March, 1978, p. 112.

Unlike his younger brother Tony, Mark cannot accept Pat, his stepmother. However she tries to be reasonable or friendly, Mark rejects her overtures; his bitterness and a rancor that emerges in harsh expletives and sarcasm spread to his relationships with his father and brother. Mark is fourteen, just the age to feel a burning shame when some other boys trick him into going to a nonexistent party. After an accident in which Tony is hurt, having gone with Mark and a friend for a stolen ride in Pat's new car, it is Pat who defends Mark and shows understanding. He overhears Pat and his father quarreling about him and realizes that, although he has tried to foment a rift between them in the past, there is no satisfaction in it. He's been getting nowhere, and the only way to change it is to change his own attitudes. A very perceptive and honest book is written with vitality; it has strong characterization and relationships, and an even narrative flow.

I AND SPROGGY (1978)

Publishers Weekly

SOURCE: A review of *I and Sproggy,* in *Publishers Weekly,* Vol. 214, No. 2, July 10, 1978, p. 136.

Adam is almost 11, living with his divorced mother near Gracie Mansion (home of New York City's mayor) and fostering two major ambitions. He wants to be the mayor's honored guest and to get rid of a new stepsister, Sproggy. She has come from England with Adam's father and second wife and the girl has many sins. She is closer to 11 than Adam, she has a crazy accent and Adam's dog likes her. Sproggy tags after her stepbrother and crowns her offenses when his best friends invite her to join their boys' club. It takes time and some jolly developments to change Adam's mind but "I and Sproggy" do become loving pals. Greene writes gracefully, with gentle humor about people who come across as human, not characters, and once again her book has the added attractions of [Emily] McCully's estimable illustrations.

Marjorie Lewis

SOURCE: A review of *I and Sproggy,* in *School Library Journal,* Vol. 25, No. 1, September, 1978, pp. 136-37.

All Adam wants out of his ten-year-old life is a chance to go to nearby Gracie Mansion and see the big shots. He spends the summer lurking outside the gates dreaming of impossible invitations. When his divorced mother announces that his father is about to return to the States with his new English wife and her daughter—Sproggy—who's about his age, his feelings are mixed: happiness about seeing his father; anguish over sharing him. Mom faces the meeting with equanimity and courtesy, but Adam revolts when he discovers Sproggy is tall, brave, and strong (she saves him from a Central Park mugger, to his own disgust)—and, further, popular with his own friends. When eternal optimist Charlie, the doorman in his building, is honored at Gracie Mansion for his involvement in Adult Education courses, Adam—watching the festivities from outside, as usual—is floored when Sproggy gets them inside the gate. He realizes that friendship, like generosity, sometimes takes work but is worth the effort. Greene's unequalled tuning-in to the preoccupations of kids (note the self-centered grammar of the title) and her knack for picking up speech rhythms and jargon without condescension make this a sympathetic, funny, and touching novel.

Ann A. Flowers

SOURCE: A review of *I and Sproggy,* in *The Horn Book Magazine,* Vol. LV, No. 5, October, 1978, pp. 516-17.

A cheerful story of a ten-year-old boy's difficulties in accepting an English stepsister. Adam lives with his divorced mother in New York City; he leads a perfectly normal, happy life until his father remarries and brings his English wife and stepdaughter Sproggy to live near them in New York. Adam is imaginative, curious, and amiable and tries to get along with Sproggy; but he finds her overpowering—aggressively friendly, bigger than he, and quite capable of taking care of herself. He alienates his friends, especially Charlie, the janitor, with his uncharacteristic meanness to Sproggy. Not surprisingly, however, the two do become friends after Adam finds that Sproggy needs

him. Especially notable are the understated description of Adam's relationship with his parents and friends; the realistic, pleasant picture of one aspect of life in New York City; and the many natural, humorous episodes characteristic of the author's work.

Zena Sutherland

SOURCE: A review of *I and Sproggy,* in *Bulletin of the Center for Children's Books,* Vol. 32, No. 5, January, 1979, p. 81.

Adam, who's ten, is dismayed when his mother tells him that his father is coming to New York to live, with his second wife (English) and her daughter, who needs his friendship. Adam's also a bit jealous when they do come and he sees how fond Dad seems to be of Sproggy, his stepdaughter. Anyway, how can he like a girl who's taller than he is, seems so self-confident, uses strange words, and—worst of all—appeals so much to his best friends that they invite her to join their hitherto all-boy club? It takes a few close encounters before Adam and Sproggy become good friends, and the moratorium is due in no small part to the sage advice of Adam's friend Charlie, the building handyman. Greene has a sharp ear for dialogue and a sharp eye for children's problems; her style is fluent and natural, lightened by humor; and her story is balanced and extended by Adam's interest in other matters than his relationship with his new stepsister.

YOUR OLD PAL, AL (1979)

Barbara Elleman

SOURCE: A review of *Your Old Pal, Al,* in *The Booklist,* Vol. 76, No. 1, September 1, 1979, p. 43.

The vicissitudes of friendship provide the central core for Greene's plot as she once again successfully pipes into the minds and hearts of two 12-year-olds. In the third follow-up to *A Girl Called Al* and *I Know You, Al,* the narrator suffers through Al's complaints at not hearing from either her father or the boy she met at his recent wedding, as well as her deliberations over her long-procrastinated letter to him. (Is "Your old pal, Al" the best closure?) Al's jealousy over the narrator's houseguest results in a spat, but eventually the girls sort out their feelings and are closer because of it. The witty dialogue is right on target, and Greene's light touch enables her remarks concerning the makings of friendship to be unobtrusive yet effective.

Mary Burns

SOURCE: A review of *Your Old Pal, Al,* in *The Horn Book Magazine,* Vol. LV, No. 5, October, 1979, p. 534.

Still reveling in her tough-minded nonconformity yet at times touchingly susceptible, Al, now nearly fourteen, declares to her best friend, the narrator of the book, that "'once you're fourteen, it seems *something* should've happened to you. Something memorable.'" Although her interpretation of "memorable" ranges from the improbable to the unlikely, she would settle for two letters—one from her father's new wife inviting her for a visit, and the other from Brian, a fifteen-year-old boy she met at the wedding. Whether or not Al should write to Brian first, just how she should phrase the salutation and conclusion, what she should say to indicate that her interest is merely platonic are the linking elements in the third book of a series which reflects the anxieties and small triumphs of young adolescents. As remarkable for their substantial vocabularies as for their brashness and their shrewd efforts to manipulate parents, the principal characters are sketched through witty repartee, such as "Thelma is a mine of unsolicited advice." As are most youngsters, the narrator is a curious mixture of naïveté and sophistication, pathos and promise—a sort of Erma Bombeck of the urban adolescent set. Vulnerable yet unsinkable, Al and her friends survive a series of microcosmic crises in a manner guaranteed to please their fans.

Christine McDonnell

SOURCE: A review of *Your Old Pal, Al*, in *School Library Journal*, Vol. 26, No. 2, October, 1979, p. 150.

A Girl Called Al is back, nervously waiting for letters from her father and new stepmother and from Brian, the boy she met at her father's wedding in *I Know You Al*. Meanwhile her best friend, the narrator, has a houseguest for two weeks and Al feels left out, so much so that their friendship is briefly threatened. But it all works out in a believable, low-key ending. The plot is less substantial than *A Girl Called Al,* but the characters have vitality. The author has an ear for the speech and humor of twelve year old girls, revealing to readers the warmth, wackiness, sturdy self-possession and moments of vulnerability that make Al so likable.

Kirkus Reviews

SOURCE: A review of *Your Old Pal, Al*, in *Kirkus Reviews*, Vol. XLVII, No. 19, October 1, 1979, p. 1145.

You'll hardly recognize old Al. What with playing dress-up, spinning show-biz fantasies, and (especially) mooning for a letter from Brian, the boy she met at her father's wedding in *I Know You, Al,* she's no longer flashing her high IQ—nor, despite her scorn for the rockettes, is her vaunted nonconformity in evidence. Here, instead of a brittle, snappy kid with some broken-home insecurity tucked away, Al is transparently love-hungry and difficult. She checks the mail every day and mulls over her chances between deliveries, but neither Brian's promised letter nor the promised invitation from her father's new family is forthcoming. Worse, Al's best friend—the nameless narrator—is putting up another friend, Polly, while Polly's parents are in Africa; and though Al is invited for dinner and sleep-overs, she clearly feels displaced. As a result Al is short with her friend, who in

turn is short with Polly—but after the jubilant celebration when Al's invitation does come through, there are apologies all round and some wise talk about the strains of friendship. This thread is well handled, and Al's followers will want to see her through this phase, but Greene gives her too few good lines here and too many breaks at the end: instead of stopping with the invitation, a postcard from Brian follows on its heels—and, in the same mail, the unfortunate pathetic note that Al had agonized over and finally mailed off to him is returned for postage due.

DOTTY'S SUITCASE (1980)

Kirkus Reviews

SOURCE: A review of *Dotty's Suitcase*, in *Kirkus Reviews*, Vol. XLVIII, No. 18, September 15, 1980, p. 1232.

This begins with 12-year-old Dotty Fickett in rare form, lording it over neighbor Jud, who's only eight, teasing him with visions of the exotic journey she will take without him when she gets her long-wished-for suitcase. Dotty is never again in such high spirits, but she does get herself and Jud into a dandy adventure, back in their 1930s' small town where excitement, like money, is hard to come by. With the town buzzing about the bank robbers who have sped off in a black car, Dotty is on hand when a tacky cardboard suitcase is tossed from just such a car. Retrieving it lands her and Jud on the road in a blizzard, picked up by a teenage truck driver who becomes threatening when he discovers that their now-busted suitcase does indeed contain money. They are lost in the storm, befriended by a once-rich hermit who doesn't want the money and gives Dotty a beautiful leather suitcase to keep it in, then shocked when they arrive at the new home, 70 miles from their own, of Dotty's old friend Olive. Since the family moved, Dotty discovers, Olive's father has died of pneumonia and she and her mother are penniless. Moved by their plight, Dotty goes home without the money—it had only come to two hundred dollars—and with a determination not to use the suitcase until Olive can go along with her, maybe to Utica. With simpler characters than those in *A Girl Called Al,* Greene's characterization itself (especially of Olive and Dotty's older, marriage-crazy sisters) tends to be flat, and she is not as effective with Depression hardship as with broken-home stings. The cold-water shock of Olive's poverty hasn't the impact that seems called for—but neither will you question the details or Dotty's reaction. With the suitcase serving neatly to convey Dotty's changing awareness, Greene has managed a successful, if far from memorable, blend of period nostalgia and back-to-basic values.

Marjorie Lewis

SOURCE: A review of *Dotty's Suitcase*, in *School Library Journal*, Vol. 27, No. 2, October, 1980, p. 146.

Times are hard during the Depression, but not all that hard for the Ficketts. Dottie's father has a job, the family is eating regularly; Dottie's only real problems are the loss of her best friend who must move, and the postponement of her dream of having a suitcase of her very own with which she can see the world. A suitcase arrives that is a mixed blessing: it's filled with money from a bank robbery. How Dottie finds it and what she does with it is the basis for a story about pride and friendship and the maturing of a twelve-year-old who finally understands the differences between dreams and realities. Only glimmers of the Greene talent for a finely honed plot, human comedy, and sharply observed characters are apparent. The book lacks the excitement or tension needed to save the far-fetched, stiffly limned story.

Publishers Weekly

SOURCE: A review of *Dotty's Suitcase*, in *Publishers Weekly*, Vol. 218, No. 15, October 10, 1980, p. 74.

In Depression-bowed 1934, 12-year-old Dottie is fixated on getting a shiny new suitcase that will lead her into the glorious adventures she describes to her friend Jud, eight. Jud sniff's but listens anyway to tales of riches that will change life for her, her sisters and widower father. No more will Mr. Fickett have to wear shoes with cardboard over the holes; the family won't worry whether they can afford hamburger at 15¢ a pound. Dottie and Jud do find a suitcase, scuffed and dirty but crammed with dollars, tossed from a car by bank robbers. Dottie grabs it and, with Jud, runs madly to evade the thieves, rushing on until the two are lost, far from home. After some hairy and sad adventures, the yearning girl discovers the difference between real and dream riches in Greene's latest novel. The author of **Beat the Turtle Drum** and other honor winners has written another buoyantly comic and moving story.

DOUBLE-DARE O'TOOLE (1981)

Barbara Elleman

SOURCE: A review of *Double-Dare O'Toole*, in *Booklist*, Vol. 78, No. 2, September 15, 1981, p. 105.

Just a whisper of the words "I double-dare you" sends Fex O'Toole into a variety of bold misdeeds—such as putting a drawing of a pig on the principal's desk—most of which he later regrets. When his older brother starts talking about "making out" and "French kissing," Fex's curiosity about the opposite sex is aroused, and he can't resist a dare to "put the moves on" an older girl at a party. The act has disastrous results, not only alienating his longtime friend Audrey but also making a fool of himself. The death of Fex's friend and store owner, Angie, seems forced into the plot; however, his triumph over his "double-dare" problem is smoothly accomplished, with Greene masterfully capturing the ups and downs of preteen adolescence with a witty, light-but-sure touch. As in the past, her characters are believable and likable, and readers will find this an amusing trip into an 11-year-old's head.

Symme J. Benoff

SOURCE: A review of *Double-Dare O'Toole*, in *School Library Journal*, Vol. 28, No. 2, October, 1981, pp. 141-42.

Francis Xavier O'Toole, unable to resist double dares, is in trouble again. When schoolmates d. d. him to place an insulting picture on the principal's desk, Francis—nicknamed Fex—feels impelled to do it. The compulsion to carry out dares, even when they are dangerous, is Fex's fatal flaw. Aside from that, in fact even *with* that, he's quite an ordinary, likable boy. Though the principal's secretary sees him leave the office and he is punished for a week, there are worse dares to come. The relationships between Fex and his friend, Audrey, and between Fex and an older neighbor, Angie, are more memorable than the plot. One of the funniest, most touching scenes is when, after a dare to "make out" with an older girl at a party, Fex tries to practice with Audrey. His awkward attempts at a first kiss are, at once, pathetic and laughable. Angie is Fex's older, wiser confidant; she is the one who explains his d. d. problem in psychological terms, and she is the one who dies at the end, leaving Fex and Audrey to share their grief and to console each other. Fex's tender feelings for Angie and the resolution of his ambivalent feelings about Audrey and his own sexuality are worth the price of the book.

Kirkus Reviews

SOURCE: A review of *Double-Dare O'Toole*, in *Kirkus Reviews*, Vol. XLIX, No. 20, October 15, 1981, p. 1296.

You guessed it—sixth-grader Fex O'Toole's main problem is that he just can't turn down a double dare. He puts an insulting drawing on the principal's desk, even though he thinks the principal is an okay guy. Later he accepts a challenge to kiss a strange girl at a party. When the lights go on he's a laughing stock, and in trouble with his good friend Audrey. Fex is cured when a four-year-old he's babysitting jumps into a dangerous river on a dare from the same bad kids who've been daring Fex. Fex jumps in after the kid and comes out a hero. Such a plot suggests a thin, contrived little story, but Greene fills it out with assorted amusing encounters that put across Fex's perplexity and discomfort appealingly. The story's course is meandering and a little slack, and the people tend to be stereotypes (the bad kid) or too-folksy "characters" (an older woman, storekeeper and Fex's confidante, who dies in the end); but Greene treats them all, and Fex especially, with sympathetic humor.

Zena Sutherland

SOURCE: A review of *Double-Dare O'Toole*, in *Bulletin of the Center for Children's Books*, Vol. 35, No. 9, May, 1982, p. 170.

Fex O'Toole, eleven, knows that he shouldn't do some of the things he's done when his friends have double-dared him. Certainly his best friends and his worried mother have tried to convince him that accepting those dares have usually meant trouble, but Fex goes right on, unable to resist the challenge. And he does get into trouble, especially with the school principal. And with his friend Audrey, who is angry because he accepted a dare and kissed a girl he hardly knew at a party. Fex finally learns his lesson when, just after he has refused to jump into a river in spate, his four-year-old friend says he'll take the dare; Fex rescues Charlie, and sees for himself how rash taking a dare can be. The story has some effective characters and relationships, and it's written in a light and lively style, but it doesn't make Fex's compulsion quite convincing.

AL(EXANDRA) THE GREAT (1982)

Kay Webb O'Connell

SOURCE: A review of *Al(exandra) the Great,* in *School Library Journal,* Vol. 28, No. 9, May, 1982, p. 62.

Less than a year has passed in the lives of Al and our narrator since the first of the three preceding books, *A Girl Called Al.* Both girls, now eighth graders, have grown: Al has designs on a boy she met at her father's wedding, and her friend has had to learn how to help Al be friends with other girls. Now a crisis occurs. Just when Al's set to fly out to visit her father's new family, Al's mother contracts pneumonia. Naturally Al stays home—there's scant suspense, although she obsesses a lot about it. The Al books are really about values and human insights, not exploits; the select characters who people these pages—unfashionable Al and her ultrafashionable mom, the narrator and her good-humored family—are endearing. The girls are looking for role models and trying people on for size—they project adult wisdom with pubescent candor.

Kirkus Reviews

SOURCE: A review of *Al(exandra) the Great,* in *Kirkus Reviews,* Vol. L, No. 9, May 1, 1982, p. 554.

Al and her nameless narrator friend haven't aged more than a year since *A Girl Called Al* hit town in 1969, though the New York background and colloquialisms keep unobtrusively up to date. Still, the focus here is on growing up to responsibility, especially as expressed through Al's feelings for her divorced, working mother. As this opens Al anticipates a visit to her father's new family in the heartland, complete with barn dance, homemade ice cream, and the chance to see the boy she's corresponded with since her reconciliatory trip to her dad's wedding in *I Know You Al.* But she's worried about her mother's health, and obviously scared when her mother ends up in hospital with pneumonia. Finally, though her mother is soon on the mend, Al decides regretfully that she must cancel her trip. "Somebody has to take care of her when she gets home. [Mr. Wright, the current 'beau,' is] not her family. She's not his responsibility. She's mine." But the story isn't that unilinear, for interwoven with Al's dilemma are scenes with her friend's intact family, including a fancy restaurant dinner both girls enjoy with the narrator's father while Al's mother is in hospital. (The narrator would have preferred to go out alone with her father, but couldn't leave Al alone.) For relief, there is Al's typical party-stopping story when the two girls are uncomfortable guests at a party of pompous 13-year-olds. The developmental pats-on-the-head are a tad mushy, with each girl envying and then sympathizing with the other, and all the parents expressing pride in their daughters' maturity. But everything is leavened by Al's characteristic snappy cracks and tough-front comebacks.

Publishers Weekly

SOURCE: A review of *Al(exandra) the Great,* in *Publishers Weekly,* Vol. 221, No. 19, May 7, 1982, p. 80.

Greene catches readers up on developments in the affairs of Al and her best friend, neighbors in a Manhattan apartment building. Again the narrator is the anonymous best friend who told the stories in *A Girl Named Al, I Know You, Al* and *Your Pal, Al.* Now she's 13 and despondent but resigned to staying in the city while Al's dream vacation takes her to her father's farm in Ohio, the home of his new wife and family. Al is also elated at the prospect of meeting Brian again, the boy she had become friendly with at her father's wedding. But her mother is hit with pneumonia and, although everyone urges the girl to go anyway since the doctor says her mother is on the mend and will be cared for, Al refuses. The story soars to a happy ending and it is written in Greene's unforced, amiable style, with salty humor balancing the poignant moments.

Nancy Sheridan

SOURCE: A review of *Al(exandra) the Great,* in *Horn Book Magazine,* Vol. LVIII, No. 4, August, 1982, pp. 402-03.

Al and her friend the unnamed narrator are back in an amusing and engaging story that takes up where *Your Old Pal, Al* left off. Al eagerly prepares to leave the hot, stifling city for a three-week trip to the country to visit her father and his new family; plans for a barn dance have been made, and Brian, the boy she met at her father's wedding, will be there. When Al's mother suddenly comes down with pneumonia, however, the girl must make what seems to be the most important decision of her life. Less than a year has passed in the series of books about Al; almost fourteen, she is still often insecure and needs the steadying hand of her reliable friend. But her final decision to stay at home and care for her mother—although made after much deliberation—is totally her own. Both girls must make sacrifices and, in doing so, learn more about themselves and the people around them. The writing style is natural, the dialogue flows with ease, and the complex feelings and relationships among children and adults are portrayed honestly and effortlessly. Once again the author creates characters that are fresh and appealing and instinctively depicts the ups and downs of a loyal friendship.

ASK ANYBODY (1983)

Publishers Weekly

SOURCE: A review of *Ask Anybody*, in *Publishers Weekly*, Vol. 223, No. 4, January 28, 1983, p. 86.

In her witty fashion Greene brings the people of a small Maine town to life, as their affairs are related by Schuyler Sweet. "I'm halfway to 12, a bad age in a woman," Schuyler says. She wants to be sweet like her name but that's hard, what with her parents divorced, the mother in love again and off on a trip. Schuyler helps her dad care for her young brothers and also hopes for redemption by cooperating with friends, planning a tag sale for their own "charity," the Chum Club. Then Nell and her ragamuffin kin move into town, and the new girl loses no time giving the club members lessons in chicanery. That means running the tag sale under Nell's direction, an event and aftermath that feature the local eccentrics fighting for the offered bargains and disclosing Nell's intended use of the profits.

Zena Sutherland

SOURCE: A review of *Ask Anybody*, in *Bulletin of the Center for Children's Books*, Vol. 36, No. 8, April, 1983, p. 149.

Schuyler lives in a small Maine town where everyone knows everyone else and few of them trust "outastaters," i.e., people not born and bred in Maine. Her friends don't like the brash new outastater, Nell, but Sky feels she ought to be nice to Nell. It isn't easy. Nell brags, steals, lies, and says insulting things, but Sky puts up with it because Nell is colorful and different—at least, she puts up with it until she learns how callous Nell is. The story is built around this uneasy friendship and around Sky's concern about her parents, who are divorced but living at opposite ends of the same house, with the children in the middle. Will Mom marry the man on whom she seems to have a crush? Or will Dad fall for Pamela, who keeps hanging around? What Greene does is end her story with unanswered questions about Mom and Dad, while the saga of Nell ends abruptly: she and her feckless family take off leaving the rent unpaid and taking the money that all the girls have garnered at a long-planned yard sale. Without filling in all the details, the author draws a trenchant, incisive picture of Nell and her carping, shiftless mother, and hints that the relationship between Mom and Dad may be improving. This has the same empathetic insight as Greene's urban stories, the same firm characterization and fluent style, and it also gives a good picture of the network of relationships in a small community.

Ann A. Flowers

SOURCE: A review of *Ask Anybody*, in *The Horn Book Magazine*, Vol. LIX, No. 3, June, 1983, p. 302.

When Nell Foster and her family came to rent the house down the street in the pretty Maine village, Schuyler Sweet was pleased to have a new neighbor. But eleven-year-old Nell seemed different; she wore green nail polish and ragged clothes and was bossy and boastful. A thoughtful, questioning girl, Schuyler could not make up her mind about Nell; while she envied the girl's apparent self-confidence and attractiveness to boys, she sometimes saw the cracks in Nell's façade—her lack of a normal family life, her mother's rejection of her, and her mistrust of others. When Nell daringly drove the Fosters' truck, she accidentally ran over their dog and cold-bloodedly hauled its body into the street to simulate a hit-and-run accident. Schuyler was horrified; yet when the Foster family left town suddenly, she was both glad and sorry. Seeing Nell through Schuyler's eyes, the reader is both sympathetic and repulsed; the story presents an often humorous, thoughtful character study of an unfortunate child.

ISABELLE SHOWS HER STUFF (1984)

Kirkus Reviews

SOURCE: A review of *Isabelle Shows Her Stuff*, in *Kirkus Reviews*, Vol. LII, No. 17, September 1, 1984, p. 70.

Isabelle the Itch is back, still ten and exasperating, but she seems dazzling to Guy Gibbs, an eight-year-old newcomer with hopes of shedding his goody-goody skin. Easily impressed, Guy quickly enlists her support in changing his image. Greene, as always, maneuvers the central two with a clean, light touch: they talk and act like kids getting to know each other. This time, though, the others, especially a gifted younger sister, an eccentric grandma, and irritating Mary Eliza Shook—add little to the proceedings. Ultimately, Guy solves his own problem (protecting a dog from some toughs) and Isabelle, with a few tidy insights, starts to curb some of her impulses. Balanced and amusing but less inspired than the original.

Ilene Cooper

SOURCE: A review of *Isabelle Shows Her Stuff*, in *Booklist*, Vol. 81, No. 2, September 15, 1984, p. 127.

Feisty Isabelle is back, and she brings with her her sparring partner, Herbie; her nemesis, brother Phillip; and a newcomer, timid, eight-year-old Guy Gibbs. Guy has recently moved to Hot Water Street, where he hopes to land in some hot water of his own. A sweet, gentle child, Guy is quickly labeled by the older kids in the neighborhood as a goody-goody, just as he has been in the past. When he meets Isabelle, he is immediately impressed with her derring-do and feels sure she can help him spiff up his image. Yet, even all of Isabelle's machinations don't work, and, in the end, he is left to tackle the job himself, which he eventually does with bravery and gusto. Greene has written a spirited story filled with memorable characters, some charming, others eccentric—even members of the supporting cast have been crafted with care. Fans of the series will be delighted by this new offering, while those previously unacquainted with Isabelle and company are in for a treat.

Publishers Weekly

SOURCE: A review of *Isabelle Shows Her Stuff,* in *Publishers Weekly,* Vol. 226, No. 13, September 28, 1984, p. 112.

In the sequel to **Isabelle the Itch,** a new boy, meek Guy Gibbs, moves into the orbit of Greene's spunky heroine. Isabelle takes on the role of protector/adviser to Guy, who longs for the reputation of a tough hombre. He is tired of being picked on by bullies who jeer at him as a goody-goody. Isabelle gives the little boy boxing lessons and tips on getting into trouble, like breaking into the school when it's closed and writing "stuff" on the walls. But Guy is too timid for such large gestures. It turns out, though, that a gang abusing a helpless dog impels Guy to act heroically, even without Isabelle backing him up. The results are mind-boggling; no one will dare to mess with Guy again. The author, as always, tells an irresistibly funny and tender story, about believable kids and the grown-ups they live with.

Lyn Littlefield Hoopes

SOURCE: A review of *Isabelle Shows Her Stuff,* in *The Christian Science Monitor,* Vol. 77, No. 68, March 1, 1985, p. B5.

In Constance C. Greene's **Isabelle Shows Her Stuff,** we meet Guy Gibbs, the new kid on Hot Water Street—"Goody-goody Guy, wouldn't hurt a fly." Guy is big on books and doesn't want to fight: How can he get the kids to stop teasing him? Even Isabelle, the "paper boy," with her flying fists and quick tongue can't seem to come up with a workable scheme. But through their friendship, Guy develops his own brand of self-confidence and determination to stand up for himself, so that when, quite unexpectedly, the need to be tough arises, he finds that he's ready.

Young readers will relish Constance C. Greene's eccentric characters and the witty lines to match. Beneath the high-energy storytelling they'll enjoy discovering the human dimension of the story when they find Isabelle, despite her bravado, as vulnerable as Guy, and Guy, under all his vulnerability, brave.

STAR SHINE (1985)

Zena Sutherland

SOURCE: A review of *Star Shine,* in *Bulletin of the Center for Children's Books,* Vol. 39, No. 2, October, 1985, p. 27.

It was hard to explain to their friends that their mother had not left them, that she had only (as a stage-struck amateur

actress) gone off to take her first chance at summer stock. When a movie company came to town to do some location shots, it wasn't pretty Mary (thirteen) they chose as an extra but boyish Jenny (twelve) with her chopped-by-hand hair that got a bit part. The theatrical razzle-dazzle lends some excitement to the book, but its strength is, as one would expect in a book by this author, in the subtleties of relationships, whether within the family or the peer group, and in the equally effective character depiction and dialogue, both of which emerge in an easy (or apparently easy) flow.

Publishers Weekly

SOURCE: A review of *Star Shine,* in *Publishers Weekly,* Vol. 228, No. 22, November 29, 1985, p. 46.

Greene's new novel may be deemed the topper of all the funny, moving unpredictable stories that have won her awards and devout fans. The excitement jets off here when Mrs. Chisholm leaves home "for a few weeks" to tour with an acting company. Jenny (11) and her sister Mary (almost 13) persuade their father to let them manage on their own in their mother's absence. The sisters stick together, despite occasional squabbles arising from Jenny's salty disapproval of Mary's adolescent airs and snippy, boy-crazy friends. When a company arrives in town to make a film, everybody gets in line to apply for the $40 per diem paid to extras, but it's raffish Jenny ("your basic gamine") who's chosen. As the girls' elderly friend Mrs. Carruthers says, the movie actors in her young days had "star shine," which is what readers will agree Jenny—and author Greene—have too.

Judie Porter

SOURCE: A review of *Star Shine,* in *School Library Journal,* Vol. 32, No. 5, January, 1986, p. 67.

The stars don't shine because this book lacks both the plot and zaniness that typifies Greene's work. Jenny and Mary's mother leaves them for the summer to go on tour as an actress; Dad must hold things together in her absence. There is a hint of insecurity about Mom's departure, but it lacks depth, as does the benign trouble the girls find. Mary is excited about the prospect of a role in a movie being filmed locally. Jenny is selected, however, and she could care less about the opportunity. Jenny, who hacks away at her hair with manicure scissors and sucks her thumb—at age 11—is well defined. Unfortunately, most of the other characters are shallow, especially the mother. Typical of Greene's books, this one also stresses values over action and tries to prove that things are not always as they seem on the surface.

JUST PLAIN AL (1986)

Publishers Weekly

SOURCE: A review of *Just Plain Al,* in *Publishers Weekly,* Vol. 230, No. 8, August 22, 1986, p. 100.

The ever-popular Al is back, in the fifth of Greene's series about Al and her best friend. With the same snappy dialogue and typical teenage humor—one of Al's current sayings is "Have a weird day"—Al anticipates her 14th birthday as a maturation milestone. In honor of approaching womanhood, Al's decided she's tired of being "just plain Al" and she and her friends spend the summer trying to decide her new name. "Alex" is snobby, "Zandra" phony, and then Al discovers Mother Zandi, the fortune-teller. Threaded through the good humor is the kids' discovery of homeless people, and Al's determination to find something to do for them, which culminates in the wacky appearance of Mother Zandi at a nursing home. This light-hearted and breezy story is sure to keep Al's fans hungry for more.

Rebekah Ray

SOURCE: A review of *Just Plain Al,* in *School Library Journal,* Vol. 33, No. 2, October, 1986, pp. 175-76.

Al is about to turn 14. She is trying to become sophisticated, have a meaningful life through selflessness, and change her name. It appears that she is succeeding at all three, but at a pace unsatisfactory to herself. *Just Plain Al* is of the same episodic type as the other Al books, with the relationships unifying the story. Al and her best friend (whose name is never given and who tells the stories) give an adolescent view of New York City which is humorous and thoughtful. Greene has a delightful talent for believable, hilarious dialogue. The characters in *Just Plain Al* are all special, with not a stereotype among them. Both the adults and the child characters are human and likable. Al's followers will continue their friendship with her, and this book is sure to make her some new ones.

Kirkus Reviews

SOURCE: A review of *Just Plain Al,* in *Kirkus Reviews,* Vol. LIV, No. 19, October 1, 1986, p. 1509.

In this fifth book about Al, she faces the landmark of turning 14 in typical Al fashion: she has what amounts to a mid-life crisis.

On the theory that Al is a baby name and lacks "pizazz," Al considers alternatives like Zandra. She also: almost celebrates a birthday at the Rainbow Room but has a more satisfying party at the home of her best friend; is bemused by the fact that her mother has a date with her best friend's grandfather; and reexamines her values in confronting a world full of people, many less materially prosperous than she. She then seriously considers divesting herself of her possessions, except for her favorite red shoes, which she will keep to remind herself of former excesses. But a more successful solution to Al's identity problems is provided when she visits a nursing home and is a roaring triumph as Madam Zandra, which allows her to improve the world in her own unique style.

This seems episodic, but Greene's skill is such that there is not a wasted scene; every line of dialogue crackles with wit. Al's fans will love this.

Zena Sutherland

SOURCE: A review of *Just Plain Al,* in *Bulletin of the Center for Children's Books,* Vol. 40, No. 6, February, 1987, p. 107.

A fifth book about Al (Alexandra) is again narrated by her best friend, who remains nameless. Al, approaching her 14th, feels that she needs a new nickname. Maybe Zandi? As in the earlier books, this is a witty account of the friendship, the family relationships, and the young teen concerns of two lively and engaging characters. The narrative is convincing as the product of a twelve-year-old, the style is yeasty, and the Manhattan background is used to stimulating effect. Strong characters, the two girls remain recognizable as their earlier selves, and both develop and mature as time marches on.

THE LOVE LETTERS OF J. TIMOTHY OWEN (1986)

Stephanie Zvirin

SOURCE: A review of *The Love Letters of J. Timothy Owen,* in *Booklist,* Vol. 83, No. 3, October 1, 1986, p. 220.

Though he tries to hide behind the guise of a laid-back intellectual, Tim Owen is a "veritable mush of romanticism" at heart, and the sight of Sophie, the beleaguered baby-sitter next door wrestling courageously with her monster charges, arouses his admiration (he's baby-sat the bunch himself) and his romantic fervor. Unfortunately, rushing in like the fabled knight on a white charger earns him little more than a "buzz off, buddy" from the damsel in distress. Still interested in Sophie—but a little more cautious about head-to-head encounters—Tim tries a different tactic to meet her. Cribbing from *One Hundred of the World's Best Love Letters,* he fires off a few anonymous billets-doux to the unsuspecting object of his desire, hoping they will attract her attention. They do, of course, but the response they provoke is not exactly the one Tim had in mind. Greene gives readers more than comedy here. She has invested Tim with sense and sensibility as well as misguided passion, and she's done a fine job of balancing the boy's wry wit and comedic encounters with some of the harsher stuff of his life. Equally skillful is the book's gently humorous close, in which Tim finds a new fairy princess of sorts—one who just happens to like letters.

Zena Sutherland

SOURCE: A review of *The Love Letters of J. Timothy Owen,* in *Bulletin of the Center for Children's Books,* Vol. 40, No. 4, December, 1986, p. 67.

Sixteen, shy, and totally smitten by Sophie, Tim uses material from an old book he's come across, *One Hundred of the World's Best Love Letters,* to send her doting but anonymous missives. Unfortunately, Sophie has a low opinion of whatever nut is writing the letters, and her father—who considers them the work of a sex maniac—is apopleptic. That just about takes care of the first crush. When a friend's younger sister (to whom Tim had been kind) suddenly blossoms from a pudgy thirteen to a slim and attractive fourteen, Tim is belatedly smitten again. This time there seems to be a response, but Tim reconsiders the whole business of love letters. Pleasant, amusing, and realistic, this is more impressive for its humor and smooth narrative flow than for depth of characterization or strong plot development. Not to be taken seriously, but easy to take.

Betty Ann Porter

SOURCE: A review of *The Love Letters of J. Timothy Owen,* in *School Library Journal,* Vol. 33, No. 4, December, 1986, p. 117.

J. Timothy Owen is one of the last romantics. When, in the same day, he discovers *One Hundred of the World's Best Love Letters* and the gorgeous Sophie, his imagination runs amok, and the result is disaster. Tim is so taken with the love letters of Rousseau, Lord Nelson, and Elizabeth Barrett Browning that he decides to send them verbatim to Sophie; he is horrified and humiliated at the reaction to his letters. Sophie's father tells the police about the pervert harassing his daughter, and Sophie herself is hurling accusations of "weird" and "sicko" at a totally crushed knight errant. True romance is not easily quashed, however, and Tim's basic good nature carries him through until a new love catches his eye. Greene, veteran of snappy dialogue, genuine humor, and warm family relationships, has created a thoroughly likable hero. With Tim's emotional highs and lows, his questions, fears, and desires, readers see the qualities that make her characters so human and so appealing. A wry and human story that beautifully captures the confusions of growing up.

John Lord

SOURCE: A review of *The Love Letters of J. Timothy Owen,* in *Voice of Youth Advocates,* Vol. 9, No. 5, December, 1986, p. 216.

The Love Letters of J. Timothy Owen is a disappointing book for several reasons. The main reason is that it never seems to get anywhere. The author's intent is good, but the action just seems to wander around, with too many diversions and not enough direction. For that reason alone, young readers will find it tedious, but some may have the perseverance to continue to the end of the book.

"I'm into writing love letters . . . , not necessarily mailing them" says Tim Owen to his friend Patrick, and that is the basic premise of the book. Tim, whose divorced parents have found other romantic interests, finds himself attracted to one Sophie Feeley. Because Tim has found some old love letters in a antique trunk in his mother's shop, he feels that he can use them as models for his own writing and his own thoughts about Sophie. However, the natural fear of rejection prevents him from sending his letters to Sophie.

The situations which develop based on this premise are trite and—essentially—boring. And that's not my opinion based on my age but rather on having read some of the Canby Hall series and the Sweet Valley High series. Those books have typical incidents and situations that are handled well, while this is tedious. Only the true romantic would bother to finish the book.

(Perhaps because the main character is a boy, the writer had difficulty making the story plausible. A girl as main character falling head-over-heels-in-love and using the letters might have worked better!)

MONDAY I LOVE YOU (1988)

Kirkus Reviews

SOURCE: A review of *Monday I Love You,* in *Kirkus Reviews,* Vol. LVI, No. 1, June 1, 1988, pp. 826-27.

Grace is 15, overweight, and wears a 38D bra. Her home life is dreary; school is bleak, friendless, and the place where the other girls once ripped her clothes in an attempt to see her "boobs." She escapes into fantasy and recollection of the past, especially the happy summer when she and her friend William became blood brothers by cutting palms (she still has a bad scar). Meanwhile, she baby-sits for a sympathetic teacher (Ms. Govoni), who helps to restore her self-esteem, and for Doris, who lives in an isolated trailer. There, a strange young man (who by the book's end is clearly identified as an armed robber, attempted rapist, and prison escapee who has recently been in the local news) breaks in and carries on an edgy, knive-waving conversation. Grace tells him about William, and shows him her scar. Although she doesn't realize till later that this is (by an astounding coincidence) William herself, the reader will identify him as he kisses her gently and departs in peace.

While this encounter holds suspense, and leads to increased self-assurance for Grace, Greene's conclusion holds a second major implausibility: not only does Grace decide not to report William to the police, but she confides in Ms. Govoni, depicted as a sensible, responsible person, and Ms. Govoni does not even debate her decision—even after an innocent man has been imprisoned in William's stead.

Ilene Cooper

SOURCE: A review of *Monday I Love You,* in *Booklist,* Vol. 84, No. 21, July, 1988, p. 1835.

Fifteen-year-old Grace Schmidt has a big problem—her size 38D breasts. Plain and lonely, she is sure that her overdeveloped bust is the main reason the other kids make fun of her; she has confirmation of this during a horrific episode in which a group of girls (including Ashley, the school's Miss Popular) tear off her blouse in the bathroom—to see if she's for real. But the incident is just one of life's burdens for Grace, who uses her bra size to avoid focusing on some of her other problems. Her father is a traveling salesman who never quite makes a living, and her mother ignores her completely. The only real friend Grace ever had was in childhood, when a beautiful boy named William became her blood brother. In an amazing (and jarring) coincidence, Grace meets up with William again at a time when he could possibly hurt her; instead he shows her a kindness that enables her to change her life. Greene writes with sensitivity, and her examination of a life unfulfilled will have meaning for those who are tormented, as well as for the tormentors. Peopled with a wealth of memorable characters, this story will effectively linger in readers' minds.

Susan F. Marcus

SOURCE: A review of *Monday I Love You*, in *School Library Journal*, Vol. 34, No. 11, August, 1988, p. 106.

Grace is 15, and she and her size 38D bosom are the objects of derision from her peers. Although her unseeing mother and ineffective father are incapable of helping her, she does get a little ego-boosting from her phys ed teacher. But it takes a very peculiar incident to give Grace the impetus to take charge of her life. A young man whom she suspects is guilty of a gas-station shooting and robbery forces his way into the house trailer in which Grace is babysitting, purportedly to call a car mechanic or a cab. Apparently unable to get help, the young man remains while Grace and her charge go to sleep. Even though his behavior is suspect, his kindness to her reminds her of William, a boy she knew when she was little. Could this man be William, the only real friend she ever had? Readers are never positive. They will be surprised, however, that neither Grace nor her teacher ever feel bound to tell the police about the incident, even when a reward is offered for a dangerous fugitive who answers to the same description. From the beginning, readers will be overcome by the grimness of Grace's relentlessly disagreeable life. At the end, they will continue to be uncomfortable, aware that Grace is protecting either a criminal or the psychotic William. This absence of a closure creates an unpleasant note and makes it difficult to recommend the book for its intended audience. Used to relying on Greene's books for believable dialogue and memorable characters, many readers will be troubled by this one

Betsy Hearne

SOURCE: A review of *Monday I Love You*, in *Bulletin of the Center for Children's Books*, Vol. 42, No. 2, October, 1988, p. 36.

This is a problem novel with a capital D—38D. That's the bra size Grace Schmitt has worn ever since she matured into a voluptuous object of ridicule at school. Contributing to her low self-esteem are low-income, lower-class parents who seem to alternate abandoning the family. Memories of a happy, un-selfconscious childhood are interspersed with tense scenes of torment, one in a washroom where several girls rip off Grace's blouse and another in a trailer home invaded by a criminal while Grace is babysitting. Past and present intersect when Grace realizes that the criminal who has spared her life may be a boy with whom she had sworn eternal friendship at age six. This encounter proves a turning point after which, with the help of a sympathetic gym teacher, she begins to value her own courage and build confidence (here one could wish she had shown a trace of anger at having her life threatened, as well as gratitude that it was spared). Considering how much is crammed into this novel, including the single gym teacher's two adopted Korean children, the stereotyped nastiness of every popular or attractive peer, and an unlikely central coincidence, the first-person narrative holds together surprisingly well. Grace has, despite her self-pity, an appealing and intense vulnerability. Unfortunate side notes include a bland cover and a single paragraph where Grace suddenly starts swearing, which she does nowhere else in the book. However, the vivid portrayal of a teenager tormented by insecurity more than makes up for these distractions.

ISABELLE AND LITTLE ORPHAN FRANNIE (1988)

Publishers Weekly

SOURCE: A review of *Isabelle and Little Orphan Frannie*, in *Publishers Weekly*, Vol. 234, No. 2, July 8, 1988, p. 56.

Isabelle, the plucky heroine of **Isabelle Shows Her Stuff**, is back to take a new look at herself and her gang. Sparring partner Herbie has grown confident, older brother Philip has discovered girls, and old Mrs. Stern has a gentleman suitor. To Isabelle, it's as if everyone else is leaving her behind. Her newest find is "little orphan Frannie," a tough, irascible kid whose semi-abandoned state evokes instant sympathy from Isabelle's mother and other adults, and whose unpredictability drives Isabelle to distraction. Then she discovers Frannie's secret—she can't read—and reluctant-reader Isabelle decides to do the teaching herself. Bright and funny, this is a terrific new adventure for Isabelle's many fans. While Frannie's plight, when explained, is quite believable, some readers may be disappointed that she disappears as quickly as she arrived.

Kirkus Reviews

SOURCE: A review of *Isabelle and Little Orphan Frannie*, in *Kirkus Reviews*, Vol. LVI, No. 16, August 15, 1988, p. 1240.

Isabelle, the lovable, troublesome perpetual-motion machine, returns for her third outing.

Out of the blue, Frannie enters Isabelle's life—saying only that she's "an orphan" who's staying with her "aunt" while her mother is off looking for a new daddy. Isabelle never knows when Frannie will turn up, what she'll be wearing, or how she'll wangle a dinner invitation from Isabelle's sympathetic mother. But when Isabelle learns that Frannie can't read or write, she captures her unwilling pupil with threats and punches and then teaches her a few of the basics. Meanwhile, old friends from the first two books make appearances—including Herbie, who's abandoned fighting with Isabelle to become the school-newspaper editor; and Mrs. Stern, who consults with Isabelle about romance. Isabelle also finds time to destroy the living-room ceiling with her bathtub skin-diving.

Greene neatly knits all these plot threads together and leaves the reader longing for the next Isabelle adventure. Newly independent readers will quickly turn the pages; teachers who need a humorous read-aloud won't be able to control the laughter.

Zena Sutherland

SOURCE: A review of *Isabelle and Little Orphan Frannie,* in *Bulletin of the Center for Children's Books,* Vol. 42, No. 1, September, 1988, p. 9.

Isabelle, the indomitable fifth-grader who gravitates toward trouble because she is inventive, ebullient, thoughtless, and determined, is back; she's as lively, appealing, and amusing as in earlier books. This time she takes eight-year-old Frannie on, having learned that Frannie can't read. A peripatetic waif, Frannie declares she is "a norphan," and in a way she is, her mother having come to stay with her friend because, as Frannie (calculatedly pitiful) explains, her old daddy died and her Mom is looking for a new one. The lessons don't go well, but after Frannie moves on, Isabelle gets a postcard: "I go to scool now. I can read some. Your a good teach." So the story ends with Isabelle happy, her project accomplished. There's no question of condescending charity, Frannie being a tough little character who knows how to get what she wants. As is usual in Greene's stories, the perceptive affection that pervades the book is balanced by light, bright humor, especially in the dialogue. This has some deliciously entertaining classroom scenes.

Ethel R. Twitchell

SOURCE: A review of *Isabelle and Little Orphan Frannie,* in *The Horn Book Magazine,* Vol. LXIV, No. 6, November-December, 1988, p. 783.

Isabelle is back to put fear into the hearts of parents and to put envy—and unholy ideas—into the minds of her peers. Although the plot line is barely discernible, Isabelle's

escapades carom amiably from pretend scuba diving in the bathtub to styling her hair with nail scissors; all the action is set pell-mell against running verbal battles with her brother, Philip, and much-relished fist fights with her good friend, Herbie. The Frannie of the title calls herself "'a norphan'" and drifts into Isabelle's life, hinting that Frannie's mother is looking for a new husband and refusing to let Isabelle meet the relative the little girl is temporarily staying with. Isabelle half-heartedly attempts to befriend Frannie, but she departs at the conclusion without having made much of a stir in Isabelle's busy, bossy, battle-strewn life. As always, Isabelle's talk is fast and funny. She tosses off quick comebacks and blistering insults without a second thought. Indeed, it is the author's gift for lively conversation and amusing characters that gives the book its sparkle and keeps the story moving along at a rapid clip.

AL'S BLIND DATE (1989)

Ilene Cooper

SOURCE: A review of *Al's Blind Date,* in *Booklist,* Vol. 86, No. 9, January 1, 1990, p. 915.

This is a disappointing addition to the popular series featuring Al(exandra) and her friend, the unnamed narrator. Previous books about Al have tackled some difficult issues—death, the homeless, divorce—warmed with humor and insight. Here, Al's concerns such as dating are realistic but so broadly handled as to make them caricatures. Al and the narrator, both 14, are set up for blind dates—to go tea dancing no less. While the girls are making up their minds (to go or not to go, that is the question), they are almost blown to smithereens at a mobster's gym and help a teacher who is lonely in New York. Though there is one party encounter with boys, the book ends just as the long-awaited blind date is about to begin. Fans of the series won't want to miss this one, since, as in most of Greene's books, there is enough witty dialogue to elicit some chuckles. It seems a shame, though, that Al isn't getting better, she's just getting older.

Eleanor K. MacDonald

SOURCE: A review of *Al's Blind Date,* in *School Library Journal,* Vol. 36, No. 4, April, 1990, p. 118.

Al is back again, and while this book will not attract new readers, it will be enjoyed by old acquaintances. Al and a friend, both 14, face the dilemma of the blind date—specifically whether to go with their classmate's cousin and his friend to a tea dance. It sounds intriguing, but Al is full of her usual doubts, and the adults in their lives offer as many horror tales as reassurances on the subject. Even Al can't fill an entire book with her dithering on this subject, so Greene has thrown in an odd episode involving an unhappy teacher, a new health club in the neighborhood, and a Mafia fire bomb. This whole part of the story feels tacked on; the girls' actions are uncharacteristically forced, and nothing is fully explained or resolved. The same can be said about the denouement. The book ends just as the girls go out to meet their dates after being assured that "they're both cute as bugs." While this seems to assure yet another in the series, it will frustrate many readers to spend all this time on the decision without finding out how it worked out. While the central core of this book is not as compelling or believable as the earlier ones, the dialogue continues to be witty, the friendship solid, and the characters real. Al's friends will be glad to see her again.

ODDS ON OLIVER (1993)

Kirkus Reviews

SOURCE: A review of *Odds on Oliver,* in *Kirkus Reviews,* Vol. LXI, No. 3, February 1, 1993, p. 147.

Greene's first foray into humorous fiction for a younger audience than her popular series about Al and Isabelle. Since preschool, Oliver has had one ambition—to be a hero. Now he's finished fourth grade and is still trying, but misses his chances in one misadventure after another until, on the Fourth of July, his dog chokes on a chicken bone and he's able to save her with the Heimlich maneuver. The book as a whole is sitcom-like—slick and fast-paced, with lots of action and little depth, and without the serious touches that distinguished *A Girl Called Al*—while Oliver lacks Al's memorable quirkiness. A graceless caricature of a fat person, U. Crumm, the town clerk, who literally has to be hoisted off a restaurant floor after consuming six helpings of chili and seven of pie, and then slipping on an ice cube, seems unfortunate.

Roger Sutton

SOURCE: A review of *Odds on Oliver,* in *Bulletin of the Center for Children's Books,* Vol. 46, No. 7, March, 1993, p. 211.

Ever since Oliver was kicked out of nursery school (just the first of many silly plot contrivances), he has wanted to be a hero. Somehow, though, he keeps screwing up: a rescue of his drowning friend Arthur proves pointless when Arthur realizes he can touch bottom; Oliver's attempt to save the grocery checkout girl from an armed robber is foiled when she rescues him instead; when he tries to get Mrs. Murphy's cat out a tree, the fire department has to be called to get Oliver out of the tree instead. The reading is easy, but the story and writing are slapdash, and Green's attempts at humor will not amuse even those used to a steady Saturday morning TV diet: "Oliver and Arthur dropped everything and went fishing. Edna [Arthur's dog] went too. Edna liked to bark at the fish. Sometimes the fish barked back. Those were the dogfish." Heh-heh.

Margaret C. Howell

SOURCE: A review of *Odds on Oliver,* in *School Library Journal,* Vol. 39, No. 3, March, 1993, p. 198.

Readers first meet Oliver in nursery school, where he and his friends are constantly hitting one another over the head. Their teacher finally has enough and sends Oliver home— a real blow to his parents. The next chapter is set the summer after fourth grade, when he tries to be a hero but meets with little success. In subsequent episodes he gets sat upon by the town clerk, is held hostage during a robbery, attempts to retrieve a cat and must be rescued instead, and is sprayed by a skunk. It is only when he saves his dog from choking that he becomes a hero. Oliver is funny and likable, but the other characters are stereotypes. Although there is the recurrent theme of Oliver trying to prove himself, the book is mainly episodic with the boy being the only connection between the easy-to-read chapters. Children who never seem to do anything right, however, will relate to him. A change of pace for a popular author.

Publishers Weekly

SOURCE: A review of *Odds on Oliver,* in *Publishers Weekly,* Vol. 240, No. 10, March 8, 1993, p. 79.

To her impressive gallery of inimitable characters, Greene adds Oliver: desperate to be a hero, but never quite making the grade. Something always seems to go awry and Oliver causes more harm than good; as with many aspiring gallants, however, Oliver triumphs when he least expects it. With deadpan humor and a snappy pace, this early chapter book sees its hero variously "Up a Tree," "Skunked" and doused in a "Tomato Juice Bath." Readers will easily identify with Oliver in his predicaments, sympathizing with him in defeat and cheering his success. Kid-appealing descriptions and dialogue abound, as when Oliver, grabbed as hostage in an attempted grocery store hold-up, mulls a possible solution: "It is a well-known fact that people don't like to hang on to a person who is throwing up." [S. D.] Schindler's drawings lend the proceedings an appropriately zany slant—his portrayals of Ms. Mabel, doyenne of Carrot Hill Nursery School, and U. Crumm, the town clerk who doubles as "a class-A eater," are particular standouts.

NORA: MAYBE A GHOST STORY (1993)

Publishers Weekly

SOURCE: A review of *Nora: Maybe a Ghost Story,* in *Publishers Weekly,* Vol. 240, No. 30, July 26, 1993, p. 73.

From the first page, masterly comic timing and sharp, witty observations (from a protagonist who could be a cousin to the narrator of the author's Al books) firmly establish that the reader has entered Greene territory. It's been three years since Nora and Patsy's mother died, and though they're eager for their father to be happy, they dread the prospect of his marrying "The Tooth" (his intended has a serious overbite). During this period of upheaval and change, Nora alone begins to hear her mother's laughter, feel her touch and find comfort in her spiritual presence. The "maybe" of the title expresses Greene's hesitancy to push her story too far from the everyday world. Instead, the mother's ghost serves as a soothing presence for the more sensitive daughter. A wise grandmother helps the girls finally to understand that they must accept their father's right to make choices for himself, just as they themselves are moving toward adulthood and making their own choices of the heart. Believable characters and snappy dialogue keep the pace brisk, and though Greene doesn't delve explicitly into the girls' deep sense of loss, she depicts how they incorporate it into their lives with a poignancy that doesn't call attention to itself.

Carol A. Edwards

SOURCE: A review of *Nora: Maybe a Ghost Story,* in *School Library Journal,* Vol. 39, No. 9, September, 1993, p. 232.

This book will be easy to sell to the kids who want ghost stories, romance, and comedy. It also deals with the death and remarriage of parents. Nora's mother died several years ago and now she and her flamboyant sister, Patsy, are determined to stop their father's marriage to "the Tooth." Meanwhile, she has recently sensed her mother's presence or smelled her favorite perfume. Then there's Chuck from Iowa whom Patsy thinks is infatuated with her, but who is actually interested in Nora. The squabbles between the girls depict sibling rivalry at its most entertaining. Friend Roberta, who has strip-poker parties with the girls, adds additional humor. For collectors of first kiss scenes there's one here to put in their top 10. The ghost story is the plot's backbone. When does a girl need the spirit of her mother most? When facing up to her father's possible remarriage to someone she thinks is phony or when she discovers that her dress has been tucked into the back of her pantyhose at a fancy restaurant. Greene balances all these threads in this first-person narrative that never ducks the psychological realities of children facing tough family issues, but keeps it all in perspective with a light touch and spirited characters. An immensely appealing story in an attractive small format guaranteed to please a broad spectrum of readers as well as the author's many fans.

Elaine M. McGuire

SOURCE: A review of *Nora: Maybe a Ghost Story,* in *Voice of Youth Advocates,* Vol. 16, No. 5, December, 1993, pp. 290-91.

Nora's mother died three years ago when she was ten. Through a series of flashbacks, we learn a little about what life was like before and during Mom's illness and a lot about Nora's challenging relationship with Patsy, her "Irish twin" younger sister by less than a year. Patsy is selfish, rude and haughty. When their father announces he is considering marrying Mrs. Ames, (The girls call her "The Tooth" became of a "fantastic overbite . . . We can't figure out how Daddy kisses her without getting bitten."), Patsy really shows her stuff. One minute she calls Mrs. Ames a witch and refuses to attend the wedding should it occur, while the next, she pictures herself as a lovely bridesmaid carefully planting black widow spiders in the bridal bouquet. Nora listens to Patsy's rantings but reluctantly thinks of her father's happiness before her own. It is during these thoughtful moments when Nora first feels a cold presence she's certain is her mother—once touching her hand, once kissing her forehead. Considering Patsy's obnoxiousness and Dad's distance, Nora decides to keep it to herself for a while. She eventually shares her experiences with Chuck, a new guy in town from Iowa where he had a 4-H prize winning pig named Nora. (He says, "It must be fate," when he tells Nora this strangely flattering tidbit.) Nora's opportunity to share her story comes at the library where she runs into Chuck while researching ghosts. He shares a similar incident with his (ghost) dog, Colonel. Once she confesses to Chuck, Nora tells the whole story to Patsy, her funky grandmother, Baba, and finally, to her father. They accept her story as the reader does. Maybe Mom *is* visiting Nora, or maybe Nora has grown toward accepting her new life even if it means getting "The Tooth" as a stepmother, losing battles with Patsy, and constantly missing her mother.

The book ends comfortably with many unanswered questions; not too neat and very appropriate. Even though the book is mainly about the aftermath of a tragic death, it is full of those hilarious incidents that really happen in families but are impossible to tell others about ("you had to be there"). Here these charming situations are more than possible, they are the perfect comic relief. *Nora* will attract readers seeking a good ghost story and they will finish it before they realize there's really no ghost . . . maybe.

Betsie D. Rugg

SOURCE: A review of *Nora: Maybe a Ghost Story,* in *Kliatt,* Vol. 28, No. 1, January, 1994, p. 8.

Greene tells a poignant tale through the eyes of 13-year-old Nora, whose mother recently died of cancer, leaving behind Nora, her 12-year-old sister, Patsy, and their father. The frustration in coping with her death is felt differently by everyone. Patsy, the outgoing, impulsive sister, is quite open about her sadness. Thoughtful Nora often feels the ghostly presence of her mother, but always wonders if she is imagining it. She is uncertain about telling even Patsy. Nora feels afraid and alone, and desperately needs to share all this with someone. Adding to the picture, their emotionally reserved father is considering remarrying a woman the girls do not approve of, whom they have nicknamed "The Tooth." This subplot serves as a source of humor, as they try to find a suitable wife for him, while remembering particular times shared with their mother. There's also the uncomfortable situation of Patsy's crush on the new boy in town, who likes Nora instead . . . and Nora likes him, too. Lots of conflict makes for an absorbing drama.

Nora is a great narrator and observer of life around her. The extremely vivid scenes and attention to detail add to the conversational tone. While creating a believable plot, Greene also gives a realistic ending to her drama, as Nora comes to terms with her mother's death, her father's impending marriage, growing up, and, of course, liking boys. The title perhaps is misleading, but eye-catching.

Additional coverage of Greene's life and career is contained in the following sources published by The Gale Group: *Authors and Artists for Young Adults,* **Vol. 7;** *Contemporary Authors New Revision Series,* **Vol. 38;** *Junior DISCovering Authors, Major Authors and Illustrators for Children and Young Adults; Something about the Author Autobiography Series,* **Vol. 11; and** *Something about the Author,* **Vols. 11, 72.**

Satomi Ichikawa

1949-

Japanese illustrator and author of picture books.

Major works include *A Child's Book of Seasons* (1975), *Suzanne and Nicholas at the Market* (1977; French edition as *Suzette et Nicolas au marché*), *Sun Through Small Leaves: Poems of Spring* (selected by Ichikawa, 1980), *Nora's Castle* (1986; originally published as *Furui oshiro no otomodachi*, 1984), *Dance, Tanya* (written by Patricia Lee Gauch, 1989).

INTRODUCTION

Ichikawa's reputation rests upon her delicate and charming picture book illustrations of children involved in their daily occupations and flights of fancy. A self-taught artist influenced by the work of French illustrator Maurice Boutet de Monvel, Ichikawa's work utilizes fine line drawings with a watercolor wash. Critics have universally lauded her books with comments such as those by Joy Fleishhacker who called *Dance, Tanya*: "bright, graceful, and filled with the joy of movement;" and Jacqueline Elsner in a review of *Nora's Surprise* (1994): "Ichikawa's watercolors are masterful. Each figure . . . is full of life, humor, and expression in every gesture. Readers will walk right into her landscapes and taste each morsel of food."

Ichikawa's two most popular series of books are about Nora, a little girl with a big imagination, and Tanya, who loves to dance. Nora is entirely Ichikawa's work. She told *Something about the Author* (SATA) that she especially enjoyed the creation of *Nora's Castle*, the first book which she developed "from beginning to end—a very satisfying experience," adding, "I have come to see that this is the best way to work." Translated from the original Japanese, the books about Nora, accompanied by dreamlike illustrations, show Nora's surroundings as she sees them in her imagination. The books about Tanya were written especially for Ichikawa by Patricia Lee Gauch in honor of Ichikawa's love of dance. These books follow Tanya, not naturally graceful or technically talented, as she dreams and dances and expresses herself in movement highly pleasing to herself. Critics have been charmed by these books, and many others from Ichikawa's large oeuvre, showing as they do the delightful, exuberant mind and imaginings of innocent young children.

Biographical Information

Adventurous and assertive, Ichikawa came late to illustration. Born and raised in Japan, she followed a general course of study through college, then traveled to Italy to meet Italian friends with whom she had become acquainted in Japan. A side trip to France was the turning point in

her life. She felt immediately at home in Paris and determined to live there, attracted by the freedom of spirit she felt, so different from the traditional Japanese culture in which she was raised. In 1971 she got a job as an *au pair*, began studying French, and started looking for what would be her life's work because, as she told *SATA*, "In Paris you are nothing if you don't work."

One of her early discoveries in Paris was the work of illustrator Maurice Boutet de Monvel, and she began to haunt the bookstalls looking for his work. Inspired by his illustrations, Ichikawa decided she would try drawing. Using Monvel's work as her guide, she taught herself to draw by observing children at play in the gardens and playgrounds of Paris, developing her own distinctive style in the process. Her combination of boldness, talent, and good luck plunged her headlong into publication of her work. On a visit to London, she visited a children's book store, wrote down a list of names and addresses of editors she found in various books, and went immediately to the one closest to the store. This happened to be the publishing house of Heinemann, and the editor, after looking at the thirty drawings Ichikawa presented, decided to publish them as *A Child's Book of Seasons*, launching Ichikawa into her new career as an illustrator.

Ichikawa lives in Paris in the famous Rue Campagna Premiere, a complex of artists' studios and ateliers that once included Pablo Picasso among its residents. She loves to dance, and she draws every day, producing between two to four books a year. Speaking of her love for Paris and the enrichment she feels from her life in that city she told *SATA*, "[An] artist must feel complete freedom in order to create. . . . Coming to Paris was a rebirth for me."

Major Works

Ichikawa's first book, *A Child's Book of Seasons*, features short simple verses illustrated in soft pastels. It shows children engaged in a variety of activities, both indoors and out, in all kinds of weather. Barbara Elleman wrote, "In each picture the artist uses care and sensitivity in shading colors and creating detail of line and pattern," and Karla Kuskin commented, "With a designer's eye the artist consistently arranges scenes that are busy but never cluttered. She combines delicate patterns and poses that are gently Oriental in feeling with elements reminiscent of late 19th-century French illustration. It is a subtle and beguiling blend."

Suzanne and Nicholas at the Market (French edition as *Suzette et Nicolas au marché*), written and illustrated by Ichikawa, is the most popular book of a series originally written in French. It follows big brother Nicholas and his little sister Suzanne as they go shopping in a French market, talking about where the things come from that they are buying. Critics thought Ichikawa's drawings were charmingly old-fashioned and delicate, although some reviewers considered them static. Other titles in the series, all illustrated by Ichikawa, are *Suzanne and Nicholas in the Garden* (1977), *Suzanne and Nicholas and the Four Seasons* (1978; written by Marie-France Mangin), *Suzette and Nicholas and the Sunijudi Circus* (1980; written by Michelle Lochak and Mangin), *Suzette et Nicolas au Zoo* (1980; written by Marcelle Verite), *Suzette et Nicolas: L'Annee en fetes* (1982; written by Resie Pouyanne), and *Suzette et Nicolas font le tour du monde* (1984; written by Pouyanne).

Ichikawa chose 15 poems and partial poems about spring for *Sun Through Small Leaves: Poems of Spring*. Poets include Dickinson, Kipling, Rossetti, and Wordsworth, among others. The drawings show active, happy children enjoying the spring, couched in the soft greens, blues, and yellows of the season. Barbara Elleman commented, "[G]race and charm reverberate through the watercolors and give the eye much to linger over."

Inspired by her summer stay at a friend's castle, Ichikawa wrote *Nora's Castle* about a little girl exploring the many rooms of an old castle and finding echoes of the past in each one. Accompanied by her dog, Kiki, and her doll and teddy, who come to life, Nora talks to the people in the paintings, plays on an old piano, and has a party with other visitors to the castle—bluebirds, a bat, and other small animals. Denise M. Wilms wrote, "Meticulous pastel drawings of castle and countryside are hushed and bucolic, as sedately self-assured as Nora's imaginings. The soft colors and refined textures, contained in the thinnest pencil line, stand clear and inviting on the white page." Subsequent titles, all written by Ichikawa, are *Nora's Stars* (1989), *Nora's Duck* (1991), *Nora's Roses* (1993), and *Nora's Surprise* (1994).

To honor Ichikawa's love of dance, Patricia Lee Gauch wrote *Dance, Tanya* specifically for Ichikawa to illustrate. It tells the story of little Tanya who loves to dance although she is too young to take ballet lessons like her big sister, Elise. Tanya dances everywhere she goes to music only she can hear, and is especially beautiful as the dying swan. The family takes great pride in Elise's performance during her recital, although Tanya falls asleep. When they return home, Tanya wakes up long enough to perform her special dance for the family, and her aunt declares, "I think you have two dancers in your family!" At the end of the book, Tanya goes happily off with Elise to take her first dance lesson. A contributor to *Kirkus Reviews* praised Ichikawa for "captur[ing] the joy and energy of the dance in her sensitive paintings," and a reviewer for *The Junior Bookshelf* enthused, "[T]he vigorous succession of little Tanyas, in constantly changing attitudes, tumbling across the pages is a real treat." Gauch and Ichikawa have pursued Tanya's adventures in *Bravo, Tanya* (1992), *Tanya and the Magic Wardrobe* (1993), *Tanya and Emily in a Dance for Two* (1994), *Tanya Steps Out* (1996), and *Presenting Tanya, the Ugly Duckling* (1999).

Awards

Awards for Ichikawa's books include a special mention for Prix "Critici in Erba" at the Bologna Children's Book Fair in 1978 for *Suzette et Nicolas au marché*, the French version of *Suzanne and Nicholas at the Market* and two Japanese prizes, the Kodansha Prize in 1978 for illustrations in *Sun Through Small Leaves: Poems of Spring* and the Sankei Prize in 1981 for illustrations in *Keep Running, Allen!* In addition, *Dance, Tanya* was named a notable book by the American Library Association.

GENERAL COMMENTARY

Herbert R. Lottman

SOURCE: "In the Studio with Satomi Ichikawa," *Publishers Weekly*, Vol. 240, No. 23, June 7, 1993, p. 19.

The itinerary of Satomi Ichikawa, whose latest productions, *Nora's Roses* and *Fickle Barbara* could make an Ichikawa children's tale—call it "Satomi Goes to Paris." A young Japanese woman picks herself up from the traditional village where her parents and their forebears were schoolteachers as far back as anyone can know, to travel alone to Tuscany—a chance meeting with Italians having given her the urge to learn their language. From Italy she visits Paris, and although she can't speak a word of the local tongue, she decides she'll never live anywhere else. So she spends her days studying French while working as an au pair. And although she never took an art lesson in her life, she is so impressed with some books she comes across by illustrator Maurice Boutet de Monvel (1851-1913) that she teaches herself to illustrate her own stories. Such were the beginnings of the children's book illustrator's career.

"I didn't know whether Boutet de Monvel was alive or dead," she says now of her favorite painter. "But I fell in love with his work and wanted to try something of my own. In Paris you are nothing if you don't work."

While collecting secondhand copies of Boutet de Monvel's books, she came upon the work of Dutch illustrator Henriette Willebeek Le Mair, perhaps best remembered for her enhancement of Robert Louis Stevenson's *A Child's Garden of Verses.* Only a few years after Ichikawa's first book, *A Child's Book of Seasons,* was published in 1976 she was stunned to receive a copy of the *Horn Book* with an article by Michael Patrick Hearn, which informed her that her heroine Le Mair was a disciple of her hero Boutet de Monvel; not only that, but the article went on to mention Satomi Ichikawa–and Maurice Sendak–as latterday pupils of the French master.

Ichikawa's initial attempts to have her work published were filled with as much verve and undaunted sense of adventure as the rest of her life. With her first sketches in hand Ichikawa visited London, copied out names of publishers while browsing in a bookshop, and walked to the address that seemed closest. It happened to be Heinemann, whose Judith Elliott soon had five copublishers for *A Child's Book of Seasons.* Indeed, Ichikawa has been so lucky with mentor-editors that she always lets her prime publisher control world rights—sometimes Heinemann in the U.K., other times Philomel in the U.S. or Kaiseisha in Japan. In any case all her books seem to go everywhere. She has been to the United States "seven or eight times," and could easily live and work in "fantastic" New York— if Paris didn't exist. In Paris she is convinced that the beauty of everyday life enriches her work.

Ichikawa found just the perfect place to experience that everyday life at 9 Rue Campagne, the well-known maze of a building fitted with more than 100 ateliers. When Pablo Picasso arrived in Paris as a young man he made a beeline for number 9, as so many artists before and since who knew they could get a studio there fast and cheap. From her diminutive duplex (living and dining corner downstairs, drawing table and bedroom alcove a half flight above), Ichikawa has been turning out a book or two a year for each of her publishers. She does the *Nora* books— picture books starring a dark-headed girl of that name— for Kaiseisha (a fifth in the series is ready in Japanese, to be called *Nora's Surprise*). *Fickle Barbara* was commissioned by Philomel's editorial director, Patricia Lee Gauch,

who wrote a book of her own (*Dance, Tanya*) for Ichikawa to illustrate. When a third Tanya book is published in 1994 it will be Ichikawa's 36th creation in 17 years.

Inspiration for the settings and subject matter for her various books come from a number of places. For instance, Ichikawa uses Raggedy Ann dolls (from her vast doll collection) as her models, together with the farms and country estates in France and England to which she gets invited (all thanks to that first au pair family).

It is also apparent that Ichikawa is moving in new directions. She has heightened her colors, intensified facial expressions and body movement—this last thanks to mornings devoted to sketching at a dance studio. The sketches are piling up; since the dancers aren't children she can't make immediate use of them, but she is sure the exercise is already having an effect on her work. "Sometimes I think that I have only one card to play—being alive, and I'll keep playing that card until I'm no longer able to."

TITLE COMMENTARY

A CHILD'S BOOK OF SEASONS (1975)

Publishers Weekly

SOURCE: A review of *A Child's Book of Seasons,* in *Publishers Weekly,* Vol. 209, No. 8, February 23, 1976, p. 120.

Low-keyed verses and appropriately soft pastel drawings make the artist's invitation easy to accept. "Please take a look inside this book to see what children do in snow and sunshine, wind and rain, the changing seasons through." Even in the rain, it would seem that clouds never darken the world of the boys and girls so lovingly examined in these pages. When they can't play outside, they make puppets indoors, play dress-up and indulge in other pleasant time-passers. One scene shows a schoolyard full of children on a brisk day—some are engaged in a tug-of-war while others watch. One loving child has her arm protectively around the shoulder of another. This picture, like all others in the book, is clearly the result of loving perceptions.

Barbara Elleman

SOURCE: A review of *A Child's Book of Seasons,* in *The Booklist,* Vol. 72, No. 15, April 1, 1976, p. 1114.

Full-page, delicately colored illustrations provide a backdrop for children who run, skip, and play through the changing seasons. Ichikawa pictures boys and girls costuming themselves on a rainy spring day, picking summer flowers, chasing the blowing autumn leaves, and building images in the winter snow. In each picture the artist uses care and sensitivity in shading colors and creating detail of line and pattern. Children of all ages will find themselves in the pictures, which provide oft-needed material on the seasons. If the accompanying jingles seem a bit trite, use the fine illustrations as a motivation for creative writing.

Ethel L. Heins

SOURCE: A review of *A Child's Book of Seasons,* in *The Horn Book Magazine,* Vol. LII, No. 3, June, 1976, pp. 280-81.

A rhymed couplet on every page provides the text for an album of charming, beautifully composed pictures. The verses are often commonplace—"In the cold and wintry sun/ Round the schoolyard children run"—or they may limp rather noticeably—"Out in the farmyard, children scatter the feed./ Hungry chicks and geese will snatch up all they need." A brief note at the end of the book states that the Japanese artist, largely self-taught, became interested in children's book illustration when she discovered in Paris the work of Boutet de Monvel. The influence of the great French illustrator is immediately apparent, although some of the paintings lack his understatement and his limpid simplicity. In the outdoor scenes, the artist has been more free, more individualistic, and less openly derivative; many of these pictures, showing the nuances of changing seasons at various times of the day, are the loveliest of all.

Marcus Crouch

SOURCE: A review of *A Child's Book of Seasons,* in *The Junior Bookshelf,* Vol. 40, No. 3, June, 1976, p. 143.

Despite the children's gear, and their freedom from inhibition, this book has a curiously old-fashioned air. Partly this is a matter of tonal values, which gives the page that softly autumnal look which characterises Kate Greenaway and Crane, partly the formally framed pages and the careful composition. Each page has a rhyming couplet—mainly either trite or terrible!—accompanying a picture in which children are busily absorbed in their own adult-free concerns. The Eastern influence is revealed only in the economy; there is never a line or a thought too much, and each element in the picture is selected and placed with enormous care and skill. The final effect is pleasing but not perhaps exciting. The book should please grandparents rather more than parents and children.

Books for Your Children

SOURCE: A review of *A Child's Book of Seasons,* in *Books for Your Children,* Vol. 11, No. 3, Summer, 1976, p. 6.

A beautifully produced picture book of what children do throughout the year. Each full page picture is softly

coloured and framed, with two lines of rhyming text. Lots for children to discover in each picture. Although the world created is an idyllic one of beautiful countryside, the children are most realistically depicted. A lovely book to escape into time and time again.

FRIENDS (1976)

Margery Fisher

SOURCE: A review of *Friends,* in *Growing Point,* Vol. 15, No. 6, December, 1976, p. 3030.

The style of this Japanese artist recalls the work of Boutet de Monvel and, more distantly, of Willebeek le Mair. Lively, touching and versatile, the pages provide in subtle colour a sequence in which children, elegantly depicted in precise detail, play games in the park or in the house, a brother and sister introducing their activities and their friends in simple words. The artist has used a horizontal format to give the effect of a frieze, with the figures of the children as it were frozen in action.

Zena Sutherland

SOURCE: A review of *Friends,* in *Bulletin of the Center for Children's Books,* Vol. 30, No. 9, May, 1977, p. 143.

First published in London, a hymn to friendship that is illustrated in the style of Boutet de Monvel, with muted colors and precise, old-fashioned drawings. The text consists of a series of activities shared by friends. "We need friends to play with, for jumping over, and bumping over, and making mean ugly faces—or beautiful smiling faces," is used for six full-page illustrations. The book has, like Halliman's *That's What a Friend Is,* the appeal of familiar activities, and the illustrations are of far better quality, but it, too, may find a limited audience because of the subdued tone.

Barbara Elleman

SOURCE: A review of *Friends,* in *The Booklist,* Vol. 73, No. 21, July, 1, 1977, p. 1653.

Friends, the brief text relates, are for sharing secrets, playing make-believe, getting dirty with, discovering treasures, doing homework, exploring meadows, drawing pictures, and having pillow fights. It is Ichikawa's illustrations, however, that magnify the mood, as full pages visualize each phrase. Using delicate shades, the artist imaginatively spaces amusing and eye-catching details against pale-hued backgrounds, effecting a warm and near dreamlike aura. Neatly combed and dressed moppets frolic through the scenes, and though the costumes are not of the Kate Greenaway era, a sense of her style lingers here.

SUZANNE AND NICHOLAS IN THE GARDEN
(translated by Denise Sheldon, 1977; originally published as *Suzette et Nicolas dans leur jardin,* 1976)

Kirkus Reviews

SOURCE: A review of *Suzette and Nicholas in the Garden,* in *Kirkus Reviews,* Vol. LIV, No. 22, November 15, 1986, p. 1722.

A brief story, translated from the French, that's a vehicle for attractive, distinctive illustrations.

Suzette and Nicholas are searching for their baby brother Choo Choo, and they find him in the garden, entranced by a bird in a tree. Choo Choo follows his older brother and sister as they explore the family's flower and vegetable gardens. Nicholas tells Suzette the names of the vegetables, and explains the other things they see. As the day ends, the children go to bed, and Nicholas plans what he will teach Suzette tomorrow.

This simple, rather dull story is accompanied by delicate, highly patterned drawings that expand and develop the text, though their static quality may limit their appeal; their draftsmanship, however, is exquisite, and children will enjoy the wealth of detail contained in the pictures. The garden scenes especially are rich and luxuriant—Suzette and Nicholas look like porcelain-doll figures imposed on a riotous nature—and the text on each page is surrounded by a border of roses, which contributes to the lush, somewhat overblown effect. One wishes only for more variety of moods in the illustrations; the two lovely, dreamy bedtime scenes that close the book are a teaser.

But charming and, within its limits, a bargain.

Publishers Weekly

SOURCE: A review of *Suzette and Nicholas in the Garden,* in *Publishers Weekly,* Vol. 230, No. 24, December 12, 1986, p. 53.

This flowery, heavily sentimental book presents Nicholas and Suzette, siblings who romp about the garden of their "happy home." Overbearing older brother Nicholas spends most of his time correcting silly Suzette. When she wishes she could pick all the flowers, for instance, he tells her, "Don't be so naughty and selfish. . . . The flowers are there for everybody to enjoy." Later he helps her climb the garden wall and shows her "the world," but "this is too much for Suzette to understand. She will think about the world another time." When we leave the children, Suzette is sleeping, but Nicholas is awake, staring at the moon. "Tomorrow he will tell Suzette all about the sky and the sun and the moon." Nicholas's patronizing attitude, cast here in a positive light, may annoy readers and parents. Ichikawa's pastel, pastoral scenes are static and not varied enough to hold interest.

SUZANNE AND NICHOLAS AT THE MARKET
(translated by Denise Sheldon, 1977; originally published as *Suzette et Nicolas au marché,* 1977; adapted by Robina Beckles Wilson as *Sophie and Nicky Go to Market,* 1984)

Books for Your Children

SOURCE: A review of *Suzanne and Nicholas at the Market,* in *Books for Your Children,* Vol. 13, No. 1, Winter, 1977, p. 11.

An appealing picture book from the illustrator featured on our last summer cover. Here she proves herself even more to be the modern Kate Greenaway. Suzanne and Nicholas go to a French market—the text is a pleasant commentary on the things they buy and what they say and think in a most reassuring read. Children around seven will enjoy it on their own.

Margery Fisher

SOURCE: A review of *Suzanne and Nicholas at the Market, Growing Point,* Vol. 16, No. 7, January, 1978, p. 3252.

From an idealised home background two small children set out on expeditions during which they watch various activities (milking, sheep shearing, the marketing of flowers) and listen to brief explanations. A book to help children to become familiar with an environment unlike their own. The bland text has influenced the artist, who has exaggerated the smooth, prosperous, static element in her art and has lost some of the vivacity and interesting composition of her earlier picture-books.

Berna Clark

SOURCE: A review of *Suzanne and Nicholas at the Market,* in *The Junior Bookshelf,* Vol. 42, No. 2, April, 1978, p. 89.

Very charming old-fashioned illustrations make this book. They are so full of detail with so much for the child to absorb. It is a simple enough story of children going shopping, and as they shop they think of places where all the things they are buying come from—fish from the sea, apples from the orchard, milk from the dairy farm and so forth. It is a bright, happy, cheerful book which every school and library will be the better for having on its shelves.

SUZANNE AND NICHOLAS AND THE FOUR SEASONS (written by Marie-France Mangin, 1978; originally published as *Suzette et Nicolas et l'horloge des 4 saisons,* 1978; U.S. edition, translated by Joan Chevalier, as *Suzette and Nicholas and the Seasons Clock,* 1982; adapted by Robina Beckles Wilson as *Sophie and Nicky and the Four Seasons,* 1985)

Margery Fisher

SOURCE: A review of *Suzanne and Nicholas and the Four Seasons,* in *Growing Point,* Vol. 18, No. 3, September, 1979, p. 3584.

Suzanne brings home her latest project, a simple season-clock, and as she turns it, imagination offers her, together with brother Nicholas and baby Benjamin, sundry typical French pleasures—picking grapes, painting Easter eggs, eating melons on a picnic. The artist's engagingly active style and the degree of formalising in her scenes are at their best when they show a number of children actively engaged, as in an autumn school scene, or in striking landscapes like a snow-scene built round a church and a fountain.

Jane F. Cullinane

SOURCE: A review of *Suzette and Nicholas and the Seasons Clock,* in *School Library Journal,* Vol. 29, No. 8, April, 1983, p. 104.

Delightful pastel illustrations follow Suzette and Nicholas through the seasons. Suzette has made a "seasons clock" at school—illustrations of the seasons around a circle, with a pointer. "'You turn the hand around the clock, like this, and the seasons change. . . . '" As Suzette turns the hands of her clock we see the seasons and the activities of children change. The book celebrates the different activities that are special to each season and if readers don't get confused by the backward cause and effect relationship between the clock and the seasons, they will enjoy it.

SUN THROUGH SMALL LEAVES: POEMS OF SPRING (1980)

Barbara Elleman

SOURCE: A review of *Sun through Small Leaves: Poems of Spring,* in *The Booklist,* Vol. 76, No. 21, July 1, 1980, p. 1612.

Ichikawa has chosen 15 poems and parts of poems to reflect the many moods of spring and has illustrated them in soft greens, blues, and yellows to catch the magic of the season. Lines from Lowell, Browning, Dickinson, Rossetti, Kipling, Wordsworth, and others offer opportunity aplenty for the artist to show her exuberant, cosily dressed children enjoying the freshness of spring. The selections are fragmentary and more ephemeral (and, in the case of the four lines from Gray's "Elegy Written in a Country Church-Yard," too advanced for the picture book) than either *Playtime* or *Under the Cherry Tree.* Still, grace and charm reverberate through the watercolors and give the eye much to linger over.

Daisy Kouzel

SOURCE: A review of *Sun through Small Leaves: Poems of Spring,* in *School Library Journal,* Vol. 26, No. 10, August, 1980, p. 52.

This slim collection contains a total of 15 poems (some snippets of longer works, some complete in themselves) ranging from two to ten lines, by such luminaries as Wordsworth, Blake, Gray, Dickinson, Kipling, Browning as well as some anonymous pieces. All were selected for being evocative of spring, and delicate watercolor illustrations complement and reinforce a mood of awakening, blossoming, and rejoicing. Indeed, Ichikawa's gentle tableaux run away with the show.

LET'S PLAY (1981)

Margery Fisher

SOURCE: A review of *Let's Play,* in *Growing Point,* Vol. 20, No. 3, September, 1981, pp. 3936-37.

Toys, like books, take their life from those who use them. *Let's Play* demonstrates this brilliantly in its sequence of favourites, from the ancient and enduring rocking-horse and teddy-bear to currently fashionable sand-pit shapes, dressing-up clothes, pedal car and Wendy house. The artist leaves no doubt about the creative element in play; the expression on the face of the small boy riding the horse or his counterpart building himself accidentally into a brick house are evidence enough. The clear colours, neat composition and energetic figures in the pictures give an impression of joyous imagination in which only the strangely toothless, gaping mouths with which the artist has endowed most of the children stand in the way of complete enjoyment—in my case, at least, and perhaps the young who look at this book will find her technical device perfectly acceptable.

M. Hobbs

SOURCE: A review of *Let's Play* in *The Junior Bookshelf,* Vol. 45, No. 5, October, 1981, p. 187.

Satomi Ichikawa's children playing together, with simple toys like a train, bricks, ball, rocking-horse and dressing-up clothes, are Western, made positive and fully extended in all their actions, but one recognises the Japanese touch in the intricacy of the abundant, delightfully humorous detail, the flowers which slip into decoration and textiles, and the colours, delicate yet somehow three dimensionally solid, with stipple suggesting from time to time mysterious distant backgrounds. In each case the first page carries a word (or as the difficulty is slightly increased, words) in bold type with its representation in colour below, then on the opposite page a scene showing it in context. Apart from the pleasure of absorbing these, the book is a useful first introduction to word-recognition.

Denise M. Wilms

SOURCE: A review of *Let's Play,* in *The Booklist,* Vol. 78, No. 9, January 1, 1982, p. 598.

In this picture book for very young children, the point is to look—and look and *look* at the familiar toys Ichikawa features first alone, and then as part of a scene in which children play with them. A toddler, a preschooler, and an older sibling provide the focus, but the book will work best with the youngest: babies and toddlers can point to the ball, blocks, doll, tambourine, or balloons that key the scenes and practice object recognition and word repetition. Any interested older onlookers might clue their younger siblings in on what is happening. The pictures are softly colored, clean-looking depictions of slightly antique interiors and fresh rural-looking backyards. The cozy feeling that emanates throughout makes this a sure pick as one of babies' first books.

Kirkus Reviews

SOURCE: A review of *Let's Play,* in *Kirkus Reviews,* Vol. L, No. 4, February 15, 1982, p. 201.

"Let's play together./ Let's play with// train// blocks// ball// dolls// tambourine// rocking horse// balloons// playhouse// car// dress-up/ clothes// pails/ one rake/ two shovels// crayons// boat// teddy bear." So reads the complete text of this picture book, in which a separate double-page (represented here by the double slash) pictures each object as the plaything of three small, fair-haired children in what might be early-20th-century dress. But there is no suggestion in the self-contained pictures of that first-page invitation to join in. A composition may be circular, against white space, or a scene's interior or outdoor background might fill the page. A tambourine frames two children holding tambourines; the ball is a beach ball seen in multiple in a beach scene, with a snapshot of a similar scene imposed on the center; other pages see the children at play with their toys in a pretty nursery, a large modern bathroom, and a peaceful lane. There's some variety, then, in design and perspective as well as object and setting, but the unvarying soft nostalgic focus, especially inappropriate for the designated one-to-three-year-old group, and the absence of genuine event (no one would think to wonder what is happening or might happen next, even of the busiest pictures) make a repeated wan impression and a weak experience overall.

NORA'S CASTLE (1986; originally published as *Furui oshiro no otomodachi,* 1984)

Denise M. Wilms

SOURCE: A review of *Nora's Castle,* in *The Booklist,* Vol. 82, No. 15, April 1, 1986, pp. 1141-42.

This story of a little girl who explores a deserted castle has a leisurely, old-fashioned air about it. It also betrays a strong affinity with the child's intensely felt world of imagination. One day Nora sets out on her bicycle with her doll, stuffed teddy, and dog, ready for a day of exploration at the castle. There, inside the empty rooms, another reality takes over. Doll and bear become animated and follow along as Nora and dog Kiki walk in silent rooms, speak to figures in old paintings, play a decrepit piano, or sit on a bed in a blue bedroom. Then Nora discovers some other visitors—bluebirds nesting in the ceiling, a bat hanging from the attic rafters, and several other animals who become her guests at a party. Afterward, when the hour is late, Nora and company curl up in straw in a nearby tower to spend the night. Meticulous pastel drawings of castle and countryside are hushed and bucolic, as sedately self-assured as Nora's imaginings. The soft colors and refined textures, contained in the thinnest pencil line, stand clear and inviting on the white page. Their allure is unmistakable, especially for children prone to indulging their own powers of imagination.

Kirkus Reviews

SOURCE: A review of *Nora's Castle,* in *Kirkus Reviews,* Vol. LIV, No. 8, April 15, 1986, p. 634.

In a mellow variation on the theme of children braving a haunted house, a French village girl with her dog, doll and toy bear explore an abandoned castle and have a party with the creatures they find there.

Ichikawa's serene paintings have always paid tribute to the French illustrator Boutet de Monvel and his pupil, Le Mair, and never more appropriately than in this fond examination of the old chateau. The simple story serves as excuse for a series of beautifully composed interior and exterior views within ovals whose boundaries are occasionally pierced by the illustration, a delicate reminder of the line between the real and the imagined. Architectural elements—cross vaults, winding stairs, and wrought-iron gates—are elegantly employed as foils for the small doings of Nora and her friends.

Children should be entranced by the marvelous evocation of a castle worthy of the rarest imagination.

Susan H. Patron

SOURCE: A review of *Nora's Castle,* in *School Library Journal,* Vol. 32, No. 9, May, 1986, p. 77.

Intrigued by a mysterious castle in the countryside, Nora sets off with her doll, her Teddy bear and her dog to explore it. Once inside, the doll and the bear come to life, and real animals who live in or near the castle are able to speak. Nora throws a party for the animals; they feast, dance and sing in the moonlight, then sleep in the tower. Nora returns home, guarding her "secret" that the castle isn't deserted—in spite of what the people of the village say. Both the text and the delicate watercolor illustrations

reflect an adult's perspective rather than a child's. Nora's dialogue does not sound natural, and her playing reflects the perception of nostalgic adulthood. The tone ("The four explorers were in high spirits. What an adventure!") is too brightly or falsely cheerful, stating rather than creating a mood. Most of the romantic illustrations are contained in oval frames, with some element of the composition extending outside of the oval—perhaps to bridge the outside (real) world and the interior imaginative play. Like an expensive greeting card, this sunny glimpse of the French countryside will have more appeal to adults than to children.

Margery Fisher

SOURCE: A review of *Nora's Castle,* in *Growing Point,* Vol. 25, No. 2, July, 1986, p. 4659.

A perfectly straightforward beginning to a small girl's bicycle excursion, with doll, stuffed bear and a small dog crammed into her basket, merges into fancy as she explores an empty castle near her home and, finding trunks full of intriguing clothes, decides to contrive a party for the local inhabitants (rabbit, toads, spider, bluebirds). An owl from the adjacent tower offers her shelter for the night and she returns home next day to cherish the secret of the ruinous but still populous castle. Superbly placed details of leaves, straw, flowers, cherries, frame the full pages; everything focuses on the round, wondering face of the kind of child who finds joy in unexpected places.

Marcus Crouch

SOURCE: A review of *Nora's Castle,* in *The Junior Book-shelf,* Vol. 50, No. 4, August, 1986, p. 141.

However typically Japanese the technique of Satomi Ichikawa's pictures their scene is vaguely Continental, and Nora's castle is a chateau rather than an English border fortress.

Trespassing one day—there is no suggestion that this is improper and potentially hazardous—Nora and her toy and animal friends find that the building is empty but not unfurnished. It also has inhabitants of a non-human kind, and for these Nora throws a party at night. Rabbit, owl, birds and a bat—who wears his napkin in spite of hanging upside down—share the goodies. By that time it is too late to go home, so Nora and her friends settle down in the hay until morning. The artist's pictures are as soft as the hay. They capture lovingly the beauty of the landscape and the charm of the castle. It is, I suppose, to match the elegance of the drawing that the text has been set in a very small type; parents and teachers might have preferred something less appropriate and more legible.

HERE A LITTLE CHILD I STAND: POEMS OF PRAYER AND PRAISE FOR CHILDREN (edited by Cynthia Mitchell, 1985)

Carolyn Phelan

SOURCE: A review of *Here a Little Child I Stand: Poems of Prayer and Praise for Children,* in *The Booklist,* Vol. 82, No. 13, March 1, 1986, p. 1019.

From sources as diverse as Africa, Europe, Asia, and North America; from Indian chants, Islamic prayers, the Svetasvatara Upanished, and the Song of Solomon; from Robert Herrick, Ogden Nash, Langston Hughes, and Eleanor Farjeon, Mitchell has drawn short poems and prayers for children. Though some are more expressive of individual concerns and desires, most of them share an essential joy, a celebration of God and creation. The spirit of the poems and the spring colors of Ichikawa's muted illustrations bring a refreshing "morning of the world" quality to the book. Pictures as well as text reflect the multicultural, multiracial theme within the universal experience of worship. If a few pictures are slightly oversweet, the balance is restored by the many that depict attitudes from quiet contemplation to wild playfulness with keen observation and lively good humor. A well-selected, well-designed, and unusually appealing collection of broadly religious verse for children, in picture-book format.

Pat Pearl

SOURCE: A review of *Here a Little Child I Stand: Poems of Prayer and Praise for Children,* in *School Library Journal,* Vol. 32, No. 8, April, 1986, pp. 76-7.

An outstanding, refreshingly different collection of poems giving thanks, asking blessings and celebrating the beauty and variety of creation. The poems are drawn from many cultures—Eskimo, Guyanan, Tewa Indian, Islamic, East African, Japanese, Hindu, European and American—and also include works of well-known poets such as Ogden Nash, Eleanor Farjeon and Langston Hughes. The text is on various levels of difficulty, from short and simple to longer and richly detailed, but all could be interpreted to small children. The elegant illustrations in dreamy soft-toned watercolors show many moods, from lively and joyful to pensive and peaceful. All are filled with meticulous details and expertly keyed to the word picture of each poem. The familiar world of cozy toys and country kitchens blends with the exotic ones of igloos, tepees and huts. A high interest level is maintained in the variety of settings and selections and the different ways in which the text and pictures are arranged on the pages. This holds up favorably against some stiff competition, such as Tasha Tudor's *First Prayers* and *More Prayers*; *And God Bless Me,* compiled by Lee Bennett Hopkins and *A Child's Book of Prayers*, illustrated by Michael Hague.

HAPPY BIRTHDAY! A BOOK OF BIRTHDAY CELEBRATIONS (written by Elizabeth Laird, 1988)

Children's Book Review Service

SOURCE: A review of *Happy Birthday! A Book of Birthday Celebrations,* in *Children's Book Review Service,* Vol. 16, No. 10, May, 1988, p. 109.

Happy Birthday! is a warmly illustrated book filled with a variety of information which should inspire a new enjoyment of birthdays. Continuity is provided by introducing a little girl and her family. Poetry, craft ideas, birthday information, and cultural traditions are woven into the story to create an unusual literary piece.

NORA'S STARS (1989)

Denise Wilms

SOURCE: A review of *Nora's Stars,* in *The Booklist,* Vol. 85, No. 17, May 1, 1989, p. 1549.

Nora and her toys visit grandmother's house, where there are fascinating treats like hibiscus flowers that open and close with the sun, fresh plum jam, and best of all, toys that have a life of their own when bedtime comes. Nora frolics with the dolls and stuffed animals, who pull down stars to fashion a glorious cape for her. Later, the night seems gloomy without its twinkling canopy, and Nora takes her cape and flings the stars back into the sky. Ichikawa's muted watercolors, brightened with the glowing stars, have a comfortable, homey ambience due in part to the story's setting—a spacious old country home that invites the kind of imaginative play the story celebrates. A quiet pleasure.

Kirkus Reviews

SOURCE: A review of *Nora's Stars,* in *Kirkus Reviews,* Vol. LVII, No. 9, May 1, 1989, p. 693.

Nora comes with her dog and her toys to visit at Grandmother's house—a lovely French villa set high on a steep hill. That night, the old toys in a trunk in Nora's room come alive and take her outdoors to play; there they collect the stars to adorn her bedcover, making her a sparkling cape. They all dance and play with the stars until Nora realizes that the sky is dark and sad; she shakes them from her bedcover back to the sky. Ichikawa has made this simple embroidery on a child's imaginative play into a joyful dream. Her style is spare and graceful; the charming illustrations—lovingly portraying the old house surrounded with flowers and the charming, unusual old toys—are precise and beautifully composed. Very nice indeed.

Sally R. Dow

SOURCE: A review of *Nora's Stars,* in *School Library Journal,* Vol. 35, No. 11, July, 1989, pp. 66-7.

While a little girl is visiting her grandmother who lives in a lovely Mediterranean setting, she discovers an old trunk full of toys that come magically to life at bedtime. That night when Nora wishes that she could have the stars that appear to be so close, the toys gather them up from the sky and bring them to her. They spend an enchanted evening playing with the stars; when Nora realizes how sad and dark the sky is without any twinkling lights, she sends them back where they belong and falls contentedly asleep. Soft pastel drawings evoke the lush tropical setting and capture the whimsical mood of this quiet bedtime fantasy. Pages are attractively laid out with ample white space to set off the cozy, detailed illustrations.

TANYA LOVED TO DANCE (written by Patricia Lee Gauch, 1989)

The Junior Bookshelf

SOURCE: A review of *Tanya Loved to Dance,* in *The Junior Bookshelf,* Vol. 53, No. 6, December, 1989, p. 261.

In delicately conceived, dreamy water colours, Satomi Ichikawa's ballet-mad little Tanya copies a much-envied elder sister old enough to go to dancing lessons already. A Japanese painter using a French setting is a fascinating combination, and the vigorous succession of little Tanyas, in constantly changing attitudes, tumbling across the pages is a real treat. After Elise's triumph at the special dancing display, when all the family, near and distant, come back home, Tanya herself, unseen at first, begins to dance, to the record of *Swan Lake*. As a result, at Christmas she finds her very own slippers and leotard under the tree, and next term she goes to ballet school too; "and Tanya knew she was not too little any more".

Margery Fisher

SOURCE: A review of *Tanya Loved to Dance,* in *Growing Point,* Vol. 28, No. 5, January, 1990, p. 5270.

Tanya Loved to Dance has [an] . . . introspective approach to imagination, showing how conscientiously a small child will try to copy its elders—in this case an older ballet student whom Tanya envies as she watches her in a school display. Eager though she is, she falls asleep in the middle of the show but when she gets home she dances her own Swan Lake, soberly working out her own version of pliés and arabesques. The story ends in wish-fulfilment as the child graduates to the ballet school but it is in the touching view of her clumsy, intent imitations, shown in pastel paint and fine line, which establish the tone of sympathetic perception of young feelings which makes the book appealing.

ROSY'S GARDEN: A CHILD'S KEEPSAKE OF FLOWERS (written by Elizabeth Laird, 1990)

Publishers Weekly

SOURCE: A review of *Rosy's Garden: A Child's Keepsake of Flowers,* in *Publishers Weekly,* Vol. 237, No. 11, March 16, 1990, p. 68.

An attractive compendium of flower lore framed within a simple story, this book by Ichikawa should appeal to practicing gardening enthusiasts and lovers of plants and flowers. During Rosy's summer-long visit to Granny's country house, she is introduced to all manner of blooming things, from roses to cherry trees. She learns how to identify herbs (and how to make "herby sandwiches"); the hallmarks of a Spanish garden (flowers there are "bigger, and bolder, and brighter" than Granny's); and how flowers have been celebrated in poetry (e.g., by Robert Burns). The illustrator's hand, though horticulturally sure, renders Granny and her beloved "Chief Assistant" in a somewhat static style.

NORA'S DUCK (1991)

Jody McCoy

SOURCE: A review of *Nora's Duck,* in *School Library Journal,* Vol. 37, No. 11, November, 1991, pp. 97-8.

Nora is back with her dog, doll, and stuffed bear in a poignant tribute to a man who loves animals. She finds a weak baby duck and takes it to Doctor John. Although not a veterinarian, he knows just what to do; while the little duck is resting, the two stroll around the man's small English farm visiting all the animals who found their way to him through injury, abandonment, illness, or neglect. When they return to Nora's duck, it is much recovered and quite talkative. Nora asks what the duckling wants, and Doctor John advises her to watch it closely. The child takes her duck back by the pond and watches until a mother duck comes along, and the baby is reunited with its family. Ichikawa's illustrations capture with exquisite detail and delicate beauty a farm with where "animals who have come to grief can live . . . peacefully." Fans of *Nora's Castle* and *Nora's Stars* won't be disappointed with this new story and animal lovers will be charmed. Although not a rousing read-aloud, it's an excellent choice to encourage discussion of the humane treatment of animals. The book can be shared one-on-one or with a group.

Kirkus Reviews

SOURCE: A review of *Nora's Duck,* in *Kirkus Reviews,* Vol. LIX, No. 21, November 1, 1991, p. 1404.

In a loving tribute to the work of her English friend "Doctor John," Ichikawa portrays the endearing child from *Nora's Stars* taking him an injured duckling she has found. Doctor John, a retired physician who now cares for many such animals, assures Nora that the duckling only needs rest; then he shows her around his establishment, introducing her other patients—birds, domestic animals, even an old parrot that used to belong to his mother. The artist's sweet, precise style is perfect for this idyll in a contemporary peaceable kingdom; the simple, uneventful story is nicely rounded when Nora returns the duckling to its mother on the way home to her own. A good addition to the sensitivity-to-other-species collection.

Denise Blank

SOURCE: A review of *Nora's Duck,* in *The Booklist,* Vol. 88, No. 6, November 15, 1991, p. 630.

Impish, gentle Nora, walking through the woods with Kiki the dog, Teddy the teddy bear, and Maggie the doll, comes across a duckling that appears hurt and rushes it to retired doctor John. While waiting for the duckling to recover, he leads Nora and her friends around his peaceful kingdom and explains how all the animals have come to be under his care. Ichikawa crafts a simple, engaging story based on a real Doctor John, and in the process, offers much information about animal welfare. In subtle but clear tones, her airy watercolor-and-pencil illustrations underline the "lion lying with the lamb" quality of the text. This warm, reassuring tale will have a wide audience, but young animal lovers will appreciate it most.

BRAVO, TANYA (written by Patricia Lee Gauch, 1992)

Luann Toth

SOURCE: A review of *Bravo, Tanya,* in *School Library Journal,* Vol. 38, No. 3, March, 1992, p. 214.

Tanya is finally old enough to study ballet, yet despite all her natural coordination, enthusiasm, and even technical mastery, she finds the structure of classes difficult and frustrating. She can't even hear the music. "She is a lovely child, and she is enjoying herself, and that is what matters" says her teacher. But Tanya doesn't experience the same joy she feels while dancing with her stuffed bear under the trees, listening to the wind. It's the helpful reassurance and gentle encouragement of her kind accompanist that makes the difference and turns the little girl into a ballerina. Ichikawa's fluid watercolors with finely etched pen-and-ink detail capture the action. The same lumpish little girl who is always one jeté behind in class is pure poetry in motion executing a pas de deux in the springtime meadow. Delicately expressive and infused with light, the illustrations and lilting prose are perfectly in step and gratifying.

Carolyn Phelan

SOURCE: A review of *Bravo, Tanya,* in *Booklist,* Vol. 88, No. 17, May 1, 1992, p. 1610.

Young Tanya and her ballerina bear, who made their first appearance in *Dance, Tanya,* dance to music that no one else can hear. Attending her first ballet lessons, Tanya's happy to don her leotard and do the barre with the older dancers. Floor exercises are her downfall, though, as she teeters in arabesque and crashes out of a pirouette. Worst of all, the teacher's insistent counting keeps her from hearing the piano accompaniment. After a few words of encouragement from the pianist, she learns to listen to the music and once again dances with joy, sometimes in class and sometimes to the music only she and her bear can hear. This sympathetic story will speak to every young ballerina whose dreams have exceeded her skill—and whose have not? The grace, joy, and poignant sadness expressed in the sunlit watercolor illustrations make this a most appealing picture book.

NORA'S ROSES (1993)

Carolyn Phelan

SOURCE: A review of *Nora's Roses,* in *Booklist,* Vol. 89, No. 14, March 15, 1993, p. 1360.

Miserable with a head cold, Nora must stay in her room and blow her nose, while others walk by and stop to pluck roses from the bush outside her window. Friends, strangers, and relatives pick one rose after another, then a cow comes by and eats quite a few more, until only one blossom remains. Determined to keep her last rose, Nora immortalizes it by drawing its picture. While the story's a bit static, Ichikawa works her familiar magic through the charming watercolor illustrations. Her expressive use of line captures with equal facility the misery of a bad cold, the beauty of a rose in bloom, and the determination of a young child. A quietly appealing picture book, particularly for fans of *Nora's Castle* and *Nora's Stars.*

Joanne Schott

SOURCE: A review of *Nora's Roses,* in *Quill & Quire,* Vol. 59, No. 4, April, 1993, p. 36.

Nora's cold keeps her in bed, where she watches through the window as Roger picks a blossom from her rosebush for his buttonhole, and Vera takes one to a tea party. Her flowers are going to interesting places while she must stay home. In a dream the roses invite her to their party but a sudden awakening reveals a neighbour's cow eating up the roses. Nora can save only one and longs to keep it, deciding finally that the best way is to draw its picture.

This is the fourth Nora story. Within the texts she is always unencumbered by parents. A lone figure free to live a life of imaginative play with her dog and her toys, she epitomizes childhood but Ichikawa gives her independence, practicality, and purpose that avoid sentimentality.

Ichikawa's illustrative technique is a delight. Her watercolours combine detail and delicacy and her feeling for colour is sure and sensitive. Roses which would do credit to a botanical illustrator seem perfectly at home with Nora in a dream sequence which keeps its magic through its simplicity.

Lori A. Janick

SOURCE: A review of *Nora's Roses,* in *School Library Journal,* Vol. 39, No. 6, June, 1993, pp. 77-8.

While sick in bed, Nora also suffers from a bad case of boredom. She watches with interest the pedestrians who stop to smell, and ultimately pick, the lovely roses that grow outside her window. Saddened by her own lack of mobility, the child drops off to sleep and dreams that the roses invite her to a party. She romps with the fairylike blossoms until she's awakened by a cow consuming the last of them. With only one bloom left, Nora decides that the only way to preserve the rose is to draw a picture of it. The story has a gentle sweetness enhanced by exquisite watercolor illustrations. The delicate flowers glow with translucent color, while Nora and her toy companions exude personality and charm. While perfect for one-on-one sharing with a sick child, all children will be able to identify with the tedium of "sick days" and budding young artists will appreciate, and perhaps imitate, Nora's creative solution.

FICKLE BARBARA (1993)

Publishers Weekly

SOURCE: A review of *Fickle Barbara,* in *Publishers Weekly,* Vol. 240, No. 45, November 8, 1993, p. 75.

The talented illustrator of *Dance, Tanya* and *Bravo, Tanya* here features her ballet-loving heroine's favorite stuffed animal. Ballerina Barbara Bear has a good life: she occupies the place of honor on Tanya's bed, and when she wants company, she tumbles to the floor to visit with her dearest friend, Ralph. Determined to expand her social circle, Barbara travels across the room one fateful day for what turns out to be a dull lesson in loyalty. Ichikawa's soft-hued watercolors capture the bears' endearing floppiness, and she infuses a large collection of teddies with raggedy individuality. Though Barbara's button eyes never shift, Ichikawa's compositions animate her characters and convey a spectrum of emotion. Too bad the text feels so vacant.

Kirkus Reviews

SOURCE: A review of *Fickle Barbara*, in *Kirkus Reviews*, Vol. LXI, No. 22, November 15, 1993, p. 1462.

"Ballerina Bear Barbara" is one of many bears living in the room of a Parisian child. She has one good friend, Ralph, but that doesn't stop her when she decides it's time to try some new relationships. What follows is a catalogue of brief encounters with various bears of distinctive character—a handsome one with a husky voice, a funny one, a baby smelling "of strawberry milk and vanilla biscuit"; the many who are quick to make friends are followed by others offering excuses (Zoe and Gatsby "said no thank you, they had each other"). Then, Ichikawa, having demonstrated the meaning of fickleness and its likely consequences, and depicted an engaging gallery of cuddly, well-worn bears with her usual charm—gets a wiser Barbara back to her loyal Ralph. The last (copyright) page discloses that the text here is by Patricia Lee Gauch; even if the idea is Ichikawa's, it would be more honest to credit Gauch, at least as coauthor, on the title page.

Ellen Mandel

SOURCE: A review of *Fickle Barbara*, in *Booklist*, Vol. 90, No. 7, December 1, 1993, p. 698.

Ichikawa's watercolor and pencil art is as soft and inviting as the panoply of bears it portrays. While toy bears of all sizes, colors, and specialties fill the child's room, Ballerina Bear Barbara is best friends only with Ralph. But one day Barbara sets out to make new friends, and she likes each bear she meets better than the one before. On and on, from one bear to the next, fickle Barbara roams, seemingly forgetting all about Ralph until a series of rebuffs by bears who don't want to get chummy makes Barbara realize the value of her old, valued friend. The story as told is flat, relying on the visual interest generated by its well-drawn, delicately detailed, and airily colored art to carry the book. Yet with sympathetic presentation, Barbara Bear's quest for companions can lead youngsters to their own evaluations of quality versus quantity in friendly relationships.

NORA'S SURPRISE (1994)

Karen Harvey

SOURCE: A review of *Nora's Surprise*, in *Booklist*, Vol. 90, No. 14, March 15, 1994, p. 1373.

In a brisk adventure, translated from the Japanese, the ever-appealing Nora returns with her friends Maggie the doll, Teddy the bear, and Kiki the dog. In this story, they receive an invitation to a tea party to be given by the "geese in the wood on the edge of the village." The tea party becomes a picnic when the geese's large neighbor, Benjy the sheep, can't fit through the house's door. Benjy proves himself a glutton and turns the picnic into a free-for-all, wreaking havoc until everyone settles down for a much needed nap. Waking to find Benjy gone, Nora and her friends run to the rescue, discovering the sheep being shorn of his wool. The story concludes with a postscript: Benjy sends Nora a note of apology along with lovely wool sweater, proving he's a kind, generous sheep after all. As always, Ichikawa's clear, delicate watercolors carry the story, delineating with equal skill the total abandon of the ruined picnic, Benjy's abashed face, and the peaceful, napping faces of Nora and her friends. Another appealing offering from the creator of *Nora's Castle*

Jacqueline Elsner

SOURCE: A review of *Nora's Surprise*, in *School Library Journal*, Vol. 40, No. 5, May, 1994, p. 96.

Stunning artwork illustrates a problematic story about a feast turned free-for-all. The tale begins when Nora accepts an invitation to a garden party hosted by two geese. There she meets Benjy the sheep, who eats everything in sight, including her gift of flowers and all of the cucumber sandwiches and raspberry jam. The child gives Benjy the business several times, telling him he is greedy, fat, and ruining the party. In the end, after he is shorn, he apologizes and gives Nora a sweater, allowing her to conclude that "He was a kind, generous sheep after all." Fatness, or bulky wool, and overeating are difficulties for Benjy, but eating flowers is doing what comes sheep-naturally! Only when the group can use him does he gain acceptance. He's not so much ungenerous, as he is out-of-bounds. Ichikawa's watercolors are masterful. Each figure, whether animal, toy, or person, is full of life, humor, and expression in every gesture. Readers will walk right into her landscapes and taste each morsel of food. Small wonder the party-goers pitch into the platters when "Benjy stuck his head into the cucumber sandwiches." A tough call overall: story conflict a bit off-target, but a perfect 10 for the paintings!

Eva Mitnick

SOURCE: A review of *Nora's Surprise*, in *The Five Owls*, Vol. IX, No. 1, September-October, 1994, p. 12.

When Nora receives an invitation to a tea party given by "the geese in the wood on the edge of the village," she is very excited and immediately sets off for the party with a large bunch of flowers. Not everything is as Nora expects, however; the geese's house is ramshackle and too small, and one of the guests is a terribly oafish sheep named Benjy. Benjy gobbles up most of the party food and even Nora's flowers, sends the guests tumbling from a tree, and splashes all the water out of the geese's pond. Everyone manages to have a good time in spite of Benjy, who, it is clear, simply finds it hard to contain his enthusiasm. At the end of the party, Benjy's owner shears his wooly coat; a few months later, Nora receives a Benjy-smelling white wool sweater in the mail, Benjy's unique way of making amends for eating Nora's flowers.

Ichikawa's delicate and lively watercolors are as appealing as ever; poor Benjy's expressions, exuberant and sheepish by turns, mirror those of any rambunctious child. Nora is an adventurous and outgoing character, and children will enjoy this summer afternoon romp with her toy and animal friends.

TANYA AND EMILY IN A DANCE FOR TWO
(written by Patricia Lee Gauch; originally published as *Tanya and Emily in a Pas de Deux,* 1994)

Cheri Estes

SOURCE: A review of *Tanya and Emily in a Dance for Two,* in *School Library Journal,* Vol. 40, No. 9, September, 1994, p. 184.

As in *Dance, Tanya* and *Bravo, Tanya,* this little girl's passion for movement shines through here, and she dances in her own, sometimes unconventional, way. She's the wiggliest in the class, always at the end of the line, but finds joy in everything about ballet. When a newcomer, Emily, joins the class, she does everything properly. On a walk through the park, Tanya teaches her new friend to find many inspirations to dance, and Emily teaches Tanya how to do a *cabriole.* Neither girl is alone anymore, and their friendship reinforces their complementary skills. Ichikawa's watercolors are equally deft in depicting Tanya's free spiritedness and Emily's grace. Like the girls, her lines are always in motion, and Tanya and Emily leap off the pages. The palette is brighter than in the first two books, and Ichikawa uses grays to paint the offsets, which show the companions working and practicing before they actually perform the steps. This book has a larger format than the previous two and reflects that Tanya, too, has grown. Children will be inspired to create their own steps and encouraged by the idea that there is room for more than one style of expression.

Carolyn Phelan

SOURCE: A review of *Tanya and Emily in a Dance for Two,* in *Booklist,* Vol. 91, No. 4, October 15, 1994, p. 424.

Tanya, the "smallest and wiggliest" student in her ballet class, looks up to the new girl, Emily, who stands, walks, stretches, and dances like a ballerina. Yet as they walk through the zoo after class, it is Tanya who shows Emily how to make a dance by mimicking the movements of the animals. They become friends, and later they perform a pas de deux in the recital. Ichikawa's charming and expertly executed line-and-watercolor wash illustrations portray the two girls and their movements to perfection. Even at the end, Tanya's positions and movements look a bit unpolished compared with Emily's more graceful ones, yet her contribution to their friendship is as clear as her energy and love of dance. Another beguiling picture book, for children who enjoyed *Dance, Tanya* and *Bravo, Tanya.*

Hanna B. Zeiger

SOURCE: A review of *Tanya and Emily in a Dance for Two,* in *The Horn Book Magazine,* Vol. 70, No. 6, November-December, 1994, p. 718.

Tanya and her love of dancing have been the subject of two previous books. Now, though she is the "smallest and wiggliest" member of her ballet class and always at the end of the line, the ballet steps never stop humming in her head. She dances to them under her covers at night and all during the day. Then, one day, Emily joins their class. Emily is truly a prima ballerina. In everything she does—standing, walking, exercising, and dancing—Emily is outstanding. Since both Tanya and Emily are loners, they each go their own way until they meet one day in the park. Emily is intrigued as Tanya dances like an ostrich and a flamingo and soon joins her to dance like two giraffes and two wild goats. A perceptive dance teacher, noticing the new friendship in class, adds a special pas de deux to the winter recital. The two friends dance, "and together they were wonderful." Ichikawa's light watercolor paintings perfectly capture the grace of the girls as they leap through the air. A delight for the dancer hidden in all of us.

ISABELA'S RIBBONS (1995)

Publishers Weekly

SOURCE: A review of *Isabela's Ribbons,* in *Publishers Weekly,* Vol. 242, No. 34, August 21, 1995, pp. 65-6.

Gaily patterned watercolors packed with playful details make this book a joy to behold—the story, unfortunately, is downright confusing. Isabela is known throughout her lush island town for her collection of hair ribbons; her other passion is for hide-and-seek. The ubiquitous green foliage provides Isabela with a perfect cover, and the vivid fruits and flowers camouflage her ribbons (this premise occasions some of Ichikawa's prettiest work). But Isabela lacks friends her own age. One day, after challenging a parrot to find her in a drab mango tree, she cunningly ties distracting ribbons among the leaves. As she waits, Isabela loses herself in a daydream—the tree becomes "deep sea, and the ribbons were fish of every color!" The fantasy suddenly evaporates as a flock of children materializes below the tree, and Isabela uses her ribbons to entice them to find her. The transitions here are blurred—what does the undersea interlude have to do with the appearance of the children? The underdeveloped prose grounds readers from plunging into Isabela's reverie.

Kathleen Odean

SOURCE: A review of *Isabela's Ribbons,* in *School Library Journal,* Vol. 41, No. 11, November, 1995, p. 74.

The strength of this book is its charming illustrations. Set on a lush Caribbean island, the fanciful tale is about a little girl who loves ribbons and the game of hide-and-seek. One day, when no one can play with her, Isabela takes a basket full of her hair ribbons up into a tree and ties them to the branches, imagining they are fish and she is swimming with them in the ocean. Then she throws the ribbons down to the children who have gathered below and plays with them. The slight story mainly exists as a vehicle for the skillful watercolors of colorful, patterned ribbons and fish, flowering trees, and brightly clad children. An additional purchase.

Hazel Rochman

SOURCE: A review of *Isabela's Ribbons,* in *Booklist,* Vol. 92, No. 7, December 1, 1995, p. 641.

Ichikawa's watercolor paintings are fresh and beautiful, creating a view of Puerto Rico as an island paradise. The story's a little cute and exclamatory with a contrived fantasy—Isabela has no one to play with one "day" so she climbs into a mango tree with all the ribbons she loves, and the ribbons turn into fishes that lead her to children who chase her ribbons and become her friends. There are better stories about imaginative play; but the dancing pictures of the child and her place and the people in her life will draw kids into her game of hide-and-seek.

TANYA STEPS OUT (written by Patricia Lee Gauch, 1996)

Joy Fleishhacker

SOURCE: A review of *Tanya Steps Out,* in *School Library Journal,* Vol. 42, No. 12, December, 1996, p. 92.

A young ballerina, first introduced in *Dance, Tanya,* gracefully leaps her way through this well-designed book. When her teacher instructs her to pose like a flamingo, Tanya imitates the animal by standing on one foot and bending her other leg. Pull the tab below the picture and vertical slats move to reveal a flamingo, standing in a very similar position. This is the basic format, as Tanya jumps like a cat, runs like an ostrich, hops like a rabbit, cavorts like a goat, leaps like an antelope, and finally takes a bow. The focus here is not on plot, but on the pictures, and the simple text works well to showcase them. Ballet terms are scattered throughout, but not translated or explained. Crafted from heavy paper, the moveable sections are sturdy and easy to operate. As one picture is replaced by another, the sections separate and move like vertical blinds. Colored in gentle pinks, yellows, and greens, the illustrations are bright, graceful, and filled with the joy of movement. A nice, but supplemental choice for young ballet fans.

TANYA AND THE MAGIC WARDROBE (written by Patricia Lee Gauch, 1997)

Dawn Amsberry

SOURCE: A review of *Tanya and the Magic Wardrobe,* in *School Library Journal,* Vol. 43, No. 10, October, 1997, p. 95.

When Tanya and her mother arrive early at the theater for a performance of *Coppélia,* the girl follows an elderly woman down a hallway and discovers a dressing room with a green wardrobe full of wonderful costumes. Tanya and the woman dress up and dance parts from *Sleeping Beauty, Cinderella,* and the *Nutcracker Suite.* Finally, they perform *Coppélia,* with Tanya as the magic doll, and the dressing room becomes a stage complete with scenery and beautifully costumed dancers. The book ends with Tanya sitting down with her mother to watch the ballet she has just seen in her own imagination. Ballet fans will snap up this latest addition to the popular series and will turn again and again to the illustrations of *Coppélia,* painted in colors just dark enough to be mysterious. The two-page spread showing all of the toys coming to life in luminous detail captures perfectly the magic of the famous ballet. The smoothly written text provides just enough narrative to keep the story flowing, letting the illustrations fill in the rest. Once again, Tanya steals the show in this well-executed picture book that pays tribute both to the beauty of dance and to the power of a child's imagination.

PRESENTING TANYA, THE UGLY DUCKLING (written by Patricia Lee Gauch, 1999)

Susan Pine

SOURCE: A review of *Presenting Tanya, the Ugly Duckling,* in *School Library Journal,* Vol. 45, No. 6, June, 1999, pp. 95-6.

Another lovely story about the young ballet student that will appeal to children who feel left out or unable to accomplish as much as their peers. In Tanya's sixth picture-book appearance, she is selected to dance the title role in *The Ugly Duckling* ballet at her school recital. As the children rehearse, the other pupils improve, but Tanya, who feels as though she has "two left feet and no wings at all," can't seem to get the movements right. Finally, at the dress rehearsal, the music, the costumes, and the drama transform her into the Ugly Duckling and Tanya is ready to perform. The expressive watercolor paintings, many of them wordless double-page spreads, capture all of the beauty of a ballet performance. As Miss Foley tells the story to the dancers, small paintings set above the text reflect the events she describes, showing a scrawny chick that blossoms into a graceful swan. Tanya's poses, motions, and emotions echo those of the duckling. In all of the paintings, Ichikawa makes effective use of line and shadow to create the illusion of movement and mood. Take a bow, Tanya!

Additional coverage of Ichikawa's life and career is contained in the following sources published by The Gale Group: *Contemporary Authors,* **Vol. 126;** *Something about the Author,* **Vols. 36, 47, 76.**

Philip Pullman

1946-

English author of fiction, nonfiction, and picture books; playwright, scriptwriter, and reteller.

Major works include *The Ruby in the Smoke* (1987), *The Shadow in the Plate* (1987; U.S. edition as *Shadow in the North*), *The Broken Bridge* (1990), *Northern Lights* (1996; U.S. edition as *The Golden Compass*), *The Firework-Maker's Daughter* (1996).

INTRODUCTION

The creator of fantasy, historical and realistic fiction, nonfiction, picture books, and plays, Pullman is a prolific and versatile writer who is regarded as one of the most talented contemporary authors of books for children and young adults. Recognized as a gifted storyteller who adds a distinctive, original touch to such literary forms as the mystery, the thriller, the horror story, and the problem novel, he is considered a writer of great range, depth, imagination, and integrity who characteristically explores moral and ethical issues in well-crafted, exciting tales. Pullman directs his works to primary and middle graders as well as to readers in high school. He is perhaps best known as the creator of a series of historical novels for young people that revolve around Sally Lockhart, a resourceful, independent young woman who solves mysteries in Victorian London, and a series of fantasies directed to readers in the middle grades through high school that are inspired by and named for a phrase from John Milton's *Paradise Lost.* Known collectively as His Dark Materials, these works outline how a girl and boy learn that they are key figures in an ancient prophecy that predicts that they are to save their world. Pullman is also the author of such works as the New Cut Gang series, comic mysteries for middle graders that feature a gang of urchins in nineteenth-century London; *How to Be Cool* (1987), a humorous satire for young adults in which a group of teenagers expose a government agency that decides which fashions are hip; *The Broken Bridge,* a realistic novel for young people in which a sixteen-year-old girl of Haitian/English descent learns the truth about her parents while searching for her identity; and *The Firework-Maker's Daughter,* a folktale-like fantasy about a young woman in an exotic country who seeks the secret ingredient of firework-making. In addition, Pullman is the creator of an informational book about the ancient cultures of several Mediterranean, Eastern, Middle Eastern, and South American countries; a tragic novel about two star-crossed teenage lovers; two graphic novels influenced by Victorian melodrama and pulp fiction that incorporate lively text and comic-book art; and a retelling of the story of Aladdin. He has also adapted *The Three Musketeers, Frankenstein,* and a story featuring Sherlock Holmes into plays and has turned the latter two into books.

Biographical Information

Born in Norwich, England, Pullman is the son of an airman in the Royal Air Force and an amateur dramatist who also worked for the British Broadcasting Corporation (BBC). Pullman spent much of his early life traveling by ship. At the age of six, he went to live in Southern Rhodesia, now Zimbabwe, where his father was stationed on assignment. After his father's tour of duty ended, Pullman returned to England, where he spent many happy times with his maternal grandparents in Drayton, a small village in Norfolk. His grandfather, a clergyman in the Church of England, was rector of the local church. "When I was young," Pullman wrote in *Something about the Author Autobiography Series (SAAS)*, "he was the sun at the centre of my life." Pullman's grandfather was also an accomplished storyteller, able to spin a tale out of the simplest events. When his father was killed on a mission in Africa, Pullman and his younger brother were sent to live in Norfolk while their mother went to London to look for work. Shortly thereafter, Pullman's father received the Distinguished Flying Cross; the posthumous award was presented to the family by Queen Elizabeth at

Buckingham Palace. Pullman received a new stepfather, an airman friend of his father, at the age of nine. When he accompanied his family to Australia as part of his stepfather's assignment, Pullman made a discovery that would change his life: comic books. He describes his fascination with Batman comics in *SAAS* as "the first stirring of the storytelling impulse." In Australia, Pullman began telling ghost stories to his school friends and other tales to his brother in their bedroom at night. Pullman noted in *SAAS,* "Many other things happened in Australia, but my discovery of storytelling was by far the most important."

After moving back to the United Kingdom, Pullman settled with his family in Llanbedr, a village on the coast of North Wales. Here, he discovered art. He recalled in *SAAS* that the book *A History of Art* was "more precious to me than any Bible." He began drawing, and fell in love with the landscape of Wales by sketching it. As a teenager, Pullman became interested in poetry. One of his English teachers introduced him to Milton, Wordsworth, and the English Metaphysical poets. He also began to learn poetry by heart and to write poems in various literary forms. After winning a scholarship to Oxford to study English literature, Pullman became the first person in his family to attend a university. Pullman realized at Oxford that he was destined to become a storyteller, not a poet. After graduation, he began to write a novel; shortly thereafter, he moved to London and worked at a men's clothing store and in a library while writing three pages a day, a regime to which he still adheres.

Pullman got his degree from Weymouth College of Education and began to teach middle school in Oxford. For twelve years, he taught Greek mythology to his students by telling them stories of the gods and heroes, including oral versions of Homer's *The Iliad* and *The Odyssey.* He wrote in *SAAS* that this experience was "something that, by a lucky chance, was the best possible training for me as a writer." In 1978, Pullman published his first novel, *Galatea,* a book for adults that describes how flautist Martin Browning, searching for his missing wife, embarks on a series of surreal adventures. Now considered a classic among aficionados of science fiction and fantasy, the novel is described by its author in *SAAS* as "a book I can't categorize"; he added, "I'm still proud of it." After completing *Galatea,* Pullman began to write and produce plays for his students. He enjoyed doing these plays so much that he decided to make young people his primary audience. After writing his informational book, *Ancient Civilizations* (1978), and *Count Karlstein* (1982), a story done originally as a play that he later turned into a graphic novel, Pullman wrote *The Ruby in the Smoke,* the first volume of his Sally Lockhart series. This volume was published in 1985, the year that Pullman became a full-time freelance writer. Inspired by some Victorian postcards he had bought years before, Pullman wrote a thriller set in Victorian London about a spirited sixteen-year-old girl, recently orphaned, who is searching for a priceless stone with seemingly hypnotic powers. "With *The Ruby in the Smoke,*" Pullman wrote in *SAAS,* "I think I first found my voice as a children's author." In 1995,

Pullman produced the first volume of the fantasy series called His Dark Materials. This work, *Northern Lights,* was published in the United States as *The Golden Compass.* It introduces Lyra Belcqua, a shrewd and feisty teen who embarks on a quest to find out who is attempting to steal the souls of abducted children. Pullman told Julie C. Boehning of *Library Journal,* "I felt as if everything I'd read, written, and done in my whole life had been in preparation for this book." He told *Books for Keeps* that His Dark Materials series, which is scheduled to be a trilogy, "is my most coherent and thought-out statement of where I am, religiously, morally, and philosophically."

Major Works

In *The Ruby in the Smoke,* Sally Lockhart, a brave young woman who is savvy about such subjects as business management and military strategy, becomes involved in the opium trade when she receives a cryptic note written in a strange hand soon after she hears of her father's drowning off the coast of Singapore. Sally is assisted in her search for the mysterious ruby by her friend and protege Jim Taylor, the young photographer Frederick Garland, and his sister Rosa. As they make their way through the London underworld, the characters encounter a series of rousing adventures, often filled with cliff-hanging suspense, as well as a number of larger-than-life characters. At the end of the novel, Sally recovers, and loses, the ruby and learns that the man she thought was her father was an impostor. The next novel in the series, *The Shadow in the Plate* (U. S. edition as *Shadow in the North*), takes place six years after the conclusion of its predecessor. Now a financial consultant, Sally joins with Frederick to investigate the failure of a shipping business that she had recommended to one of her clients as a solid investment. Sally and Frederick uncover fraud and murder; they also confront an evil industrialist who is producing a steam-powered gun that is capable of incredible destruction. The novel outlines Sally's growing love for Frederick; at the end of the story, Frederick is killed, and Sally finds that she is pregnant with his child. The third book in the series, *The Tiger in the Well* (1990), depicts Sally as a successful tycoon and the mother of a two-year-old daughter, Harriet. When Sally is sued for divorce by a man she does not know, she loses custody of Harriet as well as her home and her job; soon thereafter, Harriet is kidnapped by a man claiming to be her father. In order to find out who is behind the ruse, Sally disappears into the Jewish ghetto in London's East End. Pullman outlines Sally's developing social conscience through her experiences, which expose her to an anti-Semitic campaign, while drawing parallels between her treatment and that of the ghetto residents. Sally makes a cameo appearance in the fourth novel of the series, *The Tin Princess* (1994), as the wife of Daniel Goldberg, a Jewish political activist who appeared in the previous volume. A swashbuckling adventure set in the tiny kingdom of Razkavia, a country that lies between Germany and Austria, *The Tin Princess* focuses on Adelaide, a Cockney and former prostitute who appeared in *The Ruby in the Smoke* as Jim Taylor's childhood sweetheart. Adelaide has married into the royal family of Razkavia; when her husband is assassinated, she becomes Queen. Quickly set upon by traitors, she is aided by Becky Winter, a teenage native of Razkavia who is acting as Adelaide's tutor, and Jim, who is now a detective. The novel, which blends political intrigue and romance, includes spies, bombings, a mad prince, and a vengeful actress, as well as many twists and turns of plot.

In the first volume of His Dark Materials, *Northern Lights* (U. S. edition as *The Golden Compass*), teenage orphan Lyra Belcqua and her daemon Pantalaimon live with her uncle, Lord Asriel, at Oxford. After her uncle is imprisoned during an Arctic expedition, Lyra goes on a quest to release him, taking with her an alethiometer, a soothsaying instrument that looks like a golden compass. Lyra discovers that kidnapped children are being held in a scientific experiment station in the North, where they are undergoing operations to separate them from their daemons. Lyra also learns that her mother is the glamorous but menacing Mrs. Coulter, the leader of the group behind the abductions, and that she is destined to save her world and to move into another dimension. In *The Subtle Knife* (1997), Lyra meets Will Parry, an Oxford boy who escapes into an alternative city after killing the man who was persecuting his mentally fragile mother. Like Lyra, Will is destined to save the universe from destruction. Will possess a counterpart to the golden compass, a knife that can cut through anything; the knife allows its true bearer to part the membrane between all worlds. Lyra and Will search for Dust, a mysterious substance integral to the composition of the universe, and for Will's father, an explorer. On their journey, they encounter angels, witches, vampires, talking bears, and Specters, creatures that resemble deadly flying jellyfish. At the conclusion of the novel, Lord Asriel, Lyra's guardian, is preparing to restage the revolt of the angels against God. In addition, Lyra finds out that she has been chosen as the new Eve.

Often considered a major stylistic departure for its author, *The Broken Bridge* describes how Ginny Howard, a biracial girl living with her single father in a small Welsh town, learns that she is illegitimate, that she has a halfbrother, that her father was abused as a child, and that her mother, whom she assumed to be dead, is actually alive. Ginny, who wants to be a painter, meets her mother, who is a painter, and discovers that her mother is not interested in forming a relationship with her. By examining her heritage, character, and direction, Ginny takes a big step toward maturity. *The Firework-Maker's Daughter* is also regarded as a unique contribution to Pullman's oeuvre. In this work, Lila, the daughter of a fireworks-maker who lives in a country much like Indonesia, is in the final stages of her apprenticeship. Accompanied by a talking white elephant and its keeper, she embarks on a quest to discover the key to the creation of fireworks. Their journey takes the party to the lair of the dangerous Fire-fiend; in the process, Lila learns much about herself and finds that the firemaker's secret is wisdom. *Clockwork, or All Wound Up* (1996; U.S. edition 1998) is a fantasy that is

considered an examination of the art of storytelling as well as a particularly eerie tale. In this work, a short novel with echoes of *Faust* and the ballet *Coppelia,* the talented storyteller Fritz and the clockmaker's apprentice Carl, under duress for failing to complete making a clockwork child, are joined by the subject of one of Fritz's stories, Dr. Kalmerius, a clockmaker thought to have connections with the Devil. After Carl sells his soul to the Devil to avoid failure, he is saved by the kindness of a little girl, the innkeeper's daughter Gretl. *How to Be Cool,* Pullman's humorous novel about the exposure of the National Cool Board by a group of teenagers, is one of his most popular works. He wrote the screenplay for the television adaptation of the book that aired as a three-part series in Britain in 1988.

Critical Reception

Called "a master storyteller" by Rayma Turton and "one of today's top storytellers" by Chris Routh of *School Librarian,* Pullman is also praised for his meticulous research, his accurate recreation of Victorian England, his skill as a fantasist, and his ability to create memorable characters. The author is often lauded for his ability to write books that are sophisticated yet accessible as well as for his ability to address complex themes without compromising his exciting narratives. In addition, Pullman is acknowledged for successfully experimenting with form and theme in his works while working in traditional genres. Credited for using period settings to draw parallels to contemporary society, the author addresses such issues as feminism, prejudice, and adjustment to new technology in his historical novels. In addition, Pullman is celebrated for creating strong female characters, especially Sally Lockhart, who fights for independence and equality in a man's world; Lyra of His Dark Materials, who is destined to find redemption after her "fall"; and Lila of *The Firework-Maker's Daughter,* whom Rayma Turton of *Magpies* described as "all a feminist could ask for." Pullman's books have been criticized for being overwrought, unfocused, and overly cerebral as well as for their inclusion of sex, violence, and questionable values. However, Pullman is generally lauded as a writer of beautifully written works that are both entertaining and thought-provoking. D. A. Young noted that Pullman "has done for modern society something of the service Dickens performed for his own." Anne E. Deifendeifer of *Children's Books and Their Creators* added, "At their best, Pullman's novels, daring and inventive, are page turners that immediately hook readers into the story and often introduce them to the Victorian age." Writing about His Dark Materials, Jennifer Fakolt noted that Pullman has "the power of a master fantasist," and that his two titles in the series, "stand in equal company with the works of J. R. R. Tolkien and C. S. Lewis."

Awards

The Ruby in the Smoke received the Lancashire County Libraries/National and Provincial Children's Book Award and Best Book for Young Adults listing, *School Library*

Journal, both in 1987, as well as the Children's Book Award from the International Reading Association and the Preis der Leseratten, ZDF Television (Germany) and Best Book for Young Adults listing, ALA, both in 1988. *Shadow in the North* was Best Book for Young Adults listing, ALA, in 1988 and was nominated for an Edgar Allan Poe Award by the Mystery Writers of America in 1989. *The Firework-Maker's Daughter* won the Smarties Award in 1996. *Clockwork, or All Wound Up* was short-listed for the Whitbread Children's Book of the Year Award and the Carnagie Medal, both in 1996. *Northern Lights* received the Carnegie Medal from the British Library Association and the *Guardian* Children's Fiction Award, both in 1996. *The Golden Compass* (U. S. edition of *Northern Lights*) received the Top of the List Youth Fiction from *Booklist* in 1996 and was nominated for the American Booksellers Book of the Year in 1997.

AUTHOR'S COMMENTARY

Philip Pullman

SOURCE: "Writing about Cool," in *Books for Keeps,* No. 54, January, 1989, p. 25.

When I was a teacher, what I enjoyed most was the unofficial culture of the schools I taught in. The school uniform, for instance, might be described in the brochure, but that's only a starting point: what really matters is how the pupils wear it. If they have to wear a tie, they'll tie it in a huge big fat knot and leave two rude little bits sticking down underneath; or casually knotted halfway down the chest over an open collar; or rolled and stretched so it's as thin as a piece of string—anything to put their own mark on it, and quite right too.

I used to watch all this with fascination. And I used to listen. When kids, right, are talking together, right, I don't mean the GCSE kind of oral wossname, you know, assessment, right, but just kind of—no, shut up, listen—if they're just *talking,* okay, okay?—then if you *listen,* right, you get all the rhythms. It's all in the rhythms. Almost.

Take white socks and *well wicked.* Dated now, both of them, but I remember the first occasion I came across them. I moved from a job in one Oxford middle school to another middle school a couple of miles away across the city; and one of the first things I noticed was that the stylists, the leaders, were wearing white socks and little black low-cut shoes. And the highest term of praise in their lexicon was *well wicked. Wicked* was easy to place: words like *mean, dirty,* Michael Jackson's *Bad,* have long been terms of approval in hip slang. *Well* as an intensifier (it's well hot, he was well angry) was more intriguing; I haven't been able to work out where that one comes from.

Now neither white socks nor *well wicked* had appeared at my previous school. But as it happened, my son was a pupil there at the time, and I asked him to keep his eyes and ears open and let me know when they turned up. It took a couple of months for them to make their first appearance, and within six months they were established.

I'd been vaguely intending to write a story about style for some time; I'd even thought of the title—**How To Be Cool**—and sketched a couple of outlines, but nothing had come of it. White socks crystallised the feeling of the title into a plot. Suppose there was a sinister secret organisation controlling the spread of fashions such as white socks; the National Cool Board. And suppose some bright kid became aware of this and decided to expose it. And suppose (this was the easiest of all) that the Cool Board was about to be privatised—as British Cool, naturally. It's the sort of situation you just wind up and set going.

I still needed a protagonist, and here again classroom life came to my aid. In the class I was teaching at that time, there were three boys who were real stylists. Pink tennis shirts—exotic trainers—and there was one occasion when they all turned up with gold-rimmed folding sunglasses, and stood inside the doorway and just posed, exuding waves of cool. The girls, at whom the waves were aimed, naturally took not the slightest notice.

Well, there were my heroes. With their permission, I used their names in the book; everything else (I think) is fiction. Though when I go into one of these new mega-shopping centres and see the uniformed security guards deciding who's allowed in and who isn't, and when I consider the mysterious business of who really did first wear white socks, I begin to wonder.

GENERAL COMMENTARY

Geoff Fox

SOURCE: "May We Recommend . . . ," in *Books for Keeps,* No. 74, May, 1992, p. 25.

In the mail this morning is a xeroxed catalogue advertising old comics. I'm offered a 1939 Beano (in 'Very Good' condition, mind you) for £125.00. Its original readers must now be just about drawing their pensions, yet their grandchildren might well be chortling over much the same kind of humour in this week's issue; anarchy everywhere, chaotic chases, terrible puns, sly nudges from artist to reader and, above all, Authority Being Upset.

There's a fair bit of the enduring Beano tradition in Philip Pullman's twin volumes, *Spring-Heeled Jack: A Story of Bravery and Evil* and *Count Karlstein, or The Ride of the Demon Huntsman.* His original sources may be

Victorian Chillers or Ruritanian Romances—the stuff of Penny Dreadfuls, in fact—but he'll also mix in a dash of Janet and Allan Ahlberg or Prokofiev. The narrative is carried by print, then comic-style pictures-and-speech-bubbles, then back to print. It is a medium full of energy and wit. Both stories began as plays written when Philip Pullman was teaching at a middle school in Oxford—it's not surprising therefore that much of the comic energy stems from situations which are physically funny. A chase across the rooftops, for example, involves our sailor hero who's afraid of heights but nevertheless upends a pursuing policeman into a chimney pot. ('Right, that does it! I've lost my temper now! You're under arrest, and anything you say will be taken down in evidence . . . ' squawks the inverted rozzer, legs kicking above the tiles.)

Witty readers will also enjoy *Beano* artist Mostyn's scrawny cat and diminutive bed-bug, confiding laid-back asides on the folly of the protagonists from half-in, half-out of *Spring-Heeled Jack*'s narrative frames. They'll also like Patrice Aggs' stuffed animal heads in Count Karlstein's hunting lodge muttering, 'What rubbish!' or 'Don't listen to him'; or the ghost, about to be blasted by the globetrotting Miss Augusta Davenport's 'Bellerephon' Hydro-Atmospheric Plunger gun, with its spectral dying (?) moans of 'Down with Progress! Down with Science!'

I wrote to the author about the books and, at a loss for a genre, called them 'graphic novels'. Philip Pullman modified the description: 'The form I have evolved for these two books is a hybrid, and actually I didn't evolve it at all—I stole it lock, stock and barrel from Shirley Hughes, who developed it in *Chips and Jessie* and its sequel (and I acknowledge the theft at the back of *Count Karlstein*). The combination of text and pictures, each doing what the other wasn't or couldn't, appealed to me at once and enormously. "Novel-comic", perhaps?'

Since he is not a graphic artist ('I can't draw'), Philip Pullman had to write the text and describe the pictures, including the words *within* the pictures, in great detail and then pass the whole package over to the artist. His notes to the illustrator are precise. He suggests, for example, the angle from which the reader views the action in *Count Karlstein:* 'Over the girls' shoulders, as they look down through the window into a castle courtyard . . . '; 'From the courtyard, looking up at the grim old lawyer getting out of the carriage. He's gazing up at the towering walls of the Castle, in one high window of which we can see the two girls' heads peering down.'

Novel-reading adults can find this a slippery medium— 'Strange that,' comments Philip Pullman, 'when teenagers not thought of by their teachers as fluent readers manage them so well. The truth is that this kind of text demands a different way of reading—a non-liner way, perhaps.'

Given the chance, and they should be, young readers will pick up the rules of this particular reading game straightaway, including some not yet at home with conventional novels. They'll relish these wild versions of snakes-and-ladders with two or three heroes and heroines simultaneously sliding down or clambering up, usually just missing each other and only coinciding in the safety of 'Home'. And Philip Pullman keeps landing the characters, and his reader, on unexpected squares.

Few writers could have managed these books and also written the extraordinary *Ruby in the Smoke* trilogy (*The Shadow in the North* and *The Tiger in the Well* complete the adventures of the intrepid Sally Lockhart around nineteenth-century London, Europe and Beyond). At one level, *The Tiger in the Well,* for example, tastes delicious like the Penny Dreadfuls beloved of one of the novel's characters—there is the colour and energy, though not the excessive length, which were features of the amazing exploits of Jack Harkaway and the rest. At another level, the book is a social document with the detail of Mayhew and the compassion of Dickens, though Philip Pullman imitates neither. And, at yet another, it has a historical vision that brings alive the plight of immigrant Jews and the unemployed of London at the end of the nineteenth century. Sally Lockhart is not a simplistically drawn feminist, but she is a woman who survives in a society, or an Empire rather, of men. She values some and loves some, and opposes others whose evil is convincingly malign.

The tension between the worlds of private relationships and public concerns which marks the trilogy is also found in Philip Pullman's *The Broken Bridge:* questions of race, homosexuality, father-daughter relationships, adoption. At the outset of her A-level Art course, Ginny must determine what price she's willing to pay for her painting—and where its origins and impulse lie. Do you demand a special kind of indulgence from your friends, use them, even, for the sake of your work? And since Ginny is black and half-Haitian but brought up in white Wales, who are to be her teachers? The Europeans or her own mother, the successful Haitian painter Anielle Baptiste, whom she'd wrongly thought long dead? When they meet, Anielle says, 'I'm a painter, I'm not a mother'; and walks away. It's an uncompromising, trustworthy climax from a writer who will excite, delight and disturb many young readers.

Kit Alderdice

SOURCE: "In the Studio with Philip Pullman," in *Publishers Weekly,* Vol. 241, No. 22, May 30, 1994, pp. 24-5.

From the outside, Philip Pullman's writing studio—"the hut," as he calls it—looks like nothing more than a large gardening shed. Its location—the back garden of the British children's author and playwright's north Oxford home—seems to confirm this view. One glance at the hut's interior, however, and it is immediately evident that this is the workplace of a writer with an unusually rich and eclectic set of interests.

Masks, theater posters, postcards and artwork (by Pullman and others) cover nearly every available inch of wallspace. The bookshelves are crammed with an array of reference books as well as the many novels and picture books Pullman has published. Even the author's new computer is not exempt from the visual festivities: topped with an Indonesian-looking mask, it is wreathed with garlands of vividly colored artificial flowers.

Radiating a vibrant, contagious exuberance, the long-limbed author settles into an office chair to discuss his books, his career and his predilection for fanciful decor.

Although several of Pullman's novels for adults (including the critically acclaimed *Galatea*) had appeared in Great Britain in the 1970s, American audiences first made the writer's acquaintance in 1987, through his unabashedly melodramatic Victorian thriller *The Ruby in the Smoke*. Named an ALA Best Book for Young Adults, and awarded the International Reading Association's Children's Book Award for Older Readers, among other honors, *Ruby* was followed in fairly short order by a pair of sequels: *The Shadow in the North* and *The Tiger in the Well,* both set in Pullman's quirky, gothic version of 19th-century England and starring the staunchly independent Sally Lockhart.

Not content to be pigeonholed in a single style of children's literature, Pullman turned to what was, for him, a new genre—the contemporary, more "realistic" YA novel. The first of these to appear in the States was *The Broken Bridge* (1992), a narrative motivated, in part, by the author's desire to "go back to the landscape where I was a teenager. I loved that landscape of North Wales—I loved drawing it and painting it. And I wanted to say something about what it means to discover your sense of yourself as a painter, as someone who responds to the visual arts, which is what I got Ginny [the book's heroine] to do."

In 1993 came the taut, suspenseful novel *The White Mercedes,* which Pullman describes as "a new kind of thing for me—a short, intense tragedy," set in modern day Oxford and revolving around a pair of star-crossed teenage lovers.

Pullman's most recent book to appear in the U.S. is *The Tin Princess,* in which he returns to the world of Sally Lockhart and friends, taking up his narration several years after the events described in *The Tiger in the Well.* Since, as Pullman asserts, "Sally's story [has been] told," the free-spirited heroine makes only a cameo appearance. The novel focuses instead on the exploits of Sally's old ally Jim Taylor and his long-lost true love, the orphan Adelaide, last seen in *The Ruby in the Smoke.*

Why the return to his old literary stomping grounds? "You get stories that come to you and they want to be told," Pullman says. Another motivation was that "people kept asking me what happened to Adelaide after the first book, so I always knew she was going to come back and do something." In addition, the author says, he "wanted to write about Central Europe, and about the landscape of Prague in particular, on which I based my city in *The Tin Princess.* And I thought it would be nice to do a book which gave Jim a bit of a bigger part, because I put him on the sidelines in *The Tiger in the Well.*"

When not in the midst of producing the Sally books or his contemporary YA novels, the prolific author has kept busy with an assortment of projects that have not yet made it into print in the U.S. These include an adaptation of *Aladdin* for Scholastic in England, a version of *Frankenstein* published by OUP and numerous stage adaptations of such classics as *The Three Musketeers* for the Polka Children's Theatre in Wimbledon.

A Finger in Several Pots

As a man with more than a few interests and what seems to be an endless enthusiasm for any number of literary projects, Pullman appreciates the flexibility allowed him in the world of children's books. "Children, and children's publishers, are adaptable," says Pullman. "They don't mind if I do a contemporary novel, having done some historical ones. They're quite willing to accept that. Children are less hide-bound by what they think they're going to enjoy, so they're more willing to try a different kind of book."

Currently, Pullman is working on a picture book called *The Firework Maker's Daughter* for Doubleday and—in another departure—a novel entitled *His Dark Materials,* which Pullman describes as "the first of a trilogy of what I suppose you could call science fantasies." These will be published in the U.K. by Scholastic.

Children's books, Pullman asserts, are "a fascinating field to work in because I can simultaneously be as emotionally complex as I want to—and not hold back on the language either—yet deal with feelings and states of mind that imply a kind of innocence about them which you don't get in the field of adult books, necessarily."

Still, Pullman admits that writing for adults often offers more tangible rewards. "When you write for adults," he says "more people take notice of you, and your books sell more copies, and you get written about more prominently and this sort of thing. And people take you more seriously, too. I don't want to make a big thing of this, but people do say to children's writers, `Oh, when are you going to write a proper book? When are you going to write a book that I'd be interested in reading?' And I feel like saying, `Why the hell aren't you interested in reading the books I *have* written?'"

A Passion for Storytelling

Writing—or, more precisely, storytelling—has been of central concern to Pullman for most of his life. "I used to tell [my younger brother] stories, and I used to relish the stories my grandfather told me. I loved telling ghost stories to the other kids at school. So the business of storytelling and spinning a yarn and so on was very native to me. Almost instinctive. I don't think I could have escaped it, even if I had wanted to."

Even when Pullman was working fulltime as a middle school teacher, teaching children ages nine to 13, his passion for storytelling asserted itself. "For years and years and years, when I was teaching," Pullman reminisces, "I used to make it my practice to tell every child who passed through my hands stories from the Greek myths. First term I would teach them about the gods and the heroes. Second term, I would tell, from memory, the *Iliad*—from beginning to end. And third term I would do the *Odyssey* from beginning to end. I loved being able to do it."

In fact, it was Pullman's work as a teacher that led to the publication of his first children's book. In the era "before we had this abominable national curriculum that was foisted on us a few years ago," Pullman had both the time and the inclination to put on school plays. "One of my pupils was the daughter of a publisher," the author recalls, "and she dragged her father along to one of the plays. He wrote to me and said he had enjoyed it and if I was ever thinking of writing a children's book to let them have it and so on. And so I did, and they published it."

The name of the book was **Count Karlstein.** "It's had several incarnations and it's now in sort of picture book, comic-strip form," Pullman explains. "That was the first one, and then I wrote **The Ruby in the Smoke** and found my voice, I suppose you could say, and haven't looked back since." Several years later Pullman's "satire on fashions," entitled **How to Be Cool,** was bought by a television company and made into a TV show. "I got enough money for that to enable me to make the break. So I thought, well, this is the moment when I'm going to step off the treadmill." Pullman reduced his teaching load to two days a week at Westminster College (where he teaches a course called "The Traditional Tale") and devoted himself to writing.

Though in the States all of Pullman's books are published by Knopf, in England the author has several publishers, including Doubleday, Puffin, Macmillan, Scholastic and Oxford University Press, "who tend to publish different parts of me." This situation seems to suit Pullman just fine. As he mischievously explains, "I've got a big sort of empire here, with whole cadres of publishers. I like that, because I get taken out more times to lunch than I would with just one publisher," he jokes. "And also because, well, I like editors, actually. I like publishing, I like to hear the gossip, and I like to see who's moved from where to where and what's going on. And I think you see more of that if you've got a lot of publishers than if you've got just one."

Though his finished books are often filled with intricate plot twists, secret identities and other surprises, Pullman never prepares a fully developed plot summary before beginning writing. "With one of my early books I made the mistake of doing a detailed plan of events. And it just killed the book for me—I couldn't be bothered to finish it." He insists that "I have to be surprised by the words that come to the end of my pen or I feel it more of a chore—a slog—than it is." On the other hand, "I do have a pretty clear idea of the kind of place I want to get to. And I also have a pretty clear idea of how big the story is that I'm working on. If I get an idea, I know roughly whether it's a 130-page idea or a 300-page idea, or whatever."

When asked why so many of his novels feature female protagonists, Pullman replies candidly, "I haven't a clue! I certainly don't do it in order to make some political point. I'm glad to be providing strong images of female characters, because that's something I think is good to do. But I've always believed, in order to show women being strong, you don't have to show men being weak. I never felt the need to downplay my men in the Sally books."

But what does Pullman find most satisfying of all about his nearly full-time career as a weaver of stories? "The fundamental thing that I do find important and gratifying is that I simply have the time—never as much time as I would like—but I simply have the time to sit here and enjoy the company of my stories and my characters. That's an enormous pleasure, and a great privilege."

Clearly, it is a pleasure and privilege that he shares most generously with his readers.

Geoff Fox with Philip Pullman

SOURCE: An interview with Philip Pullman, in *Books for Keeps,* No. 102, January, 1997, pp. 12-3.

The eight-year-old Philip Pullman was enjoying 'a sort of Jennings life, you know' at his prep school near Norwich. Then, 'one day, a master called Mr Glegg, whom I liked because he was a kind man, opened a book and began to read. It was *The Ancient Mariner,* and he read it from start to finish. Fifteen of us listened spellbound by this extraordinary thing. It gripped me like nothing I'd ever heard before.'

There is something of the storytelling Mariner about Philip Pullman himself. Readers of his Carnegie medal winner, **Northern Lights,** are fixed by its glittering power; they *must* hear the story out. Those desperate for more news of his parallel worlds will be relieved to know that Philip's wife Jude (always his first reader) took the manuscript of Book 2 of the trilogy upstairs at 4 o'clock one September afternoon and finished the last sheet at 1.00 in the morning. Meanwhile, the expectant author paced about downstairs.

Eight was a good age for Philip. He was living at his grandparents' home, a Norfolk rectory, whilst his father was serving in the RAF in Kenya. His grandfather was 'the most important influence in my life, I'm certain'. A country drive in his old Ford Popular was an adventure into stories: "Now this stream—that's called Laughing Water . . . This road we're on—the Romans tramped along here . . . and you see that old tree over there, well that's why they call this The Trail of The Lonesome Pine." Bible stories mingled with tales told by murderers whose last hours before the scaffold grandfather had shared as chaplain to Norwich Jail. He was very much the Victorian head of the household—yet he was also a playful man and, occasionally, a source of unintended humour: 'he dropped a box of fireworks in the hall one Bonfire Night and struck a match to find them.' Above all, though, a man 'in whose presence you *wanted* to be good.'

Pullman is unashamedly interested in people being good, though not in the moralistic fashion of C S Lewis, a writer he finds 'distasteful', sanctimonious even. The goodness which excites him is more complex, more ambiguous. It lies at the core of *Northern Lights:*

'The trilogy is my most coherent and thought-out statement of where I am, religiously, morally, and philosophically. And it's probably the right time of my life to do it . . . What I try to do is to show people behaving well in difficult circumstances. So there isn't an overt "Do this and you'll be saved and go to heaven", but just a model that somebody could call on if they were ever in a difficult situation.'

The title of the trilogy, **"His Dark Materials,"** is drawn from Milton's *Paradise Lost,* a powerful element in the genesis of the work. Pullman's 'argument' also is The Fall—in his view, a fortunate fall (`the best thing that could have happened to us'). Before the trilogy is played out, the heroine Lyra must herself survive long enough to fall, to acquire self-awareness; only then can she win through, with study and discipline, to the redemption of a wiser state of grace. The wicked characters are not wholly evil; they have the attractiveness which Milton could not avoid giving his Satan. The alluring Mrs Coulter may be a close relative of Cruella de Vil, or the Queen in *Snow White,* but she is the more mesmeric in that her malevolence is relieved by moments of fierce love; she does, after all, save her daughter Lyra.

Pullman sometimes sees himself as much the servant of his characters as their creator. They develop lives of their own, and may insist on behaving in ways he had not envisaged ('you fight over it'). In all his novels, individual voices come talking, laughing, arguing animatedly from the page. Some of these voices were first heard in plays written when he was teaching in an Oxford middle school. 'I was a rotten teacher,' he reflects. 'Once in a while, I was brilliant—usually outside the classroom but not a *reliable* teacher.' You would not forget him, though, if you had been in one of those plays or heard him retelling *The Odyssey* or *The Iliad.*

Pullman's conversation is relaxed and ruminative, but charged by an enquiring and excited confidence to push ideas to conclusions. He knew his own mind well enough, as a sixth former, to decide he was going to Oxford—the first person to do so from his school, Ysgol Ardudwy, Harlech, and from a family with no great interest in the Arts.

That searching mind seems always to have been matched by a disciplined determination. He knew he wanted to write even when he was at school, and he has steadily written his three pages a day through a series of jobs he did after university, through all his 23 years of teaching in school and at Westminster College, and within a busy family life alongside a working wife (Jude is a clinical hypnotherapist), two sons, an amiable dog, a somnolent cat and a nimble caged finch in a house crammed

with books and pictures. In his twenties, he would even nip out at lunch time from his job at Moss Bros to write in St Paul's churchyard—poetry usually. At school, he had written an epic in heroic couplets, but over his sandwiches on the park bench he would only have time to knock out a rapid rondeau or two. From these early exercises, he feels he learned a sensitivity to the rhythms of prose as well as verse:

'It's the sound and the taste of words that give them their savour as much as what they mean . . . it's like Mr Glegg and *The Ancient Mariner,* you just have to let the splendour and the mystery have some effect.'

Pullman began a novel the morning after he finished Finals at Oxford. He had loved the undergraduate life of the mid-sixties, and thought vaguely of becoming a singer-songwriter and maybe growing up to be Bob Dylan, or at least Donovan. His course, however, had not given him much ('I read widely but not well'). He had been absorbed by John Cowper Powys, but he also read popular literature—thrillers especially. 'I've never been sniffy about that, ever since I read *The Eagle* and *Biggles;* and I loved *Dick Barton* and do you remember *Quatermass and the Pit?* I've always relished a good yarn.' Within minutes of starting that first novel, he had collided with the problem of point-of-view. Where is the writer telling from, where is the reader placed? And, he thought, 'Why wasn't I taught this? I've just done an English degree and I haven't learnt to write at all.'

He is a great reader himself—and a painstaking reviewer. He makes frequent references to contemporary novels, to the satisfying structure of the six volumes of Proust he read last year, to other children's writers. He especially admires Jan Mark and Anne Fine ('They can do so much with two or three characters in a simple setting—if I were a better writer, I could do that') and the uncompromising intelligence and range of Peter Dickinson.

His own range perhaps exceeds that of any other contemporary writer for children. There are the two gothic graphic novels, **Count Karlstein** and **Spring-Heeled Jack;** the adventures of The New Cut Gang around the streets of Lambeth—a kind of late nineteenth-century version of *Just William* with a dash of Damon Runyon (of *Guys and Dolls* fame)—these must be wonderful books to read aloud to top juniors; so much action, comedy, so many escapades—and so many voices. Victorian times have been fruitful for him. The quartet which first charted the adventures of young Sally Lockhart in **The Ruby in the Smoke** races down some of the meanest of London's streets and ends up in the tiny European kingdom of Razkavia in **The Tin Princess.** Along the way, without a hint of the didactic, the stories have embraced a woman's fight for a career in a man's world, the opium trade, the struggles of immigrant Jews in the East End—and we have met some of the most evil of double dyed villains outside Conan Doyle and the Penny Dreadfuls, and some of the chirpiest cockneys since The Artful Dodger. He stays true to what is possible historically; his research takes him far enough to free, but not to constrict, his imagination.

In his most recent book, the ingeniously crafted *Clockwork,* one narrative slides into another with enough metafictional games to satisfy the most post of post-modernists. There is a nice irony in this, for in his Carnegie acceptance speech in July 1996, Pullman launched a considered attack on contemporary British 'adult novelists' who seem embarrassed by the notion of telling good stories. ('If you were so self-conscious when you told a children's story, you'd lose the reader.') His assault hit a nerve and the headlines and leader columns of the broadsheets where, for the most part, the Press cheered him on.

That controversy was about structure as much as anything else—it is the architecture of a novel which fascinates and challenges Philip Pullman. He often drives his plots forward with three or four reins together in his hands. He will not write down to his readers. If he has anyone in mind as he writes, it is probably his own younger self, so there will be no compromise on language, or subject matter. If there is a need for a horrific death, we shall have it—and likewise the vulnerability of adolescent lovemaking in *The White Mercedes,* one of his two Young Adult novels. His readers need to match his quick intelligence, and to love roving here and there about an adventure—he sometimes leaves them hanging over a couple of cliffs simultaneously.

Driving to the station, we talk of how fictions begin. One of the things you learn to recognise, Pullman thinks, is the *scale* of a possible narrative. 'That man digging his garden,' he points, 'why's he wearing a suit? Probably up to no good. He's not a novel, he's a short story . . . '

Rayma Turton

SOURCE: A review of *Northern Lights* and *The Subtle Knife,* in *Magpies,* Vol. 13, No. 2, May, 1998, p. 41.

Philip Pullman's acceptance speech for the 1996 Carnegie Medal for his book, *Northern Lights,* was unusually widely reported for a children's book award. Why? I suppose because it was contentious. Pullman argued that *only in children's literature is the story taken seriously . . .* and that *In adult literary fiction, stories are there on sufferance. Children know they need* [stories] *and go for them with a passion, but all of us adults need them too. All of us, that is except those limp and jaded people who think they're too grown-up to need them. Northern Lights* also won the Guardian Children's Fiction Award, the Smarties Award and the prize for Children's Book of the Year at the British Book Awards. It is marketed in America as an adult book.

Now the second volume of "His Dark Materials" trilogy, *The Subtle Knife* has been published and Pullman has not wavered from his concept of what a story should be. In his Patrick Hardy lecture in 1997 he said:

> *Now if a story is a path, then to follow it you have to ignore quite ruthlessly all the things that tempt you away from it. Your business as a storyteller is with the path, not the wood.*

Northern Lights was remarkable for the driving force of the story and its adherence to the path. Woods abound on the periphery of the story: actual woods, actual towns, wintery landscapes of a world parallel to our own, fractured but recognisable by the reader. There are woods too of philosophical and moral dimensions. These woods, real and philosophical, anchor the story and give it its reality as well as its magic. But the author never loses himself in them. The protagonist of his story, Lyra, with her strange but strong sense of 'rightness' never wanders from her search to rescue her lost playmate, and the people she meets and drags into her quest are equally focussed on the destruction of those people in the northern lands who are conducting such inhuman experiments on children and their daemons. It is a great evil made universal in that whilst its physical aspects could only happen in Lyra's world, the implications resonate in our own.

And indeed the second part of the trilogy *The Subtle Knife* begins in our world. Protecting his mentally fragile mother, twelve-year-old Will accidentally kills one of her persecutors and in his flight from justice enters into another world. It is the same world that Lyra has crossed over into at the end of *Northern Lights.* Also into this world of Cittàgazze have come those that love and wish to protect her, and those that fear what she may become and wish to destroy her. Will and Lyra meet and together stumble on their way to find both the missing father Will has never known and Lyra's enigmatic and until the end of the first book undeclared father. The one father, like a prophet, preparing the way, the other central to a story that has begun to take on epic proportions. Petty scraps occur and stirring battles are fought. New allies enter onto the stage and old enemies persist. Heroes are made and human nature makes mistakes. At the end of the book we are poised on the edge of great events.

Northern Lights hinted that this was more than an exceptionally well crafted good read. *The Subtle Knife* confirms that we are in the middle of an epic of a *magnificent invention* and of a moral dimension that will sweep up readers, carrying them on to an ending which is still yet far from clear. Pullman has said that the story was inspired by Milton's *Paradise Lost.* The angels have appeared in *The Subtle Knife* and as behoves angels they are beyond the comprehension of man. Not beyond our comprehension is the universality of the story of the fight between good and evil nor our understanding that only a master storyteller can convincingly tackle such a majestic theme. Pullman is that storyteller and I for one cannot wait to see the resolution of **"His Dark Materials."**

A small tip. Even if you read and enjoyed *Northern Lights,* reread it before starting *The Subtle Knife.* I read the second book a year after I had read *Northern Lights* and although I enjoyed *The Subtle Knife* as a stand-alone I wasn't as spell-bound as I was after I went back and read both one after the other. And don't waver in your determination to buy each book of the trilogy as it becomes available.

TITLE COMMENTARY

THE RUBY IN THE SMOKE (1985; U.S. edition, 1987)

Publishers Weekly

SOURCE: A review of *The Ruby in the Smoke,* in *Publishers Weekly,* Vol. 231, No. 3, January 23, 1987, p. 73.

Pullman's Victorian melodrama boasts a sufficiency of mystery, murder and hair-breadth escapes involving a big cast of honest and ignoble types. "On a cold, fretful afternoon in early October 1872," the story begins, young Sally Lockhart is in London where she tries to find out the meaning of "the Seven Blessings." The phrase appears in a message from her recently deceased father, drowned in the South China Sea. When a colleague of her father hears the words, he dies instantly of a heart attack. That event marks the start of crises that go on with no let-up in the colorful Dickensian tale. Sally's legacy, supposedly a fantastic ruby, is nowhere to be found. A gang of cutthroats pursue the girl and her loyal allies, as the story sweeps on to a resounding close.

Kirkus Reviews

SOURCE: A review of *The Ruby in the Smoke,* in *Kirkus Reviews,* Vol. LV, No. 3, February 1, 1987, p. 229.

Set in 19th-century London, an echo of Collins' *Moonstone*—an orphaned 16-year-old unravels the mystery of her heritage and tracks down a fabulous Indian ruby, which has left murder and mayhem in its wake.

Sally Lockhart is a competent, self-reliant heroine. She walks out on the oppressive relative who's been housing her, gets her lawyer to rearrange her investments to raise her meager income by 20 percent, and finds a new home and job with an attractive, talented, but unbusinesslike young photographer and his sister, using her precocious business acumen to rescue their floundering finances. Meanwhile, trying to decipher messages from her father, recently lost at sea in the Far East, she encounters mysterious Mr. Marchbanks, who gives her a long document, which is stolen before she can read it, and also various unsavory denizens of the East End, including villainous Mrs. Holland, who has trapped Matthew Bedwell, messenger from Lockhart, by his addiction to opium. A whiff of opium smoke induces a vivid repetition of Sally's recurring nightmare, convincing her that it is actually memory; later, she deliberately breathes opium fumes in order to retrieve further pieces of the puzzle. After kidnappings and escapes, several murders, the finding and losing of the ruby and finding of a more moderate but useful inheritance hidden by Lockhart, everything is sorted out with surprisingly few loose ends, given the plot's many threads.

An entertaining yarn, enlivened by humor and vivid characters, with the added historical interest of early photography and the evils of the opium trade. Sure to please readers of historical romances.

Brooke L. Dillon

SOURCE: A review of *The Ruby in the Smoke,* in *Voice of Youth Advocates,* Vol. 10, No. 4, October, 1987, p. 206.

Alone in the world, but fiercely independent, 16 year old Sally Lockhart would not rest until she discovered why she had been told to beware of the "Seven Blessings" in the strange note she had received from Singapore. Recently orphaned by her father's death at sea, she marches into his business offices to demand an explanation, but is shocked when her questions lead to the fainting and death of her father's employee. Before the mystery is solved, Sally will find herself embroiled in an intrigue of murder, conspiracy, Chinese gangs, a ruby with almost hypnotic powers, opium, and the eventual discovery that her "father" was not her natural father. With the aid of her friends Rosa and Jim and her eventual boyfriend, Frederick, Sally fights the evil power of Mrs. Holland and also helps Rosa and Frederick establish a successful business in stereographs. She forces herself to face the terrifying "Nightmare" she has endured since childhood by smoking opium and reliving the experience which caused the nightmare.

Set in England in 1872 and by a British author, **The Ruby in the Smoke** is one of those all-too-few British novels which should appeal just as greatly to American teens as it does to British teens. Pullman uses a cliffhanger at the end of each chapter to keep readers enthralled in this fast-paced, intricate, and suspenseful novel. Sally's complex characterization as a resourceful, yet occasionally unsure, young woman, makes her both likable and memorable. The incident with the opium smoking is acceptable within the context of the novel, and the discussion of the British government's opium trade makes the novel appropriate as Social Studies supplemental reading. The beautifully crafted writing and the fact that Pullman respects his teenaged audience enough to treat them to a complex, interwoven plot will certainly make readers anxious for the upcoming sequel, **The Shadow on the Plate,** and the third novel of the trilogy, currently underway.

SPRING-HEELED JACK: A STORY OF BRAVERY AND EVIL (1989; U.S. edition, 1991)

Publishers Weekly

SOURCE: A review of *Spring-Heeled Jack: A Story of Bravery and Evil,* in *Publishers Weekly,* Vol. 238, No. 29, July 5, 1991, p. 66.

In Victorian London three children escape from the Cawn-Plaster Memorial Orphanage—a terrible place where "the porridge was as thin as the blankets, and as cold as the smiles on the guardians' faces"—only to fall into the clutches of evil villain Mack the Knife. Part narrative, part comic strip, Pullman's waggish, innovative story of this courageous trio is sure to engage even the most reluctant reader. The plot is chockablock with all the impossible coincidences, stereotypes and "meanwhile, back at the ranch" clichés of a classic spoof. The pun-filled humor is zany, even corny; the language upbeat. As they root for Spring-Heeled Jack, a superhero who bounds along in knee-high boots, readers will enjoy the underlying comedy of his appearance and actions. [David] Mostyn's black-and-white cartoon illustrations highlight the farcical elements of the text without obscuring the sharp intelligence that makes this story so successful.

Roger Sutton

SOURCE: A review of *Spring-Heeled Jack: A Story of Bravery and Evil,* in *The Bulletin of the Center for Children's Books,* Vol. 45, No. 2, October, 1991, pp. 46-7.

In a format that combines crisply inked cartoons with narrative text, Pullman and Mostyn both spoof and enjoy the conventions of Victorian melodrama. Rose, Lily, and Ned have been imprisoned in an orphanage "where the porridge was as thin as the blankets" since their father disappeared at sea and their mother died. They run away, intending to seek passage on a ship to America, but are soon in the clutches of Mack the Knife and his gang. Spring-Heeled Jack, who dresses like the devil and has springs in his shoes to help him leap, comes to the rescue: "I'm on your side, my dear! I'm good! I catch villains! I avenge wrongs. I do all kinds of stuff." Good does triumph, but not before a satisfyingly complicated sequence of events and apparent reversals of fortune. The humor is unsubtle and occasionally labored, but readers will enjoy its excesses as much as they will appreciate the novelties of the format—and the footnotes: "3. Nob him on the canister: whack him on the head."

John Peters

SOURCE: A review of *Spring-Heeled Jack: A Story of Bravery and Evil,* in *School Library Journal,* Vol. 37, No. 12, December, 1991, pp. 117-18.

The author of **Ruby in the Smoke** again pulls readers back to Victorian London for a tale of dark deeds and bright courage, aimed this time at a younger audience. Rose, Lily, and little Ned escape the Alderman Cawn-Plaster Memorial Orphanage one night, hoping to board ship and make a new life in America—but they don't reckon on running into cutthroat Mack the Knife and his evil band, or being so hotly pursued by the orphanage's nefarious supervisors, Gasket and Killjoy. With help from a good-hearted sailor, a small but fierce stray dog, and especially from Spring-Heeled Jack, a menacing caped figure in tights, top hat, and trick shoes that let him jump

over tall buildings in a single bound, the brave children win their way to safety, and even find—O Joy!—their long-lost father. Pullman's prose is appropriately melodramatic, and breaks frequently into *Mad Magazine*-style cartoon panels, with dialogue in square balloons and small creatures at the edges making asides. The author and illustrator obviously had great fun with this funny, action-packed send-up, and so will readers.

THE TIGER IN THE WELL (1990)

Barbara Hutcheson

SOURCE: A review of *The Tiger in the Well,* in *School Library Journal,* Vol. 36, No. 9, September, 1990, p. 256.

Pullman is fast becoming a modern-day Charles Dickens for young adults. The setting (Victorian London) is the same; the strong eye for characters large and small is there, as are the sometimes brooding atmosphere, the social conscience, the ability to spin plot within plot against a large landscape, and the occasional editorial comment. These last are not intrusive; the author's voice is that of a friend, filling in details in a story he has witnessed, not wanting readers to miss a thing. Sally Lockhart, first met in **Ruby in the Smoke** (1987) and **Shadow in the North** (1988), is now a young woman, left alone with a toddler since the death of her lover, Frederick Garland. Nothing prepares her for the shock of receiving a summons from a man she has never even heard of, suing her for divorce and the custody of her beloved Harriet. Two other figures emerge: Daniel Goldberg, a Jewish slum radical with a violent past; and the ironically titled Tzaddik (saint), who preys on helpless European Jewish immigrants. **The Tiger in the Well** is the story of their converging paths, as Sally struggles against the net closing around her and seeks to find out who is persecuting her and why. The writing style is lively and direct, and there's lots of action. While Sally's story is for mature readers, it is never sordid or sensational. This is a suspense novel with a conscience, and a most enjoyable one.

Roger Sutton

SOURCE: A review of *The Tiger in the Well,* in *The Bulletin of the Center for Children's Books,* Vol. 44, No. 2, October, 1990, p. 43.

"You know what your memory's for? It's for getting things to look right when you make them up." Sally Lockhart (first introduced in **The Ruby in the Smoke,** is driven to question her own memory when she receives a court summons informing her she is being sued for divorce by Arthur Parrish. Sally has never met Parrish, but that certainly is her name, in her handwriting, in the marriage registry at Southam Rectory. Parrish wants custody of Sally's daughter Harriett, now two, whose impending arrival was announced at the end of **Shadow in the North.** While occasionally distracted by a complicated subplot involving Jewish criminals and socialists and Sally's growing social conscience, this third Sally Lockhart story is suspenseful and menacing, its terrors closer to home than the exotic threats posed by Ah Ling and Axel Bellman in the previous books. The horror and effectiveness of Parrish's demand for Harriett are wound tighter as Sally takes her daughter all around London in futile attempts to protect her. When Sally eventually discovers that Mr. Parrish is in fact working for someone else, murky half-remembrances, "like a great slow fish moving a fin" begin to tell her the nature of the beast. As always, Pullman demonstrates too much integrity to resort to pastiche or melodrama; his vision of Victorian London is far from a jolly good time.

Publishers Weekly

SOURCE: A review of *The Tiger in the Well,* in *Publishers Weekly,* Vol. 237, No. 41, October 12, 1990, pp. 65-6.

This sequel to **The Ruby in the Smoke** and **The Shadow in the North** combines heart-thumping suspense, a thorough-going examination of Victorian London's underclass, a lively gang of heroes and villains and a mystery sinister enough to leave readers filled with anxiety. An unknown evildoer has made elaborate plans to steal Sally Lockhart's life away from her—by usurping her home, her business, her daughter Harriet and, finally, her sanity. Elsewhere in London, Jewish immigrants who have fled the Russian pogroms are being systematically fleeced. Daniel Goldberg, a socialist journalist, believes that the evil genius behind these brutal acts is a shadowy figure known as the Tzaddik. Rendered homeless and hounded through London's slums, Sally endures a plight that in many ways mirrors the mistreatment of the Jews. Aided by Goldberg and a handful of the city's toughest gangsters, the dauntless heroine triumphs over this malevolence. Astute readers are likely to figure out the Tzaddik's identity long before Sally does—a bit of predictability that is at odds with Pullman's otherwise tight plotting. On the whole, however, this thought-provoking romp is as rich and captivating as a modern-day Dickens novel.

Joanne Johnson

SOURCE: A review of *The Tiger in the Well,* in *Voice of Youth Advocates,* Vol. 13, No. 5, December, 1990, p. 288.

Life for Sally Lockhart, female financier and sometime detective, is going well in Victoria's England. She has financial security; friends; a secure home; and Harriet, her two year old daughter. That is, until a fateful morning in 1881 when she finds herself sued for divorce by a man named Arthur Parrish. Nothing unusual you say, but wait. Sally has never been married nor has she ever heard of this man Parrish, who claims to be her husband. British law will allow him not only to divorce her but to take her property and her child. Sally's only hope is to prove that the marriage never occurred. Her lawyers believe she does

not have a chance, and they prove right. After her day in court, Sally disappears with Harriet into the underground of the London Jewish ghetto. She must prove herself innocent, and unmarried. The only way to do so is to learn who it is who wants to destroy her so completely.

As in his two previous books in the series (**Ruby in the Smoke** and **Shadow in the North** Pullman has recreated 19th century London in good detail. His portrayal of the chauvinism rampant in British law during that time is a lesson to all. As a mystery, however, this book falls short. The perpetrator is known within the first 100 pages. However, many will keep reading to learn how or if Sally will be able to solve the mystery. This book will go where you have large numbers of Victoria Holt and Phyllis Whitney fans.

Ann A. Flowers

SOURCE: A review of *The Tiger in the Well,* in *The Horn Book Magazine,* Vol. LXVII, No. 2, March-April, 1991, p. 207.

In the third volume about Sally Lockhart, the heroine of **The Ruby in the Smoke** and **The Shadow in the North,** Sally has set up a successful career as a financial adviser and has made a comfortable life for herself and her two-year-old daughter, Harriet, who was born out of wedlock. But a net of incomprehensible circumstances begins to surround Sally: she is confronted with seemingly legal proof of her marriage to a stranger and is threatened with the loss of her home, her financial resources, and her child. In order to save her child and in an attempt to discover the motive behind her inexplicable situation, Sally takes Harriet and flees for shelter in the underworld of Victorian London. There her enemies still pursue her, but she finds help in unexpected quarters, most notably from a dedicated social worker, several Jewish immigrants, and Daniel Goldberg, a formidable political activist. Sally herself undertakes the most harrowing task of all: to insinuate herself into the household of the Tzaddik, a monstrously evil character whom Sally comes to believe is the mastermind behind the plot against her. The suspense is terrific, with the reader aware of Harriet's horrible fate if she falls into the Tzaddik's hands and with the custody of Harriet swaying back and forth between the two camps. The story, carried by Sally's independent, resolute character and an exceedingly clever, complex plot, works its way through scenes of ever-increasing crisis and excitement to a stunning conclusion.

Marcus Crouch

SOURCE: A review of *The Tiger in the Well,* in *The Junior Bookshelf,* Vol. 55, No. 3, June, 1991, p. 127.

This completes a trilogy of which the earlier volumes were **Ruby in the Smoke** and **The Shadow in the North.** Having found these books, although highly readable, unconvincing and rich in unintentional humour, I turned to the conclusion of the story with no great hopes. How wrong I was. The saga of Sally Lockhart, Victorian, unmarried mother and business tycoon, ends on a high note. Here violent action and strong emotion are held together with social significance. Not for the first time in the sequence, but with greater relevance, the name of Dickens comes to mind.

Deserted for the time being by her faithful men friends (they are exploring in South America) Sally pursues her business and enjoys her baby in great contentment. Then suddenly her world falls apart. An unknown enemy is determined to destroy her. Why? To find the answer to this question Sally goes to ground amid the squalor and misery of the East End and, in doing so, discovers that her life has so far been based on false values. In a cataclysmic climax, when everything literally falls around her ears, Sally recognises that she has been seeking the wrong enemy. It is not the evil Tzaddik (or Ah Ling) who deserves her opposition but the greed and indifference which have created the London slums. Several admirable people have contributed to her enlightenment, including the splendid Miss Robbins and Doctor Turner of the Spitalfields Social Mission and Goldberg, middle-aged Jew, tough, scruffy, with a sure instinct for finding trouble, and 'the only man in the world who. . . . ' With such a one to hand 'We don't let anyone be bad to us again', says Sally. 'Not bloody likely,' says baby Harriet, who has learnt a great deal from her harrowing experiences.

Like the earlier books *The Tiger in the Well* is compulsively readable. Unlike them the strong action runs parallel with sound social observation. Exploitation, racial violence, police corruption, all these are shown as the product of the spirit of the age, not its causes. There is much to think about while one enjoys the pace of the narrative and the colourful characters. Perhaps Mr. Pullman works too hard at his atmospheric descriptions and underlines a little crudely the villainy of his more wicked characters. But I enjoyed the downfall of the smooth Mr. Parrish—two chamberpots on the head in one day! Splendid.

Margery Fisher

SOURCE: A review of *The Tiger in the Well*, in *Growing Point*, Vol. 30, No. 2, July, 1991, pp. 5543-44.

The plots of adventure are few but infinitely variable. Conflict and confrontation, journeys with a heroic purpose, a search for a missing object, for a person, for truth and justice—with any of these ancient and well-tried themes, writers have all the scope in the world to create undiscovered places, unfamiliar characters, surprising twists of action and what the reader always hopes for, an individual voice. Boldness is all. If I say *The Tiger in the Well* is old-fashioned, it is to be understood that this is praise, not criticism. This final instalment of the fortunes of Sally Lockhart in late Victorian years (following *The Ruby in the Smoke* and *The Shadow in the North*) has the amplitude and the abounding life of a Dickens novel; it has the power to keep us shifting uneasily on our seats

as we wait to see what could possibly happen next, a power far too rare nowadays. The character of Sally Lockhart fits a stereotype of our times, as a single woman bringing up a two-year-old daughter and working in a man's world of business and finance, but the scope of her activities is precisely aligned to the year 1881 and the London in which she hides and contrives, with its slums and soup-kitchens, with a vicious anti-semitic campaign opposed by dispersed but active socialist groups, is as precisely in period as the hansom cabs, servant hierarchies and street urchins which substantiate a compelling story. Sally faces her enemies resourcefully—a rent collector Mr. Parrish, a stranger to her who claims to be her estranged husband and rightful owner of her property and her baby, and the lurking, mysterious Tzaddik whose long-planned move against her has its source in her past. Supported by many friends, by her partner, another feminist, by the shabby, indomitable Dr. Turner with her compassion for the poor and by the radical Polish journalist who alone among men seems to be her equal intellectually and emotionally, she triumphs most of all through her own courage, quick wits and tenacity. Her flight from the law and from her persecutors (the identity of one of them providing a sinister puzzle almost to the end) takes us into the seamier streets of Victorian London. In a final horrific scene Sally and the Tzaddik go down together in a welter of filthy water after the monstrous oppressor's luxurious house has collapsed from underground flooding. There is no shortage of sensation nor of surprise in this absorbing, capacious tale of danger and endeavour.

THE BROKEN BRIDGE (1990; U.S. edition, 1992)

D. A. Young

SOURCE: A review of *The Broken Bridge*, in *The Junior Bookshelf*, Vol. 55, No. 3, June, 1991, pp. 126-27.

Ginny is sixteen, black, with what Social Workers might refer to as certain features of instability in her family life. She lives with her father with whom she has a good relationship despite his tendency to take up with girl-friends from time to time. Ginny learns to accept the presence of his 'breakfast ladies' as she thinks of them without rancour. Ginny's first boy-friend turns out to be gay. The news that Robert, a brother about whom she knew nothing, was coming to join the household led to a series of revelations which might have come straight from the psychotherapist's case book.

It seems that Tony Howard, Ginny's father, had his spirit quite broken as a child. He grew up a frightened boy desperately trying to love the mother who was destroying him. He was forced into marriage with Janet the only daughter of the close friends of his parents. His affair with Ginny's mother who returned to her native Haiti after leaving her child in the care of nuns was short-lasting. In the search for her past Ginny calls on her grandparents and comes face to face with her mother, not as she had always thought dead, but very much alive, and attending a successful exhibition of her latest paintings. It is a talent that Ginny has inherited and it is that talent which is her stay and comfort when the rest of her world is collapsing around her.

The convoluted plot is spiced with Haitian Voodoo and the mystery of the motor-car accident on the broken bridge. There are other richly drawn characters who live with their own secret lives of quiet desperation. Philip Pullman has done for modern society something of the service Dickens performed for his own. It is about a 16 year old girl but she moves in a very adult world. In a conversation with her best friend Rhiannon they ponder on one of life's mysteries.

> 'He's too nice. He's kind. The trouble with kind people is they're not sexy.'
>
> 'Sexy people couldn't care less if they were kind or not, but all kind people wish they were sexy. But you are either one or the other.'
>
> 'I bet some people are both.'
>
> 'Impossible. It's tragic. Life's a tragedy, see.'

The story ends on an upbeat. Maybe you could have a boyfriend and be an artist! Anything was possible really. Even being kind as well as sexy.

Stephanie Zvirin

SOURCE: A review of *The Broken Bridge,* in *Booklist,* Vol. 88, No. 12, February 15, 1992, pp. 1099, 1102.

This is an intriguing novel, though certainly not an easy one to follow. Mixed-race Ginny, 16, is astonished to discover that she is illegitimate and that her father has another child, a legitimate son, just Ginny's age, who will be coming to live with her and her dad. Unable to get her dad to talk much about her own mother, whom she'd been told is dead, or about these strange developments, Ginny determines to find out the facts for herself. Her search leads her to a trendy art gallery, to the home of a sleazy con man, and finally to her estranged grandparents' home, where an even greater shock awaits her. Unlike Pullman's *Ruby in the Smoke,* this is a contemporary novel, set in present-day Wales and with fewer atmospheric touches. It's more puzzle than mystery in the strict sense, evolving slowly at first, then building in pace as Ginny approaches the truth about her heritage and about her own character. The weird fantasy Ginny spins about a jacket owned by a local con man is not credibly integrated into the plot, and Ginny's flashback memories, which head a few chapters, add little to the whole. Yet readers will be swept into the vortex of curious events, and though they won't come away completely clear about what occurs, they'll come away satisfied.

Barbara Hutcheson

SOURCE: A review of *The Broken Bridge,* in *School Library Journal,* Vol. 38, No. 3, March, 1992, p. 259.

Ginny, 16, has always felt somewhat an outsider in her Welsh village. Her Haitian mother is dead, but Ginny has always derived security in her relationship with her English father, and in the creative talent inherited from her artist mother. Then she discovers she has a white half-brother who is about to join the family; suddenly half-remembered scenes from her childhood begin to take on meaning. Step by step Ginny begins to peel back the mystery of her life, drawing on hitherto untapped resources of courage and resilience to raise the questions that need to be asked, and then to search out the answers, however painful that process may be. Her past and present are filled with "broken bridges" needing repair or rebuilding before she can cross them and move on with her life. As Ginny herself comments, nothing is what it seems, whether memory, event, or character. Haitian cultural details, and the influences of art in Ginny's life are clearly but unobstructively incorporated. Pullman moves as comfortably in this contemporary small town setting as he did in Victorian London in his previous novels, without sacrificing richness of plot or character. Unfortunately, the usual absurdity of translating British into American English is also maintained, while phrases in French and Welsh have been retained. The unusual setting; plot twists; and touches of pathos, humor, contemporary social concerns, and even voodoo, combine to make this an original treatment of concerns familiar to teenage readers—Who am I? How do I fit in?

Kirkus Reviews

SOURCE: A review of *The Broken Bridge,* in *Kirkus Reviews,* Vol. LX, No. 6, March 15, 1992, p. 397.

Ginny's peaceful life in a Welsh village with father Tony is disrupted when it's revealed that she has an older half brother, Robert, also 16. Her mother, she's been told, was a Haitian artist who died soon after her birth; now Ginny also learns that *Robert's* recently deceased mother—not hers—was Tony's wife, a discovery that casts doubt on the little Tony has said about her origins. Already struggling for self-identity as a teenager, a gifted artist, and almost the only dark-skinned person she knows, Ginny is drawn into a search for a past now gradually revealed as far more convoluted than she imagined, with enough woe to explain Tony's reticence and enough surprises to keep readers guessing.

Master storyteller Pullman provides an engrossing plot and a richly varied cast, including Robert (who becomes an unexpected ally); some painfully believable uptight grandparents; and a thug called Joe Chicago, who plays an important role in resolving the image of the broken bridge—a local site where a tragic misadventure is said to have taken place. Ginny is less concerned with being black than with realizing herself as an artist; as such, she is sharply realized, an intelligent and creative observer. She's also committed to finding a personal balance between qualities a friend polarizes as "sexy" (charismatic and original) and "kind" (but often boring); in the end, she survives the many dramatic revelations with the best of both. Almost impossible to put down.

Nancy Vasilakis

SOURCE: A review of *The Broken Bridge*, in *The Horn Book Magazine*, Vol. LXVIII, No. 2, March-April, 1992, p. 211.

The child of a black Haitian artist and a white British father, Ginny Howard, at sixteen, is faced with a number of nagging questions about her background. She and her father have always been a close twosome; her mother, she was told, died when Ginny was an infant. Now, however, she hears rumors that her father once spent time in jail, and when she questions him about their family history, he is curiously reluctant to discuss much with her. Skillfully manipulating the conventions of the mystery and the problem novel, Pullman constructs a story of a girl who comes of age by uncovering the secrets of her past. Ginny is confronted early in the novel with the disturbing news that she has a half-brother who is coming to live with them. Before she can fully accept quiet and sullen Robert as a brother, she learns that it is his mother, not hers, to whom her father was actually married, and that she is illegitimate. Unsettled by these revelations, which cut to the very core of her sense of self, she begins to question her artistic bearings as well as her mixed racial identity. The final blow comes when Ginny meets her mother, who is not dead after all, and realizes that this talented woman has no interest in establishing a relationship with her. Her father reveals his own secrets about his abused childhood, explaining much about his evasions and expanding her understanding of the complexities of the adult world. A series of flashbacks to Ginny's early childhood lends a level of credibility to each new disclosure, though the general effect is that of a protagonist set adrift by life's lurching vicissitudes rather than controlled by the novelist's sure hand. The contemporary Welsh setting is well realized, and the characters are flesh-and-blood people. An intriguing mystery that keeps the reader guessing and turning the pages until the very end.

Deborah Stevenson

SOURCE: A review of *The Broken Bridge*, in *The Bulletin of the Center for Children's Books*, Vol. 45, No. 8, April, 1992, pp. 219-20.

Ginny's mother, a Haitian artist, died when Ginny was only a week old; now sixteen, Ginny lives with her white father on the coast of Wales. Ginny is also an artist, proud of her black heritage and hoping to pick up where her mother left off: "I'm going to grow up, live, and be a painter in the way she couldn't." Ginny's certainty is shattered when her father announces that her half-brother Robert, of whom she's never before heard, will be coming to live with them, and her shock deepens when she discovers that her father had been married to Robert's mother, not hers. That's the beginning of a series of revelations, misconceptions, and eventual understandings that lead her through a dizzying summer of exploration of the past and contemplation of her own future; the turns are too numerous to list, but Ginny does learn that her mother is not dead—she disowns Ginny, however, when they meet. Pullman is an excellent writer and he evokes mood and relationships well, but there's way too much going on here: Haitian voodoo themes, the metaphor of the title (it involves a local legend about a bridge), Ginny's experience growing up black in a virtually all-white area, the abuse Ginny's father suffered as a child, and so on. Despite the lack of focus, this is still a thoughtful realistic novel, as well as an interesting change of pace from Pullman's *Ruby in the Smoke*.

THE WHITE MERCEDES (1992; US. edition, 1993)

Stephanie Nettell

SOURCE: A review of *The White Mercedes*, in *The Times Educational Supplement*, No. 3951, March 20, 1992, p. 46.

Philip Pullman is proving an unusually fertile writer, not only producing book after book, all grippingly readable, but experimenting stylistically and thematically with each. For adventurous readers it produces an anticipatory frisson of "What have we got this time?"

Well, this time (despite its sugared-almond binding and jacket) it is a brutal thriller, underpinned by equally savage psychology—a novel to make schools and libraries wary, not because teenage readers are incapable of handling its physical and spiritual violence and frank sexuality, but because some adults may be unable to cope with the thought of their doing so.

From its opening moment the suspense is agonising: "Chris Marshall met the girl he was going to kill on a warm night in early June." Surely he didn't mean that? prays the reader throughout the subsequent portrayal of an overwhelming first love. Chris is an unworldly 17-year-old, taking a holiday job while he comes to terms with his parents' separation. Fate delivers, then snatches away, sweet lovely Jenny, a too-worldly runaway haunted by her father's sexual abuse. By adroit plotting, Chris's search for Jenny collides fatally with the shady past of his employer. From his first act of white-knight heroism, Chris is forced to examine his high-principled ideals, pitting them against his own romantic obsession and a confusing world of adult weakness and vicious criminal intrigue.

The story, plainly told by an omniscient narrative voice that plots its terrifying course with Olympian detachment and more than a hint of didacticism—Chris has learned a lot about himself and a little about the world by the harshly unrelenting finish—asks its readers some serious questions while allowing them the exquisite pain of a tragic thriller.

Marcus Crouch

SOURCE: A review of *The White Mercedes,* in *The Junior Bookshelf,* Vol. 56, No. 4, August, 1992, p. 166.

After the stark passions and the massive destructiveness of his last Victorian Gothic three-decker, Philip Pullman now settles for a modern scene and smaller scale, though still big, emotions. The resulting novel makes for compulsive reading, but some readers, adolescent as well as adult, may be puzzled about the social and moral values of the story.

In spite of the strong plot—young man, young woman, gang warfare—it is the portrayal of the principal characters that matters most. It is Chris's book. Chris is seventeen, still at school but filling the summer with a holiday job helping Barry. Helping? He seems to be running the show, doing everything required of a qualified electrician and more with never a squeak out of the union men. Chris is a bit of a phenomenon, handsome, bright, strong, brave. He is also, it must be admitted, an innocent abroad in a harsh world. His is a simplistic view. Halfway through it becomes 'clear to Chris what things were good, and what things he was against because they were bad.' That is fine if he can tell the difference. He doesn't, and in that lies tragedy. He still doesn't learn from bitter experience. In a neat ironical conclusion the author shows Chris once again drawing the wrong conclusions. Alongside Chris, and in contrast, is his girlfriend, Jenny, to whom life has been particularly hard but who has come out of it clear-headed and resourceful. It does her no good in the end. I take Jenny's fate hard because she is an admirable girl who deserves a better fortune than that handed out by the author. The minor characters are well handled in their self-preoccupations.

This is an exciting story. The direct narrative is convincing. Unfortunately Mr. Pullman finds it necessary to fill the reader in with background information which tends to defuse the tension. Better perhaps to keep the reader guessing. Vivid individual scenes, including a love-session which would not have been acceptable in a young-adult novel ten years ago, do not fully compensate for questionable conclusions. Final opinion: a rather superior curate's egg.

Publishers Weekly

SOURCE: A review of *The White Mercedes,* in *Publishers Weekly,* Vol. 240, No. 15, April 12, 1993, p. 65.

The menacing darkness that lurked at the edges of Pullman's trilogy of Victorian-era thrillers comes to the fore in this contemporary tale of shattered innocence and betrayed love set in Oxford, England. From the first line—"Chris Marshall met the girl he was going to kill on a warm night in early June"—the sense of imminent evil and inexorable doom builds unrelentingly to the novel's violent, gut-wrenching climax. Naïve and well-intentioned, 17-year-old Chris has love, not murder, on his mind when he meets and later beds Jenny (described in lyric and intimate detail), who has run away from her abusive father. Indeed, it is precisely

Chris's trusting nature and sense of justice that cause the youth to be duped by a vengeful felon into causing Jenny's death—and only then because she is mistaken for someone else. Here is a modern-day Shakespearean tragedy, with star-crossed lovers separated by fate, a terrifyingly philosophical villain and assorted innocents, cads and buffoons. Its evocative narrative and throat-tightening suspense make this novel a compelling read; however, the graphic sex, moral ambiguity and somber ending make it most suitable for mature YA readers.

Kirkus Reviews

SOURCE: A review of *The White Mercedes,* in *Kirkus Reviews,* Vol. LXI, No. 10, May 15, 1993, p. 667.

Readers won't be able to turn the pages of this new thriller from the author of the "Sally Lockhart" trilogy fast enough. Oxford native Chris Marshall falls madly in love with Jenny, but after a single sexual encounter—in which they fail to exchange surnames or phone numbers—they lose each other. Wandering the streets, never quite coming face to face, each becomes involved with Barry Miller—an outwardly respectable businessman who is actually a small-time crook who turned state's evidence and has vengeful killer Edward Carson on his trail. These four spiral about each other until the savage climax—when Jenny is gunned down in a case of mistaken identity. Pullman stretches the tension agonizingly, presaging Jenny's murder in the first sentence, revealing facts to readers but concealing them from his characters, and salting the plot with ironic twists and bitter coincidences. The contrast between Jenny, who's self-aware but emotionally wrecked by an abusive father, and Chris, who has a fundamental innocence that's both strength and weakness, gives this engrossing, tragic story rate depth of feeling.

Marilyn Bannon

SOURCE: A review of *The White Mercedes,* in *Voice of Youth Advocates,* Vol. 16, No. 2, June, 1993, p. 93.

Chris Marshall seems, at the novel's outset, to be a normally abnormal teen, with divorced parents, a typical interest in electronics and his first real job. However, the author makes it very clear from the first line that Chris stands on the edge of an abyss, informing the reader that he will eventually be responsible for the death of the young girl to whom he is so instantly drawn. Thus begins the story of two lovers whose relationship seems destined to be destroyed.

Jenny, who has recently escaped an abusive family situation, lives a free existence with neither responsibilities nor commitment. She is a paradox, combining street smarts and innocence. Occasionally, as on the night they meet, she seems to run out of luck. In this case, Chris intervenes, saving her from a potentially violent encounter with a group of sophisticated thugs.

As the two begin their relationship, they attend a Shakespearean play, appropriately enough, the tragic story of

Romeo and Juliet. Their romance seems to be developing nicely when fate, no real friend to these two, intervenes to separate them in a series of unrelated coincidences. Throughout the remainder of the story they search in vain for each other, each realizing the other to be his/her true love.

They are soon caught in a knot of evil, with a man in a white Mercedes stalking Chris's boss, Barry. Unknown to Chris, Jenny has recently begun to baby-sit Barry's son and this relationship puts her very near Chris, although she doesn't realize it. Unfortunately, the same fate that causes their paths to cross puts Jenny in the sights of a killer. The combination of these and other events combine to create a climax liberally laced with suspense.

Pullman does a nice job with his characters, creating a modern day Romeo and Juliet who make the reader want to rewrite the ending and change fate. This reader found Chris's last chapter conclusions about Jenny forgiving her abusive father, slightly unrealistic. Whether Jenny might have done so, or not, does not seem to be supported one way or the other in the narrative of the previous chapters. However, this is a readable tale with a complex plot and a measure of action that adds interest to the romance and holds the reader's attention.

Val Randall

SOURCE: A review of *The White Mercedes,* in *Books for Keeps,* No. 81, July, 1993, p. 15.

This is a profoundly cruel book, impaling its central character, Chris, on a spike of manipulation, innocence and love. It's also an agonisingly well-written, one, snaring the reader in the same trap, building the horrifying sense of inevitability from the moment it begins.

Chris is unwittingly caught up in a gangland war, unsuspected in the quiet streets of his Oxford home and symbolised by the quiet menace of the white Mercedes whose driver's counterfeit identity draws him into a carefully set trap. He is led into a morass of betrayal and death in which Jenny, his girlfriend, loses her life.

The sense of tragedy is felt more keenly because the reader's belief in Chris is unquestioning and because the final sentence of the book is so unbearably poignant—to the last, Chris remains unaware of the whole sickening truth. *This* is what the National Curriculum should be putting before our youngsters—a work of undisputed and breathtaking excellence.

THE TIN PRINCESS (1994)

Roger Sutton

SOURCE: A review of *The Tin Princess,* in *The Bulletin of the Center for Children's Books,* Vol. 47, No. 6, February, 1994, pp. 199-200.

After two forays into contemporary "problem" fiction (*The Broken Bridge, The White Mercedes*), Pullman here returns to the Victorian sweep and setting of his three Sally Lockhart books. Sally makes a cameo appearance here, but the focus is on a young language tutor named Becky and on her student Adelaide, who will be remembered from *The Ruby in the Smoke* and who has married into the royal family of Razkavia, a *Mitteleuropa* hotbed of political intrigue. The plot is far too complicated both for its own good and to go into here; readers who appreciated the twists and turns of the Sally Lockhart stories, as well as their large measure of feminist heroics, will find plenty to keep them turning the pages. While Pullman appreciates the excesses of Victorian melodrama, he is never seduced by them, and the book has a dark, unsentimental core that banishes any sense of pastiche. The sophisticated writing and labyrinthine narrative make this a book for the more adult end of young adult; Pullman fans of any age shouldn't hesitate, but those new to the author will be better served by a first encounter with the more straightforward adventure of *The Ruby in the Smoke.*

Kirkus Reviews

SOURCE: A review of *The Tin Princess,* in *Kirkus Reviews,* Vol. LXII, No. 4, February 15, 1994, p. 232.

Pullman sets some of the younger characters from *The Ruby and the Smoke* (1987) and the other Sally Lockhart books center stage for another taut adventure. Adelaide, an intelligent Cockney who's now a lovely (but illiterate) young woman, has escaped a London brothel to marry Prince Rudolf of Razkavia, a small country tucked between Austria and Bismarck's Germany. In 1882, the couple returns to Razkavia, taking Becky, 16, a Razkavian political refugee who's been teaching Adelaide German and serves as interpreter, and Jim, now a detective, still smitten with Adelaide, his childhood sweetheart. After some unexpected deaths Rudolph becomes king, only to be assassinated at his coronation, whereupon Adelaide seizes her new subjects' fealty by heroically carrying a historic flag up a mountain to its traditional site. But traitors—not just the assassin—are at large. In the process of the trio's tracking them down, Pullman offers a grand series of maneuvers, calling on all their considerable wits and courage as well as the various loyalties of numerous other picturesque characters (helpfully listed at the outset). Still, though these exploits will appeal greatly to fans of Lloyd Alexander's Vesper Holly, in the end—after the puppets of realpolitik are unmasked and the power of the German chancellor and his banker and munitions-manufacturer cohorts can no longer be ignored—this is in the darker spirit of his *Westmark.* A mesmerizing yarn that delivers on its promises.

Publishers Weekly

SOURCE: A review of *The Tin Princess,* in *Publishers Weekly,* Vol. 241, No. 12, March 21, 1994, p. 73.

Fans of Sally Lockhart, heroine of the Victorian-era thrillers that concluded with *The Ruby in the Smoke,* may at first be disappointed that, as Mrs. Goldberg, Sally has only a minor role here. However, Pullman more than makes it up to his audience by introducing a marvelous heroine, plucky 16-year-old Becky, and by bringing back—in starring roles—the resourceful Jim, Sally's former assistant, and the incomparable Adelaide, who disappeared as a child in *Shadow in the North.* This action-packed romp, in plot and *mitteleuropäische* setting, is a breathtaking blend of Saturday matinee cliffhanger and Viennese light opera. Pullman throws in everything but the kitchen sink: a secret marriage, spies, bombings, Machiavellian schemes, regicide, a vengeful Spanish actress, even Otto von Bismarck and that hoariest of chestnuts, a secretly imprisoned mad prince. In less able hands, this bulging confection would burst apart, but it all works due to impeccable pacing, sly social commentary and superb characterizations. Adelaide and Jim make an even more electrifying couple than did Sally and her ill-fated lover. Readers are sure to clamor for more.

Ann W. Moore

SOURCE: A review of *The Tin Princess,* in *School Library Journal,* Vol. 40, No. 4, April, 1994, p. 155.

A complex tale of romance, intrigue, and adventure. Adelaide, Mrs. Holland's maid, vanished towards the end of *The Ruby in the Smoke.* Now, 10 years later, in 1882, detective Jim Taylor tracks her down. Beautiful, tough, and illiterate, 22-year-old Adelaide has secretly married Prince Rudolf of Razkavia. When his brother is shot, the couple travels to that tiny European country. Jim accompanies them, as does Becky Winter, 16, Adelaide's tutor and interpreter. In rapid succession the old king dies, Rudolf is crowned and assassinated, and Adelaide becomes queen. Surprisingly, she's remarkably good at the job. She's not without enemies, though, and Becky and Jim have their hands full as they try to stay one step ahead of the schemers. Pullman writes fluently and descriptively, and his wealth of detail brings the period alive. The unexpected twists and turns will grip readers and make it difficult to set the novel down. At times, the large cast and numerous subplots needlessly complicate matters, and the introductory list of names and family tree are more a distraction than a help. Pullman's habit of shifting perspective (from Becky to Jim to assorted others) can also be annoying. Still, this book stands above most YA novels of its type due to its richness, its fascinating characters, and its story that, while sometimes far-fetched, is firmly rooted in reality.

Susan R. Farber

SOURCE: A review of *The Tin Princess,* in *Voice of Youth Advocates,* Vol. 17, No. 3, August, 1994, p. 148.

An overwrought, unbelievable offering from a well-known YA author (*The Ruby In the Smoke,* 1985, among others).

Beck Winter sixteen, an exile from the tiny country of Razkavia, is now living in a run-down section of London and trying desperately to scrape by. To supplement her mother's income as an illustrator of cheap novels and sensational periodicals, she places an ad offering her services as a language tutor. She is hired at once to tutor Miss Bevan, whom Becky discovers is actually Adelaide, the illiterate, ex-prostitute, cockney bride of Prince Rudolph of Razkavia! Immediately after their first session together, Becky and Jim Taylor, a detective who is trying to track down Adelaide, witness an assassination attempt on Prince Rudi, and the whole entourage decides to travel to Razkavia.

Without pause, the marriage is declared valid, Adelaide is crowned princess with the enthusiastic support of the citizenry, and then crowned queen when Prince Rudolph is murdered only days after the death of his elderly father, the King. Now the various political bad guys are out to get her even as Adelaide begins to transform her flirtatious charm into political savvy to save her new country from the greedy giants surrounding it, Germany and Austria. Adelaide can only trust the Richterbund, the student faction loyal to the crown, led by Jim Taylor (who has loved her all along) to keep her safe, but even their best efforts fail to protect her from the cunning of those who would claim Razkavia for their own.

Between charging up the mountain tops, fleeing from dungeons, rescuing a mad prince from an underground cage, and fighting with their backs to the ancient castle walls with the tattered flag clutched bravely between them, the melodrama reaches a fevered pitch. While this may appeal to young adults who long for heroism and derring-do, substance and characterization suffer for the sake of action and adventure. There's just too much coincidence, bald statements of trust, and passionate swordplay for this reviewer, even though I enjoy a hearty tale of adventure as much as anyone.

THUNDERBOLT'S WAXWORK ("The New Cut Gang" series, 1994)

D. A. Young

SOURCE: A review of *Thunderbolt's Waxwork,* in *The Junior Bookshelf,* Vol. 58, No. 6, December, 1994, pp. 231-32.

The New Cut Gang are a bunch of kids living in Lambeth in 1894. As is the tradition in this popular genre they become involved in the criminal activities of grown-ups. Snide coins are circulating in Lambeth and Thunderbolt's Dad is arrested on suspicion. The gang set out to find the real culprit. All their evidence points to the owner of the Department Store and the bringing of him to justice is the main theme of the book. Sub-plots proliferate to add to the fun. There is the attempt to secure everlasting fame for Dippy, the hot chestnut vendor by smuggling his effigy into the Waxworks Museum. A lump of wax turns out to be ambergris and worth a fortune. Thunderbolt's Dad proved to be secretly working, not on counterfeit coins but electric corsets for ladies with backache.

Philip Pullman creates a convincing picture of his chosen time and place with the lightest of touches. It is never allowed to interfere with the development of the plot. He relies upon subtle references to such things as food, prices and general domestic matters to emphasise the quality of the life and times of a hundred years ago.

The pen and ink illustrations [by M. Thomas] are not so successful in capturing the atmosphere of the period but the story moves so fast this may not matter greatly.

It is to be hoped that we shall meet **The New Cut Gang** again in the not too distant future.

George Hunt

SOURCE: A review of *Thunderbolt's Waxwork,* in *Books for Keeps,* No. 102, January, 1997, p. 23.

Philip Pullman, winner of the 1996 Carnegie Medal with the epic **Northern Lights** fantasy, returns to a more domestic scale with this adventure tale, set in late Victorian Lambeth, and involving a gang of urchins, a waxworks, and a cache of counterfeit coins. When the father of a gang member is arrested, seemingly for forgery, the urchins combine their disparate and idiosyncratic talents in order to nail the real villain, but they are hampered in their efforts by the interference of various persons who are, for some reason, pursuing a dummy they've made of the local chestnut seller. The book is as rambling as this summary sounds, but it's fuelled by enough farcical japes and jeopardy to give your readers and listeners a taste for the forthcoming further adventures of the New Cut Gang.

NORTHERN LIGHTS (first volume in "His Dark Materials" series, 1995; U.S. edition as The Golden Compass, 1996)

Wendy Cooling

SOURCE: A review of *Northern Lights,* in *Books for Keeps,* No. 93, July, 1995, pp. 25, 28.

I've always loved long reads so couldn't resist the first part of a new trilogy. **His Dark Materials, Book 1: Northern Lights** by Philip Pullman is a book for serious readers. This is gripping, thought-provoking and extremely frustrating at the end, as it could be months, even years, before Book 2 is published! It's set in a world in some ways like our own and in an unspecified time; a time when everyone has their own personal daemon, a living creature often able to change shape, linked to them. Daemons are very sympathetic and able to reflect the feelings

of their particular human. Lyra's daemon is a moth at the start of the story and Lord Asriel's a snow leopard. The lives of these two characters are connected in a way that becomes apparent well into the story and Lyra's journey to reach him is the content of Book 1. Overhearing conversations and concern for her missing friend, lead Lyra to take a journey that demands all her strength and brings her into contact with animals, people and places beyond her imagination. Read this powerfully written story and you, too, will be waiting for Book 2.

Publishers Weekly

SOURCE: A review of *The Golden Compass,* in *Publishers Weekly,* Vol. 243, No. 8, February 19, 1996, p. 216.

If Pullman's imagination dazzled in the Victorian thrillers that culminated with *The Tin Princess,* in this first volume of a fantasy trilogy it is nothing short of breath-taking. Here Earth is one of only five planets in the solar system, every human has a daemon (the soul embodied as an animal familiar) and, in a time similar to our late 19th century, Oxford scholars and agents of the supreme Calvinist Church are in a race to unleash the power that will enable them to cross the bridge to a parallel universe.

The story line has all the hallmarks of a myth: brought up ignorant of her true identity, 11-year-old Lyra goes on a quest from East Anglia to the top of the world in search of her kidnapped playmate Roger and her imprisoned uncle, Lord Asriel. Deceptions and treacheries threaten at every turn, and she is not yet certain how to read the mysterious truth-telling instrument that is her only guide. After escaping from the charming and sinister Mrs. Coulter, she joins a group of "gyptians" in search of their children, who, like Roger, have been spirited away by Mrs. Coulter's henchmen, the Gobblers. Along the way Lyra is guided by friendly witches and attacked by malevolent ones, aided by an armored polar bear and a Texan balloonist, and nearly made a victim of the Gobblers' cruel experiments.

As always, Pullman is a master at combining impeccable characterizations and seamless plotting, maintaining a crackling pace to create scene upon scene of almost unbearable tension. This glittering gem will leave readers of all ages eagerly awaiting the next installment of Lyra's adventures.

Kirkus Reviews

SOURCE: A review of *The Golden Compass,* in *Kirkus Reviews,* Vol. LXIV, No. 5, March 1, 1996, p. 379.

Pullman returns to the familiar territory of Victorian England, but this time inhabits an alternate Earth, where magic is an ordinary fact of life. Lyra Belacqua and her daemon familiar Pantalaimon spend their days teasing the scholars of Jordan College until her uncle, Lord Asriel, announces that he's learned of astonishing events taking place in the far north involving the aurora borealis. When Lyra rescues

Asriel from an attempt on his life, it is only the beginning of a torrent of events that finds Lyra willingly abducted by the velvet Mrs. Coulter, a missionary of pediatric atrocities; a journey with gyptian clansmen to rescue the children who are destined to be severed from their daemons (an act that is clearly hideous); and Lyra's discovery of her unusual powers and destiny.

Lyra may suffer from excessive spunk, but she is thorough, intelligent, and charming. The author's care in recreating Victorian speech affectations never hinders the action; copious amounts of gore will not dissuade the squeamish, for resonating at the story's center is the twinkling image of a celestial city. This first fantastic installment of the **"His Dark Materials"** trilogy propels readers along with horror and high adventure, a shattering tale that begins with a promise and delivers an entire universe.

Roger Sutton

SOURCE: A review of *The Golden Compass,* in *The Bulletin of the Center for Children's Books,* Vol. 49, No. 8, April, 1996, p. 277.

Pullman here takes an intriguing break from Victorian thrillers and contemporary problem novels with this fantasy, first in a trilogy, in which a young girl follows a big destiny, the nature of which is unknown—as yet—to her or us. In a world that parallels our own, Lyra is an orphaned ward of an Oxford college, where she overhears concerns about "Dust," "the Gobblers," and an "Aurora." That she isn't really an orphan becomes apparent fairly early on, as she discovers that her father, Lord Asriel, and her mother, Mrs. Coulter, are locked into some kind of strange cosmic battle that unfortunately includes the sacrifice of children in its progress. More precisely: each human being in this world, much like our own of perhaps a hundred years ago but with sometimes startling, sometimes subtle, differences, has a "dæmon," an animal-familiar that helps and loves its human, and Mrs. Coulter—a scary descendant of Andersen's Snow Queen—is commissioning experiments in which children are separated from their dæmons. Treachery, tricks, Gypsies, polar bears, witches, and photography all play a part in the ambitious story, and Pullman is particularly inventive in the way he blends not-quite science with not-quite magic. Although the book sometimes seems overly cerebral—Lyra seems more a pawn to the plot than a personality, for example—the faithful (and sometimes nasty, depending on their humans) dæmons give it some heart; the scene in which Lyra finds a boy who has been separated from his dæmon is wrenching. There's enough resolution in this book to give it unity and a satisfying, if rushed and abrupt, closure; at the same time, the prospect of the next book (which Pullman says will be set "in the universe we know") is enticing.

Bruce Anne Shook

SOURCE: A review of *The Golden Compass,* in *School Library Journal,* Vol. 42, No. 4, April, 1996, p. 158.

A novel set in London and in the Arctic regions of a world that is somewhat like our own. Lyra, apparently an orphan, lives among the scholars at Jordan College, Oxford. She becomes aware of a nefarious plot to steal children and transport them to the far north. As Lyra is drawn deeper and deeper into this mystery, she finds that the children are being made to suffer terribly. What she does not—and must not—know is that she is the keystone in an ancient prophecy. Her destiny is to save her world and to move on into a parallel universe. She dives headlong into harrowing adventures, totally unaware of her importance. She also discovers the identity of her parents, who are major players in the unfolding drama. In Lyra's world, every human has a daemon, an animal that is sort of an extension of one's soul. This fact is central to the story as the church, the academic world, and the government seek to understand the significance of the phenomenon. Also important, but never fully explained, is a substance called Dust. This is a captivating fantasy, filled with excitement, suspense, and unusual characters. The armored bears are wonderful and more interesting than most of the humans. There is some fine descriptive writing, filled with the kind of details that encourage suspension of disbelief. The story line moves along at a rapid clip, but flags when it delves into philosophical matters. The ending is less than satisfying, but serves as a lead-in to part two of the series. Fantasy lovers will be clamoring for the next installment.

Geraldine Brennan

SOURCE: "Innocent Abroad," in *The Times Educational Supplement,* No. 4177, July 19, 1996, p. 22.

Carnegie Medal winner Philip Pullman believes that something precious is lost between the ages of nine and 13. In *Northern Lights,* his most challenging work so far, he is helping the most jaded adult regain a sense of "the grace, the innocence, the singleness that children lose".

The novel is the first volume of **"His Dark Materials,"** a trilogy inspired by Milton's *Paradise Lost* with the myth of the Temptation and Fall at its heart. This, Pullman believes, is "the central Western human myth, not only in the Christian sense . . . it's what happens to us all when we gain self-consciousness.

"Children at the stage in their lives before this happens are wonderful to write for. You can encompass large themes. They don't yet think they have other things to think about like the pressures of everyday life, emotional problems and financial problems. As adults we lose sight of the big questions, although we can come back to them."

In *Northern Lights,* that pre-pubescent energy is a commodity as sought-after as cocaine or diamonds, and the forces of cruelty and corruption are unleashed in its pursuit. Pullman's heroine Lyra, the most intriguing 11-year-old in contemporary fiction, fights back with few resources except a strange contraption—a meter for reading the truth.

Pullman sends her on a quest to an Arctic wasteland inspired by Mary Shelley's *Frankenstein,* scattered with armoured bears and flying witches, with mystical universes glimpsed beyond the Aurora. As well as her daemon—all the characters in *Northern Lights* are accompanied by their souls in animal form, like witches' familiars—Pullman has given her a charmed childhood to stave off the inevitable Fall. She has been brought up absent-mindedly by a gaggle of Oxford dons (Pullman has taken liberties with the institutions and architecture of his home town to expose a collegiate underbelly) and runs semi-wild in the clay beds and back alleys, never patronised or deceived and taught as much as she wants to learn.

"They provide for her in a casual way and leave her alone," says Pullman. "What more could a child want?" He is glad that his teaching experience—12 years in Oxford middle schools—is all prenational curriculum. He has also just stopped teaching part-time on PGCE and BEd courses at Westminster College, Oxford.

His passage into, full-time writing has been eased by the critical and commercial success of *Northern Lights,* on top of a healthy track record in fiction (his historical mysteries such as *Ruby in the Smoke* have been especially well received). "Success is hard to quantify. I used to think of publishing as throwing a stone into a swamp. You think nobody's taking any notice, the frogs are still croaking. You don't often meet other writers and you don't know if anyone's reading you. Now it seems the bubbles on the surface of the swamp are bigger than I thought."

The Carnegie Medal, awarded by librarians, has the status of the Booker Prize in the children's literature world without the hype or the big money—Pullman and the Kate Greenaway Medal winner, P J Lynch, will each receive £1,000 worth of books from the sponsors, Peters Library Service, to give to the children's library of their choice.

Northern Lights, published by Scholastic, is physically and intellectually the weightiest volume on this year's shortlist. Accessible to readers from eight-year-olds to adults, it is a deceptively learned book with a background of custom-built technology which does not emerge until a second reading.

Pullman has created his own laws of physics and his own belief system. He describes himself as "a Church of England atheist—a 1662 Prayer Book atheist in fact" and Lyra's universe is a moral one, although the Church rulers are corrupt. His grandfather was a Norfolk clergyman and, he says, "I was taught right and wrong by example rather than by threat."

A tantalising epigraph promises a second **"Dark Materials"** volume "set in the universe we know" which is at the "carpentry" stage. Pullman says, and due out next year. We haven't seen the last of the evil Mrs Coulter, or of Serafina Pekkala's witches, or of the jovial Texan pilot Lee Scores-by. The final part of the trilogy is still in Pullman's head—a strange and wonderful new treatment of an old story.

Julia Eccleshare

SOURCE: A review of *Northern Lights,* in *Books for Keeps,* No. 100, September, 1996, p. 15.

> 'Children's books still deal with the huge themes which have always been part of literature—love, loyalty, the place of religion and science in life, what it really means to be human. Contemporary adult fiction is too small and too sterile for what I'm trying to do.'

Fighting talk from Philip Pullman whose magnificent ***His Dark Materials: Northern Lights*** has just won the Carnegie Medal. 'When you're writing for children,' he says, 'the story is more important than you are. You can't be self-conscious, you just have to get out of the way.'

Pullman believes that adult fiction was radically changed by E M Forster and his contemporaries who caused 'story tellers' to move into genre fiction while 'novelists' concentrated on style. 'Luckily, in children's books, story hasn't been damaged in the same way.'

Northern Lights was a hugely ambitious concept. 'What I really wanted to do was *Paradise Lost* in 1,200 pages. From the beginning I knew the shape of the story. It's the story of The Fall which is the story of how what some would call sin, but I would call consciousness, comes to us. The more I thought about it the clearer it became. It fell naturally into three parts. Though long, I've never been in danger of getting lost because the central strand is so simple.' It's that central strand, based on the basic law that actions have consequences, that Pullman is so determined should underpin the best children's books. 'Children lack the understanding that you can do anything but that you've got to be prepared to accept the consequences. Some things cost more than others. Some things involve you in more pain. The language of rights encourages passivity and is not interesting. The language of responsibility is much more interesting. You must be subtle which is why writing is so good at dealing with it.'

The weaving together of story and morality is what makes *Northern Lights* such an exceptional book. Never for a moment does the story lose ground to the message it carries. Philip Pullman's huge cast of characters sizzle on the page. His heroine, Lyra, who, he says, 'just walked in', is cunning, deceitful, loyal and brave—a rich mixture of attributes which make her, above all, a convincing child. The adults who surround her are equally well-rounded while the device of their 'daemons', their animal familiars which reveal their innermost natures, adds a fresh level of perception. His landscapes, from the almost-Oxford where the story starts to the strange Northern wastelands at the heart of the adventure, are superbly realised. Above all, *Northern Lights* reflects Pullman's own love of storytelling. It's an immense tale, richly told and wholly satisfying. Please Philip Pullman, hurry up with volume 2.

THE GAS-FITTERS' BALL ("The New Cut Gang" series, 1995)

Robin Barlow

SOURCE: A review of *The Gas-fitters' Ball,* in *The School Librarian,* Vol. 43, No. 3, August, 1995, p. 109.

The New Cut Gang are likeable rogues, living in Lambeth at the end of the nineteenth century, who aim to solve crimes in their locality. Their names—Benny Kaminsky, Bridie Malone, Thunderbolt Dobney, Sharky Bob and Four-ball Schneider—will give a good idea of the tone and atmosphere of the book. The crime they set out to crack concerns the theft of ten thousand pounds' worth of silver from the Gas-fitters' Hall. Intertwined with this plot, we have Dick Smith and Mr Horspath both chasing the hand in marriage of Daisy Malone, the prettiest girl in New Cut. Dick is a friend of the Gang, painfully shy but a basically good lad. Mr Horspath is the oily under-manager of the Gasworks, who has no difficulty ingratiating himself with the Malone family. The two strands of the plot come together at the Gas-fitters' Ball when, lo and behold, the Prince of Wales arrives unexpectedly.

Philip Pullman's previous book featuring the New Cut Gang, **Thunderbolt's Waxwork,** was well received, and this one should be similarly so. There are some amusing incidents, the plot moves along briskly, and the background against which the book is set is original.

THE FIREWORK-MAKER'S DAUGHTER (1995)

Chris Stephenson

SOURCE: A review of *The Firework-Maker's Daughter,* in *School Librarian,* Vol. 44, No. 2, May, 1996, p. 64.

Here's a book that has it all: tradition, mission, mystery, imagination, magic, and morality; with a relish for language and a good leavening of humour thrown in. Set 'a thousand miles ago, in a country east of the jungle and south of the mountains', but probably part of Indonesia, the story's central concern is the quest of the eponymous heroine, Lila, to find the mysterious ingredient that will enable her to become a true firework-maker like her father, with whose help she has already learned the art of creating marvellous products with names like Crackle-Dragons, Golden Sneezes, Java Lights and Tumbling Demons. The quest leads, with various encounters and setbacks along the way, to the Grotto of the Fire-Fiend Razvani in the heart of a volcano, and the ultimate discovery that the fire-maker's secret is wisdom. There are also several linked comic sub-plots involving a talking white elephant and his keeper, and an incompetent band of pirates. The story ends with a dazzlingly described international firework festival in which German, Italian and American firework creators (rather stereotypically depicted) compete with Lila and her father to put on the best display. Vigorous line illustrations [by Nick Harris] framing the pages extend the fantastic imagery of the text.

Pat Clark

SOURCE: A review of *The Firework-Maker's Daughter,* in *Books for Keeps,* No. 102, January, 1997, p. 24.

Philip Pullman is a children's writer with obvious talent who can write in a variety of styles and for different age groups. **The Firework-Maker's Daughter** is reminiscent of a traditional folk story. The hero, in this case Lila, sets out on a quest to discover a secret which will enable her to fulfil her greatest ambition—to become a firework-maker. She has to overcome obstacles, face dangers and prove herself worthy of the secret. All this she does, coincidentally helping others to fulfil their ambitions, with naive confidence and determination. She passes her final test and everyone is set to live happily ever after.

One might expect a modern audience to be blasé about such a well tried and tested formula, but not so. Pullman's story has pace, the characters are appealing and the stylish black and white line illustrations help create atmosphere. I would have said this title had appeal for boys and girls of about 11 as it is quite long and the typesize small, but my copy has been passed from hand to hand in a class of less able 14-year-old students. Perhaps that, as much as anything, is testimony to Philip Pullman's art as a storyteller.

THE WONDERFUL STORY OF ALADDIN AND THE ENCHANTED LAMP (retold by Pullman, 1996)

Adrian Jackson

SOURCE: A review of *The Wonderful Story of Aladdin and the Enchanted Lamp,* in *Books for Keeps,* No. 96, January, 1996, p. 12.

An elegant picture book which manages to combine a powerful retelling of the story with richly detailed illustrations [by David Wyatt]. For many the Disney version is the standard and this may seem similar, but it has its own special verbal and visual treats. This edition is both a pleasure to read aloud and a source for much careful reading of pictures. The large format and richness of the production make it a book for all ages, but especially those who often think reading's a chore and a bore.

CLOCKWORK, OR ALL WOUND UP (illustrated by Peter Bailey, 1996; U.S. edition illustrated by Leonid Gore, 1998)

Stephanie Nettell

SOURCE: A review of *Clockwork, or All Wound Up,* in *Books for Keeps,* No. 100, September, 1996, p. 33.

I've long admired Philip Pullman for his rollicking inventiveness: a prolific storyteller, he experiments endlessly and unpredictably with style and technique, putting as much energy into his 'minor' tales as his award-winning epics. *Clockwork* is a jolly little metaphysical fairy-tale-cum-horror story set in a typically Pullman German mountain village (vaguely 18th century), where a clockmaker's apprentice sells his soul for fear of failing and the kind heart of a pretty little girl saves the day. Opinionated chorus-like commentaries pop up with Peter Bailey's pictures, and great time is had by all.

Publishers Weekly

SOURCE: A review of *Clockwork, or All Wound Up,* in *Publishers Weekly,* Vol. 245, No. 36, September 7, 1998, pp. 95-6.

In this tightly wound tale by the author of **The Golden Compass** and **Count Karlstein,** clockmaking and clockmakers serve as metaphors for fiction and its practitioners. The quaint (and aptly named) German village of Glockenheim sets great store in its clockmaking tradition: each time an apprentice becomes master of his craft, he commemorates the occasion by adding a new figure to the town's great clock. On the eve of one of these celebrations, a delectably spooky train of events is set in motion when the novelist Fritz sets out to entertain the villagers with his most recent work: the tale of Prince Florian, the deceased local ruler's son, whose fate is linked to a brilliant clockmaker. Fritz's narrative is interrupted by the arrival of a cloaked man who appears to have sprung straight from the pages of his novel: the aforementioned craftsman, enigmatic Dr. Kalmenius of Schatzberg, who has come—or so it seems—to help the gloomy apprentice clockmaker Karl achieve an unearned triumph in the next day's ceremonies. Meanwhile, poor Florian—whose time has nearly run out—stumbles into Glockenheim and finds the innkeeper's sweet daughter Gretl, the one person capable of restoring true life to the mechanical prince. In signature Pullman style, each character gets his or her just deserts with a fairy-tale ending that pays fitting and playful tribute to the story's twin obsessions: "So they both lived happily ever after; and that was how they all wound up." [Leonid] Gore's haunting black-and-white drawings both dramatize key events and reveal something of the characters' psyches. His visual artistry coupled with the luxurious design of this hand-sized volume makes this a tale to return to time after time.

Ilene Cooper

SOURCE: A review of *Clockwork, or All Wound Up,* in *Booklist,* Vol. 95, No. 2, September 15, 1998, p. 229.

Pullman, the consummate storyteller, offers deliciously spooky story combining elements of *Frankenstein,* the *Sorcerer's Apprentice,* and Faust. Set in long-ago Germany, the story brings together Fritz, a storyteller, and an inn full of men waiting to hear Fritz's latest tale. The frightening story about a king with a heart made of clockworks become horrifyingly real when a hooded, menacing figure from the tale,

the mad doctor Kalmenius, enters the inn. Pullman continues mixing elements of Fritz's tale with the real world, as an apprentice clockmaker makes an unholy deal with Kalmenius. The young man brings evil into his world when he takes possession of a mechanical knight who wields his sword with impunity eventually slaying the apprentice. Yet it is the power of love that wins out when a young girl is able to bring to life a mechanical boy, who has also wandered into the inn from Fritz's story. Deceptively simple on the first reading, the novel contains some complex reflections on the nature of reality and of good and evil. Several of the plot twists are a bit obscure, but the tale mostly runs like clockwork. Full-page black-and-white illustrations occur in each chapter. These soft-edged drawings, full of light and shadow are extremely well crafted and satisfyingly strange. Read this one aloud and discuss it afterward.

Ellen Fader

SOURCE: A review of *Clockwork, or All Wound Up,* in *School Library Journal,* Vol. 44, No. 10, October, 1998, p. 145.

In a tavern in a small town in Germany, at an unspecified time in the past, a well-respected novelist begins to read aloud his new story, "Clockwork," even though he hasn't finished it—"He was just going to wind up the story, set it going, and make up the end when he got there." He relates a tale of horror that begins with a Prince who suddenly dies and is found to have a piece of clockwork instead of a heart. The Royal Physician decides to question Dr. Kalmenius, a brilliant clockmaster who is referred to as a "philosopher of the night." When that doctor actually enters the tavern as the novelist is reading, everyone leaves in fear, except apprentice-clockmaster Karl. Kalmenius then proposes to Karl a way out of his dilemma of not having crafted a new clock figurine to mark the upcoming end of his apprenticeship. He offers him Sir Ironsoul, a perfectly sculpted mechanical knight that comes alive; only one song can stop him from killing anyone who utters the word "devil." Suffice it to say without recounting a tantalizingly complicated plot, each character gets what he or she deserves. Pullman manages to weave together the threads from both the story and the story within the story in a book filled with tension, menace, and suspense. Whether or not readers understand the references to Faust, *Frankenstein, The Velveteen Rabbit,* and *Pinocchio,* they will remain riveted until the final page. Be prepared for many requests for this easy-to-sell title.

Kirkus Reviews

SOURCE: A review of *Clockwork, or All Wound Up,* in *Kirkus Reviews,* Vol. LXVI, No. 20, October 15, 1998, p. 1536.

A gothic thriller from Pullman. In the White Horse tavern, the townspeople gather one winter night to drink and hear the latest from Fritz the storyteller, who is hoping that the ending will come to him as he tells it. Among the listeners is Karl, the clockmaker's apprentice, who faces humiliation the next day when it will be revealed that he has failed to create a new figure for the town clock. To Fritz's horror, in the middle of his story, one of his characters, the evil clockmaker Dr. Kalmenius, appears; as Fritz and the others abandon the tavern, Dr. Kalmenius offers Karl a superb clockwork figure, Sir Ironsoul, which upon hearing the word "devil," will stab the speaker in the throat. This is only the winding up of an intricate little novel, which ticks along to a gratifying conclusion that is more fable than fantasy. Gore's atmospheric, impressionistic black-and-white drawings and the workings of Pullman's fertile, Victorian imagination have been cultivated to a degree that will entrance middle graders.

THE SUBTLE KNIFE (second volume of "His Dark Materials" Series, 1997)

Kirkus Reviews

SOURCE: A review of *The Subtle Knife,* in *Kirkus Reviews,* Vol. LXV, No. 14, July 15, 1997, p. 1116.

The powerful second installment in the **"His Dark Materials"** fantasy trilogy, which began with *The Golden Compass,* continues the chronicling of Lyra Silvertongue's quest to find the origins of Dust—the very stuff of the universe.

The first chapter is vintage Pullman: gorgeous imagery, pulse-pounding action, the baiting of readers' affections as they meet Will, 12, who is trying to protect his emotionally fragile mother and to locate his lost father, an explorer who vanished years before. Instead, Will finds a window into another world, where Lyra and her daemon have also tumbled. That world holds the talisman of the subtle knife, which can cut through anything, even the space between worlds. It wounds Will, but he is bound to it by a destiny neither he nor Lyra (nor readers) yet understand. The witches of Lyra's world, the scientists of Will's, the passionately evil Mrs. Coulter (Lyra's mother), and Lyra's champion Lee Scoresby seek the source of the disorder in the worlds and shimmering spaces that connect them. Angels that bless and Specters that eat the wills of adults appear; tantalizing glimpses of the past and future abound; the whole is presented in a rush of sensuous detail that moves and entrances. Pullman has so intricately woven the textures of the two books that the outlines of the first are clearly recapitulated in the second, making it possible to read this one alone. But as it, too, ends in a tremendous cliffhanger, most readers will seek out the first volume while they eagerly await the third.

Ann A. Flowers

SOURCE: A review of *The Subtle Knife,* in *The Horn Book Magazine,* Vol. LXXIII, No. 5, September-October, 1997, pp. 578-79.

In this second book of the trilogy **"His Dark Materials,"** following *The Golden Compass,* the adventures of Lyra

Belacqua continue, with the introduction of young Will Parry as a major protagonist. Will comes from Oxford in our world; he is anxious to find his long-lost explorer father and struggles to protect his mother and some valuable papers from sinister men in black. He accidentally kills one and escapes through a window into a city, Ci'gazze, in a middle world where he joins up with Lyra. The two become friends and allies against a bewildering conglomeration of enemies. They are pursued for many reasons: they have both been prophesied to play leading parts in impending struggles of immense proportions; Will has become the owner of a knife of great powers, the subtle knife; and Lyra possesses the alethiometer—the golden compass—which can foretell the future and direct Lyra and Will to their unknown destinies. Many characters from *The Golden Compass* reappear: Mrs. Coulter continues her evil plotting; in a moving episode, Lee Scoresby, the Texas aeronaut, is killed defending a lost hope to protect Lyra; Serafina Pekkala and her witches enter this middle world to lend aid to Lyra and Will. The intricacy of the plot is staggering; it is perhaps a retelling of *Paradise Lost*—there are hints and portents that Lord Asriel, Lyra's father, is preparing to restage the revolt of the angels against God and that Lyra is destined to be the new Eve. Although this volume is very much a book between the first and third—and almost incomprehensible without having read *The Golden Compass*—each of the players in this vast game is clear and distinct, and there is no doubt that the work is stunningly ambitious, original, and fascinating. Pullman offered an exceptional romantic fantasy in *The Golden Compass,* but *The Subtle Knife* adds a mythic dimension that inevitably demands even greater things from the finale.

Pat Matthews

SOURCE: A review of *The Subtle Knife,* in *The Bulletin of the Center for Children's Books,* Vol. 51, No. 3, November, 1997, p. 98.

Once again Pullman succeeds in pushing readers headlong into other worlds in this eagerly awaited and extraordinary sequel to *The Golden Compass*. It has been worth the wait. In his quest to find his father, Will Parry collides with Lyra Silvertongue (nee Belacqua), in her quest to find Dust. The children travel through torn windows between England and a parallel universe containing the strange, sunny city of Ci'gazze, a place where only children can survive. They encounter soul-eating Specters, the earnest Dr. Malone of the Dark Matter Research Unit, angelic watchers, witches-to-the-rescue, crazed children, the sinister Sir Charles, and the knife: "This edge . . . will cut through any material in the world. . . . The other edge . . . is more subtle still. With it you can cut an opening out of this world altogether." The masterfully turned plot will alarm, electrify, and astonish readers as they see Will and Lyra journey towards a destiny which is leading up to an unthinkable conflict: "Imagine the daring of it, to make war on the Creator!" Despite its harrowing complexities, this well-crafted story never sacrifices characterization. Human dynamics and their entanglements are not only convincing but deeply moving as well. Will's tender concern for the troubled mother he has left behind haunts him throughout the book. It will be enjoyable in the extreme for readers of the first book in this series to see such diverse strands woven together so expertly in the second. We eagerly await the third.

Margaret Meek

SOURCE: A review of *The Subtle Knife,* in *Books for Keeps,* No. 108, January, 1998, p. 21.

In this, the eagerly-awaited second part of Pullman's allegoric trilogy, three universes overlap. Will, leaving home to find the real reason for his father's long absence, thinks he has killed a man. Just outside Oxford, he notices, and goes through, a gap in the transparent boundary into another world. There, in a dreary town haunted by mind-numbing vampires, he meets Lyra, the forthright, deceitful heroine of *Northern Lights,* and her daemon. They are also adrift. The children's separate quests join as they seek the subtle knife, the last powerful symbol of the ancient philosophers and the only threat to the Spectres. It allows the true bearer to part and reseal the thinning membrane between all worlds. After a near-mortal combat, Will is recognised as the knife-bearer whose inexorable responsibility is to be strong against the dark forces of evil. Lyra, her consciousness extended by Will's acceptance, knows her first task is to help him to find his father. The reader is guided through the strong, flexible cat's-cradle of the plot by the author's narrative spellbinding, and by the *sigillum,* a location symbol on each page.

After the experience of *Northern Lights* readers expect a series of surprises as part of the structure. Although here there is nothing quite the same as the titanic bear fight, nor the skincrawling gruesomeness of the silver guillotine, the inventions of suspense never flag. There is more, deeper, thought-action. Lyra's awareness of Will's concern for others lessens her egocentrism. She discovers mutual trust and learns to intuit Will's responses. (He has no visible daemon to demonstrate them.) The wise airborne guardians are constantly watchful, but we feel their power is diminishing; or rather, it has passed to the heavenly intelligences. There are threads to be gathered up; a computer lady has followed the trail, perhaps.

The dimensions of Pullman's project for **"His Dark Materials,"** its fully epic structure, emerge clearly from this novel as something more extensive, profound and resonant than anything the present generation of young readers, including those from the Star Wars annexe, has yet encountered. Pullman accepts and responsibly transforms the inevitable didactic of writing for children: to make them strong enough, wise enough, to encounter the consequences of their actions and feelings, good or evil, as they anticipate their future. The sublime has long been out of fashion in literature, especially for children. Like Milton, whose epic poem lies behind this enterprise, Pullman has little time for fugitive and cloistered virtue. One needs to draw a longer critical breath to do justice to all his subtleties, but I have seen the effect on young readers who, in his company, go further than they ever thought they could.

Gregory Maguire

SOURCE: A review of *The Subtle Knife,* in *The New York Times Book Review,* April 19, 1998, p. 32.

In a high fantasy trilogy, the first book is usually a Baedeker to a brave new world and its regulation-issue mortal conflict. The third book reveals secret identities, reverses what seemed irreversible and resolves the conflict. But the second book is prone to middle book syndrome, a parlous condition characterized by too much development and too little resolution.

"His Dark Materials," by the English novelist Philip Pullman, is the latest trilogy to step up the pulse of kids and adults alike. The first installment. *The Golden Compass,* was received with hallelujahs and literary prizes, including Britain's Carnegie Medal. Now we have *The Subtle Knife.* Though this second volume almost succumbs to middle book syndrome. Pullman, who has written many other books for children and adults, avoids it, adroitly, by force of theme.

The Subtle Knife is really two books spliced together. It continues the plot of "The Golden Compass," in which Lyra Belacqua sets out to learn the nature of a spiritual particle called, in her world, Dust. *The Subtle Knife* introduces Will Parry, a modern English boy of about 12, whose father disappeared in the Arctic. Though he doesn't remember his father, Will sets out on a rescue mission, and along the way he slips into a parallel universe and into Lyra's story. In a twist worthy of the Athenian tragedians. Will recognizes the shaman Jopari as his father only at the instant a witch's arrow finishes the shaman off.

Just when narrative sprawl is about to overwhelm, the "subtle knife" of the book's title shows up. It can slice through anything—spirit, matter and middle book syndrome. It can slash windows between worlds, allowing Will and Lyra to leap sideways out of plots as entangled as Laocoon. Young Will is anointed as the bearer of the knife, an instrument ornamented with angelic designs. Remember the sword of Michael the archangel in Milton's *Paradise Lost,* which "was given him temper'd so, that neither keen / Nor solid might resist that edge"? Our subtle knife is called Aesahaettr— "the word sounds as if it means `god-destroyer,'" says the witch Serafina Pekkala—so we know we are not in the terrain of singing mice and dancing brooms.

The Subtle Knife nears magnificence in the loftiness of its moral design. The "high" in high fantasy, in this instance, refers to the high heavens. Lyra's father, Lord Asriel, a figure of apparent majesty, is building a fortress in the frozen north from which to launch an attack upon the "Authority." Young readers will not know that in *Paradise Lost* the rebel angel, Satan, repaired to the northern realms, nor will they have any sense of the terrible glory of Milton's characterization. But they will respond to the portrayal of the totalitarian church of this parallel world. The witch queen says, "Every church is the same: control, destroy, obliterate every good feeling." Is Lord Asriel's to be a battle with a tyrannical God or with a corrupt human institution?

By the end of *The Subtle Knife* there is little clarity about which side, if any, is good and deserves to prevail. Except, of course, this is a children's book and so the child heroes deserve to prevail. This being a middle book, alas, prevail is just what these brave kids can't manage to do—yet.

Children will read *The Subtle Knife* as an adventure story rather than as an extended riff on liberty and free will derived from Books 5 and 6 of *Paradise Lost.* And adventure is abundant: cowboy shootouts, exploding dirigibles, break-ins at English country homes, tortures and assassinations, communication with spirits on computer monitors. The story gallops with such ferocious momentum that one almost forgives such cliffhangers as watching Mary Malone, a former nun turned Oxford scientist, disappear through a window into a new world, never to be heard from again—yet.

J. R. R. Tolkien, the granddaddy of modern high fantasy, asserted that the best fantasy writing is marked by "arresting strangeness." Philip Pullman measures up; his work is devilishly inventive. His worlds teem with angels, witches, humans, animal familiars, talking bears and Specters, creatures resembling deadly airborne jellyfish. (And I bet Volume 3 will reveal at least one highly placed demon. Why else would the last name of Sir Charles Latrom, who has a serpent for a familiar, spell "mortal" backward?)

Still, the strongest characterization is in Will. Will: intentionality, force. Neither bookishly wise nor cutting-edge hip, the boy is fiercely protective of his beleaguered mother, capable of violence in the good fight. And *The Subtle Knife* succeeds most resonantly in reminding us that some fights are good fights.

Children still need heroes. It's nice to see a girl who can discern the truth through a golden compass, and a boy able to slice spirit and matter with an atom-carving subtle knife. Up against heaven itself, if need be. But then what? Are Lyra and Will to be the next Adam and Eve, repopulating a fresh Eden with new, improved humans? If so, among their offspring there will be some children who will ignore paradise itself in search of the arresting strangeness of another good fantasy trilogy to read. Put Philip Pullman on the shelf with Ursula K. Le Guin, Susan Cooper, Lloyd Alexander, at least until we get to see Volume 3.

Jennifer Fakolt

SOURCE: A review of *The Subtle Knife,* in *Voice of Youth Advocates,* Vol. 21, No. 2, June, 1998, p. 133.

In *The Golden Compass,* Pullman gave us a breathtakingly rich vision of a world shades removed from and more mystical than ours, infused with magic and informed by reason, where everyone has a personal daemon in animal form that is the perfect complement of their personality, and to which they are bound with their whole soul. We met Lyra, the impudent, shrewd daughter of the powerful scholar, Lord Asriel. Left to her own wild devices under the benevolent care of elderly professors, she finds her joy running wild with the Oxford street children.

When Lyra foils an attempt to assassinate her dangerous father, events are set in motion that destroy her innocent childhood. A photograph of an alternate world, rumors of mysterious Dust, and the increasing disappearances of children all serve to move Lyra down the path of a terrible destiny. With Lord Asriel imprisoned, the glamorous Mrs. Coulter and her menacing daemon come to take Lyra from her home. Lyra receives a curious instrument—an alethiometer—which always tells the truth, if one is able to discern the layered meanings of its pictograms. Frightened when she discovers Mrs. Coulter is not only her mother, but also the leader of the Oblation board—those behind the abductions, performing unspeakable experiments, severing children from their daemons—Lyra escapes, determined to rescue her father and a missing friend. She begins a journey to the far North, making strange allies along the way, from the King of the Gyptians to Iorek Byrnison, leader of the great white armored bears. The conclusion is aching, haunting, and epically beautiful.

In *The Subtle Knife,* Pullman continues Lyra's story, as tensions escalate. Will, a boy from a parallel Oxford, is on a quest to find his own father, who had vanished on a Northern expedition. Fleeing after killing one of the mysterious men who question his mother, Will finds a hole from his modern England into the world of Cittigazze, where adults are prey to soul-eating Spectres, and where people's daemons are on the outsides. There, he meets Lyra, out to revenge the death of her friend and find out more about the elusive Dust. The two join forces and form an uneasy, fierce friendship. Victor in a bloody fight, Will learns that he is destined to be the bearer of the subtle knife, a blade able to cut holes into other worlds. As the skies of Cittigazze fill with the massive movements of angels heading to join Lord Asriel in his epic battle against the Authority, and the evil Mrs. Coulter gets nearer and nearer to Lyra, Will and Lyra are pulled into a growing maelstrom of great struggles and betrayals.

These first two volumes of **"His Dark Materials"** trilogy are, simply, magnificent. Pullman has the power of a master fantasist. He imbues an age-old classical struggle with a new mythic vision, the depth and realization of which are staggering. His style is tight, compelling, and nearly flawless. Characters quickly become friends, so layered and immediate are they, inspiring the reader to tears of loss or wonder. These two titles stand in equal company with the works of J. R. R. Tolkien and C. S. Lewis.

Additional coverage of Pullman's life and career is contained in the following sources published by The Gale Group: *Authors and Artists for Young Adults,* Vol. 15; *Contemporary Authors New Revision Series,* Vols. 50, 77; *Junior DISCovering Authors; Major Authors and Illustrators for Children and Young Adults; Something about the Author Autobiography Series,* Vol. 17; and *Something about the Author,* Vols. 65, 103.

Virginia Euwer Wolff

1937-

American author of fiction.

Major works include *Probably Still Nick Swansen* (1988), *The Mozart Season* (1991), *Make Lemonade* (1993), *Bat 6* (1998).

INTRODUCTION

Wolff is known for using unusual formats in her works for young adults, breaking away from conventional methods of presenting a story to involve the reader more deeply in the world of her characters. The young protagonists of her novels all face intense personal challenges heightened by their own peculiar circumstances: Nick in *Probably Still Nick Swansen* is a special needs teenager facing normal teenage problems; Allegra in *The Mozart Season* is a gifted musician facing the pain in her family history; LaVaughn and Jolly in *Make Lemonade* face the discouraging conditions of intense poverty; and the girls in *Bat 6* face the ugliness of racial prejudice in the aftermath of war. Wolff writes about these characters with the skill born of her love of the language and the understanding born of her life as a high school teacher. Stephanie Zvirin of *Booklist* said of Wolff, "[She has] proven herself a skilled, innovative writer with a sharp eye for the joys and disappointments of young people outside the mainstream."

Wolf paraphrased Maya Angelou in *The ALAN Review,* saying, "Writing is rarely easy and never beautiful." Her work is slow and painstaking, but she has obtained superior results. *Make Lemonade*, for example, is written in short, simple sentences that read like blank verse. Wolff wrote it that way because she believes that is how teenagers really talk. Carolyn Noah commented, "[t]he poetic form [of *Make Lemonade*] emphasizes the flow of the teenager's language and thought." Critics have described Wolff's writing as providing an emotional reading experience that is forceful, compelling, intense, and absorbing. Among the writers Wolff admires and who have influenced her is William Faulkner. She commented in *The ALAN Review*, "Faulkner said that these are the only things worth writing about: love, honor, pity, pride, compassion, and sacrifice. These things constitute the moral checklist against which I place my work."

Biographical Information

A teacher for most of her adult life, Wolff was 50 years old before she began publishing her writing, and although she writes slowly and has produced only a few books, her work has been exceptionally well received. A child of independent and strong-minded parents who left their professional lives in Pennsylvania to become fruit farmers in the

Pacific Northwest, Wolff spent her childhood surrounded by both artistic and natural beauty: a house full of books, music, and paintings in the environs of the Cascade Mountains. When she was five years old her father died, but her mother resolved to continue working the farm and raising Wolff and her brother according to plan. A New York cousin influenced her desire to play the violin, an endeavor that became a life long passion. She attended boarding school at sixteen and went from there to Smith College where she studied English. Her love for the English language was fostered by the works of her favorite writers, among them Gerard Manley Hopkins, James Joyce, and Shakespeare.

Wolff married in 1959, immediately after college, and raised two children in the vagabond world of the theater, following her husband's career all over the Eastern seaboard, and teaching English in several schools. Her children were teenagers when she began to write. Divorced in 1976, she returned to Oregon where she taught English in a public high school for ten years before publishing her first book. Although she is now a successful writer, she still teaches English during the ski season at Mount Hood Academy, a school for competitive skiers. She writes slowly, but she considers that to be a virtue. She told Stephanie Zvirin in a *Booklist* interview:

"I guess I'd rather write fewer books and have them be unusual . . . than write quantity."

Major Works

Wolff's first young adult novel, *Probably Still Nick Swansen*, was well received by critics and teachers. It tells the story of Nick, a teenager with minimal brain dysfunction, who is trying to lead an ordinary life. Told from Nick's point of view, the reader is shown the commonality of Nick's experience with those of "normal" teens. He suffers the teasing of other students, the frustrations of learning to drive, the excitement of going to the prom, the humiliation and dejection of being stood up, and a gradual growth to regain his self respect. Constance A. Mellon commented, "The brilliance in Wolff's book is that she never preaches: rather, through a series of involving events and through characterizations that are consistently sympathetic, she draws readers into Nick's life."

The Mozart Season reflects Wolff's love of the violin. It is the story of Allegra Leah Shapiro, a musician talented enough to be chosen as a finalist in a local violin competition. She spends her summer practicing Mozart's Fourth Violin Concerto, concurrently wrestling with her identity as a musician striving for excellence, an adolescent daughter of proud parents, and the granddaughter of Leah, murdered in a World War II concentration camp. A contributor to *Publishers Weekly* praised this book as "a novel of ideas for young adults that describes the delicate dance between honoring traditions of the past and being your own person in the present."

Wolff's most highly acclaimed book is *Make Lemonade*. Commended for her sensitive handling of a difficult subject, and for her innovative use of a free-verse form, she tells the story of fourteen-year-old LaVaughn and the influence she has on the life of seventeen-year-old Jolly. *Make Lemonade* is set in an impoverished inner-city neighborhood where LaVaughn, an ambitious and clever girl, is trying to earn money for college. She gets a job babysitting for Jolly's two small children while Jolly tries to sort out her life. As their friendship develops, they help each other come to terms with their individual issues and raise each other up. The title reflects LaVaughn's statement, "If life hands you lemons, make lemonade." Stephanie Zvirin remarked, "Rooted not in a particular culture, but in the community of poverty, the story offers a penetrating view of the conditions that foster our ignorance, destroy our self-esteem, and challenge our strength. . . . At once disturbing and uplifting, this finely nuanced, touching portrait proudly affirms our ability to reach beyond ourselves and reach out to one another."

Bat 6 was less favorably reviewed than Wolff's other books. Like *Make Lemonade*, Wolff experimented with form in this book, telling the story in a series of monologues. *Bat 6* takes place shortly after the end of World War II and recounts from the point of view of each of the participants the events that transpired during a girls' softball game. Aki, a Japanese-American girl newly released from an internment camp, was playing first base when she was violently assaulted by Shazam, whose racial hatred is a result of the loss of her father at Pearl Harbor. The tale unfolds as each of the girls on the two teams tells her version of what happened. Some critics found the book confusing and unsatisfying, partly because the speakers are not identified. Others thought the book a powerful portrait of an uncomfortable point in American history. Luann Toth wrote, "Wolff delves into the irreversible consequences of war and the necessity to cultivate peace and speaks volumes about courage, responsibility, and reconciliation—all in a book about softball."

Awards

Although Wolff's oeuvre is small, she has received numerous awards for her work. *Probably Still Nick Swansen* received the International Reading Association Award, young adult division, and the PEN-West Book Award, both in 1989, and was a Best Book for Young Adults selection from the American Library Association. *Make Lemonade* received the most attention with an award from the Child Study Children's Book Committee of Bank Street College and the Golden Kite Award from the Society of Children's Book Writers and Illustrators, both in 1993; the Oregon Book Award in the Young Reader's Category in 1994; Young Reader's Choice Award nominee by the Canadian Library Association in 1996; and selections for best book and top choice lists by the American Library Association, *Booklist*, *School Library Journal*, and *Parent's Magazine*. Awards granted for *The Mozart Season* include Notable Book and Best Book for Young Adults from the American Library Association and honorable mention citation in the Janusz Korczak Literary Competition from the Anti-Defamation League Braun Center for Holocaust Studies.

AUTHOR'S COMMENTARY

Stephanie Zvirin with Virginia Euwer Wolff

SOURCE: An interview in *Booklist,* Vol. 90, No. 13, March 1, 1994, pp. 1250-51.

BOOKLIST: You're still a bit of an unknown author to many of us, even though you've published three very successful novels. When curious people ask you to describe yourself, what do you tell them?

VIRGINIA EUWER WOLFF: Don Gallo edited a book about kids' authors, *Speaking for Ourselves, Too* (1993). In it, I said that three things seem to have determined a lot of what I am and what I do. I'm a woods kid—you know, the forest. I'm Pacific Northwestern. Two, I play the violin. And three, my dad died when I was a little kid. I'm also five foot three and very ordinary looking. My background is probably pretty average.

BKL: Are you a full-time writer?

WOLFF: No, I'm a teacher, and I have to go to work tomorrow. That's why we couldn't do this interview any other day this week.

BKL: Any particular subject?

WOLFF: Well, I've taught for many years. I teach high-school English now, but only during the ski season, three or four days a week from the beginning of November through the end of March. I teach at Mt. Hood Academy, a school for highly competitive skiers, kids who have gone beyond their school ski team and are aiming at the Olympics. I'm their English department. I also taught elementary school for 11 years in Philadelphia and on Long island. That was before I thought I could write, when I thought of myself as a person without skills. Actually, I got into teaching because I decided I wanted to go to school with my kids. Having taught for so many years now, I'm in a position to be profoundly respectful of teachers.

BKL: How did you make the jump from teaching to writing?

WOLFF: I just sat down and wrote one day. Actually, I was too foolish to know any different then.

BKL: You mean you wrote a book?

WOLFF: Yes, that's what I did. In the late 1970s. I had never taken a writing course, and I had never finished a short story. I just decided I would sit down and write a novel. You know "where angels fear to tread." I do everything "where angels fear to tread." I believe that's how our best writing gets done. I had a whole bunch of impulses and half-witted perceptions coming out of me, just coming out my ears, so I sat down and let stuff pour out onto the typewriter. That was my adult novel, ***Rated PG,*** which, happily, is now out of print.

BKL: It has an interesting title.

WOLFF: It's got a corny title, a terribly commercial title. I don't admire the book. I guess first novels are always embarrassing. I'd certainly never reread it. Writing it helped me find out how a book gets made, though—at least one of the ways—and by the time I sat down to write for kids, I had one humongous experience behind me.

BKL: What made you decide to write for young adults?

WOLFF: Actually, I just had a story. I really didn't know who I was going to tell it to, and I really didn't know if what I was writing would turn out to be a novel or a short story. I even thought it might turn out to be a poem. What it became was a book called ***Probably Still Nick Swansen,*** about a learning-disabled boy.

BKL: When I read that book, I wondered if you actually knew Nick or a boy like him. There aren't too many books about teenagers like Nick.

WOLFF: No. I had to do a lot of homework to write the book. I practiced being a boy.

BKL: You practiced being a boy?

WOLFF: Yes. I tried to understand how a boy would feel in the sort of situation in which Nick finds himself, and I wrote a short story and some poems. I never knew a boy like Nick, though. Lots of people ask that question, as if I were a nonfiction writer. I've never known a boy like Nick. I've never been a special-education teacher; my kids weren't in special ed, either. I write fiction. I do my research by wandering around. I watch and listen and look.

Also, I've been teaching in a public high school for a very long time. It just happened that one day I was in the cafeteria at a faculty table when I heard some teachers talking about a student who was looking forward to something. Four or five days later, I heard the same teachers talking about how the thing that the student was looking forward to hadn't occurred. I thought, boy, is that my kind of material. I major in disappointment. I guess Nick Swansen was basically me, having practiced being a boy and also having felt inept a whole lot of my life.

BKL: Was it difficult to find publishers for your first books?

WOLFF: Actually, I don't do any of that. My agent does. That's how I can live in Oregon, as far from the mainstream as I can possibly get. I also went to college with Jane Yolen, who's always been generous and kind to newcomers. After I'd written my adult novel, I asked her what to do with it. She told me to send it to her. So I got her agent. After that, the problem was writing, not selling, although ***Nick Swansen*** sat around in New York for 18 months before it found its right editor. It was turned down once before Mary Cash, who was then at Henry Holt, took it. She looked at this sow's ear and said, "I think there's a silk purse here." And she found it. She told me that the book went wrong about halfway through, and if I was going to work with her, I'd have to rewrite it. I said, "Okay," not having any idea what was involved. I found out that she meant I'd have to go back to square one and redo what I thought was perfectly fine in the first place. I did, but I cried my way through it. I no longer think anything is perfect. I know enough now to know everything can be improved.

BKL: ***The Mozart Season*** is about a girl dedicated to the violin. You play the violin. Did that make this book easier to write than ***Nick*** or ***Make Lemonade?***

WOLFF: In one way, it made the book easier. I've played the violin most of my life. I never was as good as Allegra is. I've never been an outstanding violinist, but I play in chamber orchestras a lot. I'm more comfortable in my skin when I have the violin going and have regular weekly lessons. Even so, the novel was still the most difficult of the books I've written.

BKL: Why is that?

WOLFF: Because there was so much in it. It was ambitious. I had many more characters in the world that surrounded Allegra and her violin than in my first YA book. I felt as if I were holding one of those great big bouquets of balloons and had lost all their strings. I thought the reviews were going to say "nice ambitious try that doesn't quite make it."

BKL: You've been quoted as saying that reading to children has a profound effect on who they will become. Were you read to as a child?

WOLFF: Oh yes. Winnie the Pooh and Christopher Robin left a great impression. And Eeyore and Piglet and Kanga and Roo. Winnie the Pooh keeps coming up in everything I write, either explicitly or implicitly. Those folks were in charge of my childhood. Mother read a lot of other things to us, but Milne's Pooh was the most comforting. I never got the joke about Eeyore until I was much older, though. I thought he really was unlucky, and all those terrible things were really happening to him. Mother never helped me see that he was just a self-pitying fool, and looking back, I'm glad she didn't.

BKL: In your essay for Don Gallo, you credited a number of teachers for steering you toward becoming a writer. Tell me, is that why education is such a prominent theme in your books?

WOLFF: Nobody has said that to me before, but you're absolutely right. I think so. Actually, I didn't know what education I was getting till years later. But that's the way we are. We all knew our fifth-grade teacher, Mrs. Fitzpatrick, was a strange and gifted person. I thought she was wonderfully quirky and great. We were in this little rural town on the side of a mountain, and she taught us about the structure of English—whether we wanted to learn it or not. As it turns out, I was a perfect candidate for learning it because I am in love with the English sentence. She taught us how to put the bricks in the wall to build one. Her husband was the principal and the band director to the high school, which had about 80 students in it. He embezzled the band funds and was caught, and Mrs. Fitzpatrick left in the middle of one night. They were just gone.

BKL: Let's go on to *Make Lemonade* for a bit. Where did the idea for the book come from?

WOLFF: I wish I could really pinpoint it. I watched a television series about the poor who fall into the cracks of the system and stay there generation after generation, and I was angry and sorrowful. And I watched several shows about tough, angry, loving women who take justice and safety into their own hands in inner-city projects because the city doesn't give a rip about keeping the children safe or is too snarled in bureaucracy to try. My admiration for those women was instant.

BKL: Women like LaVaughn's mother?

WOLFF: Yes, that's where she came from. But LaVaughn and Jolly really came to me first . . . their sloppy, drippy world, their world of hopelessness. I've never been hungry or gone without shelter unless I've wanted to, but I've felt hopeless and resourceless in my life. I could feel how those kids felt. I just didn't know if it would sound real to readers.

BKL: I never wondered about the reality of the situation, but I did wonder whether race was meant to be a factor in it. I kept wanting to pin labels and finding myself unable to do it.

WOLFF: Well, the idea of race went through my head at the beginning, but I settled into the writing of the book and the emotions of the characters and I honestly didn't think about it. Then I went to New York, to the public library where I was to appear on a panel, and I found 200 librarians all asking me whether the kids in the book were white or black. It's not a question I knew how to answer. I still don't, except to say that I didn't see faces so much as I heard voices when I was writing. I think that we do our best writing when we get out of the way and let our characters speak in whatever voices they have to speak in.

I also believe that it would have been very arrogant of me to try to write black talk. I am extremely white. It would be arrogant of me to write Irish talk if I'd never lived in Ireland. But I can write poor talk because I've been poor in spirit.

BKL: What about reviews for the book?

WOLFF: I was astonished and staggered by the good reviews it got. My editor, Brenda Bowen, still has a note hanging on her wall that I sent along with the last galleys. It says, "This is such a depressing story, I can't imagine reading clear through to the end. What if no one does?" We sent the book to press wondering if anyone would get the point. That was a gamble that my excellent editor took. She was willing to risk publishing a book without being sure whether or not anybody would get it. And they got it! Then, when such favorable reviews began to come in, I thought, "Now wait a minute, Wolff. One of the things you hate most is ego. Don't memorize these reviews. Put them in an envelope and file them away. Don't think about them." I've been around a lot of artistic ego in my life, and I don't want to get one.

BKL: You tried something very different with style in this book. It's written in very short, simple sentences, laid out on the page in what seem to be stanzas rather than traditional paragraphs. Why did you do the book that way?

WOLFF: Because that's the way I heard the voices. I love poetry; I read a lot of it and go to readings. Some of my favorite authors are Gerard Manley Hopkins, Dylan Thomas, Toni Morrison, and Shakespeare. Three of them are poets, and, of course, Toni Morrison is a poet in her prose. Also, I'm not unaware that kids often speak a funny kind of offbeat poetry. Nikki Giovanni put that kind of poetry on the page. People mostly talk in dashes; that's the way I speak, and I've taught school for so many eons and heard kids speak that way so long, it occurred to me that I ought to do the book that way. I hoped to do something with the rhythm of the voices that would sound real.

But I didn't ask anybody's permission. I didn't know to what extent precedent forbade me to write that way. Had I been keeping up in YA lit, as many of my author friends do, I probably would have been too intimidated to try something different. Another reason I wrote the book the way I did was that I know that mothers like Jolly have short attention spans. They are often depressed, and when you're depressed you can't concentrate well enough to read very long. I wanted to create something they could read.

BKL: I wondered if that wasn't part of the reason you wrote it the way you did . . . short lines, simple vocabulary. It might be a good choice for reluctant readers.

WOLFF: Thank you. I hope so.

BKL: How did you feel about finding out that **Make Lemonade** was *Booklist's* Top of the List winner for youth fiction?

WOLFF: I was stunned, although I always put a damper on my exuberance. I don't want it to become a matter of ego, so I haven't told many people yet. I did tell one friend who said, "Welcome to the top of the charts." But I was truly delighted. I know I'm not giving you complete answers. If you were to call me two years from now, I would have thought this through much more. Were you to interview my editor, you'd get a very articulate answer. As a matter of fact, she was flabbergasted by the manuscript when she first got it. In fact, she was intimidated by it. Not by the problems it had, but by its potential. And it wasn't nearly the novel it is now. Brenda asked tough questions to help me make the book better. Good editors do that.

BKL: Have you heard from kids who have read the book?

WOLFF: The book is still so new that I haven't heard from many kids yet. I saw kids do a couple of scenes from it in a reader's theater performance in Pittsburgh recently. I hope they'll tell their friends.

BKL: Are you working on anything at the moment?

WOLFF: I am, but very slowly. My penchant for procrastination is amazing. I'm able to delay and delay and delay, and even sabotage a book. Still, I guess I'd rather write fewer books and have them be unusual, as all three of mine are, than write quantity. The book that I'm working on now is again on the sad side. It may be for younger kids, as young as nine. And it's probably more for girls than boys. I won't give the subject away, though. I'm afraid if I do, it might bring bad luck.

TITLE COMMENTARY

PROBABLY STILL NICK SWANSEN (1988)

Stephanie Zvirin

SOURCE: A review of *Probably Still Nick Swansen,* in *Booklist,* Vol. 85, No. 6, November 15, 1988, p. 567.

Nick Swansen has a minimal brain dysfunction. Although he isn't certain what that is, he knows he has difficulty spelling and writing; he realizes that his thoughts and actions are slower, sometimes more disconnected, than those of other 16-year-olds, and that people, even his parents, treat him differently. He also understands that his slowness is the reason he remains in special education Room 19, not in regular classes like pretty Shana, who has just been mainstreamed. Different classes notwithstanding, fragile Nick asks Shana to go to the prom. Her acceptance plunges him into an agonizing round of preparations and questions about how to act and what to say. Though Nick carefully follows through, relying on lists (as Mr. Norton has taught him in class), Shana stands him up, leaving Nick the misery of wondering whether he isn't just a "drooler" from Room 19 after all. In halting, awkward sentences, punctuated by memories of the death of his sister, another "failure" that haunts him, Nick tells his own story. It is a poignant, gentle, utterly believable narrative that echoes with puzzlement and pain as Nick courageously works through his personal crisis. It is also an optimistic but real look at the difficulties faced by special kids caught between their limitations and their longing to experience life like everyone else. What Lynn Hall's *Just One Friend* does for girls, Wolff's novel does for boys.

Constance A. Mellon

SOURCE: A review of *Probably Still Nick Swansen,* in *School Library Journal,* Vol. 35, No. 4, December, 1988, p. 124.

A strong, compassionate story about a student with minimal brain dysfunction. While all 16 year olds have problems, Nick Swansen's are unique: they involve his identity outside the Special Education classroom and coming to terms with the accidental death of his sister, Dianne, seven years earlier. Told from his viewpoint, the story follows the events of several seminal weeks in Nick's maturing. Readers come to identify strongly with him and with Shana, another Special Ed. student who has "gone up" to the regular classes. The parents of both students provide a revealing contrast: Nick's are warm and understanding, Shana's stumbling and confused. The brilliance in Wolff's book is that she never preaches: rather, through a series of involving events and through characterizations that are consistently sympathetic, she draws readers into Nick's life. Unlike many books that deal with disabilities, Wolff's story stresses the similarities between Nick and other teens rather than highlighting the differences.

Barbara A. Lynn

SOURCE: A review of *Probably Still Nick Swansen,* in *Voice of Youth Advocates,* Vol. 12, No. 2, June, 1989, p. 109.

Beyond the typical problems of teenagers, Nick Swansen, 16, must cope with the identity of being in Room 19—the special education classroom—as well as coming to terms with the accidental drowning of his older sister seven years earlier. Wolff has told a vivid, compassionate story of a young man with minimal brain dysfunction trying to cope with other kids making fun of him, his disastrous prom date, and trying to learn to drive. Told from Nick's viewpoint, the reader becomes immersed in his life over several weeks time as he matures.

The phenomenal thing about Wolff's writing is that the reader is completely involved in Nick's world—his thought processes and emotions. She also stresses the similarities between Nick and other teens rather than the differences. The environment in Room 19 is portrayed as a very positive place with an exceptionally sensitive teacher. Chosen for the 1988 Best Books list, ***Probably Still Nick Swansen*** is an exceptional novel for junior and senior high teens.

Alleen Nilsen and Ken Donelson

SOURCE: A review of *Probably Still Nick Swansen,* in *English Journal,* Vol. 79, No. 1, January, 1990, p. 89.

Wolff's novel has plenty of sad moments, but it's no Kleenex book. Most of us can empathize—to a point—with Nick, doomed to spend his time at school in Room 19, home of the "droolers" and other misfits. Worse than that, Nick (with his "minimal brain damage") is attracted to Shana, who's leaving the room and heading back into a world where people don't make fun of you. Nick needs to learn whether Shana is attracted to him, so he impulsively asks her to the school prom. Shana accepts his invitation, and all seems well as Nick learns how to dance and gets himself a tux, cummerbund and all.

The prom becomes a nightmare as Nick waits forever and Shana never appears. She's not the bitch she appears to be—she's as frightened as Nick and convinces her parents that Nick has called the date off, but Nick waits, dejected and rejected, an even greater misfit than he could ever have imagined. How he makes his way back to self-respect makes up for the rest of the book.

This is Wolff's first YA book, and at times it comes close to being one of those what's-not-been-done-before-in-YA-lit and how-do-I-go-about-doing-it books. Nick's parents are never really believable, particularly his often tearful mother, and all of Nick's problems work out too neatly. But we cared about Nick and predict that other readers will, too.

One major irritation has nothing to do with the plot but with the "Author's Note" preceding the novel: "This book contains some incorrect grammar and punctuation in order to tell Nick Swansen's story in language that is consistent with his." What do you know—special-ed kids sometimes use words in ways English professors (or whoever speaks correct grammar) might object to. I'm glad that regular students don't do that. What an eye-opener, and how condescending to students and reasonably sensitive readers.

Virginia Euwer Wolff

SOURCE: "Rarely Easy and Never Beautiful," in *The ALAN Review,* Vol. 18, No. 3, Spring, 1991, pp. 2-3.

When I was in the advanced stages of writer's block, complicated by the early stages of English teacher burnout, I overheard an anecdote in a crowded cafeteria. The anecdote was two sentences long and concerned a student who had experienced a disappointment.

It went to my spine.

A vision jumped into my mind of a young person, all dressed up, outside a place of merriment, excluded from the flurried joy going on inside. Accompanying the picture were the Beatles, singing the seductive melody of "Eleanor Rigby."

> Look at all the lonely people
> Where do they all come from?

I had to find out what would happen.

The book that resulted from this scene in my head probably bears no resemblance to the original anecdote. However, the picture itself stayed with me during the coming years as ***Probably Still Nick Swansen*** took shape, underwent reshaping, traveled back and forth between my desk in rural Oregon and my editor's desk in Manhattan, and got born.

In the beginning, I decided that my character would be a Special Ed or Special Needs student, and that he would be left out of something he wanted to be included in.

What on earth entitled me, a lifelong English major, to invade the mind of this boy and find out what he was thinking? In order to help answer that question, I want you to reach back into your youth and recall one moment when you noticed that one kid was left out of something. Look back there and notice how that boy or girl looked: shoes, hands, hair, mouth—where was s/he standing? Where were you standing? Recall what it was like.

Those moments entitled me.

Next, I want you to reach back into your own life and recall a time when you yourself felt left out, or rejected, or incompetent—inferior in any way. One instant in your entire life.

Those moments entitled me.

I do my research by wandering around. I'd been researching kids for years. And bolstering me was Hemingway's remark, "I learned to write by looking at paintings in the Luxembourg Museum."

It had occurred to me, having lived in the world for a while, that life might be looked at as an oscillating system of expectancy and loss. Optimistic anticipation on the one hand and disappointment on the other—as if we'd been asked to hold our hands up for someone to wind yarn around them in preparation for building a sweater. Back and forth: expectancy and loss. At its dramatic worst, it becomes a vertical process in the manner of Sisyphus and his rock: he finally heaves it up over the summit, only to see it plunge to the bottom once again.

I'd looked at Special Needs students—those kids who are always quietly under siege—and I'd supposed that at times *their* expectancy-loss burden must be intolerable.

From my fellow Oregonian Ken Kesey I borrowed a device. When he was writing *Sometimes a Great Notion*, whose central character is Hank Stamper, he kept an index card at his side: "Try to make Hank Stamper give up." I wrote on an index card, "Try to make Nick Swansen give up," and I taped it on the wall above my typewriter.

In order to try to find Nick Swansen's breaking point—his "indomitability level"—I had to immerse him in events and surround him with a supporting cast who would play out the drama of testing his strength. How would the supporting cast behave?

It wasn't as simple as it had looked at first. Nothing is.

Now, although we live in the era of Public Law 94-142 and we're aiming at civil rights for everybody, we've inherited from the past a set of attitudes, a cultural paradox, a pattern that's hard to break. The pattern is one of pity and fear.

The disabled—those who look different or behave differently—arouse pity and fear in the "regulars." The pity we can handle with some ease. It even makes us feel good. It enables us to endow the disabled with disproportionate amounts of saintliness, to consign them to a special position "a little closer to God."

Imagine Dickens's Tiny Tim complaining, "Gimme a break. I want medical attention and I want it *now*." Would we still be adoring him and weeping over him nearly 150 years later? We much prefer that he bless us every one.

Tiny Tim's endearing meekness allows us our annual catharsis of tears. It provokes the most stony-hearted of us to say to ourselves, "See? I'm still capable of feeling *something*."

So much for the pity. It has its place.

The fear is far more dangerous. Leslie Fiedler, in his 1977 book, *Freaks*, suggests that the fear has a logic of its own. He points out that we like to imagine that we're made in some kind of divine image. We see someone who looks different. We immediately wonder: Did the same figure of omnipotence who made me make that creature? What is that creature being punished for? Essentially, if the creator could punish that creature, surely the same thing could happen to us. We feel an immediate need to put some distance between that creature and ourselves.

Illustrations of this need for distance abound in literature. In William Faulkner's novel, *The Sound and the Fury*, one of the narrators is thirty-three-year-old intellectually deficient Benjy Compson. Another character says of Benjy, "Folks don't like to look at a looney. Taint no luck in it." (Notice that Faulkner, who rarely disappoints, has included the punning "taint.")

One of the easiest methods of distancing ourselves is the laughter of ridicule. We're taught it as children: Laugh at the thunderstorm, the monster, the big bully; show them we're not afraid.

"Regulars" are drawn to the disabled by pity, and repelled by fear. We give the disabled a wide berth, and make jokes to cover our fright.

There's even a word for it. *Teratophobia*, from the Greek *teras*, "monster." Fear of, especially of giving birth to, monsters. What does every pregnant woman in every culture hope and/or pray for? "Let my baby be normal."

Only those who understand how this pity-fear paradox operates—who understand it *on some level*—can work successfully with Special Ed or Special Needs students. We've all noticed that "regular" kids in the same age group often work wonderfully with them; clearly, they understand this system somewhere in their solar plexus, although they might reject Fiedler's analysis of it.

I didn't know about Fiedler's thinking on the subject when I wrote **Probably Still Nick Swansen;** I'd forgotten the Faulkner quotation; I didn't even think about Tiny Tim. Consciously, that is. I worked purely on hunches, but hunches informed by more than twenty years in classrooms and by a subconscious sense of paradox. I knew things in my solar plexus.

A clerk in a florist's shop patronizes Nick; a schoolmate taunts him; a policeman gives him funny looks; and a dance chaperon refers to Special Ed students as "droolers." On the other side, Nick's teacher, his classmates, his parents, the family doctor, and even the girl he wants to go to the prom with—all of these acknowledge him and allow him to take himself seriously.

On the wall above my typewriter, not far from the "give up" card, was my list of Faulkner's Six. In his Nobel Prize acceptance speech in 1949, Faulkner said these are the only things worth writing about: love, honor, pity, pride, compassion, and sacrifice. These things constitute the moral checklist against which I place my work.

One of the things **Nick Swansen** is about, I think, is the examined life. The courage it takes. Nick examines his life awkwardly, using a blind-men-and-the-elephant approach—but he keeps on trying. And he makes millimeters of progress, just as most of us do.

Many books contain a conspiracy between author and reader, pushing and nudging the character to get the point. Such a conspiracy exists in **Probably Still Nick Swansen.** He moves between two unlikely extremes: One of his favorite amphibians is the pig frog, a lime-green frog that is very beautiful in nature but which scientists have given an ugly name. At the other extreme, the book contains several references to Beethoven, the genius who was deaf, who wasn't a good dancer, and who couldn't easily do math. Somewhere between these two far-fetched poles, Nick must find his way, must find some patterns that help him construct his life.

Writing **Nick Swansen** was scary. I didn't like the discomfort of going around inside the ribcage of somebody who sometimes couldn't read bumper stickers and whose torments were at times nearly more than I could bear. Looking at the world through his eyes made me angry, made me want to shake my fist at heaven.

One of my most perennially useful quotations is from Maya Angelou, who has said, "Preparation is rarely easy and never beautiful." This, too, was on the wall above my typewriter. I sometimes think that if she hadn't said that, and if I hadn't found out about it, Nick Swansen might have given up.

THE MOZART SEASON (1991)

Publishers Weekly

SOURCE: A review of *The Mozart Season,* in *Publishers Weekly,* Vol. 238, No. 23, May 24, 1991, p. 59.

At the beginning of summer, 12-year-old Allegra Leah Shapiro finds out that she has been selected as a finalist in a local violin competition. She spends the summer practicing Mozart's fourth violin concerto, preparing for the competition and sorting through her conflicting feelings about wanting to be herself and wanting to please her parents and grandmother. *The Mozart Season* is long on rumination and short on action, as Allegra wrestles with everything from what it takes to be a musician to what it means to be half Jewish and half Gentile to the exact nature of her connection with her grandmother, murdered in a concentration camp during World War II. Unfortunately, Wolff's constant repetition of themes is hardly hypnotic, as was probably intended, but simply mind numbing. However, Wolff's slightly flawed work contains some redeeming qualities—it is a pleasure to have a novel of ideas for young adults that describes the delicate dance between honoring traditions of the past and being your own person in the present.

Hazel Rochman

SOURCE: A review of *The Mozart Season,* in *Booklist,* Vol. 87, No. 19, June 1, 1991, p. 1869.

It's cool to be a high achiever in our feel-good culture, and YA fiction name-drops the Juilliard with casual respect. But it has to stay casual. No sweat. It's like you become a concert violinist—a celebrity—on your way to the mall, without even stopping to tune your instrument. What the stories ignore is the hard work, the obsession, the tenacity, and also the exhilaration. Only in sport is it accepted that the breakthrough is difficult, that you have to practice, exercise, give up things, fail, hurt, in order to reach beyond yourself.

Wolff uses compelling sports analogies in her story of 12-year-old violinist and softball player, Allegra Leah Shapiro of Portland, Oregon, who's the youngest of six finalists chosen to play Mozart's Fourth Violin Concerto in a big youth contest. Allegra's first-person narrative is chatty and intense. "In both music and softball you get breathless with effort, you surprise yourself sometimes," she says. She calculates that she'll play the concerto maybe 1,000 times before the contest in September. And, like sports, it's not just a matter of technique and will. Watching the Boston Celtics and seeing "one of those beautiful shots go exploding down through the basket. . . . That guy has in his memory every basket he's ever shot—and at the same instant he's making up a new one." She compares her elation with what she sees in the face of a skier on TV: "It's a kind of alertness that comes on you, as if somebody has turned on all your lights inside. Sometimes it can get almost too bright in there."

The problem is that Wolff's characters are too brightly lit, their roles too purposive. Allegra's teacher is a model of wisdom and sensitivity. Her two artistic friends are nice and supportive. Her parents, musicians themselves, help without pressuring her. Even the poor brain-injured man she sees dancing at Portland's free outdoor concerts is like a figure from a Chagall painting. Her confrontation with the Holocaust death of her Polish great-grandmother, Leah, seems pulled into the story to raise Allegra's sensitivity. Only her older brother mocks all the fervor and insists that "everything isn't a matter of life and death." This is pedantic stuff compared with the stories of teenage artists in Cole's *Celine* or Oneal's *In Summer Light* or Brooks' *Midnight Hour Encores.* Yet, Wolff's story is more focused on the artistic experience, and she makes it both special and a part of ordinary life.

Like MacKinnon's *Song for a Shadow,* this is about making music, listening to it, practicing it, playing it, alone and with others. Allegra keeps trying to understand how to play Mozart, to merge with the music without letting herself get in the way, to find the song. As she practices, works with her teacher, practices, learns from another musician, reaches out to others, plays well in a concert, fails, learns about herself, picks herself up, practices, tries a new way, is interviewed on TV, and finally plays in the competition, the story has the suspense and conflict and terror of all good performance stories. It has the feel of a survival adventure. Not only musicians, but any kid who's really *into* science, sports, theater, writing, art, chess, will recognize the concentration, the drudgery, the dailiness, and the imaginative leap into the unknown.

Allegra's no elitist. There's no jargon about creativity, no talk of prodigies or even of the gifted. There are unusual people who love music. In a quiet episode, Allegra plays with a small, rural orchestra that bonds farmers, pharmacists, and white-haired little old ladies. The Mozart contest winner's a surprise, a klutzy girl Allegra once thought she had to pity. It's interesting that talented Allegra has some of the same great qualities as Nick, the slow learner in Wolff's award-winning *Probably Still Nick Swansen*— qualities of empathy and drive and courage.

Allegra's privileged, she's happy, but she knows—from Mozart, from her own experience, and from her feelings for those around her—that happiness is fragile, that suffering and joy are very close. She imagines the life of the relative who died in Treblinka. She knows that, like the brain-damaged dancing man, she could lose her song. A simple image combines the universal and the elusive: looking down at the scroll of her violin, Allegra sees that her instrument is "like a seashell, as if there's such a story inside that you could never find out all of it."

Connie C. Rockman

SOURCE: A review of *The Mozart Season,* in *School Library Journal,* Vol. 37, No. 7, July, 1991, p. 91.

Allegra Leah Shapiro is happily making the transition from seventh-grade softball season to summertime when she can concentrate on her violin lessons. At their first session, her teacher informs her that she has been chosen as a finalist in a competition for young musicians, probably the youngest of those selected. Allegra, a gifted violinist, plays in a youth orchestra in her hometown of Portland, Oregon, but she is also a three-dimensional, real 12-year-old who wrangles good-naturedly with her older brother, chafes at her parents' restrictions on late-night bike riding, is loyal to her friends, and is intensely curious about the world around her. As the summer progresses, several themes weave in and out of Allegra's consciousness and growth as she struggles with the Mozart concerto she will play in the competition. A strange dancing man who appears at outdoor concerts, the mysterious sadness surrounding her mother's friend Deirdre, and a very special gift from her grandmother in New York—all these find their way into Allegra's awareness and eventually into her own interpretation of the concerto. With a clear, fresh voice that never falters, Wolff gives readers a delightful heroine, a fully realized setting, and a slowly building tension that reaches a stunning climax at the competition. . . . Wolff interweaves the themes of adolescence, music, and striving for excellence with great success. A book that will richly reward its readers.

Ellen Fader

SOURCE: A review of *The Mozart Season,* in *The Horn Book Magazine,* Vol. LXVII, No. 5, September-October, 1991, pp. 599-600.

Having just completed seventh grade, Allegra Shapiro is looking forward to a relaxing summer of bike rides and twice-a-week violin lessons. But when she is chosen as the youngest of six finalists in one of Oregon's most prestigious music competitions, her days are filled with practicing Mozart's Fourth Violin Concerto. Like Patricia MacLachlan's cellist in *The Facts and Fictions of Minna Pratt,* Allegra tries to define her relationship with music as well as find her way through the increasingly complicated world of a young teenager. Advice comes from all directions: her musician parents and her violin teacher offer her the freedom to make her own musical decisions, while her brother reminds her that "'it's a concerto; it's not the future of the universe.'" A long-time friend of her mother, who is a gifted singer, reminds Allegra that nobody ever really makes music, it is rather "'a matter of letting the music out.'" Her grandmother attempts to interest her granddaughter in Judaism, believing that her religious education has been neglected because of Allegra's parents' mixed marriage. In the end, while she does not take first place in the competition, Allegra emerges a winner. She comes across as sometimes uniquely wise and gifted and sometimes genuinely bewildered, and her multitextured first-person story will speak strongly to many young people. Although Wolff's style is leisurely, lacking the strong emotional impact of her impressive first novel, *Probably Still Nick Swansen,* readers who are musically inclined and those who enjoy a story with strong and intriguing characters as well as a touch of romance will savor each word of this distinctive novel.

Julie Jaffee Nagel

SOURCE: A review of *The Mozart Season,* in *American Music Teacher,* Vol. 41, No. 5, April-May, 1992, p. 84.

Virginia Euwer Wolff has written a charming and sensitive novel that, upon first inspection, appears to appeal to the young adolescent musician who is involved in music lessons and music competitions. But after reading *The Mozart Season,* I am left with the opinion that this engaging book presents contrapuntal themes that go beyond the obvious.

The story of Allegra Shapiro spans the summer of her twelfth year and allows the reader to be a part of her life and thoughts as she prepares for the Ernest Bloch Young Musicians' Competition. The name of the central character, Allegra, gives a clue to the tempo of this story which reads quickly and is written with sensitivity to the musical and emotional development for a talented violinist. The reader is drawn into Allegra's world of violin lessons, family interactions (both parents are Juilliard graduates and professional musicians), friendships with peers, competition with other contestants, and curiosity about the mysteries of growing up. In Allegra's words, "I'm supposed to be a child and stay in my bed at night, and I'm supposed to be an adult and be responsible. How can I be everything at the same time?"

Woven into this background (for the benefit of non-musicians or young music students) are numerous references about musical terminology. And we truly see Allegra's character develop as she explores in a very touching way her feelings about her great grandmother's painful sacrifice.

In summary, Allegra Shapiro's twelfth summer is one of maturation for her, and it is through her involvement with music that we witness her growth. This book provides not only an interesting and well-written story but also an example of how music can be an integral part of one's life.

MAKE LEMONADE (1993)

Stephanie Zvirin

SOURCE: A review of *Make Lemonade,* in *Booklist,* Vol. 89, No. 19-20, June 1 & 15, 1993, p. 1813.

Wolff's latest novel stretches her considerable talents in a new direction. Written in a riveting, stream-of-consciousness fashion, with the lines laid out on the page as if they were the verses of a poem, the book plunges into the depths of inner-city poverty. But instead of focusing on the gangs that spread fear in city tenements, Wolff writes about ordinary folks trying to get by as best they can. Fourteen-year-old LaVaughn, clever yet still naive, wants to go to college, a word that bears such weight in her home "you have to walk around it in the rooms like furniture." To earn money, she takes a baby-sitting job with 17-year-old Jolly, a proud young woman with two small children. LaVaughn's reactions to Jolly and the children, described in her colorful personal idiom, are mixed with the stories that anchor her own life and enriched by a strong sense of place. There's humor as well as anguish in the tableaux she sets before us, with some of the funniest and most stirring scenes revolving around Jolly's children, both fully realized characters. Revealing as well are interactions between LaVaughn and her single-parent mother, from whom LaVaughn has obviously inherited stubbornness and a healthy measure of good sense. Jolly's problems provide the book's drama. Barely more than a child herself, she has no idea how to "take hold," as LaVaughn's mother says, and it's ironic that it is someone younger than Jolly, an outsider, who shows her the way. Rooted not in a particular culture, but in the community of poverty, the story offers a penetrating view of the conditions that foster our ignorance, destroy our self-esteem, and challenge our strength. That education is the bridge to a better life is the unapologetic, unmistakable theme, symbolized by the sprouting of the lemon seeds LaVaughn plants for Jolly's children. At once disturbing and uplifting, this finely nuanced, touching portrait proudly affirms our ability to reach beyond ourselves and reach out to one another.

Carolyn Noah

SOURCE: A review of *Make Lemonade,* in *School Library Journal,* Vol. 39, No. 7, July, 1993, p. 103.

"This word COLLEGE is in my house,/ and you have to walk around it in the rooms/ like furniture." So LaVaughn, an urban 14-year-old, tries to earn the money she needs to make college a reality. She and her mother are a solid two-person family. When LaVaughn takes a job babysitting for Jolly, an abused, 17-year-old single parent who lives with her two children in squalor, her mother is not sure it's a good idea. How the girl's steady support helps Jolly to bootstrap herself into better times and how Jolly, in turn, helps her young friend to clarify her own values are the subjects of this complex, powerful narrative. The themes of parental love, sexual harassment, abuse, independence, and the value of education are its underpinnings. LaVaughn is a bright, compassionate teen who is a foil for Jolly, whose only brief role model was a foster parent, Gram, who died. The dynamics between the two young women are multidimensional and elastic—absolutely credible. LaVaughn's mother is a complete character, too, and even Jolly's kids become real. The tale is told in natural first-person, and in rhythmic prose arranged in open verse. The poetic form emphasizes the flow of the teenager's language and thought. The form invites readers to drop some preconceptions about novels, and they will find the plot and characters riveting. *Make Lemonade* is a triumphant, outstanding story.

Ellen Fader

SOURCE: A review of *Make Lemonade,* in *The Horn Book Magazine,* Vol. LXIX, No. 5, September-October, 1993, pp. 606-7.

Wolff's third novel for young adults tackles the theme of poverty, not only that of LaVaughn, a fourteen-year-old determined to earn enough money to go to college, but also that of a seventeen-year-old single mother ironically named Jolly. LaVaughn accepts the job of baby-sitting Jolly's two small children but quickly realizes that the young woman needs as much help and nurturing as her two neglected children. Jolly's problems—she is nearly illiterate; neither of the fathers of her two children provides any assistance; her apartment is unbelievably filthy; and she loses her job because of sexual harassment—threaten to take over LaVaughn's life. But the four become something akin to a temporary family, and through their relationship, each makes progress toward a better life. Notably, Jolly enrolls in a program for young mothers at the high school and begins to develop the skills she needs to move her life forward, to "make lemonade" from lemons. Wolff's stylistic experiment will intrigue young readers; sixty-six brief chapters, with words arranged on the page like poetry and sometimes composed of ungrammatic sentences, perfectly echo the patterns of teenage speech. With a plot that develops incredible dramatic momentum, this fast-reading book may appeal to readers just like Jolly.

Vague in setting—the story could take place in an inner city—as well as ethnicity, Wolff's characters grab hold and don't let go The author's fans will celebrate this new book that provides the same emotional reading experience as her earlier novels, *Probably Still Nick Swansen* and *The Mozart Season.*

Wendy Cooling

SOURCE: A review of *Make Lemonade,* in *Books for Keeps,* No. 93, July, 1995, p. 28.

You can't help but notice the cover of **Make Lemonade** by Virginia Euwer Wolff, another American writer published in this country for the first time. Fourteen-year-old LaVaughn wants to earn money for college and so responds to a notice on the school bulletin board, 'Babysitter Needed Bad', and her involvement with single-parent Jolly, two-year-old Jeremy and baby Jilly, begins. Jolly is 17 and as she says, 'I can't do it alone' for the third time, LaVaughn finds herself agreeing to babysit so that Jolly can work the evening shift at the factory. The story is warm and compulsive as LaVaughn takes on the family and sticks with them even when there's no money to pay her. She offers a kind of optimism reflected in her attempts to grow a lemon tree from lemon pips. But, against all the odds, she helps Jolly to take some control of her life. This is a very special book, it reflects the lives of a growing number of young people in our inner cities and is both disturbing and cheering. There are young people like LaVaughn who take on the problems of others, and by telling her story in a form of naturalistic monologue it becomes very accessible to teenage readers. Forget your preconceptions about the novel and read this one.

Geraldine Brennan

SOURCE: A review of *Make Lemonade,* in *The Times Educational Supplement,* No. 4131, September 1, 1995, p. 24.

Virginia Euwer Wolff celebrates humanity's resourcefulness in dire circumstances—the ability to produce a tiny stash of sugar to sweeten the sour fruit of experience. Her familiar material—urban poverty, the hard grind of parenting on the margins of society and children's enduring capacity for fun and learning—is lifted into something extraordinary by the prose poem form and the energy of the narrator Verna La Vaughn's rap rhythms.

La Vaughn is a bright working-class high-school student whose brain is her ticket out of her run-down neighbourhood. The inner-city United States setting and the characters' ethnic background are deliberately non-specific: any reader can identify with La Vaughn or Jolly, the 17-year-old single mother who hires her as a babysitter.

The intense, forceful narrative, compelling enough to read in one sitting, is a subtle treatment of the shifting power balance between the two teenagers and the walk-on roles which relative privilege and exploitation play in the drama of their relationship. La Vaughn earns money to save for college from Jolly, who had to drop out of school; the employee takes on responsibility for her employer's problems; eventually Jolly can't afford to pay La Vaughn, but needs her help. Who is exploiting whom?

Fear is another key player. Jolly's history of homelessness and abuse and her "dropout" lifestyle spells dreaded destitution and moral decline for the respectable, upwardly mobile poor, such as La Vaughn and her mother (also a single parent, but a widow and therefore socially acceptable). La Vaughn, reared to strive for self-improvement, feels threatened by the chaos in Jolly's home: "I put one finger up/just a little bit of yuck off the glass/to see me better/and I'm afraid . . . and I'll end up old and no college/with back rent to pay/and looking at cockroaches for my entertainment". Finally, this is a study of growing up through a series of breakthroughs. As Jolly's two children learn to walk, count and grow lemon trees, both their mother and their career become better equipped to face the future.

BAT 6 (1998)

Publishers Weekly

SOURCE: A review of *Bat 6,* in *Publishers Weekly,* Vol. 245, No. 16, April 20, 1998, p. 67.

Wolff's ambitious but ultimately unsuccessful novel explores prejudice via a baseball game between the sixth grade girls of Bear Creek Ridge and Barlow Road Grade Schools on May 28, 1949. "Now that it's over, we are telling. We voted to, it's fairer than not," begins Tootie, the catcher for Bear Creek Ridge, in what appears to be the start of a series of flashback testimonials. But not all of the 21 girls' accounts adhere to this format, and readers never discover whom the girls are addressing. Some of the characters speak only a few times, and since readers never get to know them, their voices run together in a miscellany. The actual conflict—when Shazam, whose father died at Pearl Harbor, in a run to first base, assaults Aki, the Japanese first baseman—occurs more than halfway through the book. The most distinct voices belong to Shazam (who speaks in a stream-of-consciousness style, "Sneaky Japs never warned nobody they snuck behind our backs dropped bombs right in my fathers ship the *Arizona* he was down in it without no warning") and to Aki, whose perspective is markedly different from the other girls'. Shazam exposes much of her troubled background through her narratives, and Aki reveals some fascinating cultural details as well as provides insight into life in an internment camp. However, because readers are only acquainted with the two through a few lengthy accounts interspersed among the other 19 girls, the change in both of them (especially in Shazam) at story's end seems sudden and hollow. While readers cannot help but admire the stalwart Aki, they will likely walk away from this book trying to make sense of who these characters were and what they were trying to say.

Luann Toth

SOURCE: A review of *Bat 6*, in *School Library Journal*, Vol. 44, No. 5, May, 1998, p. 150.

Since the turn of the century, two rival Oregon farm communities have put their differences behind them and come together once a year to watch their sixth-grade girls' teams play softball. In the spring of 1949, the "50-year girls" excitedly anticipate their moment of glory. *Bat 6* is their story, reconstructed just after it happened. The narrative is comprised of firsthand reporting from girls on both sides. This year, each team has a ringer. For the Bear Creek Ridge Mountaineers, it's Japanese-American first-baseman Aki, whose family has just moved back to the community after spending most of the war years in an internment camp. The Barlow Pioneers' marvel is their center fielder who calls herself Shazam, a troubled youngster who does everything, except her schoolwork, with an unsettling, single-minded intensity. Her father was killed at Pearl Harbor and she has maintained a deep-seated hatred of the Japanese ever since. In the book's pivotal scene, Shazam violently attacks Aki during the big game, and play (and time itself, for that matter) is suspended. The period details and use of the vernacular are right on the money and always reflect the adolescent female point of view. At some point comes the liberating realization that it isn't necessary to keep the multiple voices straight and that the well-crafted account has taken on a life of its own. Wolff delves into the irreversible consequences of war and the necessity to cultivate peace and speaks volumes about courage, responsibility, and reconciliation—all in a book about softball.

Michael Cart

SOURCE: A review of *Bat 6*, in *Booklist*, Vol. 94, No. 7, May 1, 1998, p. 1517.

Three years after the end of World War II, 11-year-old Aki Mikami and her family return to their home and orchard in Bear Creek Ridge. They've been gone for six years—since the day in 1942 when they were forced to join tens of thousands of other Americans of Japanese ancestry in internment camps. Coinciding with their return, the Japanese-hating Shazam, whose father died at Pearl Harbor, comes to live with her grandmother in the nearby town of Barlow. The ultimate, explosive meeting of the two girls on a softball field as members of opposing sixth-grade teams will demonstrate that wars may end, but the passions they foster—if unexamined—can make victims of the survivors. This ambitious novel is told in 21 different first-person voices; each member of the two girls' softball teams has one or more "turns" at bat as narrator, recounting bits and pieces of the story. Inevitably, a few of the voices sound distractingly similar, but a gratifyingly large number reveal complex, fully realized characters. Gradually, their individual vignettes merge into an extraordinarily artful portrait of a moment in American history that challenged our comfortable assumptions about who we were and what we believed. None of the 21 girls emerges unchanged from what happens during that fateful encounter nor, one predicts, will most readers of this powerful novel.

Nancy Vasilakis

SOURCE: A review of *Bat 6*, in *The Horn Book Magazine*, Vol. LXXIV, No. 4, July-August, 1998, p. 500.

Set against the backdrop of a softball game played between two small rural towns in Oregon in 1949, this novel reveals, among other things, the lingering aftereffects of war. The sixth-grade girls from Barlow and Bear Creek Ridge have spent the year practicing for a softball game that has been an annual event since 1900. Now, during the fiftieth anniversary game, an incident occurs that upsets the sanguine assumptions of the citizens. The central action revolves around Shazam, a deeply troubled girl whose father was killed at Pearl Harbor and who has been nursing an abiding hatred for the Japanese ever since, and Aki, a Japanese-American girl. Aki and her family have recently returned home after spending the war years in an internment camp. Early in the game (but late in the novel), Shazam attacks Aki, injuring her severely. The game ends abruptly, and all the players—and many of the adults as well—are left to wonder what share of the responsibility they bear. The story is narrated in brief first-person retrospective accounts from all twenty-one girls on both teams, and it is sometimes difficult to distinguish one voice from another. But the characters are engaging for the most part, and while Aki's characterization seems a bit too stereotypical, Shazam is a complex and compelling protagonist. Wolff's evocation of period and place, on the other hand, is indisputably masterful. The question she raises about war, race, and cherished beliefs are difficult and honest and welcome antidote to more romanticized versions of the years following the "last good war."

Additional coverage of Wolff's life and career is contained in the following sources published by The Gale Group: *Authors and Artists for Young Adults,* Vol. 26; *Contemporary Authors,* Vol. 107; *Something about the Author,* Vol. 78.

Cumulative Indexes

How to Use This Index

The main references

> **Calvino, Italo**
> 1923–1985 .... **CLC 5, 8, 11, 22, 33, 39,**
> **73; SSC 3**

list all author entries in the following Gale Literary Criticism series:

BLC = *Black Literature Criticism*
CLC = *Contemporary Literary Criticism*
CLR = *Children's Literature Review*
CMLC = *Classical and Medieval Literature Criticism*
DA = *DISCovering Authors*
DAB = *DISCovering Authors: British*
DAC = *DISCovering Authors: Canadian*
DAM = *DISCovering Authors: Modules*
      DRAM: *Dramatists Module;* *MST*: *Most-Studied Authors Module;*
      MULT: *Multicultural Authors Module;* *NOV*: *Novelists Module;*
      POET: *Poets Module;* *POP*: *Popular Fiction and Genre Authors Module*
DC = *Drama Criticism*
HLC = *Hispanic Literature Criticism*
LC = *Literature Criticism from 1400 to 1800*
NCLC = *Nineteenth-Century Literature Criticism*
PC = *Poetry Criticism*
SSC = *Short Story Criticism*
TCLC = *Twentieth-Century Literary Criticism*
WLC = *World Literature Criticism, 1500 to the Present*

The cross-references

> See also CANR 23; CA 85-88;
>   obituary CA116

list all author entries in the following Gale biographical and literary sources:

AAYA = *Authors & Artists for Young Adults*
AITN = *Authors in the News*
BEST = *Bestsellers*
BW = *Black Writers*
CA = *Contemporary Authors*
CAAS = *Contemporary Authors Autobiography Series*
CABS = *Contemporary Authors Bibliographical Series*
CANR = *Contemporary Authors New Revision Series*
CAP = *Contemporary Authors Permanent Series*
CDALB = *Concise Dictionary of American Literary Biography*
CDBLB = *Concise Dictionary of British Literary Biography*
DLB = *Dictionary of Literary Biography*
DLBD = *Dictionary of Literary Biography Documentary Series*
DLBY = *Dictionary of Literary Biography Yearbook*
HW = *Hispanic Writers*
JRDA = *Junior DISCovering Authors*
MAICYA = *Major Authors and Illustrators for Children and Young Adults*
MTCW = *Major 20th-Century Writers*
NNAL = *Native North American Literature*
SAAS = *Something about the Author Autobiography Series*
SATA = *Something about the Author*
YABC = *Yesterday's Authors of Books for Children*

Children's Literature Review
Cumulative Nationality Index

AMERICAN

Aardema, Verna **17**
Aaseng, Nathan **54**
Adkins, Jan **7**
Adler, Irving **27**
Adoff, Arnold **7**
Alcott, Louisa May **1, 38**
Alexander, Lloyd (Chudley) **1, 5, 48**
Aliki **9**
Anderson, Poul (William) **58**
Angelou, Maya **53**
Anglund, Joan Walsh **1**
Armstrong, William H(oward) **1**
Arnold, Caroline **61**
Arnosky, James Edward **15**
Aruego, Jose (Espiritu) **5**
Ashabranner, Brent (Kenneth) **28**
Asimov, Isaac **12**
Atwater, Florence (Hasseltine Carroll) **19**
Atwater, Richard (Tupper) **19**
Avi **24**
Aylesworth, Thomas G(ibbons) **6**
Babbitt, Natalie (Zane Moore) **2, 53**
Bacon, Martha Sherman **3**
Ballard, Robert D(uane) **60**
Bang, Molly Garrett **8**
Baum, L(yman) Frank **15**
Baylor, Byrd **3**
Bellairs, John (A.) **37**
Bemelmans, Ludwig **6**
Benary-Isbert, Margot **12**
Bendick, Jeanne **5**
Berenstain, Jan(ice) **19**
Berenstain, Stan(ley) **19**
Berger, Melvin H. **32**
Bess, Clayton **39**
Bethancourt, T. Ernesto **3**
Block, Francesca (Lia) **33**
Blos, Joan W(insor) **18**
Blumberg, Rhoda **21**
Blume, Judy (Sussman) **2, 15**
Bogart, Jo Ellen **59**
Bond, Nancy (Barbara) **11**
Bontemps, Arna(ud Wendell) **6**
Bova, Ben(jamin William) **3**
Boyd, Candy Dawson **50**
Brancato, Robin F(idler) **32**
Branley, Franklyn M(ansfield) **13**
Brett, Jan (Churchill) **27**
Bridgers, Sue Ellen **18**
Brink, Carol Ryrie **30**
Brooks, Bruce **25**
Brooks, Gwendolyn **27**
Brown, Marcia **12**
Brown, Marc (Tolon) **29**
Brown, Margaret Wise **10**
Bruchac, Joseph III **46**
Bryan, Ashley F. **18**
Bunting, Eve **28, 56**
Burnett, Frances (Eliza) Hodgson **24**
Burton, Virginia Lee **11**
Byars, Betsy (Cromer) **1, 16**

Caines, Jeannette (Franklin) **24**
Calhoun, Mary **42**
Cameron, Eleanor (Frances) **1**
Carle, Eric **10**
Carter, Alden R(ichardson) **22**
Cassedy, Sylvia **26**
Charlip, Remy **8**
Childress, Alice **14**
Choi, Sook Nyul **53**
Christopher, Matt(hew Frederick) **33**
Ciardi, John (Anthony) **19**
Clark, Ann Nolan **16**
Cleary, Beverly (Atlee Bunn) **2, 8**
Cleaver, Bill **6**
Cleaver, Vera (Allen) **6**
Clifton, (Thelma) Lucille **5**
Coatsworth, Elizabeth (Jane) **2**
Cobb, Vicki **2**
Cohen, Daniel (E.) **3, 43**
Cole, Brock **18**
Cole, Joanna **5, 40**
Collier, James L(incoln) **3**
Colum, Padraic **36**
Conford, Ellen **10**
Conrad, Pam **18**
Cooney, Barbara **23**
Cooper, Floyd **60**
Corbett, Scott **1**
Corcoran, Barbara **50**
Cormier, Robert (Edmund) **12, 55**
Cox, Palmer **24**
Creech, Sharon **42**
Crews, Donald **7**
Crutcher, Chris(topher C.) **28**
Cummings, Pat (Marie) **48**
Curry, Jane L(ouise) **31**
Cushman, Karen **55**
Dalgliesh, Alice **62**
Danziger, Paula **20**
d'Aulaire, Edgar Parin **21**
d'Aulaire, Ingri (Mortenson Parin) **21**
Davis, Ossie **56**
Day, Alexandra **22**
de Angeli, Marguerite (Lofft) **1**
DeClements, Barthe **23**
DeJong, Meindert **1**
Denslow, W(illiam) W(allace) **15**
dePaola, Tomie **4, 24**
Dillon, Diane (Claire) **44**
Dillon, Leo **44**
Disch, Thomas M(ichael) **18**
Dixon, Franklin W. **61**
Dodge, Mary (Elizabeth) Mapes **62**
Domanska, Janina **40**
Donovan, John **3**
Dorris, Michael (Anthony) **58**
Dorros, Arthur (M.) **42**
Draper, Sharon M(ills) **57**
Dr. Seuss **1, 9, 53**
Duke, Kate **51**
Duncan, Lois **29**
Duvoisin, Roger Antoine **23**

Eager, Edward McMaken **43**
Ehlert, Lois (Jane) **28**
Emberley, Barbara A(nne) **5**
Emberley, Ed(ward Randolph) **5**
Engdahl, Sylvia Louise **2**
L'Engle, Madeleine (Camp Franklin) **1, 14, 57**
Enright, Elizabeth **4**
Epstein, Beryl (M. Williams) **26**
Epstein, Samuel **26**
Estes, Eleanor (Ruth) **2**
Ets, Marie Hall **33**
Feelings, Muriel (Grey) **5**
Feelings, Tom **5, 58**
Ferry, Charles **34**
Field, Rachel (Lyman) **21**
Fisher, Aileen (Lucia) **49**
Fisher, Leonard Everett **18**
Fitzgerald, John D(ennis) **1**
Fitzhugh, Louise **1**
Flack, Marjorie **28**
Fleischman, (Albert) Sid(ney) **1, 15**
Fleischman, Paul **20**
Forbes, Esther **27**
Foster, Genevieve Stump **7**
Fox, Paula **1, 44**
Freedman, Russell (Bruce) **20**
Freeman, Don **30**
Fritz, Jean (Guttery) **2, 14**
Fujikawa, Gyo **25**
Gaberman, Judie Angell **33**
Gag, Wanda (Hazel) **4**
Gaines, Ernest J(ames) **62**
Galdone, Paul **16**
Gallant, Roy A(rthur) **30**
Gantos, Jack **18**
Garden, Nancy **51**
Gauch, Patricia Lee **56**
Geisel, Theodor Seuss **53**
George, Jean Craighead **1**
Gibbons, Gail **8**
Giblin, James Cross **29**
Giovanni, Nikki **6**
Glenn, Mel **51**
Glubok, Shirley (Astor) **1**
Goble, Paul **21**
Goffstein, (Marilyn) Brooke **3**
Gordon, Sheila **27**
Gorey, Edward (St. John) **36**
Graham, Lorenz (Bell) **10**
Gramatky, Hardie **22**
Greene, Bette **2**
Greene, Constance C(larke) **62**
Greenfield, Eloise **4, 38**
Grifalconi, Ann **35**
Grimes, Nikki **42**
Gruelle, Johnny **34**
Guy, Rosa (Cuthbert) **13**
Hadley, Lee **40**
Haley, Gail E(inhart) **21**
Hamilton, Virginia **1, 11, 40**
Hansen, Joyce (Viola) **21**
Harris, Joel Chandler **49**

Nationality Index

Title Index

Title Index

Title Index

Title Index

Title Index

Title Index

Title Index

Title Index

ISBN 0-7876-3227-9